LAW AND ADMINISTRATION IN EUROPE

Carol Harlow FBA
Emeritus Professor

Law and Administration in Europe

Essays in Honour of Carol Harlow

Edited by

PAUL CRAIG

and

RICHARD RAWLINGS

OXFORD

UNIVERSITY PRESS

OXFORD
UNIVERSITY PRESS

Great Clarendon Street, Oxford OX2 6DP

Oxford University Press is a department of the University of Oxford.
It furthers the University's objective of excellence in research, scholarship,
and education by publishing worldwide in

Oxford New York

Auckland Bangkok Buenos Aires Cape Town Chennai
Dar es Salaam Delhi Hong Kong Istanbul Karachi Kolkata
Kuala Lumpur Madrid Melbourne Mexico City Mumbai Nairobi
São Paulo Shanghai Taipei Tokyo Toronto

Oxford is a registered trade mark of Oxford University Press
in the UK and in certain other countries

Published in the United States
by Oxford University Press Inc., New York

British Library cataloguing in Publication Data

Data available

Library of Congress Cataloging in Publication Data

Data available

ISBN 0–19–926537–2

1 3 5 7 9 10 8 6 4 2

Typeset by Newgen Imaging Systems (P) Ltd., Chennai, India
Printed in Great Britain
on acid-free paper by
Biddles Ltd., Guildford and King's Lynn

Preface

It is a pleasant duty to edit this collection of essays in honour of Carol Harlow. Carol has been one of the major figures in public law over the last thirty years. She has made leading contributions to Constitutional Law, Administrative Law, and EU Law, and continues to do so even though she has formally retired from her post of Professor of Public Law at the London School of Economics.

'Oviferous scholarship' is one description. As shown in the bibliography of Carol's writing in the annex to this volume, her contribution is notable both for the range of subject matter and the rich variety of perspectives—'law' and 'context', theory and practice, the contemporary, the historical, and (especially) the comparative. Titles such as *Politics and Public Law* and *Lawmaking in the European Union*, and on through *Compensation and Government Torts* to classic articles like ' "Public" and "Private" Law: Definition without Distinction' and 'Codification of EC Administrative Procedures' serve to convey the general flavour. This is the generous LSE tradition in public law writ large.

A second main feature of Carol's scholarship is introduced: her willingness to engage in critical and lively debate, as also to pin her colours to the mast. Designedly then this set of essays honouring Carol is no exercise in hagiography. In reflecting the main corpus of interests of her work, many of the chapters develop themes she has addressed or take issue with her approach. A true strength in the scholar, Carol would not have had it otherwise.

Law and Administration in Europe: the title was deliberately chosen both as a suitable vehicle for a set of themed approaches and as a celebration of Carol's own intellectual journey. An early and enduring interest in domestic public law, as shown in two editions of *Law and Administration*, is now seen to be matched by a major pioneering role in European public law, from her inaugural lecture 'A Community of Interests?' to her most recent book *Accountability in the European Union*.

'A life in the law': Carol will hate the idea. Nonetheless, to her oviferous scholarship must be added a long list of related activities (and distinctions); from the Legal Action Group to the British Academy, not forgetting the various dents along the way in the glass ceiling, for example as convenor of the LSE law department. A reflection of Carol's generosity of spirit, in editing this volume we were able to call upon a wide range of her friends and colleagues. Far from having to drum up contributions, a major challenge was to keep *Law and Administration in Europe* to a reasonable length. In so doing, we hope to have facilitated a genuinely interesting and stimulating book, surely the best reason of all for *Festschriften*.

Contents

Tables of Cases

EUROPEAN COURT OF JUSTICE AND COURT OF FIRST INSTANCE

European Court of Human Rights

International Criminal Tribunal for the Former Yugoslavia

PERMANENT COURT OF INTERNATIONAL JUSTICE

NATIONAL CASES

Australia

Canada

Denmark

France

Germany

Greece

Ireland

Italy

New Zealand

Pakistan

Rhodesia, now Zimbabwe

Uganda

United States

Tables of Legislation

SECONDARY LEGISLATION

UK Concordats

EU Materials

European Convention on Human Rights

INTERNATIONAL TREATIES AND DECLARATIONS

National Legislation

Canada

Denmark

Germany

Ireland

Netherlands

New Zealand

United States

List of Contributors

Rodney Barker, Professor of Government, London School of Economics and Political Science, London.

Peter Cane, Professor of Law, Research School of Social Sciences, The Australian National University, Canberra.

Paul Craig, Professor of English Law, St. John's College, Oxford.

Mark Freedland, Professor of Employment Law, St. John's College, Oxford.

Elspeth Guild, Professor of European Migration Law, University of Nijmegen, Netherlands, Partner, Kingsley Napley, London.

Trevor C. Hartley, Professor of Law, London School of Economics and Political Science, London.

Jeffrey Jowell, Professor of Public Law, University College London, Faculty of Laws, London.

Martin Loughlin, Professor of Public Law, London School of Economics and Political Science, London.

Dawn Oliver, Professor of Constitutional Law, University College London, Faculty of Laws, London.

Richard Rawlings, Professor of Law, London School of Economics and Political Science, London.

Martin Shapiro, James W. and Isabel Coffroth Professor of Law, University of California, Berkeley.

Alec Stone Sweet, Official Fellow and Chair of Comparative Government, Nuffield College, Oxford.

Michael Taggart, Professor of Law, University of Auckland, Faculty of Law, Auckland.

Adam Tomkins, Fellow and Tutor in Law, St. Catherine's College, Oxford. John Millar Professor of Public Law, elect, University of Glasgow.

PART I

PUBLIC LAW

1

Theory and Values in Public Law

PETER CANE*

At the heart of Carol Harlow's scholarship is a strong belief that our understanding of legal rules and principles, the law in the books,[1] can be greatly enriched by normative argument on the one hand, and by empirical investigation of social practices on the other. So far as social practice is concerned, she was one of the very first English public lawyers to ask searching questions about the impact of administrative law on the behaviour of administrators.[2] On the normative side, the distinction between 'red light' and 'green light' approaches to administrative law that she and Rick Rawlings laid as the theoretical foundation of their path-breaking materials-and-commentary volume[3] has achieved near-cult status.[4] 'The academic', she says, 'is a professional cynic who must never be afraid to ask awkward questions nor to observe that the emperor has no clothes'.[5] She contrasts the academic *naïf*, who 'accepting things at face value',[6] unsatisfactorily limits his or her activities to 'descriptive analysis of judicial performance',[7] with the *faux naïf* who 'questions what we tend to take for granted or hope to hide'.[8] In the course of Carol Harlow's academic life (and in no small part as a result of her eloquent and passionate advocacy), such sentiments have become academic equivalents of mothers and apple pie, so obviously wholesome as to be unassailable. For this very reason, it may be time, in the spirit of our honorand's own intellectual open-mindedness, to stand back and subject them to some of the sort of sceptical questioning that gave them birth.

* Thanks go to Paul Craig, Niki Lacey, Janet McLean, Declan Roche, and Colin Scott for insightful and helpful comments.

[1] And of legal institutions: C. Harlow, 'Refurbishing the Judicial Service', in C. Harlow (ed.), *Public Law and Politics* (Sweet & Maxwell, London, 1986), 183–90.

[2] C. Harlow, 'Administrative Reaction to Judicial Review' [1976] *PL* 116–33.

[3] C. Harlow and R. Rawlings, *Law and Administration* (Weidenfeld, London, 1984); 2nd edn (Butterworths, London, 1997).

[4] For critical reflection on the distinction see L. Hancher and M. Ruete, 'Forever Amber?' (1985) 48 *MLR* 236–43; and for a doubt about its continued usefulness see M. Taggart, 'Reinvented Government, Traffic Lights and the Convergence of Public and Private Law' [1999] *PL* 124, 128.

[5] C. Harlow, '*La Huronne au Palais-Royal* or a Naïve Perspective on Administrative Law' (2000) 27 *J of Law and Society* 322, 327. [6] N. 5 above, 327.

[7] C. Harlow, 'Changing the Mindset: The Place of Theory in English Administrative Law' (1994) 14 *OJLS* 419, 420. [8] N. 5 above, 327.

It would, of course, be absurd to suggest that empirical study of the impact of legal rules (both statutory and judge-made) on the behaviour of those subject to them, and on the interests of their intended beneficiaries, is not a desirable and potentially valuable activity. In recent years, for instance, researchers have investigated the impact of judicial review on administrative behaviour in various contexts;[9] and systematic study of court records has thrown much light on the incidence of judicial review in the UK.[10] Such research has considerably increased our understanding of administrative law. On the other hand, empirical socio-legal research is expensive, time-consuming, and methodologically difficult. Experience in areas such as tort law,[11] where there is a larger corpus of empirical data than we have in relation to administrative law, warns us not to be too optimistic about the possibility of discovering the sort of causal generalizations that we associate with the natural sciences. Moreover, as contemporary debates about genetic engineering (for instance) attest, it is one thing to know how the world works, but quite another to decide what use ought to be made of that knowledge. For example, it is sometimes argued that courts exercising judicial review jurisdiction should be better informed than they typically are about how the administration actually operates. The implication seems to be that courts should be wary of laying down rules about the way administrators should exercise their powers that would be difficult, inconvenient, or expensive for them to comply with given existing administrative practice. This latter assertion might be thought by some to rest on a contestable view about the desirable balance between efficiency in the conduct of government business and the protection of individual rights.

Difficult and important as such issues undoubtedly are, in this essay I will focus on the other core proposition of Carol Harlow's scholarship, namely that moral and political values are central to the public law enterprise. Recent British debates around this proposition have displayed two noteworthy characteristics. One is a concern with the role of the public law academic, and the other is the identification of values with 'theory'. Both of these features (I will argue) potentially hinder examination of the relationship between public law on the one hand, and political and moral values on the other, by diverting attention away from the values of the law. In the first case, attention is focused on the values espoused by public law scholars (in the terms used by Harlow and

---

[9] For a survey see G. Richardson and M. Sunkin, 'Judicial Review: Questions of Impact' [1996] *PL* 79; and for some recent research S. Halliday, 'The Influence of Judicial Review on Bureaucratic Decision-Making' [2000] *PL* 110; G. Richardson and D. Machin, 'Judicial Review and Tribunal Decision-Making: A Study of the Mental Health Review Tribunal' [2000] *PL* 494; M. Sunkin and K. Pick, 'The Changing Impact of Judicial Review: The Independent Review Service of the Social Fund' [2001] *PL* 736.

[10] L. Bridges, G. Meszaros, and M. Sunkin, *Judicial Review in Perspective* (Cavendish, London, 1995); 'Regulating the Judicial Review Case Load' [2000] *PL* 651–70; T. Mullen, K. Pick, and T. Prosser, *Judicial Review in Scotland* (Wiley, Chichester, 1996).

[11] See, e.g., D. Dewees, D. Duff, and M. Trebilcock, *Exploring the Domain of Accident Law* (Oxford University Press, New York, 1996).

Rawlings, on whether they are 'red-light' or 'green-light' theorists), and in the second on values espoused by various groups of political theorists and philosophers (liberals, republicans, and so on). My aim in this essay is to focus on the values of public law and to consider how and to what extent our understanding of the law and its values can be improved by recourse to political theory. For present purposes, a (normative) 'theory' can be understood as a recommendation of a set of values to be used for the guidance and assessment of human conduct, coupled with an explanation of how those values interact with one another.

The first section of the essay introduces distinctions between background and foreground theories and between immanent and critical values. In the second section I consider whether Harlow and Rawlings' distinction between red-light and green-light approaches to administrative law can help us to understand the relationship between public law and values. The third section contains a list of a few of the most important values immanent in English public law, followed by some general points about the nature of public-law values. In the fourth section I discuss the relationship between law, values, and theory, and argue that the contribution political theory can make to our understanding of public law is limited by the abstractness of political values on the one hand, and by disagreement about values on the other. When, as a result, 'theory runs out', law can fill the normative gap and in this way make a positive contribution to the political life of a society.

1. IMMANENT AND CRITICAL VALUES

The relationship between law on the one hand and political and moral values on the other is a complex topic, intimately tied up with ideas about the autonomy of law and the relationship between law and other normative systems. The theory of autopoiesis recommends that we think about law as normatively closed (and in that sense, an autonomous system of rules and principles), but cognitively open—meaning that it is influenced by and can absorb non-legal norms, making them its own, as it were.[12] This insight may provide a foundation for the distinction that Harlow[13] and others have drawn between 'background' and 'foreground' normative theory. Background theory is 'immanent' in the law;[14] and it is often implicit rather than explicitly stated. In terms of autopoietic theory, we might say that the background values of the law are the values

---

[12] G. Teubner, *Law as an Autopoietic System* (Oxford University Press, Oxford, 1993).
[13] N. 7 above.
[14] 'Indwelling', 'inherent'. Harlow also distinguishes between 'shallow' and 'deep' theory. These seem to be varieties of what I am calling 'background theory'. She applies the term 'shallow' to theory immanent in legal rules and principles, and the term 'deep' to theory about 'the function of law in general, or public law in particular, in modern societies' (n. 7 above, 422). For her, background theories can also be immanent in legal treatises such as Dicey's famous account of the British Constitution in *An Introduction to the Study of the Law of the Constitution*, which was first published in 1885.

we discover by treating law as an autonomous normative system. One of the motivations for academic analysis of judicial decisions is a desire to uncover the more-or-less implicit background values on which they are (arguably) based. A reason the background values of the common law are often at least partly implicit is that the prime function of courts is to decide concrete disputes, not to lay down general rules. Of course, rule-making (in the context of dispute-settlement) is an important function of appellate courts. But making a rule is not the same thing as providing a normative justification for it; and the prime social function of appellate courts is to make rules, not to justify them.[15] This is equally true of legislatures; and the background values of legislation, the 'intention of the legislator' or the 'purpose of the legislation', can be every bit as difficult to discern as the values on which adjudicative rules rest.

This is not to say, of course, that courts and legislatures are free of any obligation to justify the rules they make. On the contrary, courts are expected to provide supporting reasons that (at least) show the rules to be consistent and coherent with the existing body of legal materials. In common-law systems, the prime role of courts is the essentially conservative one of maintaining values expressed in society's existing legal culture.[16] By contrast, subject to constraints imposed by constitutions and human rights documents, we expect legislators to justify their rule-making primarily by reference to outcomes. Unlike courts, legislators are not required to respect the values of consistency and coherence for their own sake. Conversely, although courts cannot and do not ignore consequences in justifying common law rules, the prime responsibility of judges is for the integrity of the legal system, not the social consequences of the law. By choosing to use legislation (i.e. law) to further desired social goals, governments make major contributions to legal culture. In Westminster-style political systems, it is by this means that society's legal culture can be rapidly changed in fundamental ways. Courts can and do change that culture slowly and incrementally; but their main task is to maintain its integrity by interpreting and applying legislation, and by making and applying the common law, in ways that respect and preserve traditional legal values. Because courts are required to promote consistency and coherence not only in common-law rule-making but also in the interpretation and application of legislation, judge-made law provides a framework of values into which legislation is introduced and within which the forward-looking outcome-oriented values of legislation have to be accommodated.[17] The background values of the law are to be found in this complex interaction between legislative and judicial activity.[18]

---

[15] S. Fish, *There's No Such Thing as Free Speech and It's a Good Thing Too* (Oxford University Press, New York, 1994), chaps. 11–13.

[16] J. Raz, *Ethics in the Public Domain* (Oxford University Press, Oxford, 1994), chap. 16.

[17] M. Krygier, 'The Traditionality of Statutes' (1988) 1 *Ratio Juris* 20.

[18] Lord Lester of Herne Hill, 'Developing Constitutional Principles of Public Law' [2001] *PL* 684. An illuminating case-study of this interaction is provided by the history of regulation in the United States. See C.R. Sunstein, *After the Rights Revolution: Reconceiving the Regulatory State*

By contrast to background values, foreground values are found outside the law. In this sense, the political theories discussed in Craig's *Public Law and Democracy in the United Kingdom and the United States of America*,[19] pluralism, liberalism, republicanism, and so on are in the foreground, not the background.[20] For lawyers, such foreground normative theories may assist the search for the background values of the law by providing theoretical models which, it can reasonably be assumed, are also accessible to, and therefore may have influenced, lawmakers. In terms of autopoietic theory, the cognitive openness of the law suggests that foreground normative theories may become absorbed into the law as background theory. Another use of foreground theories is to provide critical standards against which to assess the law.

Harlow and Rawlings have this to say about the relationship between background and foreground theory and values:[21]

... administrative law raises fundamental questions about our constitutional and political arrangements ... the argument is made that students must learn the law before they criticise it. This is to put the cart before the horse. The danger is that background theory, by which is meant the underlying values of a legal or constitutional system, will be absorbed uncritically along with the rules ... This book does not set out to propound a single, consistent theory of the state or the constitution ... civic-republican, post-modern, or legal-positivist ... a variety of views about administrative law are presented and subjected to critical scrutiny.

An assumption underlying this passage is that foreground values stand to law and its background values as critical standard to social practice. Students must first be provided with critical normative tools before being exposed to the potentially corrupting influence of the law and its immanent values. Despite the authors' disavowal of a consistent theory 'of the state or its constitution', this approach fairly clearly associates them with the positivist approach that distinguishes between 'the law' on the one hand and, on the other hand, the moral and political values that underlie it. Although Harlow and Rawlings see a close connection between positivism and the 'red-light', 'classical tradition of English administrative law' from which they distance themselves,[22] their basic objection is apparently not to positivism as a theory of the nature of (public) law, but rather to a rights-based, anti-communitarian political individualism which they attribute to its red-light adherents.[23] Craig, by contrast, aligns himself with Ronald Dworkin's anti-positivist 'interpretivist' approach to the relationship

---

(Harvard University Press, Cambridge, Mass., 1990). For a very different approach see G. Calabresi, *A Common Law for the Age of Statutes* (Harvard University Press, Cambridge, Mass., 1982). See also P.S. Atiyah, 'Common Law and Statute Law' (1985) 48 *MLR* 1; J Beatson, 'Has the Common Law a Future?' [1997] *CLJ* 291, 298ff.

[19] (Oxford University Press, Oxford, 1990).

[20] But note that Craig calls them 'background theories'.

[21] C. Harlow and R. Rawlings, *Law and Administration* (Butterworths, London, 2nd edn., 1997), p. vii. [22] *Ibid.*, 30.

[23] *Ibid.*, 36.

between law on the one hand and political and moral values on the other.[24] According to that approach, there can be no clear separation between rules of law and the values that best explain them. On the contrary, for the interpretivist, the reason that (in Craig's words) 'the content of public law can only be properly understood against the background political theory which a society actually espouses'[25] is that such theory is (part of) the law.[26] For the positivist, but not for the interpretivist, values can be immanent in the law without being part of it: the rules are one thing and their normative foundations are another.

For present purposes, the importance of the distinction between background and foreground values is that whatever view is taken about the relationship between law and its background values, that relationship is necessarily different from the relationship between law and foreground values. For most people, foreground values (identified as 'moral', 'political', or whatever) provide a basis for evaluating and criticizing law and its background values, but not vice versa. For this reason, in the rest of this essay I will use the term 'critical' instead of 'foreground', and the term 'immanent' instead of 'background'.

The attribution of such priority in practical reasoning[27] to critical values should be distinguished from claims of 'objectivity' or 'truth'. Pettit distinguishes between three different senses in which values may be said to be objective.[28] 'Semantic' objectivity involves only the claim that values express the truth from the speaker's perspective. A claim of 'ontological' objectivity additionally involves saying that value-statements are like colour-statements. Just as we see things as red because they are red, so we judge things as being morally good or bad because they are morally good or bad, and not vice versa. 'Justificatory' objectivism

---

[24] P.P. Craig, 'What Should Public Lawyers Do? A Reply' (1992) 12 *OJLS* 564; 'Public Law, Political Theory and Legal Theory' [2000] *PL* 211, 228–30.

[25] Craig, n. 19 above, 3. Craig elaborates his position in 'Public Law, Political Theory and Legal Theory', n. 24 above. He criticizes Sir William Wade's view that the sovereignty of Parliament is nothing but a 'political fact' (H.W.R. Wade, 'The Legal Basis of Sovereignty' [1955] *Cambridge LJ* 172). Craig's view, by contrast, seems to be that it is the normative (legal) conclusion of an argument premissed on normative (political) principles ('political theory'). A third possibility is that Parliamentary sovereignty is a legal norm based on facts about what relevant people think the role of Parliament ought to be. On this basis, we could say that Parliament is legally sovereign because relevant people *in fact* believe (or act as if they believe) that, as a matter of political norms, it ought to be sovereign. In other words, the sovereignty of Parliament can be based on facts without being merely a fact. The position Craig attributes to Wade he calls 'positivist', but the third position has at least as good a claim to that title. Note that in his discussion of the rule of law, Craig apparently aligns himself with positivism: P.P. Craig, 'Formal and Substantive Conceptions of the Rule of Law: An Analytical Framework' [1997] *PL* 467.

[26] Or, as Dyzenhaus puts it, because the 'legal materials [such as cases and statutes] are the legal data that have to be accounted for in deciding what the law is': D. Dyzenhaus, *Hard Cases in Wicked Legal Systems: South African Law in the Perspective of Legal Theory* (Clarendon Press, Oxford, 1991), 27. I leave aside complications associated with the distinction between inclusive and exclusive positivism, as to which see J. Coleman and B. Leiter, 'Legal Positivism', in D. Patterson (ed.), *A Companion to Philosophy of Law and Legal Theory* (Oxford University Press, Oxford, 1996), chap. 15.

[27] i.e., reasoning about what one ought to do.

[28] P. Pettit, 'Embracing Objectivity in Ethics', in B. Leiter (ed.), *Objectivity in Law and Morals* (Cambridge University Press, Cambridge, 2001), 234–86.

involves the further belief that there is a single set of values that everyone must use for assessing human conduct.

The difference I am pointing out between critical and immanent values does not depend on the view that critical values are objective in any of these three senses, but only on the attribution to critical values of priority in practical reasoning. It makes no sense to accord immanent values such priority over the law because even if immanent values are not part of the law, they are necessarily congruent with the existing law because they are read out of (or in to) it. It should also be noted that a person could rationally adopt a critical evaluative attitude to the law and its immanent values without believing that their own critical values were objective in either the justificatory or the ontological (or perhaps even the semantic) sense.

2. GREEN LIGHT AND RED LIGHT APPROACHES TO ADMINISTRATIVE LAW

Amongst English public lawyers and their critics, debate about the relative merits of positivism and interpretivism has taken place in the context of an occasionally acrimonious methodological dispute about 'what public lawyers should do' and, in particular, the extent to which lawyers should concern themselves with political theory and political science.[29] Framing the issue in this way unfortunately smacks of academic turf warfare, and it has encouraged a certain preoccupation with the views of influential individual writers and with 'styles of public law scholarship' rather than sustained analysis of legal rules and values. It has also produced some over-simplified polarities.

Consider, for instance, the distinction between so-called 'red-light' and 'green-light' theories of administrative law.[30] The typical red-light theorist (or so the story goes) views law 'positivistically' as an 'autonomous' system of norms. In the view of red-lighters, the prime concern of administrative law is (and should be) to control public executive power through formal, external mechanisms such as courts and tribunals. Red-lighters see the main function of such external control as being the protection of individual rights against undue encroachment in the name of the public interest. Consequently, they favour restrictive interpretation of the scope of public powers. At the same time, they consider the proper focus of external control to be the process and procedures of public decision-making, not its substance. Even though they subscribe to this normatively rich account of administrative law, red-lighters are depicted as thinking that administrative law is value-neutral, if not value-free.

[29] See especially B. O'Leary, 'What Should Public Lawyers Do?' (1992) 12 *OJLS* 404; Craig, 'What Should Public Lawyers Do? A Reply', n. 24 above; Harlow and Rawlings, n. 21 above, 25–8; M. Loughlin, *Public Law and Political Theory* (Oxford University Press, Oxford, 1992).

[30] Loughlin, n. 29 above, draws a similar distinction in terms of 'normativism' and 'functionalism'. Although these various categories are apparently intended as ideal-types rather than descriptions, their proponents freely apply them to named scholars.

By contrast, the paradigm green-light theorist (or so the story goes on) views law functionally as an instrument of power. In the view of green-lighters, the prime concern of administrative law is (and should be) to facilitate the execution of public programmes and the promotion of government policies. Consequently, they favour generous interpretation of the scope of public powers; and they emphasize the role of law in regulating the distribution of public powers between different organs of power as opposed to the relationship between public organs and the individual. Green-lighters favour internal control mechanisms (such as intra-departmental complaint and appeal mechanisms) over external mechanisms, and political control (by Parliament, for instance) over control in the name of law. Political control is preferred because it is more concerned with outcomes than with procedures, and because it is more 'democratic'. Unlike red-lighters, green-lighters do not hide their ideological light under a bushel of rule-based formalism. For them, administrative law is value-laden and ripe for critical assessment against moral and political criteria.

This story may well be useful as a pedagogical tool (as Harlow and Rawlings appear to have intended) or as an exercise in academic politics. But as a contribution to legal theory, it is problematic because (as Harlow and Rawlings acknowledge, especially by the addition of 'amber light theorists' to the ranks of the reds and greens) its power depends on various false dichotomies. A complete account of the relationship between public law and public power, whether descriptive or normative, would consider the role of law in both facilitating and constraining the exercise of power; and in both furthering public purposes and protecting individual interests. An account that gave undue weight to internal or political controls would be just as deficient as one that paid excessive attention to external or legal controls. A complete account would deal with relations between citizens and organs of public power as well as relations between the various organs themselves. A complete account would concern itself with both the procedure and the substance of public decision-making. This is not to say, of course, that an account must be complete in order to be useful or valuable. Indeed, the notion of the 'complete picture' is an ideal rather than a practical aspiration. The fact that a scholar emphasizes one scene of the complete picture does not justify the conclusion that they cannot distinguish the part from the whole.

At a somewhat deeper level, the contrast between (red-light) normativism and (green-light) functionalism is misleading. There is no inconsistency involved in thinking that law is both a normative institution and a purposive human practice; indeed, it is law's very normativity that makes it so useful as an instrument of power and a source of legitimation for those who exercise power. The most enduring insight of the realist movement in legal theory, from which green-light functionalists are often said to have taken inspiration, did not involve a denial that law is a normative enterprise, but rather insisted that because legal norms are indeterminate, they cannot explain or justify judicial decisions.[31] Also misleading is the association of the idea that law is value-neutral with positivism (understood as a school of legal theory). The point I wish to make here is different from that which Craig makes in answer to O'Leary's puzzling suggestion that positivism is the background theory of public law (as opposed to law in general) espoused in many liberal democracies, and his conclusion that public lawyers should therefore concern themselves exclusively with the law, and forget about the values which it embodies or promotes.[32] Craig replies that even if O'Leary's suggestion is correct, the conclusion does not follow because there may be gaps in the law which courts (i.e. lawyers) have to fill; and because, more generally, the question of what the law ought to be 'is an appropriate concern for public lawyers, whether academics or practitioners'.[33] On one reading of this exchange, Craig and O'Leary concur in the belief that, for positivists, 'what the law ought to be' is a matter of values, but that the same cannot be said about 'what the law is'. This perhaps helps to explain why Craig espouses Dworkinian interpretivism. According to this latter theory, legal theorists and lawyers (both academic and practising) are necessarily concerned with moral and political values because determining what the law is on any particular topic involves giving the best possible interpretation of relevant legal materials in the light of such values.

It is a mistake to think that because positivists draw a distinction between what the law is and what it ought to be, they are committed to the view that law (as it is) is value-neutral or value-free. Indeed, one of the prime motivations for insisting on the distinction is 'to enable men [*sic*] to see steadily the precise issues posed by the existence of morally bad laws, and to understand the specific character of the authority of a legal order'.[34] There is an important difference between Dworkinian interpretivism, which is anti-positivistic, and what Julie Dickson (building on Joseph Raz's work) calls 'indirectly evaluative theory', which is not.[35] There is no inconsistency between the propositions that law is identifiable by its institutional sources and that it embodies and promotes moral and political values.[36] Rather it is primarily by reference to its norm-generating

---

[31] B. Leiter, 'Legal Realism', in D. Patterson (ed.), n. 26 above, chap. 16. On Llewellyn's statement that '[w]hat . . . officials do about disputes is . . . the law' see M.J. Horwitz, *The Transformation of American Law, 1870–1960* (Oxford University Press, New York, 1992), 247–50.

[32] O'Leary, n. 29 above, 407–8.

[33] Craig, 'What Should Public Lawyers Do? A Reply', n. 24 above, 566.

[34] H.L.A. Hart, *Essays in Jurisprudence and Philosophy* (Oxford University Press, Oxford, 1983), 53. See also R. Cotterrell, *The Politics of Jurisprudence: A Critical Introduction to Legal Philosophy* (Butterworths, London, 1989), chap. 5. One of the preoccupations of jurisprudence in the middle decades of the 20th century was the question whether 'natural law or positivism best encouraged or resisted totalitarianism': Horwitz, n. 31 above, 248.

[35] J. Dickson, *Evaluation and Legal Theory* (Hart, Oxford, 2001).

[36] J. Raz, *The Authority of Law: Essays on Law and Morality* (Oxford University Press, Oxford, 1979), chap. 3. This is true even in relation to exclusive (or 'hard') positivism which (unlike inclusive, or 'soft', positivism) says that what the law is must always be ascertainable without reference to 'morality'. It does not follow from this proposition that law does not embody and

institutions (legislatures and courts) that we are able to differentiate law from other normative systems such as morality and politics. The idea that law in general, or public law in particular, is value-neutral, let alone value-free, is certainly a mistake. But it is not a mistake that can be pinned on positivism or, by a loose association of ideas, on public lawyers who think that there is an important sense in which law is distinguishable from morality and politics, and that law and legal institutions play a vital role in controlling the exercise of public power. If some public lawyers have made this mistake, it should not be attributed to their having been positivists or red-lighters. More likely it was the product of a crude and untenable conception of separation of powers according to which judges do not make law and the only function of courts is to apply law.

The contrast between red-lighters and green-lighters is misleading in another way, too. Red-lighters, we are told, see law as autonomous and value-neutral, whereas green-lighters see it as an instrument of values. However, at least in extreme versions (such as that espoused by Griffith),[37] functionalism rests on the view that law is merely an instrument of power, available to be turned to whatever ideological use is chosen by those who control or can engage the legal system. By denying that law is autonomous of politics, such views rob it of any ideological content of its own: the values of the law are the values of the powerful. On one reading, Craig's position is similar: public law is a reflection of political values that are found outside the law in 'society'. For Harlow and Rawlings, by contrast, law has an ideology of its own from which students need to be protected by being equipped with some political theory before their first encounters with legal materials, especially cases. Herein lies an irony, for Craig is certainly not a green-light functionalist in the sense in which Griffith is a functionalist,[38] while Harlow and Rawlings identify themselves, albeit tentatively, as green-lighters. This suggests to me that the distinction between red-lighters and green-lighters does not capture the differences between various approaches to the relationship between public law and political values.

In my view, the most important difference between green-lighters and red-lighters does not concern the relationship between law and values, but rather resides in the role they respectively assign to courts in regulating the exercise of public power. Green-lighters distrust judges because, as Griffith powerfully argued in *The Politics of the Judiciary*,[39] while the judicial role is inherently and inevitably 'small-p' political, judges are politically unrepresentative and unaccountable. According to the green-light creed, the balance of public decision-making power,

---

promote 'moral' values: J. Raz, *Ethics in the Public Domain* (Oxford University Press, Oxford, 1994), chap. 10.

[37] '. . . laws are merely statements of a power relationship *and nothing more*': J.A.G. Griffith, 'The Political Constitution' (1979) 42 *MLR* 1, 19 (emphasis added).

[38] See previous note and Loughlin, n. 29 above, 197–201. See also M. Loughlin, 'The Pathways of Public Law Scholarship', in G.P. Wilson (ed.), *Frontiers of Legal Scholarship: Twenty Five Years of the Warwick Law School* (Wiley, Chichester, 1995), 170–4.

[39] First published 1977; 5th edn. (Fontana, London, 1997).

as between the judiciary on the one hand and the legislature and the executive on the other, should rest firmly with the legislature and the executive. In this view, the institutions of government should be designed in such a way as to minimize judicial opportunities to constrain the exercise of public power by the 'democratic' branches. It is in this spirit that Carol Harlow opposes broad standing rules[40] and the expansion of state liability for damages under European law.[41] Red-lighters, by contrast, believe that precisely because courts are immunized from political and social pressure, they play a crucial and significant role in regulating the exercise of public power by promoting traditional legal values.

Of course, the difference between the two positions is only one of degree. The typical green-lighter does not advocate the abolition of judicial review of the exercise of public power any more than the typical red-lighter denies the value of non-judicial review mechanisms and of judicial restraint in the exercise of the review jurisdiction. More importantly, whether any particular scholar espouses red-light or green-light views is likely to depend, to some extent at least, on their personal ideology. Those who are broadly sympathetic with the substance of judge-made (administrative) law will tend to be red-lighters, whereas those who are not will tend to be green-lighters. At the same time, individual attitudes towards 'activist' judicial review may be related to espousal of a larger set of political values. Thus, Harlow and Rawlings suggest an association between red-lightism and liberal individualism; and there is some reason to think that green-light views may be particularly attractive to those of a communitarian or welfarist persuasion and to people who favour what McAuslan calls 'collective consumption'.[42]

However, such coincidence of commitments (to the extent that it exists) is likely to be contingent.[43] For instance, communitarians are more likely than liberal individualists to be concerned about the 'accountability deficit' allegedly generated by phenomena, such as out-sourcing of the provision of government services and the creation of 'Next Steps' agencies, which were designed to replace traditional 'public' forms of accountability with market(-type) forces. And it is surely no cause for surprise that the rapid growth and development of representative and public-interest judicial-review litigation coincided with the political sea-change of the 1980s and 1990s which saw pressure groups representing social (as opposed to economic) interests increasingly relegated to the status of outsiders in the great game of interest-group politics. The courts have responded to these developments in a proactive, red-light way by, for instance, extending the reach of judicial review to private-sector regulators,[44] and by developing rules of standing that give representative applicants easy access to the courts.[45]

---

[40] C. Harlow, 'Public Law and Popular Justice' (2002) 65 *MLR* 1.
[41] C. Harlow, 'Francovich and the Problem of the Disobedient State' (1996) 2 *ELJ* 199.
[42] P. McAuslan, 'Administrative Law, Collective Consumption and Judicial Policy' (1983) 46 *MLR* 1.
[43] For an excellent exposition of this point see Horwitz, n. 31 above, 240–6.
[44] J. Black, 'Constitutionalising Self-Regulation' (1996) 59 *MLR* 24.
[45] P. Cane, 'Standing up for the Public' [1995] *PL* 276.

Incidentally, such developments graphically illustrate the value-laden nature of the common law—they could, without strain, be interpreted as undermining the political thrust of the changes to which they were a reaction.

The contingency of the link between attitudes to judicial review and particular political commitments can be seen also in the fact that neither the 'incorporation' of the European Convention on Human Rights into English law by the Human Rights Act 1998, nor Scottish, Welsh, and Irish devolution, lacked a goodly measure of support from the Left,[46] even though these developments have brought with them greatly increased opportunities for judicial control over executives and legislatures.

Finally, we should note another respect in which the red-light/green-light dichotomy provides a less than satisfying account of approaches to public law. Both red-lighters and green-lighters define their positions in relation to judicial review, internal complaint and review mechanisms, and parliamentary scrutiny of the executive—all hierarchical forms of accountability in which an 'inferior' is required to answer to a 'superior'. As a result, they give little or no help in understanding market-based and quasi-market-based forms of accountability, the introduction of which has characterized public sector reform in the past twenty years or so.[47]

My basic argument, then, is that the debate between red-lighters and green-lighters should be understood as being concerned with the proper role of the courts *vis-à-vis* the executive and the legislature, and not with the relationship between law and values. Green-lighters are just as likely as red-lighters to be positivists; and there is no reason why a red-lighter should not be an interpretivist. The erroneous view that law is value-free or value-neutral is not a feature of positivism, and the correct view that law is value-laden is not exclusive to interpretivists.

3. Values in English public law

It was argued earlier that the English debate about the relationship between public law and political theory has diverted attention away from legal values and on to styles of legal and theoretical scholarship. Because this essay is chiefly about the relationships between law, values, and theory, I must say something at this point about the values of English public law before moving on, in the final section, to discuss those relationships. Space does not permit anything more than the most cursory account of some of the values immanent in English public law. They include the following:

Representation. This is the basis of what is often treated as the most fundamental principle of English public law, namely the priority of law made by or under the authority of Parliament over law made by courts.

---

[46] The natural home, one might expect, of green-lighters.
[47] C. Scott, 'Accountability in the Regulatory State' (2000) 27 *J of Law and Society* 38.

Accountability. This value underpins (for instance) the doctrine of individual ministerial responsibility to Parliament, the principle that governmental power must be exercised according to law, and the existence of multiple mutually reinforcing forms and criteria of accountability[48]—political accountability to Parliament, legal accountability to courts and tribunals, financial accountability to auditors, administrative accountability to ombudsmen, and so on.

Judicial deference. This value is based on a set of ideas about the unrepresentative and unaccountable nature of the judiciary, the characteristics of court procedure, and the limits of judicial expertise.

A public/private dichotomy. The law utilizes a complex set of public/private distinctions for two broad purposes: to justify the existence and exercise of powers to interfere with the freedom and autonomy of individuals in order to protect and promote social interests ('public powers'); and to justify the imposition of distinctive duties and obligations on public functionaries in order to protect the interests of individuals, groups within society, and society as a whole.

Equality before the law. The equality principle creates a presumption that rules of private law apply to public functionaries in the same way that they apply to citizens, so that departures from equality should be allowed only to the extent necessary for the proper performance of public functions.

Protection of the individual. In Westminster-style democracies, promoting social interests by law-making is primarily the function of Parliament and its delegates. Law-making by courts (common law) is centrally concerned with individual rights, not social interests. As a result, promoting social interests through law is typically conceived of as belonging to the 'political' as opposed to the 'judicial' realm. As traditionally understood, the distinctively judicial public-law task, expressed in common-law principles of judicial review and statutory interpretation, is the protection of individual rights and interests against undue encroachment in the name of social interests. The enactment of the Human Rights Act 1998 greatly increased the capacity of the courts to protect individual rights.

Access to the courts. In theory (so the traditional view holds), Parliament could abolish the power of the judicial branch to review conduct of the executive branch. On the other hand, in modern times at least, courts have gone to considerable lengths to interpret ouster provisions narrowly in order to afford maximum scope to the judicial review jurisdiction.

Executive authority. The monarchical origins of British government explain the existence in English public law of an authoritarian strand that reflects the dominance of the central executive ('the Crown') in the constitution. For instance (and somewhat inconsistently with the value of representation) central government has certain 'prerogative' powers that have no statutory source.

Diffusion of public power. Monarchy is a centripetal influence in British public law. But there are powerful centrifugal forces as well—local and devolved

---

[48] Scott, *ibid.*, calls this phenomenon 'redundancy'.

government, the institutions of the EU, and the ideology of outsourcing and the New Public Management.

Transparency. This value is most obviously embodied in the Freedom of Information Act 2000. Contrapuntally, the value of secrecy is most obviously embodied in the Official Secrets Act 1989.

Participation. Participation by citizens in governmental processes takes various forms, including self-regulation and public/private partnerships for the delivery of public services. The principle that individuals should be heard before decisions are made that affect them personally is more deeply embedded in English legal culture than the principle that citizens should be allowed to participate in public policy-formation processes.

Promotion of the public interest. Counterposed to the pluralist/individualist value of participation is an elitist notion of 'the public interest'.[49] Elements of public law that reflect the value of facilitating the promotion of a politically defined 'public interest' include strong judicial deference to legislation; judicial restraint in reviewing policy decisions; concern not to hinder 'efficiency' in the conduct of government business in the context, for instance, of defining notions of procedural fairness; relatively short time-limits for challenging administrative decisions in the courts; explicit reference to 'public interest' in the rules governing extensions of time; and so on.

The superiority of European law. Like the passage of the Human Rights Act 1998 and the various devolution statutes, EC membership has brought about a huge shift of power in the British polity away from the political process and into the courts. Griffith's thesis that Britain has a 'political' rather than a 'legal' constitution,[50] however plausible it may have been in 1979, has become increasingly difficult to sustain.

Even this breathless recitation of a few of the immanent values of English public law suffices to support several pertinent general observations. First, as is illustrated by the value of protecting the individual, the immanent values of public law are a product of complex interaction between legislative and judicial activity.[51] Secondly, the red/green light metaphor, focused (as I have argued that it is) on issues of accountability, can throw only partial light on the wide array of values underlying public law. Thirdly, public law values may be in competition with one another, transparency with secrecy, executive authority with representation, public interest with the protection of the individual, and so on. This is not surprising. Public law reflects the plurality of commitments characteristic of moral and political life.

Fourthly, a value may be honoured more in the breach than the observance. For instance, it has been argued that the Freedom of Information Act 2000 is a

---

[49] For a general account of elitist political theory see P. Dunleavy and B. O'Leary, *Theories of the State: The Politics of Liberal Democracy* (Macmillan, Basingstoke, 1987), chap. 4. Concerning pluralism see chaps. 2 and 6. See also D. Feldman, 'Public Law Values in the House of Lords' (1990) 106 *LQR* 246.　　　　　　　　　　　　　　　　　　　　　　　[50] Griffith, n. 37 above.

[51] See page 6 above.

'sheep in wolf's clothing, masquerading as a Freedom of Information Act, yet in reality reserving to government near absolute control over all sensitive government information'.[52] Fifthly, the values are dynamic rather than static. This is obviously true of values that find expression in legislation. For instance, enactment of the Freedom of Information Act greatly enhanced promotion of the value of transparency in English law. But it is also true of those that are part of the common law. For instance, the doctrine of Parliamentary sovereignty (which is underpinned by the value of representation) has been adapted to accommodate the superiority of European law. Although courts have a special responsibility for preserving well-established legal values, they must also adapt those values to accommodate legislation and changes in political practice.

Sixthly, some of the values, as one would expect, reflect the particular features of the British Constitution, most obviously, perhaps, the fact that Britain has a parliamentary as opposed to a presidential system of government. This suggests that theories (such as American-style republicanism) that were developed against a different constitutional background may have only indirect relevance to understanding or assessing English public law and its values. It also suggests that descriptive political science may make just as important a contribution to understanding public law as normative political theory can.[53]

4. THE DEPENDENCE OF POLITICAL THEORY ON PUBLIC LAW

The values listed in the previous section are more or less abstract and subject to various mutual conflicts. It is of the very nature of normative principles that purport to explain and justify legal rules that they will be more general and abstract than the rules themselves; and the larger the number of rules such a principle covers, the more this will be the case. Because the immanent values of (public) law are abstract, people may disagree about what concrete rules they require or justify. For instance, people who agree that procedural fairness is valuable may disagree about what detailed procedural rules would best promote this value. Moreover, people who subscribe to a common set of values may disagree about how to resolve conflicts between those values either in the abstract or in concrete situations. Normative 'political theories', such as pluralism, liberalism, and republicanism, may be understood as sets of values worked into a system which shows how those values relate to one another and how conflicts between them ought to be resolved. Such theories are inevitably even more abstract than principles of the sort we have been considering. As a result, people who profess to hold the same theory may disagree about the details of the theory, i.e. about how the values they hold relate to one another, and about how conflicts between them ought to be resolved.

---

[52] R. Austin, 'Freedom of Information: The Constitutional Impact', in J. Jowell and D. Oliver (eds.), *The Changing Constitution* (Oxford University Press, Oxford, 4th edn. 2000), 371.

[53] A point also made in an unfortunately aggressive and theory-phobic way by O'Leary, n. 29 above.

The argument in this section concerns the implications of disagreement about values, and the abstractness of values, for our understanding of the relationship between values and law. In particular, I want to question the idea, which is at least implicit in much recent writing about public law and political theory, that the relationship between the two is asymmetrical in the sense that we need political theory in order to understand public law, but that public law has no distinctive contribution to make to our understanding of political values.

(a) Disagreement about Values

Let us first consider disagreement about values. As Harlow and Rawlings rightly observe, '[d]iscussion, debate and disagreement are the very nature of politics'[54] and, one might add, of theorizing about politics. Disagreement about values is a pervasive feature of our moral and political lives. In practice, disagreements about the detailed implications of immanent and critical political values may be unresolvable. Unresolvable disagreements about basic values may threaten the stability of social life and undermine social co-operation.[55] In order to deal with and manage unresolvable disagreements about how political values should be concretized and about how conflicts of value should be resolved, society needs authority. Law is an authoritative (i.e. an authority-claiming) normative institution. Legislation and judicial rule-making concretize political (and moral) values by applying them to particular social problems and issues. Adjudication concretizes values even more by applying legislative and common-law rules to individual cases. This process of authoritative concretization of values in legal rules does not purport to resolve disagreement at the level of basic values. But if the legal rules are accepted as legitimate by those to whom they apply, they will be used as a guide to behaviour by those who disagree with them as well as by those who agree with them. Legitimate laws provide people with authority-based reasons for action that are independent of the normative content of the laws. It is by virtue of its authoritativeness that law can manage value-based disagreement.[56]

Adjudication makes a central contribution to law's function of managing moral and political disagreement because courts are under an obligation to decide disputes that are properly brought before them. This means that disagreements that may be left unaddressed outside the law have to be addressed when they are legalized. As a result, courts can make a contribution to the management of political disagreement that the political system may not be able to make by reason of the fact that no-one has a sufficiently strong incentive to address the disagreement in issue. However, the potential of courts to address disagreements which the political system ignores is limited for several reasons.

---

[54] Harlow and Rawlings, n. 21 above, p. vii.
[55] T. Honoré, 'The Dependence of Morality on Law' (1993) 13 *OJLS* 1, 12–17.
[56] J. Raz, *The Authority of Law* (Oxford University Press, Oxford, 1979), 50–2.

First, courts deal only with concrete disputes; secondly they deal only with disputes that are presented to them (i.e. they are reactive); thirdly, they are tradition-bound; fourthly, they lack democratic legitimacy; and fifthly, their procedures are unsuited to addressing many complex moral and political issues. Even so, because legal disputes have to be resolved, and because courts have at their disposal coercive tools for the resolution of disputes (such as the power to quash decisions and to make mandatory and prohibitory orders), courts are frequently required to choose between competing concrete applications of abstract values in a way that other social institutions are not required to do.

The basic point is that by virtue of the authoritative nature of law and the social and constitutional function of courts, law and legal institutions make a distinctive and significant contribution to the normative life of society. At the least, this contribution takes the form of managing disagreement about basic political values by authoritatively adopting a position on disputed issues. But the law's importance may not be limited to this negative regulatory role. Although the law does not purport to resolve underlying normative disagreement when it adopts one position rather than another on a disputed issue, the very fact that legal institutions which are widely regarded as legitimate have adopted a particular normative position may cause those who disagree with it to reconsider their own views. Such people may come to think that the normative position adopted by the law is superior to their own, and may come to comply with the law not merely because it makes legitimate demands on them as an authority, but also because they accept that what it demands of them is rightly demanded as a matter of substantive values. The possibility that law may lead people to alter their values in this way is an important reason why we should think of the relationship between law and values as being symbiotic. It is a mistake, it seems to me, to view the 'normative traffic' as being all one way from critical values to law. Law may not only reflect critical values, but may also mould them.

The point can be made more theoretically in terms of the idea of autopoiesis. Law and politics can be thought of as distinct normative systems that are open to influence from each other. When law absorbs political values it translates them into the language of law—the politically valuable becomes the legal, and the politically unacceptable becomes the illegal. Just as law can absorb political values, so the political system can absorb legal values. In this direction, the legal becomes the politically valuable and the illegal becomes the politically unacceptable. If one accepts the now almost universal view that the law is 'cognitively open' to political values,[57] there is no reason to deny that the political realm may be cognitively open to legal values.[58] It follows (adapting Craig's words[59]) that

---

[57] One of the most basic insights of the 'law-in-context' approach to administrative law, of which Harlow is a leading exponent, is that administrative law is permeated by politics or, in Loughlin's words (adopted by Harlow and Rawlings), that it is 'a sophisticated form of political discourse'.

[58] For a valuable discussion of the relationship between 'legal reasoning' and 'political argument' see T.R.S. Allan, *Constitutional Justice: A Liberal Theory of the Rule of Law* (Oxford University Press, Oxford, 2001), 288–90.　　　　[59] Craig, n. 19 above, 3.

just as public law cannot be 'properly understood' without reference to political values and theory, so political values and theory cannot be properly understood without reference to public law.

(b) The Abstractness of Values

Now let us consider the implications of the abstractness of political (and legal) values and theory. It is the abstractness of values and normative theories that gives them explanatory power and enables them to contribute to our understanding of law. But the abstractness of values and theory also limits their explanatory power as well as their normative force. For instance, it is unlikely that any value or normative theory would dictate a choice between unreasonableness and proportionality as standards of judicial review, or between oral and written 'hearings' as a requirement of procedural fairness. Just as many people think that there comes a point where 'the law runs out' and needs to be supplemented by extra-legal values, so there may come a point where values and normative theories run out and need to be supplemented by law. In the context of the relationship between law and morality, Honoré calls this latter phenomenon 'the dependence of morality on law'.[60] Sometimes we need the law to tell us what is the morally right thing to do. Morality may tell us that we ought to pay taxes or that we should take care for the safety of others. But we need the law to tell us how much tax we ought morally to pay, or on which side of the road we ought morally to drive. There are obvious ways in which the law is dependent on morality, but there are also important ways in which morality needs the law.

The same is true of the relationship between law and political values. The idea that there are political values immanent in the law expresses the dependence of law on political values. But there may be situations in which we need the law to tell us what behaviour is politically appropriate. For instance, although the political principle of respect for individual rights might tell us that people should be heard before the making by a government official of a decision that affects them adversely, that principle may not tell us whether the hearing should be oral or whether an opportunity to put one's case in writing is sufficient. In that case, a legal rule requiring an oral hearing would tell us what was the right thing to do politically.

By saying that the law tells us what is the right thing to do morally or politically I do not mean that the law has the quality of an ultimate standard of behaviour. Rather, the point is that law possesses institutional resources (in the form of legislative and adjudicative organs) that enable it to provide determinate answers to moral and political questions that would not otherwise be forthcoming. But the answers it provides are, of course, open to critical assessment in moral and political terms. Some of the questions to which the law provides answers, for instance, on which side of the road to drive, may be normatively

---

[60] Honoré, n. 55 above.

neutral; but others, for instance, how much tax to pay or whether an oral hearing is required, may themselves generate normative disagreement. The general point is that while it seems obviously true that we cannot properly understand public law without taking account of the political values that underlie it, the converse is also true, namely that we cannot fully understand the demands made on us by political values immanent in public law without knowing what public law says, because law possesses institutional resources that enable it to generate answers to political questions that political theory may lack the resources to provide.

5. CONCLUSION

In this essay I have argued that by focusing on 'values' rather than on 'theory' and 'styles of scholarship' we can learn valuable lessons about the relationship between law and politics. I have briefly analysed some of the political values immanent in English public law. Building on this analysis, I have argued that the relationship between public law and political values is symbiotic. Although public law is dependent on political values, it also makes a distinctive contribution to society's political culture by managing unresolvable conflicts of political values and by providing guidance for behaviour when that provided by abstract political values runs out.

2

Theory and Values in Public Law: A Response

PAUL CRAIG*

Peter Cane has, in the previous chapter, presented a challenging argument as to the role of theory and values in public law. The challenge is directed in part towards the utility of the distinction between red- and green-light theories of administrative law used by Harlow and Rawlings. The argument is also directed more generally against the use of political theory by public lawyers, the claim being that it has diverted attention away from legal values.

Debate is good. This essay will present an opposing argument to that put forward by Cane. The discussion will begin with an exploration of Cane's legal values. It will then be argued that discussion of legal values will often throw into sharp relief contestable issues that take one back to political theory/theory of the state, and that such theory can enrich our understanding of these values. This will be followed by an analysis of the limits of political theory. The last two sections of the essay will be concerned respectively with the relationship between public law, political theory and political science, and between public law, legal theory, and political theory.

1. VALUES IN ENGLISH PUBLIC LAW

It is central to Peter Cane's argument that concerns with political theory, or theory of the state, have hindered examination of the relationship between public law on the one hand, and political and moral values on the other, by diverting attention away from the values of the law.[1] Debate about the relationship between public law and political theory has, he argues, diverted attention away from 'legal values and on to styles of legal and theoretical scholarship'.[2] He then provides a list of some of the values that are immanent in English public law.

It is important at the outset to be clear in what sense the matters thus listed are to be regarded as public law values, since this is of significance more generally for Cane's argument.

---

* I am grateful for comments from Peter Cane, Richard Rawlings, and Adam Tomkins.
[1] P. Cane, 'Theory and Values in Public Law', 4.   [2] *Ibid*.

A criterion might be that the *items included in any such list are to be found in positive law*. This would be the most obvious test for deciding whether a value should be included within a list of values that are central to English public law. We would, on this view, have to find a source in positive law, in terms of statute or common law doctrine, that justified the inclusion of any particular value on the list. This criterion cannot however justify the list that we are presented with. Consider the following examples. If recognition through positive law were the criterion then there would, for example, have been little or no basis for including transparency prior to the Freedom of Information Act 2000. The value of participation would have to be re-drafted, since neither courts nor legislature provide any general protection for participation in rule-making. The protection of individual rights would have to have been given a very different spin prior to the common law jurisprudence on the protection of rights in the late 1980s, and prior to the Human Rights Act 1998. The meaning, and perhaps very existence, of diffusion of power as a value would have been read wholly differently prior to devolution. It is however the case that those concerned with public law regarded these issues as of importance, and discussed them as being integral to public law, before they were included within positive law. It is for this reason that transparency was talked about on the 'public law agenda' long before the 2000 legislation, why participation rights in rule-making is a regular subject of discussion among public lawyers, and why discourse about rights and public law took place long before common law or legislative initiatives.

Another possible criterion is that the list *comprises values that are immanent within public law*. This is what Cane appears to have in mind, since he speaks in these terms.[3] What Cane terms background values are immanent within the law, and are those values that can be discovered by treating the law as an autonomous normative system.[4] For the positivist, such values can be immanent in the law without being part of it, in the sense that the rules are one thing and their normative foundations another.[5] However, we are also told that even if 'immanent values are not part of the law, they are necessarily congruent with the existing law because they are read out of (or in to) it'.[6] This does not resolve the problem adverted to above. Public lawyers regard the values listed by Cane as being important, notwithstanding that a particular value has or had no secure place in positive law. This problem cannot be overcome by referring to the values as being immanent within public law, since, as Cane himself states, immanent values are necessarily congruent with the existing law, being read out of or into it.

The real criterion is surely that *the list captures the values that public lawyers think are or should be important in a regime of public law*. On this view, inclusion within positive law may be a sufficient, but not a necessary, condition for inclusion within the list of public law values. If this is indeed the real criterion

---

[3] P. Cane, 'Theory and Values in Public Law', 5–9.   [4] *Ibid.*, 5–6.   [5] *Ibid.*, 6.
[6] *Ibid.*, 9.

then it requires us to think about the list in a very different light. It begs the question why we regard such values as being central or integral to public law. This is because of complex assumptions about, for example, the rule of law, separation of powers, the degree of autonomy of different levels of government, and, most fundamentally, the relation of individual and state. If this is so it invites the question why, for example, 'citizenship' does not feature in the list as a topic in its own right: the political, social, and economic rights of an individual against the state are surely central to public law. It also more fundamentally calls into question whether it is possible to interpret these 'legal values' without recourse to background assumptions drawn from political theory. This latter issue will now be considered in more detail.

2. POLITICAL THEORY AND LEGAL VALUES

Cane argues that political theory has diverted attention away from the legal values discussed in the previous section. There is, however, no evidence that preoccupation with theory has hindered consideration of, or diverted attention from, these issues by those writing in the public law field. There is a very large volume of literature dealing with such matters. Public lawyers who evince an interest in political theory would moreover contest this claim as it applies to them. Those who 'do' political theory, or theories of the state, do not ignore these values. The authors taken to task, Harlow and Rawlings, Craig, Loughlin, etc, have addressed many, if not all, of these particular values in their own work. We do, however, believe that the interpretation accorded to such values will often throw into sharp relief contestable issues that take one back to political theory/theory of the state, and that such theory can enrich our understanding of these values, in the different ways discussed within this section. The conclusions drawn from such theory are not mechanistic, and they may be contestable. This is, however, also true of legal reasoning in general, and is not an objection to the enterprise itself.

(a) The Nature and Object of Public Law: Red, Green, and Amber Light Theories

It is fitting to begin with the colour nomenclature used by Harlow and Rawlings, of red, green, and amber light theories. Tomkins has provided a valuable summation of these theories.[7] Red-light theorists believed that law was autonomous to and superior over politics; that the administrative state was dangerous and should be kept in check by law; that the preferred way of doing this was through adjudication; and that the goal should be to enhance liberty,

---

[7] A. Tomkins, 'In Defence of the Political Constitution' (2002) 22 *OJLS* 157.

conceived in terms of the absence of external constraints.[8] Green-light theorists challenged these tenets. They believed that law was not autonomous from politics; that the administrative state was not a necessary evil, but a positive attribute to be welcomed; that administrative law should seek not merely to stop bad administrative practices, but to encourage and facilitate good administrative practice, and that there might be better ways to achieve this than adjudication; and that the goal was to enhance individual and collective liberty conceived in positive and not just negative terms.[9] Tomkins describes amber-light theory in the following terms. There is a belief that law is discrete from and superior to politics; that the state can be successfully limited by law; that the best way of controlling the state is through the judicial articulation of broad principles of legality; and that the ultimate goal is to safeguard a particular vision of human rights.[10]

There is force in Cane's argument on this issue. He questions the theoretical assumptions underlying the dichotomy between red- and green-light theories, more particularly the sense in which law can be seen to be separate from politics, and the sense in which it can be regarded as value free. I would, in particular, accept that the sense in which red and green, or indeed amber, light theories perceive law and politics to be distinct or not is a controversial and complex issue. The overarching critique is, however, that, while the distinctions between red and green light might be useful as a pedagogical tool, they are problematic, since they are dependent upon various false dichotomies. A complete account of the relationship between 'public law and public power, whether descriptive or normative, would consider the role of law in both facilitating and constraining the exercise of power, and in both furthering public purposes and protecting individual interests'.[11] We must, says Cane, have due regard to internal/political controls, and also to external/legal controls.

There are, however, two senses in which this critique misses the mark, one historical, the other conceptual.

The fact that a particular view might now be regarded as defective does not mean that, in historical terms, it did not capture the dominant mode of thinking about administrative law extant at that time. The fact that a red-light approach might no longer exert the dominance that it once had does not mean that we can or should ignore it in seeking to understand the development of the subject over time. Thus scholars in, for example, the USA will, in a similar vein, advert to transmission belt theories of administrative law, based on protection of private autonomy narrowly conceived, which once held sway.

There is, equally importantly, a sense in which this critique misses the mark in more conceptual terms. Red and green light theories encapsulated, as Tomkins' summation reveals, very different attitudes to the administrative state, very different views as to the appropriate legal and political response, and very different views on the overall objective of administrative law. Cane would argue

---

[8] A. Tomkins, 'In Defence of the Political Constitution' (2002) 22 *OJLS* 157.
[9] *Ibid.*, 158–9.   [10] *Ibid.*, 160.   [11] Cane, n. 1 above, 10.

that these are false dichotomies and that we must, for example, have both internal/political and external/legal controls, and that we must recognize the role of law in facilitating and constraining the exercise of power. It is, however, precisely the blend of these that is at stake. The fact, for example, that a green-light theorist should also acknowledge the need for external/judicial controls does not mean that such an advocate would be driven to accept the same types of legal controls as an advocate of the red-light approach. What judicial controls a green-light theorist might be inclined to accept is itself an under-explored issue. It is however perfectly possible to configure judicial controls that accord with green-light theory, which would differ markedly from those of the traditional red-light school.[12] There are moreover some things that cannot be 'blended'. A perception that administrative law is concerned to enhance liberty, conceived in negative terms as the absence of external constraints, cannot be reconciled with the view that the goal is to enhance individual and collective liberty conceived in positive and not just negative terms.

(b) The Nature and Object of Public Law: The Changing Boundaries of State Action

It is clear that there have been significant changes in the nature of government, more especially in the last two decades. The move towards privatization, contracting out, new public management, and the like is the concrete manifestations of this. The discussion of the particular values listed by Cane, as they relate to the Thatcher reforms, has not been hindered by discussion of the political theory of the New Right, which initially informed these changes. It is, to the contrary, difficult to see how one could discuss those particular issues at all without adverting to the background political theory that informed those policies. The fact that some aspects of this theory have survived the passing of its original protagonists, and have informed the policy of successive governments, does not diminish the force of the point.

This theory is, in more particular terms, central to an understanding of the resulting institutional landscape, and the public–private divide. It has implications for the conceptions of accountability that we employ. It raises in acute form the balance between political and market accountability. It prompts important questions as to regulation, standard setting, and the emergence of the 'cost/benefit' state.[13] All would agree that public law is not solely concerned with judicial review. Most, if not all, books on the subject will include discussion of the administrative system. The background theory that has driven the changes to the institutional landscape helps to enrich our understanding of the new status quo.

---

[12] P. Craig, *Administrative Law* (Sweet & Maxwell, London, 4th edn., 1999), 31–7.
[13] C. Sunstein, *Free Markets and Social Justice* (Oxford University Press, New York, 1997); E. Fisher, 'Drowning by Numbers: Standard Setting in Risk Regulation and the Pursuit of Accountable Public Administration' (2000) 20 *OJLS* 109.

The theory also provides the necessary backdrop against which to consider the application of doctrinal legal issues that require resolution. We do not, it should be made clear, claim that this theory necessarily 'dictates' a particular legal outcome. It may nonetheless be of significance in evaluating arguments that arise for judicial resolution. Whether a private party to whom power has been contracted out should be subject to the Human Rights Act 1998 and whether it should be amenable to review are important issues that the courts must resolve. When doing so they will, for example, be faced with issues such as whether the 'logic of contracting out' inclines to the conclusion that the private service provider should be subject only to private, and not public, law. There is in fact no such logic, but an argument of this nature has influenced the courts' reasoning. An understanding of the theory driving the changing nature of government can itself be of help in avoiding such erroneous reasoning.[14]

(c) Central Concepts in Public Law: Sovereignty

The relevance of political theory to legal discourse can also be exemplified by reflecting on the meaning and interpretation of central concepts within English public law, such as sovereignty, the separation of powers, and the rule of law.

In relation to sovereignty I have argued in detail elsewhere[15] that from the sixteenth century parliamentary sovereignty was premissed on the existence of justificatory arguments drawn from legal and political theory which served to legitimate the ascription of this power to Parliament. These arguments were of central importance in framing the resultant legal rule. Nor should this be regarded as surprising. Political thinkers and lawyers alike were formulating a rule about the power of Parliament. They realized that the ascription of power required justification, and the greater the power ascribed the more important was the nature of that justification. They did not content themselves with any general argument based on representation. The justifications offered for sovereignty altered over time, but normative arguments couched in terms of political theory were central throughout.

Parliamentarian theorists in the seventeenth century argued that sovereignty resided in the 'King-in-Parliament'. The seeds of this view were in part contractarian. God was held to have conferred power on the community as a whole, not just on a single person. The community had delegated these powers to the King to enable them to be exercised effectively. This delegation was however subject to the condition that laws could be made and taxes could be imposed only through Parliament and with its consent. Parliamentarian claims in the first half of the seventeenth century were directed principally at denying absolute power to the King, rather than claiming it for the two Houses of Parliament.[16] Critics

---

[14] P. Craig, 'Contracting Out, the HRA and the Availability of Judicial Review' (2002) 118 *LQR* SSI.
[15] P. Craig, 'Public Law, Political Theory and Legal Theory' [2000] *PL* 211.
[16] C. Hill, *The Century of Revolution 1603–1714* (Norton, London, 1980), 52.

of James I formulated their argument in terms of the 'sovereignty of the King in Parliament, or more often of a mixed monarchy, a balanced constitution'.[17] If contractarian ideas helped to justify the locus of sovereignty as the King-in-Parliament, other arguments were used to justify the absence of any limits to this sovereign power. A commonly expressed view was that the Parliament thus conceived was bound to act for the common good, and hence that no limits on its powers were needed. A closely related idea was that the very composition of Parliament served to ensure that all estates of the realm were proportionately represented, and hence that no single part thereof could predominate over the rest. It was also felt that the imposition of any constraints on sovereign power would be absurd since the needs of the country could not be readily predicted in advance. There was little support for any judicial role, or what would, in modern parlance, be described as constitutional review. This was in part because the judges were felt to be too much under the influence of the King. They were therefore not to be trusted with ultimate authority over the validity of statutes.

In the eighteenth century the Blackstonian rationale for sovereignty cast in terms of institutional balance came to prominence. This was itself expressly framed against the background of republican ideals of a balanced polity. This in turn was overtaken by the Diceyan rationale for unlimited sovereignty, explicitly set against the background of a self-correcting unitary democracy.

Modern legal discussion of sovereignty, as articulated by Sir William Wade, is very different. There is no discussion of the justification for the sovereign, unlimited, power of Parliament. The question why Parliament should be regarded as legally omnipotent is not addressed. The issue is conceived of in terms of the content of the ultimate legal principle or rule of recognition, which might be said to exist within society at any one point in time. There is no argument put as to whether the current rule is normatively justifiable. This absence of any principled justification for the status quo is mirrored by the way in which the courts are said to go about their task as interpreters of the content of the top rule. The courts will make a political choice at the point where the law 'stops'. There is no need for the courts to engage in a principled discourse on the answer to this question at any particular point in time, since the issue is never perceived in these terms.

(d) Central Concepts in Public Law: The Rule of Law

This is not the place for any general exegesis on the rule of law. It is rather to consider the way in which discussion about the rule of law casts light on the present topic, concerning the relationship between political theory and legal values. This is especially interesting, given the centrality of the rule of law to discussion about judicial review.

---

[17] *Ibid.*, 53.

There is, as is well known, a lively debate concerning formal and substantive conceptions of the rule of law. The formal conception of the rule of law addresses the manner in which the law was promulgated, the clarity of the ensuing norm, and its temporal dimension. It does not however seek to pass judgment upon the actual content of the law itself. On this view, we are not concerned with whether the law was a good law or a bad law, provided that the formal precepts of the rule of law are met. The rationale for limiting the rule of law in this manner is, for Raz,[18] that if the rule of law is the rule of the good law then to explain its nature is to propound a complete social philosophy, in which case it lacks any useful, independent function.

Those who espouse substantive conceptions of the rule of law accept that the rule of law has the formal attributes mentioned above, but they wish to take the doctrine further. Certain substantive rights are said to be based on, or derived from, the rule of law. The concept is used as the foundation for these rights, which are then used to distinguish between 'good' laws, which comply with such rights, and 'bad' laws, which do not. Thus, as Dworkin states,[19] those who have a formal conception of the rule of law care about the content of the law, 'but they say that this is matter of substantive justice, and that substantive justice is an independent ideal, in no sense part of the ideal of the rule of law'.[20] Dworkin, by way of contrast, adopts a rights-based or substantive conception of the rule of law.[21] On this view citizens have moral rights and duties with respect to one another, and political rights against the state as a whole. These rights are to be enforced upon the demand of individual citizens through courts. This conception of the rule of law does not distinguish between the rule of law and substantive justice; on the contrary it requires, as part of the ideal of law, that the rules in the book capture and enforce moral rights. This does not mean that the substantive conception of the rule of law is consistent with only *one* theory of justice. There is no such argument. It does mean that the substantive conception is not independent of the *particular* theory of justice which constitutes its content at any point in time. A substantive conception of the rule of law, delineating individual rights, which then determines the outcome of the case in the manner described by Dworkin, will collapse the rule of law into the particular theory of justice being espoused. This may be utilitarianism, liberalism, or communitarianism.

Allan has advanced a position, avowedly mid-way between the formal and substantive conceptions of the rule of law. He argues that we should go beyond the formal conception of the rule of law, but that we should stop short of regarding the rule of law as the expression of any particular theory of substantive justice.[22] The rule of law should embrace, in addition to its formal attributes,

---

[18] 'The Rule of Law and its Virtue' (1977) 93 *LQR* 195, 196.
[19] R. Dworkin, *A Matter of Principle* (Harvard University Press, Cambridge, Mass., 1985), 11–12.
[20] *Ibid.*, 11.   [21] *Ibid.*, 11–12.
[22] T.R.S. Allan, 'The Rule of Law as the Rule of Reason: Consent and Constitutionalism' (1999) 115 *LQR* 221. For more detailed explication of the approach see T.R.S. Allan, *Constitutional Justice, A Liberal Theory of the Rule of Law* (Oxford University Press, Oxford, 2001).

ideals of equality and rationality, proportionality and fairness, and certain substantive rights. These are said to constitute central components of any 'recognisably liberal theory of justice',[23] while being 'compatible with a variety of liberalisms',[24] and while 'leaving the scope and content of the rights and duties which citizens should possess largely as a matter for independent debate and analysis'.[25] It is necessary, in order to understand this approach, to delve a little further into the substantive aspects of the theory. Formal equality is to be supplemented by a more substantive equality, which requires that relevant distinctions must be capable of reasoned justification in terms of some conception of the common good. It is said not to embody any particular theory of equal justice, but to 'require that government should adhere faithfully and consistently to some conception of justice, however controversial'.[26] The rule of law on this view does not entail commitment to any particular vision of the public good or any specific conception of social justice. It does require that all legal obligations be justified by appeal to some such vision.[27] Allan's theory also embraces certain substantive rights, namely freedoms of speech, conscience, association, and access to information. These are regarded as being part of the rule of law, because they 'assist in preserving the citizen's autonomy in the face of governmental authority',[28] and because they foster rational criticism of governmental action.[29]

It is readily apparent that if one adopts the Dworkinian substantive conception of the rule of law, political theory, or theories of justice, will be integral to deciding on the interpretation of that conception. This can be exemplified by the extra-judicial writing of Sir John Laws.[30] He presents an essentially non-positivist, rights-based conception of law and the role of the judge in cases involving fundamental rights. He posits a higher order law, binding on the elected Parliament, with the courts as the guardian of both fundamental individual rights and what may be termed structural constitutional rights.[31] He indicates what he perceives to be the content of constitutional rights which individuals possess.[32] The argument is based explicitly on Kantian liberalism. The conception of individual autonomy, the content of individual constitutional rights, and the divide drawn between positive and negative rights, with priority being accorded to negative rights, are all aspects of the argument expressly posited on this philosophical foundation. The rule of law on this view encompasses an attachment to freedom, certainty, and fairness. The first of these elements is the substantive component of the rule of law, while the second and the third bring in the more traditional attributes of the formal rule of law.[33]

It is equally interesting to consider the relationship between political theory and the rule of law on the thesis advanced by Allan. It is, as we have seen, central to

---

[23] *Ibid.*, 224.   [24] *Ibid.*, 224.   [25] *Ibid.*, 224–5.   [26] *Ibid.*, 231.
[27] *Ibid.*, 237.   [28] *Ibid.*, 238.   [29] *Ibid.*, 238.
[30] 'Is the High Court the Guardian of Fundamental Constitutional Rights' [1993] *PL* 59; 'Law and Democracy' [1995] *PL* 72; 'The Constitution: Morals and Rights' [1996] *PL* 622.
[31] 'Law and Democracy', n. 30 above.   [32] 'Morals and Rights', n. 30 above.
[33] *Ibid.*, 630–2.

his thesis that we can go beyond the formal conception of the rule of law, and
that we can imbue it with certain substantive content, without thereby embracing
a particular theory of justice. There are however two general points to be made
about this thesis, which relate respectively to equality and substantive political
rights.[34]

The rule of law does not, on Allan's view, embody any particular theory of
equal justice. It requires rather that relevant distinctions must be capable of reasoned justification in terms of some conception of the common good, and that
government should adhere faithfully and consistently to some conception of justice, however controversial. We must, on this view, articulate the particular conception of justice that underpins governmental action. We must then decide
whether the distinctions drawn can be justified in terms of that conception, since
it is clear that conceptions of justice differ markedly in relation to precisely this
issue. Thus, for example, libertarians take a very different view of legitimate
distinctions from classical liberals or republicans. We must moreover then
decide how far such distinctions, even if fully and consistently justified by the
particular conception of justice embraced by the government, should be
accepted in law. The fact that the existing government adheres consistently to a
particular conception of justice that incorporates distinctions that are felt, given
the longer-term history of that society, to be suspect may justify judicial intervention on a Dworkinian theory of adjudication.

The argument that substantive political rights should be regarded as part of
the rule of law is also problematic in the following sense. It is true, of course,
that we value such rights. That is not the point. It is rather what the inclusion
of such rights within the rule of law tells us about the assumptions underlying
Allan's conception of the rule of law. Allan argues that his liberal theory of the
rule of law is consistent with many different liberalisms. It is itself central to the
thesis that his version of the rule of law does not entail any commitment to a
particular theory of justice. It is however by no means self-evident that 'differing
liberalisms' would accord privileged status to such rights as part of the rule of
law. If, for example, utilitarianism were the societal conception of justice then it
is by no means certain that a speech right would be afforded this status. It is also
by no means self-evident that 'differing liberalisms' would necessarily treat such
rights as being more important than others. For example, adherents of public-
choice pluralism may well believe that property rights are as important, or more
important, than speech rights in 'preserving the citizen's autonomy in the face of
governmental authority'. Advocates of this theory regard many redistributive
policies as constitutionally suspect. The reality is that the inclusion by Allan of
rights of speech, association, and conscience as part of the rule of law reflects
the prominence accorded to these interests by a particular version of liberalism,
such as that proffered by Rawls. Allan's conception of the rule of law is, in this
respect, itself based on a particular political theory.

---

[34] P. Craig, 'Constitutional Foundations, The Rule of Law and Supremacy', [2003] *PL* 92.

(e) Central Concepts in Public Law: The Separation of Powers

The separation of powers is rightly regarded as a central construct in our constitutional structure. We draw from it precepts about the relationship between courts and the political arm of government. The concept operates as a source of judicial legitimacy, with the courts defending their role as the rightful interpreters of legislation, and of the legality of executive action. It serves also as the foundation for judicial restraint, with the courts being mindful of not substituting their view on matters of discretion for that of the body to which Parliament has granted the power.

The separation of powers also purports to tell us something about the relationship between executive and legislature. The 'lessons' from this aspect of the separation of powers have always been more difficult for a parliamentary system, such as ours. This is reflected in the standard treatment, which indicates the plethora of ways in which the executive and the legislature interact, with the result that the former controls the latter.

It is, in the light of this, interesting and informative to recall our history. The reality was that whereas the judiciary focused on placing limits to the existence or extent of prerogative power, Parliament sought not only to do this, but also to limit the manner of exercise of this species of power. The prerogative powers of principal importance from the seventeenth to the nineteenth century were those of ministerial appointment and the dissolution of Parliament. These were the main powers through which the King could maintain control over Parliament. In the seventeenth and eighteenth centuries Parliament sought, both directly and indirectly, to constrain these prerogative powers through statute and convention.

The accommodation between King and Parliament which resulted from these constraints on the manner of exercise of prerogative power constituted an essential feature of the balanced constitutionalism said to characterize political life in the eighteenth century, at least between 1716 and 1784. It was this republican conception of balanced constitutionalism, and not Montesquieu's vision of separation of powers, which captured the essence of the division of authority within the state. The constitutional order was perceived to be one of balance, in which the King, Commons, and Lords each possessed important powers. Their respective powers were seen as justified in two complementary senses. They were perceived as representing different legitimate interests within society; and the division of power between them was seen as a bulwark against tyranny. Indeed, for writers such as Blackstone and de Lolme, the very essence of tyranny was a form of constitutional ordering in which power was not distributed and counterbalanced in this manner.

This is not intended to be an exercise in atavistic romanticism. It is rather designed to show that republican conceptions of government were of central importance here, not just in the USA. It reveals moreover that we have lost sight of an important principle, which should properly be regarded as within the list of 'legal values', which may well be of use when reasoning as to constitutional propriety and accountability in the modern day.

(f) Doctrinal Issues: The Vertical Dimension

Those who believe that political theory is important to understand public law do not deny that there are public law values, in the sense of values that public lawyers think are or should be important in a regime of public law. We write about them the whole time. We do believe that the meaning accorded to them will throw into sharp relief contestable issues that take one back to political theory/theory of the state. This is readily apparent if you 'scratch' any of the issues on Cane's list. We may all agree that these concepts are central to public law, but the more particular conception or meaning attributed to them will reveal disagreement that is reflective of deeper tensions as to the appropriate background theory. Space precludes detailed analysis, but this point can be exemplified in two complementary ways, vertically and horizontally.

The vertical approach involves reasoning through the implications of a background theory as a way of elucidating and understanding the particular meaning accorded to a range of public law values. I have attempted to do this in my own work, in relation to four different theories.[35] This can be demonstrated through a very brief summation of the Diceyan model, and the way in which it shaped public law doctrine.

It was premised on explicit assumptions as to how our democracy did and should operate. Democracy was 'unitary', in the sense that all public power was channelled through Parliament. The democratic system was also 'self-correcting', in that Dicey believed that the Commons accurately reflected the will of the people and controlled the executive. The all-powerful Parliament would not therefore be likely to pass legislation contrary to the wishes of the electorate. Dicey used the rule of law to reinforce sovereignty in the sense of parliamentary monopoly. It was assumed that the regular law predominated, that exercise of broad discretionary power was absent, and that all people were subject to the ordinary law of the realm. Notwithstanding this, it is readily apparent that the execution of legislation may in fact require the grant of discretionary power to a minister or agency, since Parliament may not be able to foresee all eventualities and flexibility may be required to implement the legislation. Judicial review was designed to ensure that the sovereign will of Parliament was not transgressed by those to whom such grants of power were made. If authority had been delegated to a minister to perform certain tasks on certain conditions, the courts' function was to check that only those tasks were performed and only where the conditions were present. Judicial review was therefore the tool used to protect Parliament's monopoly and to police its boundaries. Dicey's rule of law reinforced this exercise of judicial power by entrenching the idea that it was

---

[35] P. Craig, *Administrative Law* (Sweet & Maxwell, London, 4th edn., 1999), chap. 1.

natural, right, and a matter of constitutional principle that the ordinary courts should be supreme and that the ordinary law should be all pervasive.

The Diceyan model had implications for many of the doctrinal issues within public law. It shaped the particular conception of the public law values, in the following ways. It shaped the *very form* of judicial intervention, by linking the basis for intervention to the enforcement of the legislative will. It lent force to the idea that when the court was enforcing the legislative will it was only undertaking review and not appeal. The court was simply determining the 'validity' of the administration's behaviour. It had a profound effect upon the *shape and scope* of judicial intervention. It accorded centre stage to control by the courts of administrative bodies. This was regarded as the main purpose of administrative law. The vigorous assertion of the supremacy of the ordinary law was directed towards controlling the bureaucratic organs of the state, which were viewed with implicit distrust. It fostered a generalist as opposed to a functionalist approach to administrative law. It legitimated judicial activism in the following sense. Where there was a difference of opinion between the courts and an agency as to the meaning of a legislative condition, the tendency was to prefer the opinion of the reviewing court, operating through the ordinary law.

The Diceyan model had implications for standing and natural justice, both of which are concerned with the *range of protected interests* recognized by administrative law. A notable feature of administrative law has been the insistence that only those who possessed private rights in the traditional sense of a cause of action in contract or tort, etc, were to be allowed into the system. The gateways were barred to those who did not possess such rights. The common law's preoccupation with traditional rights was a partial explanation of this phenomenon. However the judicial attitude fitted well with the traditional model. The idea that the ordinary law was being applied by the ordinary courts reinforced this restriction on the range of protected interests. It strengthened the belief that the court was doing no more than applying standard notions of contract or tort to cases where the defendant happened to be a public body. The traditional model also had an influence upon the *meaning of process rights*. The rules of natural justice assume that the method of decision-making is adversarial adjudication. The assumption that the ordinary law was being applied by the ordinary courts to administrative agencies led naturally to the assumption that the process rights which such agencies should have to follow would be the same as those used by the ordinary courts. This in turn helps to explain the prevalence of the distinction between 'administrative' and 'judicial' proceedings. If the procedure before an agency was to assume the form of adversarial adjudication then certain courts felt that this was only suitable if the agency was itself in some sense 'judging' a matter between two opposing litigants. If it could not be said to be doing this and was only engaged in 'administration', then no procedural rights should be available to these parties. It also helps us to understand the unwillingness of the courts to grant process rights in 'legislative' contexts. This was in part because it might be difficult to apply process rights designed for 'judging' to a situation when someone was 'legislating'. It was in part because even to accept that any process rights might be necessary would be to challenge the foundation of the unitary vision of democracy, by acknowledging that there rules of a legislative nature were being made independently of Parliament itself.

The Diceyan model shaped thinking about the application of *tort and contract* to public bodies. Dicey believed that the French gave advantageous treatment to public officials who committed a wrong. The situation in England was different. The ordinary law applied to all. Special regimes did not exist. If a public officer committed a wrong then standard principles of tortious liability were applied. How far the ordinary principles of tortious or contractual liability ought to be modified when dealing with public bodies is a complex topic. The Diceyan legacy was, however, to preclude, or at least forestall, reasoned discussion on this issue by insisting that any such distinct regime would be contrary to the rule of law. When such discourse did surface in the case law it assumed a defensive, almost apologetic, air.

(g) Doctrinal Issues: The Horizontal Dimension

The idea that there may be disagreement about the particular conception of the public law values, which is reflective of deeper tensions as to the appropriate background theory, can also be examined from an horizontal perspective. The focus here is on individual public law values in order to determine how the detailed interpretation of that value is affected by different background political theories. This exercise could be undertaken for any of the values on Cane's list. The following are but examples.

Consider, for example, the *public–private divide* and the way in which Oliver approaches the subject.[36] The stimulating discussion is framed, at beginning and end, by consideration of theories of democracy, government, and citizenship. Oliver posits four theories: positivist authoritarianism, liberal majoritarianism, considerate altruism, and participative communitarianism. She argues that 'implicit in these theories are assumptions about citizenship, the relationship between the individual and the state'.[37] The relevance of these theories is brought out at various stages of the substantive discussion. The book ends where it began, with a discussion of these same theories. Oliver concludes that 'in both public and private law theories of democracy—civic and civil democracy—are influential'.[38] She acknowledges also that theories of democracy and citizenship lie behind the common values that she identifies in her work, arguing that these theories give decreasing weight to the demands of authority and majoritarianism, and increasing weight to arguments for 'consideration of others, altruism, communitarianism and participation'.[39]

---

[36] D. Oliver, *Common Values and the Public–Private Divide* (Butterworths, London, 1999).
[37] *Ibid.*, 7.   [38] *Ibid.*, 273.   [39] *Ibid.*, 273.

Consider a detailed doctrinal issue such as *the content of procedural rights accorded through natural justice*, an example raised by Cane himself. Any legal system will perforce have to decide what process rights to accord, whether these should include oral or written hearings, legal representation, a hearing before or after the challenged determination, as well as a plethora of other such issues. The courts will, in general, balance between the nature of the individual's interest, the likely benefit to be gained from an increase in procedural rights, and the costs to the administration of having to comply with such process rights. This approach is well recognized in the USA, but it is equally apparent in the UK case law. The existence of judicial balancing should not lead us to conclude that all such balancing is necessarily premised on the same assumptions. A law and economics approach to judicial balancing[40] focuses principally upon an instrumental connection between the presence of process rights and the correct determination on the substance of the case. The process rights are accorded in so far as they constitute an efficient mechanism for ensuring the correctness of the substantive outcome. The foundations of this approach are utilitarian, and can be traced back to Bentham.[41] This approach to judicial balancing has been criticized.[42] Critics recognize that some species of balancing must, nonetheless, be undertaken, since the costs of such protection have to be borne by society.[43] Dworkin has articulated a rights-based approach to procedure, which still entails some balancing, but is distinctive from utilitarian cost-benefit analysis.[44]

Consider the debate about *participation in rule-making*. The reasons we might wish to move towards a more general right to participate in rule-making are eclectic. The fact that Parliament scrutinizes only a fraction of secondary legislative norms, those designated as statutory instruments, is one argument. The fact that there would, in practical terms, be real difficulties in demanding that it should scrutinize all rules of a legislative nature is another. It is then necessary, against this backdrop, to consider why a more generalized right to participate in rule-making might be felt to be desirable. This immediately raises important issues as to the relationship between representative democracy through Parliament, and more direct forms of democratic input through participation in rule-making. It also throws into sharp relief the issue of how such participation, were it to exist, should be regarded. It might be viewed as a form of interest representation, in which the public interest is seen as the outcome of the contending interests of those proffering their views. This view is itself premised on a theory of interest-group pluralism. The rationale for such participatory rights might, on the other hand, be cast in very different terms. The primary rationale might be to enable individuals to take part in governance, and to regard this as an integral part of citizenship. Individuals will of course have preferences, but

---

[40] R. Posner, *Economic Analysis of Law* (Little Brown, Boston, Mass., 2nd edn., 1972), 430.
[41] J. Mashaw, *Due Process in the Administrative State* (Yale University Press, New Haven, Conn., 1985), 104–8.   [42] *Ibid.*, 115.
[43] *Ibid.*, 154–5.
[44] R. Dworkin, *A Matter of Principle* (Harvard University Press, Cambridge, Mass., 1985), chap. 3.

these do not have to be seen as givens that they bring to the bargaining table in the manner of interest-group pluralism. Participation can, alternatively, be seen as part of a more deliberative discourse, in the manner suggested by modern republican theory.[45]

It is also instructive to consider the *standard of judicial review*. It is a basic precept that the court should not simply substitute its view for that of the agency. Parliament has assigned the discretionary choice to the agency, and the court should not overturn its decision simply because it would prefer a different decision. The judicial response has been to retreat to the opposite end of the spectrum, represented by the *Wednesbury* test, and only countenance judicial intervention in cases of extreme arbitrariness. This has survived for so long only because the courts used various devices to justify intervention, notwithstanding the actual wording of the test.[46] Recent debate has centred on the spectrum between substitution of judgment and extreme arbitrariness, the candidates being proportionality or some strengthened form of reasonableness. It is interesting to reflect on why this shift is felt to be desirable, quite independently of the pressures from EU law and from the ECHR. The answer is, of course, at some basic level that we want a more testing criterion than traditional *Wednesbury*, and we feel that this can be achieved without damage to hallowed notions of the separation of powers. We can however press further and consider why this is so. Different theories can shed light on this. The conclusion reached might be the same, but the emphasis might well be different. A pluralist would argue that there must be some meaningful review beyond traditional *Wednesbury*, because otherwise one cannot realistically foster participation rights. We have to ensure that the agency does not just go through the motions of listening to people. If we wish seriously to enhance participation rights then we must be prepared to listen to arguments that the agency did not give adequate consideration to the views of interested parties. We cannot sanction judicial intervention only when the resultant agency decision is substantively arbitrary, because there may be many instances when it falls far short of this, but still wholly or partially ignores the views of concerned participants. A liberal might regard the structural properties of a proportionality test as being most important. The three-part test would, on this view, engender more accountable administration by forcing it to defend its challenged policy through the specific lenses of necessity, sufficiency, and *stricto sensu* proportionality, as opposed to the monolithic *Wednesbury* formula. The reviewing court would also be rendered more accountable, in the sense of having to justify its intervention in terms that were related to the specific arguments presented via the proportionality test. The modern republican might regard the principal virtue of

---

[45] C. Sunstein, 'Interest Groups in American Public Law' (1985) 38 *Stanford LR* 29.

[46] The courts applied the test to situations that were, on the facts, not manifestly arbitrary. They re-defined it in cases of fundamental rights. The courts also, most importantly, could, if they so desired, classify cases as 'going to' propriety of purpose or relevancy, in which instances all bets were off, and they would substitute judgment.

a proportionality test as being a defence against naked political bargain. Participation in decision-making would foster citizen involvement in the governmental process, and prevent any one group from gaining exclusive hearing rights before the decision-maker. The proportionality test would help to ensure that the public body properly considered the relevant evidence, that there was some rational connection between the evidence presented and the resultant decision, and that the decision did not unduly reflect the concern of a particular faction as opposed to the overall good.

Consider, as a final example, the way in which *we think about the protection of individual rights*. It may well be true, as Cane states, that law-making by courts is centrally concerned with individual rights, not social interests, and that the protection of social interests is typically conceived as belonging to the political and not the judicial realm.[47] This still leaves open the crucial issue as to the content of political, social, and economic rights that should be held to constitute citizenship in the Marshallian sense. This will inevitably take one back to political theory. It also leaves open the issue as to how far any such social or economic rights, if they are held to exist, can and should be enforced through the judicial process. Both issues may fall to be resolved by the courts, although the political branch of government may address either issue directly, or indirectly. We can see the conjunction of both issues in the EU Charter of Rights. The European Council decided that the Charter, the precise legal status of which will be decided in 2004, should include economic and social, as well as political, rights. In relation to judicial enforcement, some have drawn a distinction between rights enforceable in the courts and principles that could be relied on against official authorities, as a basis for censuring their acts, which would not however ground a legal action. There clearly are Charter provisions, such as that concerned with consumer protection, which by their wording are indicative of a principle and not a right. It is tempting to think more generally that there is an equation between rights and the civil Charter provisions, and principles and the social/economic provisions of the Charter. This would be mistaken. The matter is more complex. There are provisions of the Charter dealing with social matters that can properly be thought of as rights, capable of individual legal enforcement. The injunction in Article 29, that everyone has the right to a free placement service, provides one such example. There is no reason why an individual should not be able to bring a legal rights-based claim against a state that sought to charge for such services. The same is true for the right to working conditions which respect the health, safety, and dignity of the worker, Article 31. This is amenable to an individual rights-based legal claim by a particular worker that, for example, the conditions of his employment were unsafe. The injunction against unfair dismissal in Article 30 provides a further example.

---

[47] Cane, n. 1 above, 6.

3. The 'dependence of political theory on public law'

The discussion within the previous section has elaborated a number of ways in which political theory is implicated in, and enriches our understanding of, the values that we regard as important as public lawyers.

We must however address Cane's argument that political theory is to a certain extent dependent upon public law. He argues that it is 'implicit in much of the writing about public law and political theory, that the relationship between the two is asymmetrical in the sense that we need political theory in order to understand public law, but that public law has no distinctive contribution to make to our understanding of political values'.[48] There are two stages to the argument.

(a) Disagreement about Values

Cane contends that disagreement about values is endemic within society, that law performs a valuable function by concretizing values through legislation and adjudication, and that the authoritative nature of law thereby makes a distinctive contribution to the normative life of society. Moreover the very fact that legal institutions regarded as legitimate decide a matter in a certain way may then cause people to reconsider their previously held views. The 'normative traffic' should not therefore be seen as being only one way from critical values to law, since law may not only reflect critical values but also mould them.[49]

This argument would be accepted by most, if not all, of those who use political theory in the field of public law. Law can indeed make a contribution to the resolution of disagreement about values. This is true of legislation and adjudication. There is however no 'implicit asymmetry' at work here. It is, to the contrary, central for those who work with political theory that law as an authoritative system, can mould values, and make a contribution to the resolution of disagreement. It is precisely because this is so that it is important to understand the theoretical foundations that drive or affect the legal contribution.

(b) The Abstractness of Values

Cane also focuses directly on the abstractness of values and theory. He argues that the fact that theory and values are set at an abstract level limits their explanatory power. It is this very abstractness which means that such theories or values are unlikely to provide any solution to the choice between proportionality and unreasonableness as the standard of review, or between oral and written hearings as a requirement of procedural fairness. There will therefore be a point at which values and normative theory run out and need to be supplemented by law.[50]

---

[48] Cane, n. 1 above, 18.   [49] *Ibid.*, 18–19.   [50] *Ibid.*, 20–1.

There are two points to be made concerning this argument. They are related, but distinct.

It is, on the one hand, of course true that the public lawyer using the tools of political theory will have to reason through the implications from that theory. By definition any background theory that is being used to explicate legal doctrine will be set out at some level of generality, which then has to be applied to the particular legal context in question. The lawyer will then seek to reason through those implications in order to cast light on the discrete problem at hand. It should be made clear that this is equally true for Cane's list of abstract legal values as it is for political theory. There is however nothing inconsistent in the claim that political theory is integral to an understanding of public law, and the fact that public lawyers using such work will of necessity have to reason through the implications of that theory to particular public law problems. This point can be made in relation to those who seek to understand tort law through using corrective justice, or criminal law through notions of moral responsibility. They too will have to reason through the implications of those moral precepts in order to work out the implications for particular doctrinal issues. This is also true for lawyers that draw on anthropology, sociology, etc to explicate an area of the law, as it is for public lawyers that draw on political theory. The point applies moreover to non-legal disciplines. Scholars in international relations who seek to draw on insights from economics, game theory, and the like will have to consider how these background precepts affect the detailed problems that they tackle within their own discipline.

There is, on the other hand, the issue as to how far such reasoning can take one. There is no claim by those who use political theory that it will in itself resolve all detailed issues that arise in, for example, judicial review. This limitation is however also true for the 'legal values' that Cane lists. They will not provide ready answers to the detailed examples that he poses. It should not however be assumed that background theory will be irrelevant when it comes to such matters. There may be issues where the background theory, or abstract legal values, fail to provide concrete guidance, even when one has reasoned through the implications. There may be other issues where guidance is forthcoming. The previous analysis has shown how this can be so in relation to even detailed issues such as the content of natural justice.

4. Public Law, Political Theory, and Political Science

There is another aspect of Cane's critique that should be addressed directly. He argues that 'descriptive political science may make just as important a contribution to understanding public law as normative political theory'.[51] There are two points that should be made in this respect.

---

[51] *Ibid.*, 17.

There is, on the one hand, no sense in which a commitment to the importance of political theory/theories of the state entails the ignoring of material from descriptive political science. This is not a zero-sum game.

There is, on the other hand, implicit within this critique a view about political theory and political science that colours the argument as a whole.

There is a tendency to regard political theory as 'theoretical', in the sense of not being grounded in reality. This is mistaken. Political theories will be based on certain empirical evidence and assumptions, from which normative conclusions will be drawn. This can be exemplified by the pluralist political theory developed in the UK in the first half of the twentieth century. The Diceyan view of administrative law was premissed upon a particular view of how our democracy functioned. Democracy was conceived of as being unitary, in the sense that all public power was and should be channelled through Parliament, which body possessed a legislative monopoly. The pluralists revealed the historical foundations of the unitary view of the state. The idea that sovereignty was indivisible appeared initially in the writings of, among others, Hobbes as a defence against anarchy. Only if the state was all-powerful could a breakdown in society be prevented. If groups or associations were rivals to the state then chaos would ensue. This political justification for the unitary state was unsurprising, given the turmoil that occurred in the English Civil War. Having revealed the historical foundations for the unitary state, the pluralists then proceeded to challenge them in descriptive and prescriptive terms. In descriptive terms, they contested the idea that all public power was in fact wielded by the state. They pointed to pressure groups which shaped and constrained state action. Religious, economic, and social associations exercised authority, and took part in decisions of a public character. 'Legislative' decisions would often be reached by the executive, after negotiation with such groups, and would then be forced through the legislature. In prescriptive terms, group power was applauded rather than condemned. The all-powerful unitary state was dangerous. Liberty was best preserved by the presence of groups within the state to which the individual could owe allegiance. Decentralization and the preservation of group autonomy were to be valued. This vision of political pluralism was complemented by a concern with the social and economic conditions which existed within the state. There was a strong belief that political liberty was closely linked with social and economic equality.

There is also a tendency among some lawyers to see descriptive political science as 'factual', in the sense of not being rooted in any theoretical frame. Some descriptive political science is of this nature, telling us who did what, how a certain scheme operated, and the like. There is however much political science that is squarely rooted within a theoretical frame. Thus a dominant stream of political science seeks to describe or measure phenomena against an explicit backdrop drawn from economics. This can be seen in the work of those who employ rational choice, public choice, and principal/agent theory to describe certain action, as well as to evaluate it. Critics[52] have described the foundations of this approach as being contextualism, reductionism, utilitarianism, instrumentalism, and functionalism.[53] Contextualism captures the idea that politics is not to be differentiated from the remainder of society. Reductionism is expressive of the tendency to assume that political phenomena are best understood as the aggregate consequences of individual or group behaviour, acting so as to maximize their exogenous preferences. For the critics, utilitarianism is indicative of the related inclination within modern political science to see action as stemming from calculated self-interest. Instrumentalism connotes the idea that much political science has given primacy to outcomes, expressed in terms of resource allocation. This is at the expense of an historical tradition which 'portrayed political decision making primarily as a process for developing a sense of purpose, direction, identity and belonging', as 'a vehicle for educating citizens and improving cultural values'.[54] Functionalism signifies the tendency to regard history as an efficient mechanism for the attainment of some equilibrium, as exemplified by the primacy accorded to the idea of optimality, as opposed to an earlier approach which placed emphasis on the singular or unique within a particular historical context. This is not the place to engage in a debate between advocates of rational choice and the new institutionalists. It is simply to point out that if public lawyers use political science, which they should, they will not thereby avoid theoretical issues or the need to evaluate the theoretical assumptions on which the literature is based.

5. PUBLIC LAW, LEGAL THEORY, AND POLITICAL THEORY

There are a number of points at which Cane adverts to legal theory within his own analysis. It is therefore important to be clear about the relationship between public law, legal theory, and political theory for the purposes of the current debate. It will be argued that the centrality of political theory for public law is compatible with the principal contending legal theories.

This is most obviously so for the *Dworkinian theory of adjudication*, based on the idea of law as integrity. Propositions of law are true if they figure in or follow from the principles of justice, fairness, and procedural due process that provide the best constructive interpretation of the community's legal practice.[55] Law as integrity does not demand consistency in principle 'over all historical stages of a community's law'.[56] It does require a consistency of principle across the 'range of standards the community now enforces'.[57] The law must be held

---

[52] J. March and J. Olsen, *Rediscovering Institutions, The Organizational Basis of Politics* (Free Press, New York, 1989). [53] *Ibid.*, 2–8.
[54] *Ibid.*, 6. [55] R. Dworkin, *Law's Empire* (Fontana, London, 1986), 225.
[56] *Ibid.*, 227. [57] *Ibid.*, 227.

to consist of not only the rights and duties which the community now enforces, but also the scheme of principles necessary to justify them.[58] Ideas of 'fit' and 'justification' are central to the concept of law as integrity. The former provides 'a rough threshold requirement that an interpretation of some part of the law must meet if it is to be eligible at all'.[59] This threshold serves to eliminate interpretations which ignore the 'brute facts of history', and serves also to 'limit the role any judge's personal convictions of justice can play in' reaching a particular decision.[60] The latter element, that of justification, is engaged when the threshold test of fit is passed. There may be more than one possible interpretation which passes the threshold test. The judge 'must choose between eligible interpretations by asking which shows the community's structure of institutions and decisions—its public standards as a whole—in a better light from the standpoint of political morality'.[61] The process at this second stage is itself interpretative, in the sense that there may be interpretations which surmount the threshold test but do not fit perfectly with all elements of past practice.[62] The Dworkinian analysis is designed to determine what the law actually is; it is not an elaborate structure for deciding what the law ought to be.

It might be felt that the relevance of political theory for public law will be more problematic for *positivists* who adopt a source-based view of law. They do not, however, deny that courts can have recourse to moral considerations or conceptions of justice or fairness when deciding a case. Positivists, such as Raz, accept that courts should reason in this fashion when they are faced with cases for which the existing source-based law provides no answer.[63]

According to [the sources thesis], the law on a question is settled when legally binding sources provide its solution. In such cases judges are typically said to apply the law, and since it is source-based, its application involves technical, legal skills in reasoning from those sources and does not call for moral acumen. If a legal question is not answered from legal sources then it lacks a legal answer—the law on the question is unsettled. In deciding such cases courts inevitably break new (legal) ground and their decision develops the law (at least in precedent-based legal systems). Naturally, their decisions in such cases rely at least partly on moral and other extra-legal considerations.

Raz provides further insight into when there will be a gap in the established sources. He distinguishes between what he terms regulated cases, those which fall under a common law or statutory rule which does not require judicial discretion for the determination of the dispute, and unregulated cases, where there is some gap in the law applicable to the case.[64] The latter include cases where there is some indeterminacy of language or intention, or those where there are two conflicting rules potentially applicable to the case.[65] Raz argues that courts

---

[58] R. Dworkin, *Law's Empire* (Fontana, London, 1986), 227–8.   [59] *Ibid.*, 255.
[60] *Ibid.*, 255.   [61] *Ibid.*, 256.   [62] *Ibid.*, 257.
[63] J. Raz, *The Authority of Law, Essays on Law and Morality* (Clarendon Press, Oxford, 1979), 49–50.   [64] *Ibid.*, 181.
[65] *Ibid.*, 193–4.

should be regarded as making law in cases of unregulated disputes, and that when they do so they should adopt those rules which they believe to be best, in the same manner as a legislator. He accepts that this may well entail taking into account moral considerations, but that there may, nonetheless, be constraints which cause courts to be less adventurous than legislators. Law application and law making may both be present within a particular case, but the judicial law-making function is not dependent upon the courts necessarily realizing that this is what they are doing.[66]

Cane draws, at a number of points, on the *theory of autopoiesis*.[67] He argues from this theory that law can be thought of as normatively closed, and in that sense an autonomous system of rules and principles, but cognitively open, 'meaning that it can be influenced by and can absorb non-legal norms', making them its own.[68] This is not the place to enter into debate about this view of the relationship between law and other normative systems. Suffice it to say for the present that if one does subscribe to this view, then it is all the more important to reveal the nature and content of the non-legal norms that have been absorbed into the law. This cannot be revealed *per se* through a list of abstract legal values, for the very reasons adverted to in the previous discussion. These values, in their abstracted form, tell one relatively little about the non-legal norms that have been absorbed. The more particular conception of any of these values will differ markedly depending, in part, on the political theory which imbues them with such content.

The view that political theory is central to an understanding of public law is therefore central to the Dworkinian view of law, and perfectly compatible with positivist accounts. Which particular legal theory any public lawyer subscribes to is, of course, an entirely different matter. It is not relevant to the present debate, save in one respect. Cane contends[69] that Craig, and Harlow and Rawlings, apparently believe that, on a positivist account the law as it is, is value-free. I have never said any such thing, nor do I believe that Harlow and Rawlings ever meant this either. It is of course true that the existing corpus of legal rules, derived from positivist 'sources', embody values. This is true of any legal rule derived from an accepted source, whether it be the relatively mundane, such as 'wills must be witnessed', to grander rules. My own preference for a Dworkinian view of adjudication is based on quite different grounds.

6. CONCLUSION

There will be no attempt to summarize the preceding argument. Two points should however be emphasized by way of conclusion.

---

[66] *Ibid.*, chap. 10. This is a complex topic. For further discussion see J. Raz, *Ethics in the Public Domain, Essays on the Morality of Law and Politics* (Oxford University Press, Oxford, 1994), chaps. 10, 13; J. Coleman, 'Negative and Positive Positivism' (1982) 11 *J of Legal Studies* 139.
[67] Cane, n. 1 above, 5–6.   [68] *Ibid.*, 5.   [69] *Ibid.*, 11.

The first relates to the use of theory within public law itself. There is no claim by those who use political theory that the entirety of the legal status quo can be captured by any one theory. This should be readily apparent from the analysis within this essay. The impact of theories may alter across time, and different theories may exert an influence at any one point in time. It should also be recalled that different theories may lead to the same conclusion on certain issues, sometimes for the same reason, sometimes for different reasons. The conclusions drawn from such theory may well be contestable. This may also be true of more conventional analysis. There are moreover dangers of not adverting to such background assumptions. It is all too easy to deny the relevance of theory, and then to advance arguments which draw implicitly on theoretical assumptions without revealing or realizing that one is doing so.

The second point relates more generally to theory and law. Criminal lawyers draw on moral theory, and tort lawyers draw on corrective and distributive justice, and there is a vibrant scholarship on the theoretical foundations of contract law. Public international lawyers have used political theory, as have those concerned with EU law. It seems that Cane's strictures would be equally applicable to the many and varied uses of theory in these divergent legal disciplines. It would be possible to put the same type of argument, to the effect that recourse to such theory has diverted our attention away from the legal values that operate within these disciplines, towards theoretical debate that is unhelpful. The fact that use of theory is commonplace within these subjects does not of course 'prove' that Cane is wrong. It does however, give comfort to those in public law who believe that such theory can enrich our understanding of the legal values with which we work.

3

Representation and Constitutional Theory

MARTIN LOUGHLIN*

All modern, self-proclaimed democracies base their systems of government on the foundation of representation. The question might therefore be asked: what is it that is being represented? For many, the answer to that question is obvious: it is the people that form the objects of representation. In modern societies, so this argument runs, government does not claim to rule the people; by electing politicians to act on their behalf, government today is representative of the people. Representative government should therefore be viewed as the method by which the people are able to govern themselves.

This idea of representative government as a form of self-government must be placed in question. Self-government, government by the people, is in reality a thoroughly ambiguous, even an incoherent, notion. If representative government is taken to be the means by which the people rule themselves, then it is a rather indirect method of their so doing. And it is the indirect nature of this ostensible exercise in self-government, exemplified by the distance which exists today between governors and governed, that should be of particular interest to those concerned with constitutional arrangements. In the formation of constitutional authority, self-government is not only 'accomplished by agents appointed out of themselves' but, as Mansfield notes, is also undertaken by agents who have been vested with 'sovereign powers in an artificial, public status'.[1]

If the importance of representation within constitutional theory is to be grasped, it is essential that both aspects of this process be properly acknowledged. All too often it is supposed that the issue of representation in constitutional theory is bound up solely with the former question. That is, it is assumed that representation focuses on the nature of the relationship between the people and their representative agents and therefore exemplifies a modern understanding of

* In 1985 Carol Harlow argued that the concept of representation was one that constitutional lawyers had unjustifiably neglected: see C. Harlow, 'Power from the People? Representation and Constitutional Theory', in P. McAuslan and J. McEldowney (eds.), *Law, Legitimacy and the Constitution: Essays marking the Centenary of Dicey's* Law of the Constitution (Sweet & Maxwell, London, 1985), chap. 3. This essay is an attempt to respond to that concern. For comments on a version of the essay, I am grateful to Neil Duxbury, Janet McLean, Neil Walker, and Michael Taggart, and to the participants at a staff seminar in the School of Law, University of Glasgow.

[1] H. C. Mansfield Jr., 'Hobbes and the Science of Indirect Government' (1971) 65 *Amer. Pol. Sci. Rev.* 97.

democracy. But the latter issue, the way in which such 'sovereign powers' are given 'an artificial, public status', also has important representational aspects, and these must not be overlooked. Only by examining the two together can the ambiguities of representation in modern constitutional arrangements properly be addressed. Only by considering both aspects will we be able to understand how representative government, which initially was conceived in explicit opposition to democracy, today is seen as its predominant form.[2]

1. THE REPRESENTATION OF SOVEREIGN AUTHORITY

Governance is founded on a capacity to fashion a form of collective order and establish some apparatus of rule. The system of order that is instituted develops as a consequence of an evolving variety of political practices which tie rulers and people together in a bond of protection and allegiance, and in a set of reciprocal duties and rights. But whenever a form of political order is drawn into existence, at some time or other the question is invariably asked: wherein lies the source of political authority?

Attempts to answer that question have most commonly taken the form of trying to identify a particular locus of ultimate authority, whether that be the king (as divine right theorists suggested), the people (as advocates of popular sovereignty proclaim), or (as constitutional scholars have occasionally argued) an institution such as parliament. This question proved troublesome for medieval jurists who, although obliged to acknowledge the pre-eminence of monarchical authority, also contended that the king was under the law. The most celebrated of such formulations, Bracton's statement that the king 'must not be under a man, but under God and under the law',[3] may have satisfied many medieval scholars,[4] but it has puzzled modern commentators. If Bracton had intended to suggest that certain institutional legal constraints on the powers of the king existed, he did nothing to explain how, in what circumstances, and by whom these were to be applied.[5] Much of the difficulty surrounding this exercise flows from an almost inherent ambiguity in the concepts deployed, a point which is concisely suggested by the continuing influence during the Middle Ages of the

---

[2] See B. Manin, *The Principles of Representative Government* (Cambridge University Press, Cambridge, 1997), 236.

[3] *Bracton on the Laws and Customs of England*. (S.E. Thorne trans., Belknap Press, Cambridge, Mass., 1968) ii, 33 (folio 5): *ipse autem rex non debet esse sub homine, sed sub deo et lege, quia facit legem*.

[4] See K. Pennington, *The Prince and the Law 1200–1600: Sovereignty and Rights in the Western Legal Tradition* (University of California Press, Berkeley, Calif., 1993), esp. chap. 3; B. Tierney, 'Bracton on Government' (1963) 38 *Speculum* 295.

[5] See C. H. McIlwain, *Constitutionalism: Ancient and Modern* (Cornell University Press, Ithaca, NY, rev. edn. 1947), 73: 'It is somewhat surprising that historians have been content to leave such an apparent discrepancy as this so largely unexplained. Was Bracton, then, an absolutist or a constitutionalist, or was he just a blockhead?'

rather elusive prescription of the ancient Romans: *imperium in magistratibus, auctoritatem in Senatu, potestatem in plebe, maiestatem in populo*.[6] The question of where ultimate authority lay did not begin to receive a clear answer until the early-modern period.

The first systematic treatment appears in the work of Thomas Hobbes. Hobbes built a theory of the state from the human desire for order and security in a world of perpetual struggle. Starting from a graphic image of life in a state of nature, one of 'war of every man against every man' in which 'the life of man [is] solitary, poor, nasty, brutish and short',[7] Hobbes tried to demonstrate that the only way to secure peace and security would be for everyone to covenant to relinquish their natural rights and submit to the authority of a sovereign power. This great Leviathan, Hobbes argued, 'hath the use of so much Power and Strength conferred on him, that by terror thereof, he is inabled to conforme the wills of them all, to Peace at home and mutual ayd against their enemies abroad'.[8] The solution which Hobbes proposed to the pervasiveness of conflict was to establish an awesome political power equipped with the authority to rule.

Hobbes's great achievement was to have provided us with the first unequivocally modern conception of the state as a political authority differentiated not only from the people who originally established it, but also from the personality of those office-holders for the time being. In his opening words to *Leviathan*, Hobbes indicates that he intends to speak 'not of the men, but (in the Abstract) of the Seat of Power'.[9] He seeks to show how 'by Art is created that great *Leviathan* called a *Common-wealth*, or *State*'.[10] In Skinner's words, it is Hobbes 'who first speaks . . . in the abstract and unmodulated tones of the modern theorist of the state'.[11] Hobbes is the first to provide us with a clear idea of the concept of the sovereign authority of the state.

(a) Representation

Hobbes was unequivocal in his characterization of the nature of the sovereign power. He maintained that this power was in no sense personal: the power belongs entirely to the status of 'the office of the soveraign representative'.[12] Elaborating, Hobbes stated that the 'office of the soveraign (be it a Monarch, or an Assembly) consisteth in the end, for which he was trusted with the sovereign power, namely the procuration of *the safety of the people*'.[13] Hobbes

---

[6] 'Command [is] in the magistrates, authority in the Senate, power in the commons, and sovereignty in the people'. See Jean Bodin, *Six livres de la république*, Bk.I, chap. 10, 218. See also J.P.V.D. Balsdon, 'Auctoritas, Dignitas, Otium' (1960) 54 *The Classical Quarterly* 43, at 43: 'Thus *auctoritas*, which was the Senate's function in government, was, as Mommsen said, "an indefinite word, evading strict definition".'

[7] Hobbes, *Leviathan* (R. Tuck (ed.), Cambridge University Press, Cambridge, 1996), 88, 89.

[8] *Ibid.*, 120–1.   [9] *Ibid.*, 3.   [10] *Ibid.*, 9.

[11] Q. Skinner, 'The State', in T. Ball, J. Farr, and R. Hanson (eds.), *Political Innovation and Conceptual Change* (Cambridge University Press, Cambridge, 1989), 90, 126.

[12] *Leviathan*, n. 7 above, chap. 30.   [13] *Ibid.*, 231.

here ties the question of the locus of political authority directly to the issue of representation. Hobbes's status as a great political philosopher has been widely acknowledged. Once we focus on his analysis of representation, he is revealed also to be a profound juristic thinker.

Hobbes builds his theory from the concept of the 'person'. A person is not to be equated with a human being. There are two types of personality, natural and artificial.[14] The words and actions of a natural person are his own, but those of an artificial person are the representations of another. What is especially important about this characterization is that Hobbes builds his theory of government entirely on the foundation of artificial personality. Government is established as a result of the competence of artificial persons to represent natural persons. A commonwealth thus comes into existence whenever a multitude of individuals agree and covenant amongst themselves that an individual or group shall have 'the *right* to *present* the Person of them all (that is to say, to be their *Representative*)'.[15]

The nature of this regime cannot be grasped without appreciating its representative character. Hobbes explains that a 'multitude of men, are made *One* Person, when they are by one man, or one Person Represented' and it is 'the *Unity* of the Representer not the *Unity* of the Represented, that maketh the Person One'.[16] In the office of the sovereign 'consisteth the Essence of the Commonwealth; which . . . is *One Person*'.[17] The sovereign thus represents a single person, and to that unit we can give the name 'commonwealth' or, in modern language, 'the state'.

From this explanation, we gather that 'the people' exists as such only when a sovereign power is established: 'prior to the formation of a commonwealth a *People* does not exist, since it was not then a person but a crowd of individual persons'.[18] Although noting the three classical types of commonwealth, monarchy, aristocracy and democracy, Hobbes recognizes that if the people meet 'to erect a commonwealth, they are, almost by the very fact that they have met, a *Democracy*' and 'a convention whose will is the will of all the citizens has sovraign power'.[19] Under such circumstances, an aristocracy or monarchy is derived from the power of the people as a result of the transfer of sovereign power to a small group or to a single individual. But once a sovereign is instituted, the sovereign's authority knows no bounds; the sovereign is 'their Representative unlimited'.[20] Hobbes makes this explicit in the distinction which he draws between a people and a crowd.[21]

[M]en do not make a clear enough distinction between a *people* and a *crowd*. A *people* is a *single* entity, with *a single will*; you can attribute *an act* to it. None of this can be said

---

[14] *Leviathan*, n. 7 above, chap. 30, 111: 'A person, is he, whose words or actions are considered, either as their own, or as representing the words or actions of an other man, or of any other thing to whom they are attributed, whether Truly or by Fiction.'   [15] *Ibid.*, 121.

[16] *Ibid.*, 114.   [17] *Ibid.*, 121.

[18] Hobbes, *On the Citizen* (R. Tuck and M. Silverthorne trans., Cambridge University Press, Cambridge, 1998), 95.   [19] *Ibid.*, 94.

[20] *Leviathan*, n. 7 above, 156.   [21] *On the Citizen*, n. 18 above, 137.

of a *crowd*. In every commonwealth the *People* Reigns; for even in *Monarchies* the *People* exercises power; for the *people* wills through the will of *one man*. But the citizens, i.e. the subjects, are a *crowd*. In a *Democracy* and in an *Aristocracy* the citizens are the *crowd*, but the *council* is the *people*; in a *Monarchy* the subjects are the *crowd*, and (paradoxically) the *King* is the *people*.

The crowd, in short, lacks political agency; such agency is intrinsically representative.[22]

Utilizing this concept of representation, Hobbes does nothing less than lay down the foundation for a comprehensive system of public law. The full implications of the principle of representation become evident once the allocation of responsibilities in a mature political system is considered. In this situation, the sovereign body invariably needs to appoint representatives, executive and judicial officers, to carry out the tasks of government. The power of such representatives must always be limited since 'Power Unlimited is absolute Soveraignty' and the limits of the powers of such officers are for the sovereign to determine.[23] But Hobbes is clear about the representative character of the task:[24]

A Publique Minister, is he, that by the Soveraign (whether a Monarch, or an Assembly,) is employed in any affaires, with Authority to represent in that employment, the Person of the Common-wealth.

Similarly with judges: those 'to whom jurisdiction is given, are Publique Ministers' because 'in their Seats of Justice they represent the person of the Soveraign; and their Sentence, is his Sentence'.[25]

For Hobbes, this public capacity of representatives (artificial persons) must be differentiated from the private role of the individual (the natural person) who exercises these responsibilities. Further, it is not only ministers who have two personalities: medieval jurists developed an intricate notion of 'the king's two bodies', precisely for the purpose of demonstrating that the monarch, the titular sovereign, also possesses two personalities or capacities, the natural and the political.[26] Following through the logic of this medieval doctrine, Hobbes notes that 'they that be servants to them [the sovereign] in their naturall Capacity, are not Publique Ministers; but those onely that serve them in the Administration of the Publique businesse'.[27]

---

[22] The formula, *SPQR* (*Senatus Populusque Romanus*/the Senate and People of Rome) under which the legions of Rome marched and which provides a formula of elite rule, is illustrative of this point. As Crick has noted, this was not just a constitutional dictum; it could also present itself as 'a warning maxim addressed to the patrician class—do not forget the dreadful power of the people [i.e., the crowd] if things go wrong or if agitators stir them up'. See B. Crick, 'Introduction', to Niccolò Machiavelli, *The Discourses* (Penguin, London, 1970), 24. On the character of this relationship see E. Canetti, *Crowds and Power* (C. Stewart trans., Penguin, Harmondsworth, 1973), esp. 'Rulers and Paranoiacs', 475.   [23] *Leviathan*, n. 7 above, 155.

[24] *Ibid.*, 166.   [25] *Ibid.*, 168.

[26] See E. H. Kantorowicz, *The King's Two Bodies: A Study in Mediaeval Political Theology* (Princeton University Press, Princeton, NJ, 1957).   [27] *Leviathan*, n. 7 above, 166.

Hobbes's analysis helps us to appreciate how representation provides the key to understanding the structural unity of public law. The principle of representation requires a distinction to be drawn between the public and private aspects of a representative's personality. Since the concept of representation indicates that certain standards are attached to, and certain limits are imposed on, the office of the representative, it underscores the idea that public law is mainly concerned with duties that attach to such offices. This is elementary so far as the executive officers of the state are concerned. But what of the office of the sovereign? Pitkin has argued that when Hobbes calls his sovereign a representative, 'he implies that the man is to *represent* his subjects, not merely to do whatever he pleases' since the 'concept itself contains the idea that the sovereign has duties'.[28] This seems essentially correct. Hobbes, nevertheless, is clear in holding that subjects can have no rights against the sovereign. These positions are not, however, irreconcilable. Once it is recognized that Hobbes is developing a juristic theory, the conundrum disappears. The duties of the sovereign inhere in the nature of the office (to promote the *salus populi*). And to argue that subjects have no right, that is no institutional mechanism, to enforce these duties of which the sovereign is (in law) the sole judge is not in the least paradoxical. But since a full elaboration of this point requires some discussion of the political aspects of the issue, this must be deferred until the latter half of this essay.

(b) The State

Building a juristic theory on the foundation of representation, Hobbes is able to provide the basis for a fairly comprehensive account of the sovereign authority of the state. But there remains a core question that must now be addressed: what is the state?

In order to answer this phenomenological question it is necessary to return to Hobbes's analysis of persons. As we have seen, Hobbes draws a basic distinction between natural and artificial persons and builds a theory of public law on the foundation of artificial personality. Certain natural persons, such as ministers, are also artificial persons. When dealing with the question of the personality of the state, however, we are concerned with an artificial person that has no natural personality. The state does not stand alone in this category. The world can be divided into 'men' and 'things' and there are many inanimate things that are capable of being 'represented by Fiction'.[29] To illustrate this point, Hobbes uses the example of a church, a hospital, or a bridge which 'may be Personated by a Rector, Master, or Overseer' respectively.[30] Hobbes observes that since inanimate things cannot give authority to their representatives to procure their maintenance, 'such things cannot be Personated, before there be some state of Civill Government'.[31] These artificial persons acquire their personality,

---

[28] H. Pitkin, *The Concept of Representation* (University of California Press, Berkeley, Calif., 1967), 33.
[29] *Leviathan*, n. 7 above, 113.   [30] *Ibid.*   [31] *Ibid.*

and the ability to authorize representatives to act on their behalf, entirely through the operation of the law. Can this analysis of artificial personality be extended to the personality of the state? Hobbes writes that a state is instituted,[32]

when a *Multitude* of men do Agree, and *Covenant, every one with every* one, that to whatever *Man*, or *Assembly of Men*, shall be given by the major part, the *Right* to present the person of them all, (that is to say, to be their *Representative*), every one, as well he that *Voted for it*, as he that *Voted against it*, shall *Authorise* all the Actions and Judgements, of that Man, or Assembly of men, in the same manner, as if they were his own, to the end, to live peaceably amongst themselves, and be protected against other men.

The unity of the 'Man, or Assembly of Men'—that is, 'the *Unity* of the Representer, not the *Unity* of the Represented'[33]—is what creates the personality of the state. And the name which is given to this Representer, who 'carryeth this Person, is called SOVERAIGNE, and said to have *Soveraigne Power*; and every one besides, his SUBJECT'.[34]

Hobbes here is in effect seeking to clarify the meaning of, and relations between, the concepts of state, sovereign, and sovereignty. Thus, the state is the name of the person created as a result of this process of authorization by a multitude.[35] The sovereign is the name given to the representative of the person of the state. Sovereignty is the name given to the relation between sovereign and subject.

Although technically the sovereign can be a natural or artificial person, the important point is to recognize its intrinsically public nature: the sovereign holds an office impressed with political responsibilities (to promote peace and security) and for the realization of these purposes is vested with absolute sovereign authority. This authority is exercised mainly through the power of law-making. And although these laws are enacted by the sovereign, the sovereign is a representative who is acting in the name of the state. In this purely juristic sense, then, the sovereign's acts can be understood to constitute an exercise in self-government.

But what kind of person is the state? It has been suggested that because Hobbes founds juristic order on the unconditional allegiance of subjects, the idea of vesting personality in the state does not make much sense.[36] A further difficulty arises since, although Hobbes states at several points in *Leviathan* that the Commonwealth or state is a person,[37] he never articulates precisely

---

[32] *Ibid.*, 121.   [33] *Ibid.*, 114.   [34] *Ibid.*, 121.

[35] In *The Logic of Leviathan: The Moral and Political Theory of Thomas Hobbes* (Clarendon Press, Oxford, 1969), chap. 4, D. Gauthier argues that Hobbes's use of the notion of authorization in *Leviathan* (as compared with subjection or surrender of rights in earlier works) represents a major, and more democractic, shift in his thought. Cf. J. Hampton, *Hobbes and the Social Contract Tradition* (Cambridge University Press, Cambridge, 1986), chap. 5.

[36] D. Runciman, *Pluralism and the Personality of the State* (Cambridge University Press, Cambridge, 1997), 32.

[37] It is not clear, however, that Hobbes is entirely consistent on this matter. In *Leviathan* he states that 'the Multitude so united in one Person, is called a COMMON-WEALTH' (n. 7 above, 120). But later he seems to deny this: 'But the Common-wealth is no Person, nor has the capacity to doe anything, but by the Representative, (that is, the Soveraign)' (*Ibid.*, 184). This is best resolved by reading the latter as stating that the person of the Commonwealth has no independent will, but can act only through the will of the sovereign as representative.

what kind of person the state is supposed to be. Skinner has recently argued that for Hobbes the state must be viewed as analogous to a church, hospital, or bridge and treated as a 'purely artificial person'.[38] Notwithstanding the lucidity of Skinner's reconstructive account, Runciman's criticisms of Skinner's claim are compelling.[39] Runciman notes that although Hobbes treated the state as a single person, the state could not be a real person for the rather basic reason that it is not capable of acting for itself. The state, it is generally agreed, cannot act other than through the person of its representative. But who does the sovereign represent? It is common ground that the state itself cannot authorize the sovereign to act, and it is similarly accepted that the sovereign must represent something other than a multitude. The most sensible answer, Runciman suggests, is that the multitude 'separately perform the real actions [i.e. covenanting] which allow responsibility to be attributed to the state as a single unit'.[40] And the consequence of this type of attribution of unity means that the state must be understood to be a person by fiction.

That the state is a *persona ficta* is justified by Runciman on various grounds.[41] But there is a more basic juristic reason for regarding the state as *sui generis*, and for recognizing its fictitious personality. The person of the state must first be differentiated from other artificial persons such as churches, hospitals, and bridges. This is not difficult: as Runciman recognizes, the state, unlike a bridge, does not exist at all before its representative is set in place.[42] Unlike a bridge, the state is entirely created out of the act of representation. But even more fundamentally, the personality of the bridge is, as we have seen,[43] created as a result of the operation of law; it acquires, we might say, a form of juristic personality. This cannot be so with respect to the person of the state, however, since the state and its representative, the sovereign, are instituted precisely for the purpose of creating law. The state stands alone as a fictitious person.

The argument of whether the state is a 'purely artificial person' or a 'person by fiction' might appear one that is in danger of dissipating into a sterile scholastic question. But underpinning the exercise lies an attempt to instil some clarity into our understanding of the most basic concepts on which constitutional order is founded. In this respect, Hobbes's great achievement is to have produced a coherent explanation of the ideas of state, sovereign, sovereignty,

---

[38] Q. Skinner, 'Hobbes and the Purely Artificial Person of the State' (1999) 7 *J of Political Philosophy* 1. Contrary to a number of commentators, Skinner thus argues (at 22) that Hobbes does not regard the state as a *persona ficta*. Cf. M. Oakeshott, *On Human Conduct* (Clarendon Press, Oxford, 1975), 204; Runciman, n. 36 above, chap. 2.

[39] D. Runciman, 'What Kind of a Person is Hobbes's State? A Reply to Skinner' (2000) 8 *J of Political Philosophy* 268.   [40] *Ibid.*, 273.

[41] Runciman (*ibid.*, 278) contends, first, that Skinner's term, 'purely artificial person', is not a phrase that Hobbes uses; secondly, that it 'does not sufficiently distinguish the person of the state from those artificial persons who are capable of action, such as assemblies'; and finally that Hobbes's own phrase, 'person by fiction', seems 'best to conjure up the kind of state we actually encounter in the political world we do inhabit, the world that Hobbes helped to create'.

[42] *Ibid.*, 273–4.   [43] See text to n. 31 above.

and law, and in the process to have demonstrated that, far from being a natural phenomenon, political power, being generated by artifice, is rooted in the principle of representation.

The specifically juristic aspects of Hobbes's work on the state have been relatively neglected. When in the late nineteenth century they were taken up by Maitland, he complained that while a 'theory of the State . . . may be interesting to the philosophic few . . . a doctrine of Corporations, which probably speaks of fictitious personality and similar artifices, can only concern some juristic speculators, of whom there are none or next to none in this country'.[44] While continuing to focus on the practical legal questions which provoked this philosophical inquiry,[45] however, Maitland never got much beyond acknowledging that 'there seems to be a genus of which State and corporation are species'.[46] If this inquiry does reveal one basic insight it is that Hobbes's *Leviathan* is not only a 'masterpiece of political philosophy',[47] but also a work of profound juristic sophistication. *Leviathan* should be read essentially as an explication of the idea of juristic order founded on sovereignty and exercised through law. From this perspective, the state's power to command is absolute. For Hobbes, all notions of charisma, dignity, and honour are subsumed within the idea of power, honour being simply 'an argument and signe of Power'.[48]

This juristic reading of Hobbes also highlights the limitations of his thought. In *Leviathan*, Hobbes utilizes the device of the social contract, covenanting in the state of nature, ostensibly for the purpose of providing a solution to the question of the source of political authority. But once the text is read as a work of jurisprudence, it is evident that although it provides a clear analysis of the basic concepts of which a system of public law is to be founded, it does not resolve the question of the source of political authority. This perhaps is not surprising since the establishment of political order is no mere juristic exercise. By highlighting the centrality of the concept of representation, Hobbes directs us along the right path. In *Leviathan*, representation is used primarily to set in place the foundations of a system of positive law. But if an answer is to be found to the question of the source of political authority, his method must be extended and a broader conception of political representation embraced.

[44] F.W. Maitland, 'Introduction', in O. Gierke, *Political Theories of the Middle Age* (Cambridge University Press, Cambridge, 1900), p. ix.

[45] See Maitland's essays on this subject which have helpfully been collected in F.W. Maitland, *Selected Essays* (H.D. Hazeltine, G. Lapsley, and P.H. Winfield (eds.), Cambridge University Press, Cambridge, 1936).

[46] Maitland, n. 44 above, p. ix; Maitland, 'Moral Personality and Legal Personality', in *Selected Essays*, n. 45 above, chap. 5. See further M. Loughlin, 'The State, the Crown and the Law', in M. Sunkin and S. Payne (eds.), *The Nature of the Crown: A Legal and Political Analysis* (Oxford University Press, Oxford, 1999), chap. 3; D. Runciman, 'Is the State a Corporation?' (2000) 35 *Government & Opposition* 90.

[47] M. Oakeshott, 'Introduction', in Thomas Hobbes, *Leviathan* (Blackwell, Oxford, 1946), p. viii: 'The *Leviathan* is the greatest, perhaps the sole, masterpiece of political philosophy written in the English language.'   [48] *Leviathan*, n. 7 above, 65.

2. Political representation

In *Leviathan*, Hobbes was concerned mainly to provide a coherent account of the person of the state and the office of the sovereign. The concept of sovereignty, the relation between sovereign and subject, is one that remained underdeveloped. This question of sovereignty was not squarely faced until the following century, when, as a consequence of the French Revolution, the idea of covenanting by a multitude moved from the world of books to the world of action. The political debates which the revolution provoked suggested that the idea of covenanting to institute a state was one that required closer scrutiny.

Of the French revolutionary thinkers, the impact of this Hobbesian moment was most deeply examined by the Abbé Sieyes.[49] The main achievement of Sieyes was, in the words of one of his most sensitive commentators, to have 'transformed the modern theory of the state that had gradually been developing in the wake of the Reformation, that is to say the theory of the state as the creation of the social contract, into a practicable, realizable idea'.[50] This idea, which Forsyth has argued was latent in Hobbes,[51] is that of 'the people', or what Sieyes calls 'the nation', as the constituent power of political establishment. Before considering directly the relevance of sovereignty to the issue of political representation, it is necessary first to examine this idea of constituent power.

(a) Constituent Power

Sieyes emphasized the necessity of drawing a clear distinction between the constituted power (*pouvoir constitué*) and constituent power (*pouvoir constituant*). Holding an authority delegated from the people, government is a form of constituted power. But it is the government, not the nation, that is constituted. 'Not only is the nation not subject to a constitution', argued Sieyes, 'but it *cannot* be and *must not* be'.[52] The nation, he emphasized, must not be identified with its constitutional forms. Although constitutional law may be fundamental law with respect to the institutions of government that are established, this simply means that no type of delegated power can in any way alter the conditions of its delegation.[53] The constituent power remains: 'The nation is prior to everything. It is the source of everything. Its will is always legal; indeed, it is the law itself.'[54]

---

[49] There is some confusion over the spelling of Sieyes's name and Sieyes himself does not appear to have maintained consistency. I have therefore followed Pasquino in spelling without accents: P. Pasquino, 'Emmanuel Sieyes, Benjamin Constant et le "Gouvernement des Modernes" ' (1987) 37 *Revue Française de Science Politique* 214: '*L'orthographe sans accents semble la plus vraisemblable*'.

[50] M. Forsyth, *Reason and Revolution: The Political Thought of the Abbé Sieyes* (Leicester University Press, Leicester, 1987), 217.

[51] M. Forsyth, 'Thomas Hobbes and the Constituent Power of the People' (1981) 29 *Political Studies* 191. Cf. Runciman, n. 36 above, 12 (n. 13).

[52] E.J. Sieyès, *What is the Third Estate?* (1789) (M. Blondel trans., Pall Mall Press, London, 1963), 126.   [53] *Ibid.*, 125.

[54] *Ibid.*, 124.

Although Sieyes identified 'the nation' as the constituent power, he also recognized that that body could not govern. Once the fundamental political tenets of Machiavelli are embraced, that is, that conflict and tension are basic features of all collectivities and that politics exists to provide a way of managing these irreducible conflicts,[55] it should be evident that the idea that authority rests in the 'will of the people' takes us nowhere. Although political tensions can be treated as positive phenomena, they need to be managed. Recognizing this basic facet of modern political conduct, Sieyes argued that the way this is to be achieved is through the principle of representation.[56]

Sieyes accepted both that the establishment of government is a necessary precondition for enabling citizens to realize their freedoms and also that there could never be an identity of rulers and ruled. This is a distinctively modern condition.[57] In the words of Istvan Hont, Sieyes 'saw representation as a fundamental fact of modern society, as something indelibly inscribed in the division of labour and commercial sociability, and political representation as a permanent necessity in any large and populous country in which it was virtually impossible to unite the voice of the people directly'.[58] But representation should not be treated merely as a mechanism that has been devised for the purpose of addressing the problem of ensuring that in a mass society the views of all citizens can be heard. Representation is not simply the product of necessity. Because of its ability to manage conflict effectively, representative government must also be seen as a superior form of government.[59]

For Sieyes, political power originates in representation. Pure or direct forms of democracy are conceived to be ineffective methods of rule. A properly constituted

---

[55] Niccolò Machiavelli, *The Discourses* I.4.

[56] Cf. J. de Maistre, 'Study on Sovereignty', in J. Lively (ed.), *The Works of Joseph de Maistre* (Allen & Unwin, London, 1965), 93: 'It is said that the people are sovereign; but over whom?—over themselves, apparently. The people are thus subject. There is something equivocal if not erroneous here, for the people which *command* are not the people which *obey*. It is enough, then, to put the general proposition, "The people are sovereign", to feel that it needs an exegesis. . . . The people, it will be said, exercise their sovereignty by means of their representatives. This begins to make sense. The people are the sovereign which cannot exercise their sovereignty'.

[57] See Pasquino, n. 49 above, esp. 223–5; Manin, n. 2 above, esp. chap. 6. See also B. Manin, 'The Metamorphoses of Representative Government' (1994) 23 *Economy and Society* 133.

[58] I. Hont, 'The Permanent Crisis of a Divided Mankind: "Contemporary Crisis of the Nation State" in Historical Perspective', in J. Dunn (ed.), *Contemporary Crisis of the Nation State?* (Blackwell, Oxford, 1995), 166, 198.

[59] Citing *Federalist* No. 52, Pitkin assumes that Madison, Hamilton, and Jay were of the view that 'representative government is a device adopted instead of direct democracy, because of the impossibility of assembling large meetings of people in a single place, "a substitute for the meeting of the citizens in person" ' (Pitkin, n. 28 above, 191). This seems to be a not entirely faithful reading of the Federalist Papers. Madison in particular was concerned about the inability of 'a pure democracy' to deal with 'the mischiefs of faction' and suggests that a 'republic, by which I mean a government in which the scheme of representation takes place, opens a different prospect and promises the cure for which we are seeking'. J. Madison, A. Hamilton, and J. Jay, *The Federalist Papers*, No.10 Publius (Madison). Cf. Manin, n. 2 above, 3: 'For Siéyès, . . . as for Madison, representative government was not one kind of democracy; it was an essentially different and furthermore preferable form of government.'

political order must therefore be based on the notion of 'indirect rule', in which the representative retains a degree of independence from the people. The 'people' establishes a mode of government, a system of public offices to represent the 'general will', and must then elect the persons to hold such offices. Contrasting classical and modern systems, Manin argues that the fact that representative governments have never used selection by lot, a method which ensures that there will be an equal probability of citizens being called on to perform governmental functions, shows that the difference between representative and direct systems concerns their method of selection rather than limited number of those selected. 'What makes a system representative', Manin concludes, 'is not that a few govern in the place of the people, but that they are selected by election only'.[60] Representation is a fundamental feature of modern government. This is not because representation legitimates power; rather it is 'because all legitimate power arises exclusively in and through political representation'.[61]

It is only by focusing on this idea of political representation that we are able properly to address the question of sovereign authority. Although, following Sieyes, it might be said that constituent power vests in the nation, this does not mean that political authority is located in the people (*qua* the multitude), as theorists of popular sovereignty seem to suggest.[62] Sieyes believed that sovereignty was fused with representation and cannot be exercised except through representation. But neither does this mean that political authority is bound up entirely in the authority of an established ruler, as theorists of the authoritarian state advocate. Sovereignty may have been fused with representation, but, contrary to Hobbes, Sieyes argued in effect that the people never leave the state of nature and retain the possibility of re-acquiring constituent power. One of the most fundamental tasks of politics, understood as a set of practices for managing conflict, is to ensure that this situation never arises. But the implication of this argument is that sovereign authority does not rest in any particular locus; it is a product of the relation between the people and the state. Political power is a complex phenomenon: it is rooted in the division between governors and governed, rests on the principle of representation, and gives effect to the concept of sovereignty.

[60] Manin, n. 2 above, 41.

[61] F.R. Ankersmit, *Aesthetic Politics: Political Philosophy Beyond Fact and Value* (Stanford University Press, Stanford, Calif., 1996), 51. This point is one that recent advocates of more participatory forms of democracy often tend (erroneously) to reject: see, e.g., B. Barber, *Strong Democracy: Participatory Politics for a New Age* (University of California Press, Berkeley, Calif., 1984), 135, 145–6: 'Representation is incompatible with freedom . . . Representation is incompatible with equality . . . Representation, finally, is incompatible with social justice.' Cf. D. Plotke, 'Representation is Democracy' (1997) 4 *Constellations* 19.

[62] Cf. G.W.F. Hegel, *Philosophy of Right* (1821) (T.M. Knox trans. Oxford University Press, Oxford, 1952), §279: 'the sovereignty of the people is one of the confused notions based on the wild idea of the "people". Taken without its monarch and the articulation of the whole which is the indispensable and direct concomitant of monarchy, the people is a formless mass and no longer a state. It lacks every one of those determinate characteristics—sovereignty, government, judges, magistrates, class-divisions, etc.—which are to be found only in a whole which is inwardly organized'.

Political power is thus derived from those tensions and conflicts which exist in all collectivities. These tensions must be properly handled, and it is for the purpose of fulfilling this function that the practices of politics have evolved. But such conflicts are not resolved by the act of vesting absolute legal power in the sovereign authority. Such action does not eliminate the problem of generating a real, sustainable political will. Furthermore, especially if the concepts of juridical and political will are confused and assumed to be united, it carries the danger of collapsing the system into tyranny. And apart from other considerations, tyranny is a grossly ineffective political regime. Hobbes was conscious of this distinction. Although an authoritarian, Hobbes was no absolutist. He recognized that 'the power of the mighty hath no foundation but in the opinion and belief of the people',[63] and acknowledged implicitly the significance of Machiavelli's belief that freedom flourishes through the maintenance of the tension between state and society.[64]

But if political authority does not flow simply from the establishment of an entirely top-down system of authority, then neither does it rest in 'the will of the people', whatever this confused notion may mean. If the expression is intended to reflect a belief that this 'will' is discerned by an aggregation of the desires of the multitude,[65] then it leads not to authority but to impotence. As Sieyes's analysis of the idea of constituent power suggests, political power is the product of representation. It is only through representation that social conflicts are positively harnessed, appropriate institutional arrangements of government devised,[66] and real political will established.[67]

(b) Sovereignty

This analysis leads to a relational concept of sovereignty. A relational perspective enables us to draw out the nuances inherent in, and perhaps also to resolve

---

[63] Thomas Hobbes, *Behemoth, or the Long Parliament* (1682) (Cass, London, 1969), 16.

[64] See *Leviathan*, n. 7 above, chap. 30.

[65] Cf. J.-J. Rousseau, *The Social Contract* (1762) (M. Cranston trans., Penguin, Harmondsworth, 1968), Bk. III, chap. xv. See M. Cranston, 'The Sovereignty of the Nation', in C. Lucas (ed.), *The French Revolution and the Creation of Modern Political Culture. Vol.2: The Political Culture of the French Revolution* (Pergamon Press, Oxford, 1988), 97, 100: 'Rousseau's concept of a general will is often dismissed as a rather absurd notion, but it is a crucial element of his system. Without it, republican theory must lean heavily on a concept of representation: the senators and officers rule as representatives of the people. But Rousseau had no patience with representation'.

[66] By this I mean the elaborate arrangements of government which have become associated with parliamentarism, deliberation, trusteeship in office, and notions of accountability for the exercise of governmental power. For classic illustrations see: E. Burke, 'Speech to the Electors of Bristol, 1774', in his *Speeches and Letters on American Affairs* (Dent, London, 1908), 68; J.S. Mill, *Considerations on Representative Government* (1861), in Mill, *Three Essays* (Oxford University Press, Oxford, 1975), 145. For a recent analysis of these issues see: A. Przeworski, S.C. Stokes, and B. Manin (eds.), *Democracy, Accountability and Representation* (Cambridge University Press, Cambridge, 1999).

[67] Cf. C. Schmitt, *The Crisis of Parliamentary Democracy* (1923) (E. Kennedy trans., MIT Press, Cambridge, Mass., 1985), 34: 'The *ratio* of Parliament rests in a "dynamic-dialectic", that is, in a process of confrontation of differences and opinions, from which the real political will results.'

some of the confusion that surrounds, the concept of sovereignty. To make these advances, however, it is necessary first to return to that critical moment when a multitude covenant to found a state. Hobbes argued that the state is the person created by the authorization of the multitude and the sovereign is the represent-ative of the person of the state. But if sovereignty is a relational phenomenon, which is the determinative relationship, that between the state and the people, or between sovereign and subject? For Hobbes the answer is clear. Since the state has no will except through that of its representative, the critical relation-ship is the latter: it is the sovereign who reduces the 'plurality of voices, unto one Will', and who is 'to beare their Person',[68] and it is 'his Command, that maketh Law'.[69] But is this adequate?

To some extent, Hobbes's answer is a consequence of the way in which he conceives his task as an essentially juristic exercise. The issue becomes more complicated, however, once Sieyes's distinction between 'the nation' and 'the government' is introduced. It seems evident that, as the bearer of constituent power, 'the nation' is a representative form which is to be differentiated from the people as a multitude or crowd. But this would then suggest that the nation should best be understood as a synonym for the person of the state. This has a certain merit, especially since, even in juristic terms, this personality is capable of having an existence over and above a formal constitutional ordering. Consider, for example, Maitland's practical concern about the ability of states to borrow money.[70] Does this debt continue to be owed even if the government collapses and, as a result of a new constitutional settlement, an entirely new governmental regime is established? The answer suggested by international law is that it does: in the international arena at least, the state has a personality which is distinct from that of the constituted governmental order.[71] Maitland in fact argues that '[w]e cannot get on without the State, or the Nation, or the Commonwealth, or the Public, or some similar entity', though he added that, given the confusions of the British system, 'this is what we are proposing to do'.[72] Notwithstanding the ambiguities of British arrangements, it seems evident that in order properly to grasp the relational character of sovereignty both the state/people and sovereign/subject (or government/citizen) relationships need to be considered. Each brings out a slightly different dimension of sovereignty: neither can be ignored without skewing our understanding of the concept.

If the sovereign/subject aspect provides the focus of inquiry, the primary con-cern is likely to be the question of ultimate legal authority. In this dimension,

---

[68] *Leviathan*, n. 7 above, 120.   [69] *Ibid.*, 187.

[70] See, e.g., Maitland, 'The Crown as Corporation', in his *Selected Essays*, n. 45 above, 113–15 which discusses the idea of 'the Publick' which by statute becomes responsible for the national debt.

[71] See *Tinoco Concessions* arbitration (1923) RIAA i. 369; I. Brownlie, *Principles of Public International Law* (Clarendon Press, Oxford, 5th edn. 1998), 86–9.

[72] Maitland, n. 70 above, 112. One of the complexities in the British system concerns the status of the monarch: 'It is true that "The people" exists, and "the liberties of the People" must be set over against "the prerogatives of the King"; but just because the King is no part of the People, the People cannot be the State or the Commonwealth': *ibid.*, 113.

sovereignty in the British system can be understood to be an expression of the ability of the crown in parliament to legislate without any legal limitation on its competence.[73] Notwithstanding recent complications arising from the accession of the United Kingdom to the European Union,[74] the legal doctrine of sovereignty does not cause many conceptual difficulties. But the question of sovereignty cannot be reduced to an issue of positive law, and one which deals solely with the sovereign/subject relationship, without distorting the concept's overall juristic significance.

For the purpose of explaining this point, it is necessary to return to Sieyes's claim that the will of the nation 'is the law itself'. From a modern legal perspective, this is a peculiar statement. We get a deeper sense of its meaning once it is noted that immediately following this statement Sieyes wrote: 'Prior to and above the nation, there is only *natural* law'.[75] The claim, nevertheless, remains puzzling. The concept of natural law does not much help us here. But if we accept that the relationship between sovereign and subject is expressed in the language of positive law, what term can be used for that conception of law embodied in 'the nation' that is 'the source of everything', including positive law itself, if it is not that of natural law? What I would suggest is that Sieyes is here referring to the vital, but now neglected, idea of *droit politique*, politic law.[76] And it is only by deploying the concept of *droit politique*, those precepts of political conduct which are needed to ensure the maintenance of the state, that the full juristic significance of the concept of sovereignty, quintessentially a political concept, can adequately be grasped.

Because of the longstanding dominance of legal positivism within the British tradition of government, expressed most clearly in the idea that sovereignty solely concerns the relation of sovereign and subject, the conception of law understood as *droit politique* is one that cannot easily be acknowledged. But there is evidence that in the early-modern period its logic was readily understood. Shortly after *Leviathan* was published, for example, Lawson published his *Politica Sacra et Civilis*.[77] In this work, Lawson drew a distinction between two types of sovereignty, real and personal. Personal sovereignty is 'the power

[73] For the classic expression of the legal doctrine see A.V. Dicey, *Introduction to the Study of the Law of the Constitution* (London: Macmillan, 8th edn., 1915), chap. 1.

[74] See, e.g. P. Craig, 'Britain in the European Union', in J. Jowell and D. Oliver (eds.), *The Changing Constitution* (Oxford University Press, Oxford, 4th edn. 2000), chap. 3; N. MacCormick, *Questioning Sovereignty: Law, State, and Nation in the European Commonwealth* (Oxford University Press, Oxford, 1999); N. Walker, 'Sovereignty and Differentiated Integration in the European Union' (1998) 4 *ELJ* 355.

[75] Sieyes, n. 52 above, 124; and see above, 56–7.

[76] Cf. the full title of Rousseau's *The Social Contract*, n. 65 above: *Contrat Social, ou Principes du droit politique*.

[77] G. Lawson, *Politica Sacra et Civilis or, A Modell of Civil and Ecclesiasticall Government* (1660) (C. Condren (ed.), Cambridge University Press, Cambridge, 1992). Lawson had earlier written an explicit critique of *Leviathan*: G. Lawson, *An examination of the Political Part of Mr Hobbs, his Leviathan* (privately published, London, 1657). See C. Condren, *George Lawson's Politica and the English Revolution* (Cambridge University Press, Cambridge, 1989).

of a commonwealth already constituted',[78] the power, it might be said, of the office of the sovereign. Real sovereignty, by contrast, belongs to the community itself. And real sovereignty, Lawson claimed, is superior to personal sovereignty. Lawson noted that the holders of personal sovereignty 'cannot alter or take away the cause whereby they have their being, nor can they meddle with the fundamental laws of the constitution, which if it once cease, they cease to be a Parliament'.[79] The sovereignty vested in the community, however, 'hath the power of constitution', which includes the power 'to alter the forms of the government'.[80]

This type of statement is apt to be misconstrued. Today, legal scholars seek to re-interpret its meaning either by elevating the notion of 'real sovereignty' to the language of natural law,[81] or by reducing it to a positivist statement about the rule of recognition.[82] Both these tendencies are distortive. Real sovereignty, which is analogous to Sieyes's concept of *pouvoir constituant*,[83] must be understood as an expression of politic law. And this complex notion, one that is concerned with the intrinsically political precepts of conduct between the state and the people,[84] lies at the core of the subject of public law.

Once we turn directly to Lawson's idea of 'real' sovereignty, then, matters, perhaps not surprisingly, become somewhat complicated. The focus on real sovereignty, or on constituent power, helps us to understand how the institutionalized separation of powers can be treated as an explication, rather than a division,[85] of sovereignty.[86] But if it helps us to understand how the institutional forms of

---

[78] G. Lawson, *Politica Sacra et Civilis or, A Modell of Civil and Ecclesiasticall Government* (1660) (C. Condren (ed.), Cambridge University Press, Cambridge, 1992), 47.   [79] *Ibid.*, 48.

[80] *Ibid.*, 47.

[81] See, e.g. T.R.S. Allan, *Law, Liberty, and Justice: The Legal Foundations of British Constitutionalism* (Clarendon Press, Oxford, 1993), 4: 'In the absence of a higher "constitutional" law, proclaimed in a written Constitution and venerated as a source of unique legal authority, the rule of law serves in Britain as a form of constitution.' Allan makes it clear (*Ibid.*, 5) that the rule of law 'entails the subjection of government to the law . . . in the sense of its being bound to comply with "rules of just conduct".'

[82] See, e.g. J. Goldsworthy, *The Sovereignty of Parliament: History and Philosophy* (Clarendon Press, Oxford, 1999), chap. 10. Cf. T.R.S. Allan, *Constitutional Justice: A Liberal Theory of the Rule of Law* (Oxford University Press, Oxford, 2001), 216–25.

[83] See P. Pasquino, 'The Constitutional Republicanism of Emmanuel Sieyès', in B. Fontana (ed.), *The Invention of the Modern Republic* (Cambridge University Press, Cambridge, 1994), 112–13.

[84] Although Dicey acknowledged the force of this point, because of his adherence to legal positivism he was unable to invest it with juristic significance. Thus, he recognized that 'the word "sovereignty" is sometimes employed in a political rather than in a strictly legal sense' and that in this political sense 'the electors of Great Britain may be said to be, together with the Crown and the Lords, or perhaps, in strict accuracy, independently of the King and the Peers, the body in which sovereign power is invested'. 'But this', Dicey concluded, 'is a political, not a legal fact': Dicey, n. 73 above, 70–1.

[85] Cf. the American revolutionary debates in which 'American thinkers attempted to depart sharply from one of the most firmly fixed points in eighteenth-century political thought [i.e. the indivisibility of sovereignty]; and though they failed to gain acceptance for their strange and awkward views, they succeeded nevertheless in opening this fundamental issue to critical discussion, preparing the way for a new departure in the organization of power': B. Bailyn, *The Ideological Origins of the American Revolution* (Belknap Press, Cambridge, Mass., 1967), 198.

[86] E. J. Sieyes, *Préliminaire de la Constitution* (July 1789): 'In a large society individual liberty has three kinds of enemies to fear. The least dangerous are malevolent citizens . . . Individual liberty is far

constitutionalism bolster sovereignty, it also suggests that this entire framework should be treated as being conditional rather than absolute.

This latter conclusion is one that most jurists operating in the framework of modern liberal constitutionalism are unwilling to accept. Their general objective has been in effect to suppress the idea of sovereignty and to assert the absolute supremacy of 'the rule of law'.[87] In this sense, it might be said that the French Revolution, the moment at which the constituent power asserted itself, is something of an embarrassment to liberal juristic thought.[88] Thus, although the opening sentence of Carl Schmitt's *Political Theology*, 'sovereign is he who decides on the exception',[89] is today generally considered 'infamous',[90] it is in reality a fairly conventional, though admittedly dramatic, presentation of the concept of political sovereignty. It is not necessary to embrace Schmitt's personalistic and decisionistic reading of the issue of the exception to recognize that his formulation is capable of offering acute juristic insight. Schmitt, for example, contends that although the sovereign 'stands outside the normally valid legal system, he nevertheless belongs to it, for it is he who must decide whether the constitution needs to be suspended in its entirety'.[91] In the context of the turbulent politics of the Weimar Republic, Schmitt's political message was highly provocative.[92] But if his work is read as an explication of (in Lawson's language) 'real' sovereignty, the general message, that any coherent constitutional theory is obliged to take seriously the indivisible and absolute nature of the constituent power,[93] is one that cannot be ignored.

more endangered by [the second enemy: the] undertakings of the *Officers encharged to exercise some part of public power*. . . . The separation, and a good constitution of public powers are the only guarantee that nations and citizens might be preserved from this extreme evil' (cited in Pasquino, n. 83 above, 113–14). The third threat is that of a foreign enemy.

[87] See, e.g. Allan, n. 81 above, chap. 11; Allan, n. 82 above, chap. 7; R. Dworkin, *Law's Empire* (Fontana, London, 1986), chap. 11. Although this theme appears most prominently in the work of contemporary anti-positivists, it is worth noting that this is a feature which they share with legal positivists who, by differentiating legal from political sovereignty, aim to marginalize the significance of the latter conception. Cf. C. Schmitt, *Théorie de la Constitution [Verfassungslehre, 1928]* (L. Deroche trans., Presses Universitaires de France, Paris, 1993), 270: 'It is imagined first, that the constitution is nothing but a system of legal norms; secondly, that it is a closed system; and thirdly that it is "sovereign"—that is to say, it can never be interfered with or even influenced by reason or necessity of political existence.'

[88] Cf. J. Derrida, 'Declarations of Independence' (1986) 15 *New Political Science* 7, who states (at 10), in relation to the 'We the People' statement in the American declaration, that 'this people does not yet exist. They do *not* exist as an entity, it does *not* exist, *before* this declaration, *as such* . . . The signature invents the signer'.

[89] C. Schmitt, *Political Theology: Four Chapters on Sovereignty* (1922) (G. Schwab trans., MIT Press, Cambridge, Mass., 1988), 5.

[90] See, e.g. J. P. McCormick, *Carl Schmitt's Critique of Liberalism: Against Politics as Technology* (Cambridge University Press, Cambridge, 1997), 213. [91] Schmitt, n. 89 above, 7.

[92] See P. C. Caldwell, *Popular Sovereignty and the Crisis of German Constitutional Law: The Theory and Practice of Weimar Constitutionalism* (Duke University Press, Durham, NC, 1997), esp. chap. 4.

[93] Schmitt, n. 87 above, 215: 'The people, the nation, remains the true origin of all political events. It is the source of all those energies which manifest themselves in ever-new forms, and although it generates new forms and organisations, it is never able conclusively to subordinate its political existence to a particular form.'

If the constitutional form is not to be treated as definitive, however, this does not mean that we descend into a pure decisionism, in which concrete will is substituted for abstract form. This was Schmitt's basic error, an error which stemmed in part from his scepticism about the intrinsically representative character of the constituent power.[94] Once the representative dimensions of the constituent power are taken seriously, we can begin to understand *droit politique* as a set of precepts and maxims, even as a mode of conduct, which enables the state to maintain itself and to flourish. From the perspective of *droit politique*, sovereignty is as much concerned with capacity as with competence, with power and not just with authority. From such a relational perspective, we can appreciate how institutional restraints on the powers of government can operate to enhance the state's capacity to mobilize public power for common purposes. By reassuring the people that the power of the state will be used to promote the public welfare, and by establishing checking and reviewing mechanisms into the basic arrangements of state power, constitutionalism's significance can properly be recognized. Constitutionalism is to be viewed neither as a set of fundamental moral principles nor as the 'unpolitical principles of the bourgeois *Rechtstaat*', but as 'one of the most effective philosophies of state building ever contrived'.[95] Constitutional values are conditional, not absolute; constitutional discourse is political, not moral.

3. CONCLUSIONS

The main objective of this essay has been to reveal the extent to which our understanding of constitutional ordering is dependent on the concept of representation. The foundations of this understanding were laid bare primarily by Hobbes's remarkable exposition of the subject. By building a theory of government on the foundation of representation, Hobbes was able to offer a clear and coherent explanation of the concepts of state, sovereign, and sovereignty, concepts which lie at the heart of modern political order.

However, once *Leviathan* is viewed as a work of jurisprudence, and therefore as an early elaboration of legal positivism, certain limitations in Hobbes's treatment of the concept of sovereignty are evident. These have been highlighted with the aid of Sieyes's elaboration of the concept of constituent power. Sieyes agrees with Hobbes's contention that representation is a foundational concept. But by drawing on a broader notion of political representation, one which explicitly recognizes that the role of representation is the management of conflict, Sieyes

---

[94] From this perspective, Schmitt does not present himself consistently. Notwithstanding his tendency to treat political authority as personal, in *Verfassungslehre* he appears to modify his position and acknowledges the representative character of the constituent power of the people: n. 87 above, chap. 18.

[95] S. Holmes, *Passions and Constraint: On the Theory of Liberal Democracy* (University of Chicago Press, Chicago, Ill., 1995), p. xi.

provides us with the basis for understanding sovereignty as an intrinsically political concept.

From this perspective, we are able more clearly to recognize that sovereignty is relational. Sovereignty is not found to reside in any particular locus; it is generated as a product of the political relationship between the people and the state. Here too the idea of representation is pivotal, especially in fashioning images both of the relationship between governors and governed and of the way in which government acquires an 'artificial, public status'. This relational perspective enables us to appreciate more fully the legal and political aspects of sovereignty, and especially to grasp the relation between the two. It suggests that if lawyers seek to analyse the legal conception without properly acknowledging its inextricable links with the political, then unless the confines of legal discourse are acknowledged, this surely will lead to distortion.

The concept of representation thus lies at the root of political power. It is only through representation that those exercising governmental power become fixed with certain responsibilities; similarly, it is only as a result of the work undertaken by this concept that the people are transformed into citizens.[96] In this sense, it might be said that political power is both generated and utilized through representation. The notion of pure or direct democracy must as a consequence be recognized to be a thoroughly ineffective method of rule. Drawing a distinction between 'aesthetic' and 'mimetic' representation, Ankersmit has succinctly captured the essence of this concept of political representation. The latter, rooted in the notion that representation is a mirror of society, finds its expression in calls for direct democracy, a concept that 'dishonours democracy by extraditing it to the boundless and unlimited desires of a collective political libido'.[97] It is only through aesthetic representation, a symbolic representation which acknowledges that political actors possess some duty of trusteeship but are also equipped with the power of creative political action, that conflict in society is capable of being properly managed.[98]

Finally, if the juristic aspects of this exercise in state-building are to be fully revealed, each of the predominant conceptions of law in contemporary

---

[96] One of the main thrusts behind the growing contemporary interest in such themes as civic republicanism and deliberative democracy, it might be noted, has been precisely to remind governors of their civic duties in the exercise of their public offices, and to educate the people in the responsibilities of the office of citizenship. See P. Pettit, *Republicanism: A Theory of Freedom and Government* (Oxford University Press, Oxford, 1997); J.S. Dryzek, *Deliberative Democracy and Beyond: Liberals, Critics, Contestations* (Oxford University Press, Oxford, 2000).

[97] Ankersmit, n. 61 above, 347. It follows that those seeking to promote mimetic representation—the aim of ensuring that government and its agencies (including the judiciary) somehow mirror society—fail to appreciate the vitally important role which aesthetic representation—and the maintenance of a division between state and society—plays in the constitution of political authority. This is not to deny that there are important questions to be addressed concerning political exclusion: on which see A. Phillips, *The Politics of Presence: The Political Representation of Gender, Ethnicity, and Race* (Clarendon Press, Oxford, 1995). But the politics of inclusion must be recognized also to constitute a form of symbolic representation.

[98] See G. Kateb, 'The Moral Distinctiveness of Representative Democracy' (1981) 91 *Ethics* 357.

jurisprudence, that is, both those that treat law as the command of the sovereign and those promoting an image of law as a moral force that transcends the
political, must be jettisoned. The specifically juristic dimensions to constitutional
ordering can properly be grasped only by resurrecting a conception of law which
explicitly draws on the affinities between the legal and the political; that is, by
adopting a concept of public law as *droit politique*.

4

Judicial Deference and Human Rights: A Question of Competence

JEFFREY JOWELL*

As our Human Rights Act unfolds, two views are emerging about the extent to which the courts should defer to Parliament and other bodies exercising public powers. The first contends that courts should in principle bow to the decisions of the legislature and those exercising power on its behalf on matters of public interest (sometimes referred to as matters of public policy or expediency). The second view contends that judges should assess those decisions by the standards of 'legality' under domestic administrative law, allowing little or no 'discretionary area of judgment'[1] to the primary decision-maker.

I shall suggest that both these views are based upon a mistaken notion of the relative competence of courts and other institutions in our now altered constitutional order. In my view the Act does permit some limited room for deference by the courts to the views of the bodies they are reviewing. But such deference no longer rests upon the superior constitutional status of those bodies. It should be contingent upon the relative institutional competence or capacity of courts and other bodies to decide the matter, in the context of the particular right under review.

1. Two foundational questions

Before proceeding to consider these two opposing contentions, two foundational questions need to be considered:

(a) Does the Human Rights Act possess constitutional status? and
(b) To what extent does Parliamentary sovereignty survive under the Act?

* My thanks to Anthony Lester and Dawn Oliver for their helpful comments on an earlier draft—and Carol Harlow for being such a supportive and responsive colleague over the years.
[1] A term employed by A. Lester and D. Pannick, *Human Rights Law and Practice* (Butterworths, London, 1999), 74, para. 3.21; cited by Lord Hope in *R v. DPP, ex p. Kebilene* [2000] 2 AC 326, 380–1 and Lord Bingham in *Brown v. Stott* [2001] 2 WLR 817, 834–5.

(a) The Constitutional Status of the Act

Prior to the implementation of the Human Rights Act, such implied constitutional principles as we possessed could merely temper, but not override, the clearly expressed will of the elected representatives of the people.[2] By contrast, the Human Rights Act establishes an expectation that all official power, including Parliament's powers, will be limited by those rights set out in the European Convention on Human Rights ('Convention rights'). The constitutional significance of the Act is grounded in the fact that the Convention rights are not a mere random catalogue of freedoms, set out in an instrument with no greater force than, say, a statute establishing rights of way or social benefits. The Convention incorporates a coherent set of civil and political entitlements that are inherent to a new conception of democracy for the United Kingdom. The Convention was conceived for a Europe where, in the first half of the twentieth century, it was tragically and conclusively demonstrated that the infringement of certain fundamental rights and freedoms, even if fully supported by the majority of the electorate, fatally undermines democracy itself. The respect for and protection of those rights is thus not merely desirable, but a necessary feature of democracy; constitutive of democracy itself.[3] Even where the breach of a right is sanctioned under the Convention, the breach is normally permitted in order to preserve democracy (when 'necessary in a democratic society') and not to deviate from it.[4]

The most convincing indication of the constitutional departure intended by the Human Rights Act is the fact that it permits the courts to review not only the decisions of public officials for conformity to Convention rights. It also permits judicial review of Acts of Parliament.[5] Prior to the Act, outside European Community law courts could review whether officials had properly carried out Parliament's designs, but could not question the scope of those designs. It is now recognized that the legislature too is expected to observe the imperatives of the new order. It is clear therefore that the Act provides a higher-order framework, a constitutional order, which constrains all public institutions and is expected to constrain even the elected legislature itself.[6]

---

[2] *R v. Secretary of State for the Home Department, ex p. Simms* [2000] 2 AC 115, *per* Lords Steyn and Hoffmann (referring to the constitutional principle of 'legality' which could only be—but nevertheless could be—overriden by the legislature's clear words).

[3] 'When the [Canadian] Charter [of Rights and Freedoms] was introduced Canada went, in the words of former Chief Justice Brian Dickson, from a system of Parliamentary supremacy to constitutional supremacy [where] each Canadian was given individual rights which no government or legislature could take away': Iacobucci J in *Vriend* [1998] 1 SCR 493, cited by Laws LJ in *Roth and Others v. Secretary of State for the Home Department* [2002] EWCA Civ 158 (CA).

[4] Some of the Convention rights specify that condition (Arts. 8–11); others do not (e.g. Art. 1 of Protocol 1); but that condition should nevertheless be assumed under the general requirement of constitutionality.   [5] Human Rights Act 1998, ss. 3 and 4.

[6] Judicial recognition of the constitutional status of the Human Rights Act is as follows: Lord Bingham in *Brown v. Stott* [2001] 2 WLR 817 at 835; Lord Steyn at 839; Lord Woolf in *R v. Offen* [2001] 1 WLR 254 at 275; Laws LJ in *Roth* (note 3 above) at paras. 69–75 and in *Thoburn and others v. Sunderland City Council and others* [2001] EWHC Admin 934, [2002] EuLR 253, para. 62. See W. Eskridge and J. Ferejohn, 'Super-Statutes', (2001) 50 *Duke LJ* 1215.

It is sometimes said that such an arrangement reassigns power from the legislature to the judiciary. In reality, Parliament has itself limited its own power under the Act and has assigned to the courts the function of adjudicating, in the event of a dispute, whether a Convention right is offended by Parliament or its representatives. Yet the courts are also constrained under the Act to observe Convention rights, along with all other 'public authorities'.[7]

Although Parliament is not designated under the Act as a 'public authority', it is of high significance to the Act's status that, in performing their reviewing function, the courts are also instructed by the Act to make the presumption that all legislation is and was intended by Parliament to conform with Convention rights. The injunction to read and give effect to primary and subordinate legislation 'so far as it is possible to do so'[8] in a way which is compatible with Convention rights does of course not permit the courts to legislate themselves.[9] But it provides a clear indication that all legislation is expected to comply with the new constitutional order.

A further indication of this expectation and of the constitutional status of the Human Rights Act is the fact that courts give precedence to that Act even over subsequent legislation. The doctrine of implied repeal does not apply to the Act. Future legislation will have to be explicit in order to evade the Act's requirements.[10]

(b) Parliamentary Sovereignty under the Act

If the Human Rights Act does have constitutional significance, the content of which embodies the expectation that even Parliament should conform to its

---

[7] Under s. 6 of the HRA. See also Lord Lester QC, 'The Magnetism of the Human Rights Act 1998' [2002] *Judicial Review* 179, who says, at para. 20, that the Act 'has created a magnetic field in which all three branches of government must work to secure a fair balance between individual rights and the general interest of the community'.

[8] *Ibid.*, s. 3. See C. Gearty, 'Reconciling Parliamentary Democracy and Human Rights' (2002) 118 *LQR* 248. See also R. Clayton, 'The Limits of What's "Possible": Statutory Construction Under the Human Rights Act' [2002] *EHRLRev* 559.

[9] *Poplar Borough Council* v. *Donoghue* [2001] 3 WLR 183, *per* Lord Woolf. Nor to amend existing legislation. See *R (Anderson)* v. *Secretary of State for the Home Department* [2002] UKHL 46, [2002] 4 All ER 1089, at para. 81.

[10] See *Thoburn and others* v. *Sunderland City Council*, n. 6 above, where Laws LJ said that we should recognize a distinction between 'ordinary statutes' and 'constitutional statutes'. In the latter category are the Magna Carta, the Bill of Rights 1689, the Act of Union, the Reform Acts, the Scotland Act 1998, the Government of Wales Act 1998, the European Communities Act 1972, and the Human Rights Act 1998. According to Sir John, ordinary statutes may be impliedly repealed, but constitutional statutes may not: 'For the repeal of a constitutional act or the abrogation of a fundamental right to be effected by statute, the court would apply this test: is it shown that the legislature's *actual*—not imputed, constructive or presumed—intention was to effect the repeal or abrogation? I think the test could only be met by express words in the later statute, or by words so specific that the inference of an actual determination to effect the result contended for was irresistible. The ordinary rule of implied repeal does not satisfy this test. Accordingly, it has no application to constitutional statutes'. It is noteworthy that during the passage of the Human Rights Bill the Government expressly rejected an amendment to preserve implied repeal along the lines of Section 4 of the New Zealand Bill of Rights Act: HL Debs., Vol. 583, cols. 518 ff. (18 November 1997). See further Lord Lester QC, n. 7 above.

terms, how do we explain the fact that Parliament is entitled under the Act to legislate in violation of Convention rights and to ignore judicial declarations of incompatibility with those rights? It is often said that the Human Rights Act offers a subtle compromise between two models of democracy: the model based upon Parliamentary sovereignty, and the rights model, sometimes called the model of 'constitutional supremacy', which limits governmental power to interfere with specified individual rights. Under the terms of this compromise it is said that Parliament's sovereignty is preserved because it retains the ultimate power to override Convention rights. In so far as there is a partnership between the legislature and the judiciary, the legislature, according to this view, remains the senior partner.

The metaphor of partnership does not fit comfortably with the scheme of the Act. The courts are empowered under the Act to pronounce whether the standards of the new constitutional order have been honoured. Parliament may then decide to ignore such pronouncements. In so doing, however, Parliament does not purport itself to overrule the view of the courts that Convention rights have been infringed. Parliament simply retains the raw power (call it sovereign power if you like) to act, or to continue to act, in breach of the Convention, even in opposition to the sole authoritative interpretation of the scope of a Convention right, that of a declaration issued by a court. Such a power permits Parliament to defy the expectations of the new order, but not to define them (for that task rests squarely with the judiciary). It may be that if Parliament were to defy a declaration of incompatibility it would be acting lawfully, but it is open to question whether it would be acting in accordance with the principles underlying the altered constitutional expectations. It is not necessary in this essay to explore that difficult question.[11] What is clear, and relevant, for these purposes is that in view of the constitutional significance of the Human Rights Act, Parliament's ultimate power of defiance in no way implies that the courts are expected to acknowledge or submit to the ultimately superior constitutional status of the legislature *when exercising their adjudicative functions under the Act.*

---

[11] For an attempt to differentiate legality and constitutionality in this context see M. Elliott, 'Parliamentary Sovereignty and the New Constitutional Order: Legislative Freedom, Political Reality and Convention' (2002) 22 *Legal Studies* 340. Elliott considers that although Parliamentary violation of Convention rights in the face of a court's declaration to the contrary may not be an illegal act, it could be unconstitutional in the 'political' and 'moral' sense of that term. However, following an adverse ruling of the European Court of Human Rights, the continued violation of a Convention right by Parliament would be unlawful in international law. He also submits that over the course of time a convention may arise binding Parliament not to override Convention rights, which could in turn provide an interpretative tool to the courts to restrain violations of those rights. Compare David Feldman, who considers that a declaration of incompatibility is simply an indication that Parliament has committed a non-legal wrong: D. Feldman, 'The Human Rights Act 1998 and Constitutional Principles' (1999) 19 *Legal Studies* 165, 187.

2. THE FIRST VIEW: DEFERENCE AND PUBLIC INTEREST

In the recent case of *Roth*,[12] Sir John Laws postulated as one of the principles that now emerge from the authorities under the Human Rights Act that 'greater deference is to be paid to an Act of Parliament than to a decision of the executive or subordinate measure'. Lord Woolf has said that:[13]

... legislation is passed by a democratically elected Parliament and therefore the courts under the Convention are entitled to and should, *as a matter of constitutional principle*, pay a degree of deference to the view of Parliament as to what is in the interest of the public generally when upholding the rights of the individual under the Convention.

To accord the legislature superior constitutional status to decide matters of public interest or policy normally recognizes the appropriate divisions of power in a democracy. But should constitutional superiority apply where matters of public interest are engaged under the Human Rights Act? In the case of *Alconbury*,[14] Lord Hoffmann noted the distinction between a decision as to the public interest, which he called a 'policy decision', and a 'determination of right', which was 'a judicial or quasi judicial act' involving a decision about the 'rights or interests of particular persons'. Policy decisions, said Lord Hoffmann, are not for the courts. In a democracy, they should be made by 'democratically elected bodies or persons accountable to them'. In a subsequent lecture Lord Hoffmann repeated this theme, saying:[15]

The courts should not, under cover of interpretation of the human rights of the individual, make decisions about what the general public interest requires. There is no individual right to have the law changed to accord with the court's perception of the general public interest. Once this happens, we have government by judges rather than government by the people.

Lord Hoffmann's general analysis of the constitutional division between what Dworkin would call the forum of principle (which is a matter for the courts), and that of policy (which is for the elected representatives) in general sustains the notion of separation of powers in any model of democracy.[16] Under the model which enshrines the sovereignty of Parliament, the legislature possesses the supreme power to override individual rights in favour of the general interest. Under the rights model, however, the legislature's policy-making power is constrained in favour of individual rights. Even the most passionate policy, fully supported by the electorate, in favour of the suppression of terrorism, should

---

[12] *Roth and others v. Secretary of State for Home Department* [2002] EWCA Civ. 158 (22 February 2002).   [13] *R v. Lambert* [2001] 2 WLR 211, 219 (emphasis added).

[14] *R (on application of Alconbury Developments Ltd) v. Secretary of State for the Environment and the Regions* [2001] 2 WLR 1389.

[15] Lord Hoffmann, 'COMBAR Lecture 2001: Separation of Powers' [2002] *Judicial Review* 137.

[16] R. Dworkin, *Taking Rights Seriously* (Duckworth, London, 1978), and *Freedom's Law, The Moral Reading of the American Constitution* (Oxford University Press, Oxford, 1996).

not permit the torture of suspects. This policy is removed from the domain of majority choice; blocked by the individual's right not to be subject to inhuman and degrading treatment.[17] Lord Hoffmann recognizes this when he says, in *Alconbury*:[18]

There is no conflict between human rights and the democratic principle. Respect for human rights requires that certain basic rights of individuals should not be capable in any circumstances of being overridden by the majority, even if they think that the public interest so requires. Other rights should only be overridden in very restricted circumstances. These are rights which belong to individuals simply by virtue of their humanity, independently of any utilitarian calculation.

The question of the extent of any judicial deference is brought into high relief in relation to 'qualified rights', those rights which the Convention permits to be breached, but only in pursuit of a number of stipulated interests. Thus free expression, under Article 10 of the Convention, may be breached if necessary in a democratic society for the preservation of a number of specified interests, including national security. In *Alconbury* Lord Hoffmann referred to the qualified right to the peaceful enjoyment of property under Article 1 of Protocol 1 to the Convention. The qualification there permits the state to impair property rights 'as it deems necessary to control the use of property in accordance with the general interest'. Lord Hoffmann comments on this provision as follows:[19]

Importantly, the question of what the public interest requires for the purpose of Article 1 of Protocol 1 can, and in my opinion should, be determined according to the democratic principle—by elected local or central bodies or by ministers accountable to them. There is no principle of human rights which requires such decisions to be made by independent and impartial tribunals.

Lord Hoffmann is here specifically referring to the underlying issue in *Alconbury*, which was whether a decision about large-scale planning made by the Minister offended the need for an 'independent and impartial tribunal' under Article 6 of the Convention. The right to property under Article 1 of Protocol 1 is also a relatively weak right under international law (which is engaged by that Article). Nevertheless, this illustration raises the question whether in general the nature of qualified rights resurrects the normal 'democratic principle' under which courts should defer, on constitutional grounds, to the legislature on matters of public policy.[20]

I shall argue below that on many of these matters of general or public interest the courts may defer to another body on the ground that the body in question

---

[17] Under Art. 3 of the Convention.   [18] Above n. 14, para. 70.

[19] Lord Hoffmann is here specifically referring to the underlying issue in *Alconbury*, which was whether a decision about large-scale planning made by the Minister offended the need for an 'independent and impartial tribunal' under Art. 6 of the Convention. But here and elsewhere he makes it clear that the courts should defer to his 'democratic principle' on such matters of public interest.

[20] As Sir John Laws put it in *Roth* (n. 12 above): 'Parliament remains the sovereign legislator. It, and not a written constitution, bears the ultimate mantle of democracy in the state'.

has the better *institutional competence* to decide the question in hand. Institutional competence refers to the *capacity* of a body to make the relevant decision. The question asked is whether the court's structures and procedures equip it to decide the matter better than the body being reviewed. Factors to be taken into account in answering this question include the respective expertise of the two institutions, access to information, and so on. *Constitutional competence*, on the other hand, refers to the *authority* of the body to decide the relevant question. The question asked is whether the body is authorized to take the relevant decision under the constitutive rules and principles which allocate decision-making power to bodies (including the courts) exercising public functions in a democracy.

In the case of *Rehman*,[21] Lord Hoffmann enunciated this distinction (without employing those terms). Although not decided under the Human Rights Act, *Rehman* raised a question central to that Act, namely, whether it is for the courts to pronounce upon matters of national security, or whether courts should instead defer on that matter to the executive. Lord Hoffmann insisted that, in the context of that particular case,[22] matters of national security were not for the courts for two reasons. The first was that 'the executive has special expertise in these matters'. This reason is based upon the superior institutional competence of the executive; its structural capacity to decide matters of national security, by virtue of its special access to intelligence information, etc. Lord Hoffmann's second reason was as follows:[23]

[These decisions] require a legitimacy which can only be conferred by entrusting them to persons responsible to the community through the democratic process. If the people were to accept the consequences of such decisions, they must be made by persons whom the people have elected, and whom they can remove.

This second reason for judicial deference to the executive lies squarely within the realm of constitutional competence; upon the authority (rather than capacity) of the executive to take these decisions. The authority is based in turn upon the accountability of the executive to Parliament and thence to the public.

If this approach were to extend to all Convention rights (and Lord Hoffmann was by no means implying in that case that they should), courts would be required automatically to defer, on constitutional grounds, on any occasion on which a qualified right was claimed to be sacrificed on the altar of the public interest. Courts would thus be required to submit to the view of the legislature or executive whenever decisions were based on criteria such as 'public' or 'general' interest (under Article 1 of or Protocol 1 to the Convention), 'national security' (under Articles 8, 10, 11), 'public safety' (under Articles 8, 9, 10, 11), 'the economic well-being of the country' (under Article 8), 'public order' (under

---

[21] *Secretary of State* v. *Rehman* [2002] 1 All ER 122 (HL).
[22] Which concerned whether it would be contrary to the national interest to harbour an alien who was alleged to have aided terrorism in a foreign country.   [23] *Rehman*, n. 21 above, para. 62.

Article 9), 'the protection of health or morals' (under Articles 8, 9, 10, 11), or 'the prevention of disorder or crime' (under Articles 8, 10, 11).

It must be emphasized that most of the interests referred to in the previous sentence may only provide a valid reason for overriding the right in question if 'necessary in a democratic society'. Three crucial features of this notion need emphasizing.

The first is that the interests specified may only prevail when necessary (and not merely desirable). The second is that the measures may be taken to support democracy, but not to subvert it (thus, freedom of speech may not be restricted for the purpose of the 'prevention of disorder' if the real reason is to prevent the opposition from holding public meetings during an election period). Thirdly, it bears repeating that the concept of democracy which has to be supported should not be wholly subsumed by the imperative of majority rule. There is no longer a dichotomy between the 'democratic principle' (which ensures the supremacy of bodies representing the electorate) and individual rights. The new dispensation considers the protection of rights to be integral to democracy, not opposed to it. Wisely, however, it is not rigid in its application. It permits the representatives of the people to override some, but by no means all, of the protected rights in order to achieve specified goals (for example, national security, public health, etc). Other rights may be derogated from, under Article 15 of the Convention, provided there is a 'war or other public emergency threatening the life of the nation'. But even in the case of qualified rights it is the courts, rather than the representative bodies, which are charged with the responsibility of deciding the democratic necessity of those public interest goals or, in the case of a derogation under Article 15, whether the measures are 'strictly required by the exigencies of the situation'. In so doing, the courts are neither constitutionally disabled from making those decisions themselves nor constitutionally required to defer either to the executive *or to Parliament* on these matters. As has been recently decided by the Court of Appeal, even the urgent policy need to control illegal immigration does not justify the imposition by Parliament of unfair procedures upon lorry drivers who are discovered carrying immigrants, or the arbitrary impounding of their vehicles.[24]

That is not to say that all determinations of policy may infringe Convention rights. The scope of the right to a fair and unbiased hearing does not, for example, extend to a requirement that all decisions on whether to grant or refuse planning permission for large areas of land must be conducted by a judge who is free of any political connection.[25] The new democratic order retains broad opportunity for the legislature, or those acting on its behalf, to take decisions of policy and to allocate scarce resources free of the constraints of rights. The extent to which that opportunity is inhibited by the scope of a particular right is the concern of much of the new constitutional review.

---

[24] *Roth and others* v. *Secretary of State for the Home Department* [2002] EWCA Civ 158 (22 February 2002).   [25] *Alconbury*, n. 14 above.

Where rights do inhibit legislative action, there is no need for the courts to observe the constitutional propriety of the old order. This is true even where, as with the qualified rights, Convention rights may be overridden on matters concerning the public interest. That is why the *Wednesbury* standard of judicial review[26] has no place under the Human Rights Act.[27] *Wednesbury* review is a child of the old order. This is because when the then sovereign Parliament conferred broad discretion upon officials to decide in the public interest, the courts would presume that those officials, as delegates of the elected representatives of the people were, constitutionally, under the then-prevailing 'democratic principle', the appropriate body to make those decisions. The burden of proving unreasonableness was therefore placed squarely upon the claimant and the courts interpreted their power to intervene narrowly.[28]

The *Wednesbury* presumption is reversed under the new constitutional order. In respect of qualified rights, the court must decide whether a breach of a right is justified in a democratic society because it promotes certain necessary public interests. It is for the body concerned, whether public official or Parliament, positively to justify that breach. The courts would be acting under the conditions of the old order if they were to presume that the reviewed bodies were constitutionally best suited to decide the matter simply because of their representative character and the fact that they are politically accountable to the electorate. The primacy of representative status and political accountability has been erased under the altered constitutional settlement. It cannot revive even in times of stress. A breach of Convention rights has always to be positively justified to the satisfaction of the courts. Constitutional deference should have no part in this process. In the words of McLachlin J in respect of the Canadian Charter of Human Rights:[29]

Parliament has its role: to choose the appropriate response to social problems within the limiting framework of the Constitution. But the courts also have a role: to determine, objectively and impartially, whether Parliament's choice falls within the limiting framework of the Constitution. The courts are no more permitted to abdicate their responsibility than is Parliament. To carry judicial deference to the point of accepting Parliament's view simply on the basis that the problem is so serious and the solution difficult, would be to diminish the role of the courts in the constitutional process and to weaken the structure of rights upon which our constitution and nation is founded.

---

[26] *Associated Provincial Picture Houses* v. *Wednesbury Corporation* [1948] 1 KB 223.

[27] See Lord Phillips MR in *R (Mahmood)* v. *Secretary of State for the Home Department* [2001] 1 WLR 840, 857: 'When anxiously scrutinising an executive decision that interferes with human rights, the court will ask the question, applying the objective test, whether the decision-maker could reasonably have concluded that the interference was necessary to achieve one or more of the legitimate aims recognised by the Convention.' See also *R (Isiko)* v. *Secretary of State for the Home Department* [2001] HRLR 295; *R (Samaroo)* v. *Secretary of State for the Home Department* [2001] UKHRR 1150 (*per* Dyson LJ).

[28] Perhaps too narrowly. See e.g. Lord Cooke in *R (Daly)* v. *Secretary of State for the Home Department* [2001] 3 WLR 1622.

[29] *RJR McDonald* v. *Canada Attorney General* [1993] 3 SCR 199, paras. 133–137, cited in R. Clayton, 'Regaining a Sense of Proportion: The Human Rights Act and the Proportionality Principle' [2001] *EHRLRev* 504. Compare Lord Hoffmann, 'Bentham and Human Rights' (2001) *CLP* 61, esp. at 73.

3. The second view: illegality review

The second view contends that it is for the courts to decide the scope of Convention rights, including matters of public interest, and to leave little or no discretionary area to the decision-maker. This view assumes that the ground of review which the courts are engaging under the Act is that of illegality, which requires the courts themselves to determine whether a body has exceeded the terms of the statute, has strayed outside its 'four corners' or offended any of its provisions.[30] If this view were correct, then much of our existing common law standards under the ground of procedural propriety would be subsumed under Articles 5 and 6 of the Convention,[31] and review on all matters of substance would be determined not by the timid standards of irrationality review (of whatever intensity), but by the standards of illegality, under which it is for the courts to decide whether the terms of the Human Rights Act have been exceeded and whether Convention rights have been breached.

Is illegality the appropriate ground of review under the Human Rights Act? At first glance the Act seems simply to introduce a new statutory tort, that of breach of Convention rights, and the question to be decided is therefore conceptually straightforward, namely, whether the relevant act or decision strayed outside the scope of the Act. It would thus be illegal for a public body to act in breach of most of the terms of an international instrument (the ECHR), which the governing statute (the HRA) incorporates and sets out in Schedule 1 to the Act.[32] In other words, to act within the four corners of the Human Rights Act, the body must act within the corners of the ECHR. Judges therefore assess the boundaries of the statute by reference to the boundaries of the ECHR. This is illegality review at one remove, but still perhaps, strictly speaking, illegality review.

More difficult to fit into illegality review is the review of Parliamentary legislation under the Human Rights Act.[33] Does it make sense to say that a statute can be illegal because it offends the terms of another statute (at least in the absence of the doctrine of implied repeal)? Is it 'illegal' for Parliament to pass (or have passed) a statute which offends against the Human Rights Act? This question is finessed because the Act permits courts only to issue a declaration that the offending statute is incompatible with the Convention rights. Nevertheless,

---

[30] See e.g. I. Leigh, 'Taking Rights Proportionally: Judicial Review, the Human Rights Act and Strasbourg' [2002] PL 265; and to some extent Clayton, n. 29 above.

[31] When Lord Diplock, in the GCHQ case, employed the term 'procedural impropriety' as one of the grounds of judicial review, he included under that head 'failure by an administrative tribunal to observe procedural rules that are expressly laid down in the legislative instrument by which its jurisdiction is conferred, even when such failure does not involve any denial of natural justice': Council for Civil Service Unions v. Minister for the Civil Service [1985] AC 374, 410–11.

[32] S. 6(1) of the HRA states that: 'It is unlawful for a public authority to act in a way which is incompatible with a Convention right.'

[33] Parliament (except for the House of Lords in its judicial capacity) does not qualify as a 'public authority' under the Act.

the fact is that the courts are empowered by the terms of one statute, the Human Rights Act, to review all other legislation. This does not feel like illegality review, which engages the narrower question whether the implementation or enforcement of a particular statute by public officials is authorized by its terms.

The grounds of conventional judicial review fit awkwardly as organizing categories under the Human Rights Act. The reason relates again to the constitutional status of the Act. The essential aims of review under our administrative law differ from those of the new constitutional review.[34] Administrative review asks either whether the decision under review meets standards of fairness, procedural or substantive (under the general grounds of procedural impropriety or irrationality). Or it asks whether the terms and purpose of a statute have been evaded (under the ground of illegality). Constitutional review asks whether the matter fulfils or offends against the requirements of a modern democracy (based on the new rights-based constitutional model).[35] The answer to that question is not found wholly in the terms of the Human Rights Act or in the concepts of our administrative law. It is discussed in the jurisprudence of the European Court of Human Rights, to which the judges have to have regard under the Act. It is also well rehearsed in the rich case law of other constitutional democracies. It is to be forged by our own judges in the light of the imperatives of new constitutional expectations. Up to now their principal aid to interpretation has been the doctrine of proportionality.

4. PROPORTIONALITY: GROUND OF REVIEW OR TEST OF CONSTITUTIONALITY UNDER THE ACT?

The question whether an interference with a Convention right is justified is assessed by the European Court of Human Rights by the standard of proportionality. Our courts have also adopted proportionality to determine the scope of a Convention right, particularly (although not entirely) in respect of qualified rights.[36] Does proportionality guide us on the question of the intensity of review, or the degree of deference, which the courts must accord the legislature and other public bodies?

---

[34] I have expanded on this point in: Jeffrey Jowell, 'Beyond the Rule of Law: Towards Constitutional Review' [2001] *PL* 671.

[35] See the recent case of *P (Pro Life Alliance)* v. *BBC* [2002] 2 All ER 756 where Laws LJ referred to the courts' 'overarching constitutional responsibility' to protect political speech. He said: 'This responsibility is most acute at the time . . . of a general election. It has its origin in a deeper truth, which is that the courts are ultimately the trustees of our democracy's framework.' The Court of Appeal held that the BBC's refusal to transmit images of aborted foetuses could not be justified under Art. 10 of the Convention.

[36] See e.g. *Roth*, n. 24 above, where proportionality was employed in respect of the interpretation of Art. 5 which is not, on its face, a right which permits of qualification.

To answer this question we must ask first whether proportionality is applied in relation to Convention rights as a general ground of judicial review or, as has recently been suggested, as a matter of law?[37] In other words, is it an independent interpretative common law standard or is it a requirement which is engaged by the terms of the Human Rights Act and Convention rights? Proportionality as a judicially-fashioned standard requires all discretionary powers to be exercised with due regard to the balance between the ends pursued and the means to achieve those ends.[38] It seeks to ensure substantive fairness in the exercise of any discretionary power. It has been applied in our domestic administrative law under other names, most notably unreasonableness, although it is probably emerging as a separate ground of review.[39] By contrast, proportionality under the Human Rights Act is an instrument tailored for a specific purpose, namely, to test the scope of Convention rights and to ensure that they are overridden only for compelling reasons.

It is often forgotten that the Convention makes no express mention of proportionality. The term is found nowhere in the Human Rights Act. Therefore, in so far as it is a test required by the Act, and is thus a requirement of law, proportionality is merely convenient shorthand to describe the standard which, by implication, the Convention requires to justify the limitation of certain rights for the purpose of furthering some designated interests. In that, rather tortuous, sense, proportionality is perhaps a matter of law. Its purpose and intent become clearer, however, when it is seen as an instrument of constitutional review, a standard to ensure that the fundamental requirements of a democracy are not curtailed or infringed except where necessary to sustain democracy.

The content of proportionality now accepted in our courts is that set out by Lord Clyde in the Privy Council in *de Freitas* v. *Permanent Secretary of Minister of Agriculture, Fisheries, Lands and Housing*:[40]

[w]hether: (1) the legislative objective is sufficiently important to justify limiting a fundamental right; (2) the measures designed to meet the legislative objective are rationally connected to it; and (3) the means used to impair the right or freedom are no more than is necessary to accomplish the objective.

---

[37] See *B* v. *Secretary of State for the Home Department* [2000] 2 CMLR 1086, 1098, where Simon Brown LJ stated that proportionality involved a 'question of law' and if the court's view of the matter differed from that of the Immigration Appeal Tribunal 'then we are bound to say so and to allow the appeal, substituting our decision for theirs'. Sedley LJ said that the requirements of the ECHR 'means making up our own minds about the proportionality of a public law measure—not simply deciding whether the Home Secretary or the IAT's view of it is lawful and rational': *ibid.*, 1095. It was held that the deportation of a person who had lived in the UK for 39 years following his release from prison violated Art. 8 of the ECHR (via Art. 6 of the EC Treaty).

[38] See Lord Steyn's distinction between proportionality and *Wednesbury* unreasonableness in *R (Daly)* v. *Secretary of State for the Home Department* [2001] 3 WLR 1622, 1634–6.

[39] See P. Craig, 'The Courts, the Human Rights Act and Judicial Review' (2001) 117 *LQR* 589; M. Elliott, 'The Human Rights Act 1998 and the Standard of Substantive Review' [2001] *CLJ* 301. See in particular Lord Bingham's adoption in *Daly*, n. 38 above, of Lord Steyn's employment of proportionality in *R* v. *Secretary of State for the Home Department, ex p. Leech (No. 2)* [1994] QB 198.

[40] [1999] 1 AC 69, adopted by the House of Lords in *Daly*, n. 38 above.

Even under the terms of this structured inquiry, we are none the wiser as to the precise degree of deference, if any, which the courts should accord the legislature and other bodies. We have established this much: that the level of judicial scrutiny of Convention rights will be more intense than that undertaken under common law rationality review because the burden of justifying the limitation of the right is placed upon the body being reviewed. In addition, under Lord Clyde's third test, the 'least restrictive alternative', official decision-makers will now have to demonstrate that they considered alternative courses of action and have selected the least onerous of them. This requirement in itself will introduce a new culture of justification, requiring officials to expose their methodology and reasoning and to consider alternative courses of action. Our administrative review has never gone so far. The second of Lord Clyde's questions, rational connection, is familiar under our administrative law review, but again does not provide any guidance on how deeply the official's view on that matter should be probed by the courts.

Lord Clyde's first question, whether the objective is 'sufficiently important' to justify the limitation of the right, bristles with problems about deference. In answering that question, the courts must first ask whether the objective of the curtailment or restriction of a right is genuinely to defend one of the interests that the Convention permits. In the words of the European Court's jurisprudence: was the curtailment of the right in pursuit of a 'legitimate end'? As in classic legality review, the courts here seek to ensure that the decision-maker has not taken into account improper, extraneous, or irrelevant considerations. Thus free speech may be curtailed in the interest of national security, but not in the interest of preventing legitimate criticism of the government during an election period. The determination of this issue is clearly for the court. Having established the existence of a legitimate end (proper purpose), the key question is then whether the pursuit of that end by the means employed justifies the infringement of the relevant Convention right. Here the investigation seeks to determine not merely whether the need to achieve the objective is desirable. It must be so pressing ('sufficiently important') as to fulfil the test of being 'necessary in a democratic society'. This question is steeped in constitutionality, steering the decision-maker by the star of the fundamental qualities and requirements of a democracy. Yet neither the identification of that question, nor the appellation proportionality provides any help on the question of the degree of deference the courts ought to accord to Parliament, the executive, or other decision-maker on this matter. If there is an 'area of discretionary judgment' within which the courts ought to defer to the legislature and other public bodies,[41] on what basis can its contours be determined?

---

[41] See n. 1 above.

5. INSTITUTIONAL DEFERENCE

As we have seen, the new democratic model often requires a balance to be struck between what Lord Steyn has called a 'triangulation of interests'.[42] In this context the three interests include the right in question, the public interest in overriding that right, and the essential requirements of a democratic society. The ultimate judgment whether that balance has been correctly struck is for the courts. It would be an abdication of their constitutional responsibility to yield that decision to the legislature or any other body. But the possession of constitutional authority does not mean that the courts should not be sensitive to the limits of their own institutional competence to determine the public interest. The courts are limited in their capacity to determine a number of subjects because of lack of expertise, lack of investigative techniques, or because of the limits to the structure of the adversarial process. It is not easy for the courts to second-guess the executive's assertion as to whether national security is likely to be endangered. The executive does have special information and expertise on this matter.

It is important to note, however, that the reason why the courts might defer to Parliament on this matter is not that the majority of the representatives of the electorate declared themselves on the issue. Nor because the responsible minister is accountable to the representatives of the electorate. The fact that the decision has been made by 'persons whom the people have elected, and whom they can remove'[43] should not, in itself, lead the court to delegate its decision to that body on 'democratic grounds'. That was the way of the old order. The ultimate question for the courts now is not: 'Do the people want it?' but rather: 'Does democracy need it?'. In determining this question, however, the courts are perfectly entitled to recognize that institutions which connect to public opinion more closely than the courts are best able to determine matters such as 'the economic well-being of the country'.[44] Similarly, the courts should acknowledge the limits of their procedures to decide questions involving the allocation of scarce resources.[45]

---

[42] *R* v. *A (No 2)* [2001] 2 WLR 1546, 1560, referring in that case to the accused, the victim, and society.　　　[43] Lord Hoffmann in *Rehman*, n. 21 above.

[44] But see *R* v. *Lichniak* [2002] 4 All ER 1122, where the issue was whether a statute requiring all convicted murderers to serve a mandatory period of imprisonment, whether a danger to the public or not, offended Arts. 3 and 5(1) of the Convention. The House of Lords held that it did not so offend, and Lord Bingham said: 'The fact that [the statutory provision] represents the settled will of a democratic assembly is not a conclusive reason for upholding it, but a degree of deference is due to the judgment of a democratic assembly on how a social problem is best tackled. . . . It may be accepted that the mandatory life penalty for murder has a denunciatory value, expressing society's view of a crime which has long been regarded with particular abhorrence.'

[45] Largely because such decision contains an element of polycentricty which is not suited to a judicial-type decision. Lord Hoffmann puts this issue clearly in his COMBAR Lecture (n. 15 above, para. 19): '[A] court deciding a case which will affect one form of public expenditure—for example, impose a burden of expenditure upon education authorities—has no way of being able to decide whether such expenditure should or should not have a prior claim over other forms of expenditure. It may

Equally, the executive may sometimes (if not always) be better placed than the courts both to determine, first, whether the public interest (in, say, national security, or public order, or the protection of health or morals) is under a real threat and, secondly, whether the continued protection of the relevant right (to free speech or to a fair trial) may endanger those interests. The first of those questions (is there a threat to the interest?) is a matter of fact and degree often best suited to be decided by the primary decision-maker which is likely to have superior fact-finding capacity. The second question (would the exercise of the relevant right endanger the interest?) involves a value judgment and the weighing of uncertain risk.[46] The courts may again defer to the decision-maker on that second question, where compelling reasons of institutional capacity so dictate. In either case, however, the burden of justifying the infringement of rights rests upon the decision-maker. In the words of the Canadian Charter of Rights and Freedoms and the New Zealand Bill of Rights Act, the limits on rights must be 'demonstrably justified'.

The reasoning process does not, however, stop there. The courts then have to decide a third question, namely, whether the overall benefit of limiting the relevant right is necessary to democracy. This requires a consideration of whether the damage to the new, rights-based constitutional order is outweighed by the benefit of the measure in question, to the overall detriment of that order. This decision is for the courts alone, firmly within their constitutional authority and without the need to defer to the majority of the electorate or their representatives.[47]

Under the Human Rights Act there is no reason why the courts should not appreciate the limits of their own capacity to decide certain questions best answered by the body being reviewed. The new constitutional review does not empower the courts to act as if they were in the shoes of the primary decision-maker. Nor, however, does it permit the courts to shirk their ultimate responsibility as guardians of the new constitutional expectations, irrespective of Parliament's ultimate power to defy their declarations.

---

consider that, viewed in isolation, it is fair and reasonable that children in schools should receive certain benefits or financial compensation for not having received other benefits. But because it can only view the matter in isolation, it has no way of knowing whether this means that other people dependent upon social security, police protection and so on will have to make sacrifices because there is less money for them. The only people who can make such decisions are the democratically elected bodies who are in charge of the budget as a whole'.

[46] See e.g. *A, X and Y and Others* v. *Secretary of State for the Home Department* (CA, 25 October 2002) where the Court of Appeal upheld the Home Secretary's submission that the criteria for satisfying a derogation (under Art. 15 of the Convention) from Art. 5 was satisfied and therefore permitted legislation to detain immigrants suspected of terrorist activities without trial.

[47] Indeed, the court may even appropriately decide that a body which owes allegiance to the popular will (such as a government Minister) is disqualified *on that ground* from making certain kinds of decision (e.g. to order the continued extension of the detention of a prisoner). See, e.g., the ECHR's judgment in *Stafford* v. *UK* (2002) 13 BHRC 260 and the recent case holding that the Home Secretary's part in the fixing of the tariff of a convicted murderer violated Art. 6(1) of the Convention, as well as the rule of law and separation of powers: *R (Anderson)* v. *Secretary of State for the Home Department* [2002] 4 All ER 1089.

5

English Law and Convention Concepts

DAWN OLIVER

1. INTRODUCTION

Among Professor Harlow's many contributions to public law have been her writings on the public–private divide in English law, or more accurately on the absence of any real such divide. In her article ' "Public" and "Private" Law: Definition without Distinction'[1] she argued that the distinction is 'wholly incompatible with the English tradition and is unlikely to contribute in any meaningful way to the solution of the many problems which modern administrative law has to overcome'. Other scholars too have challenged the workability of a public–private distinction in English law, including Allison in his book *A Continental Distinction in the Common Law*.[2] He says that 'in the absence of a rough consensus about the state administration, and thus about the scope of public law, the distinction would be reduced to a rhetorical tool'.[3] And he argues that there is no such consensus in English law. Indeed, '[t]hose who advocate the distinction's retention should countenance fundamental reforms, reforms that are theoretical, institutional and procedural'.[4]

Although the UK is currently going through a period of deep and wide-ranging constitutional reform, none of those reforms represents, it seems to me, even a rough consensus about the state administration, and they do not meet the requirements envisaged by Allison to enable us to be able to accommodate a public–private divide coherently in England and Wales. We are nowhere near the institutional, procedural, and theoretical reforms that Allison refers to.

To take *institutional reforms* first, the Administrative Court is far from being an equivalent of the French Conseil d'Etat, for instance, with members who are separate from the judiciary, and its own exclusive jurisdiction, procedures, and substantive law. It is really no more than a list of judges who spend only part of their time on judicial review, and it is part of the High Court. Nor do we have any real concept of the state[5] as a set of institutions which could enable our system to develop substantive rules applicable only to those institutions. The courts for

---

[1] (1980) 43 *MLR* 241, 242. [2] (Oxford University Press, Oxford, 2nd edn., 1999).
[3] *Ibid.*, 38. [4] *Ibid.*, 246.
[5] See K.H.F. Dyson, *The State Tradition in Western Europe* (Oxford University Press, Oxford, 1980).

England and Wales, having developed the procedural exclusivity principle in relation to the claim for judicial review,[6] have found it difficult to apply because we have no developed criteria for determining what are rights protected by public law or private rights,[7] or whether particular 'fringe' institutions, for instance, universities, charities, self-regulating bodies in sport and other areas of activity, the BBC, are 'public' bodies, or whether they are exercising functions of a public or governmental nature, or which have 'a public character or stamp'.[8] Similar problems have arisen under the Human Rights Act, which has direct vertical effect only in relation to the acts of 'public authorities' or those exercising 'public functions'.[9] The problems of defining the state, or what is public or what is private, are exacerbated by the processes of privatization of previously state-run or state-owned enterprises, the contracting out of once-state-delivered functions, the private finance initiative, public–private partnerships, and other such devices which form part of the network system[10] by which nowadays public policy is commonly delivered. Indeed we seem to be moving away from regarding the state and what is public as institutional questions but rather functional ones, and even here the distinction between public and private functions is hard to make workable, a point to which we return in due course.

As far as separate public law *procedures* are concerned, Allison's second requirement for a system of public law, the Civil Procedure Rules (CPR) (which replace the former Order 53 of the Rules of the Supreme Court) have actually *reduced* the distinctiveness of the judicial review procedure by linking it with private law procedures under Part 8 of these Rules, which apply where a claim is unlikely to involve a substantial dispute of fact.[11] This change represents a positive step away from the Conseil d'Etat model. .Case law on procedural exclusivity which rested on the question whether public or private rights were at issue has reduced its importance by establishing many exceptions to it, thus permitting judicial review issues to be raised in ordinary actions.[12] The architect of the Civil Procedure Rules, Lord Woolf, has written with approval of the bridging of the previous procedural and substantive public–private divides.[13] This runs quite counter to the requirements Allison has identified as necessary if a distinctive system of public law were to develop.

Nor do we have a coherent *theory* of substantive public law as being distinct from substantive private law. The strong trend in English law has been towards

---

[6] *O'Reilly v. Mackman* [1983] 2 AC 237.   [7] *Ibid.*, 284–5.

[8] See Lord Woolf CJ in *Donoghue*, below n. 95, at para. 65(v).

[9] See s. 6 Human Rights Act 1998.

[10] See R.A.W. Rhodes, *Understanding Governance. Policy Networks, Governance, Reflexivity and Accountability* (Open University Press, Buckingham, 1997).

[11] See D. Oliver, 'Public Law Procedures and Remedies—Do We Need Them?' [2002] *PL* 91.

[12] For summaries of the exceptions see S. de Smith, Lord Woolf, and J. Jowell, *Judicial Review of Administrative Action* (Sweet & Maxwell, London, 5th edn., 1995), chap. 3; M. Supperstone and J. Goudie (eds.), *Judicial Review* (Butterworths, London, 2nd edn., 1997), chap. 3.

[13] Lord Woolf, 'The Human Rights Act 1998 and Remedies', in M. Andenas (ed.), *Judicial Review in International Perspective* (Kluwer Law International, The Hague, 2000), 429–30.

integrating substantive public and private law: supervisory jurisdictions using similar grounds for review and awarding similar remedies can be found in judicial review and in equity, in company and employment law, in contract, in restraint of trade, and in many other areas.[14] Both public and private law are concerned with common principles, that power, whether in public or private hands, should not be abused, and the rights and interests of individuals should be protected against abuses of power. The remedies, the prerogative orders, to which substantive rules have been linked in the past are no longer exclusively linked to those rules, since the reforms of 1977 enabled the court to award *either* prerogative orders *or* injunctions or declarations where substantive public law principles have been breached.

All this is not to imply that the absence of the distinguishing characteristics which Allison identified is a defect in English law. In my view it is entirely consistent with the deepest historical roots of the common law and equity. It fits well with processes of public–private partnerships and the operation of networks, noted above. Indeed it may be that the common law system can cope better with these changes in governance than civil law systems based on the concept of state can do.

Nor is all this to say that public law does not exist in England and Wales, or the rest of the UK; only that there is no set of criteria for distinguishing it institutionally, procedurally, or substantively from the rest of the law. There is no hermetically sealed category of public law.

And yet judges dealing with judicial review cases and statutory appeals claim from time to time that the courts of common law have fashioned a system of developed principles of public law and, via *O'Reilly v. Mackman*,[15] a public–private divide. Others have, in my view rightly, expressed caution about such a divide. For instance, Lord Wilberforce in *Davy v. Spelthorne BC* considered public law and private law to be convenient expressions for descriptive purposes, but he suggested that they should be used with caution, for typically English law fastens not on principles but on remedies.[16] The rule of procedural exclusivity that goes with a public–private divide can result in fruitless litigation, and recognition of this fact has influenced the courts' development of exceptions to the rule over the years.

Although public–private distinctions in English law are blurred, the European Communities Act 1972 and the Human Rights Act 1998 (HRA) compel our courts to work with phrases and concepts in various texts, the EC Treaties, the European Charter of Fundamental Rights, the European Convention on Human Rights and the jurisprudence of the associated courts, which *assume* a range of

---

[14] See D. Oliver, *Common Values and the Public–Private Divide* (Butterworths, London, 1999) and 'Review of (Non-statutory) Discretions', in C. Forsyth (ed.), *Judicial Review and the Constitution* (Hart, Oxford, 2000), chap. 14. Scotland, supposedly closer to civil law jurisdictions than England, has never had a substantive, procedural, or jurisdictional public–private divide: annex to *Common Values*, above.   [15] [1983] 2 AC 237.

[16] [1983] 3 All ER 278, 285.

divides between public and other law. They include distinctions between civil
and criminal law, between civil and public law, between public authorities and
functions and other institutions and functions, and between vertical and horizontal effect. The concepts in these texts are often autonomous, in that they do
not have direct equivalents in all, or even in many, of the legal systems in the
states parties to them, and in particular they may not have equivalents in
English law. But nevertheless our courts are obliged to give effect to them. They
may even force our courts to import new concepts into English law, and these
may not all be liberal or democratic concepts. As we shall see, the concept of
'the hard core prerogatives of the state' is one such.

The idea of 'autonomous concept' was first elaborated by the European
Court of Human Rights (ECtHR) in *Engel* v. *Netherlands*.[17] The Court decided
that the categorization of proceedings as disciplinary and not criminal in the law
of the Netherlands was not determinative of whether charges were criminal for
the purposes of Article 6 of the ECHR. 'Criminal charge' is an autonomous concept. Certain concepts in the Convention were autonomous, and this was essential to prevent states from evading the Convention protections by relying on
their own definitions of concepts. In *Karakurt* v. *Austria*[18] the Court defined
autonomous concepts as those whose 'definition in national law has only
relative value and constitutes no more than a starting point'; and in *RL* v.
Netherlands[19] the Court stated that certain concepts must be interpreted as
'having an autonomous meaning in the context of the Convention and not on
the basis of their meaning in domestic law'.

How the English courts are coping with these categories and autonomous
concepts is the subject of the following sections of this essay.

2. CIVIL V CRIMINAL LAW

Blackstone made a distinction between public and private wrongs, the former
being 'crimes and misdemesnors'.[20] 'Private wrongs' were often termed 'civil
injuries'.[21] Blackstone's focus on wrongs, rather than rights, pervades much
of English law: Sedley J in *R* v. *Somerset County Council, ex parte Dixon*[22]
observed: '[p]ublic law is not at base about rights . . . it is about wrongs—that
is to say misuses of public power . . .'. He then includes irrationality, illegality,
and unfairness, the grounds for judicial review, among these wrongs. Given this
background, the new language of rights in Community law and under the
Human Rights Act 1998 will take time to integrate itself into our system.

---

[17] See *Engel* v. *Netherlands (No. 1)*, 1 EHRR 647 (1976).
[18] Judgment of 14 September 1999; see also *Chassagnou and others v. France* (1999) 7 BHRC 151.
[19] Judgment of 18 May 1995.
[20] *Blackstone's Commentaries on the Laws of England* (10th edn., London), iv, 1.
[21] These were the subject matter of vol. iii of the *Commentaries*.
[22] [1998] Env LR 111, 121.

The principal natural division in English law has been between civil and criminal law.[23] While a distinction between civil and criminal law is one with which English lawyers have been relatively comfortable, it has become blurred in domestic law. A number of formerly criminal offences have been decriminalized and reclassified as civil. How are such offences to be treated under Article 6 ECHR? We have already noted that 'criminal charge' is one of a number of autonomous concepts under the ECHR, and this fact has surfaced in our courts.

Article 6 provides that everyone charged with a criminal offence, in addition to the right of access to a fair and public hearing before an independent and impartial tribunal, has rights to be presumed innocent, and to an interpreter and other facilities for the purpose of his or her defence. Are decriminalized, civil penalty proceedings brought in the tax tribunals to be regarded as 'criminal' so that they attract the special protections of Article 6(2) and (3) of the Convention? Or are they civil, attracting only the protection of Article 6(1)?[24]

The introduction of civil penalties for VAT offences of dishonest evasion was recommended by the *Keith Report*, 1983.[25] The provisions are to be found in the Value Added Tax Act 1994, sections 60 and 61. The principal justifications for this measure were twofold: the reduction in the workload of the Commissioners, since a lower burden of proof was laid upon them than in criminal prosecutions; and the fact that the taxpayer would avoid the stigma of a criminal conviction.

In *Customs and Excise Commissioners* v. *Han*[26] the Customs and Excise Commissioners had assessed a number of taxpayers to penalties for dishonestly or fraudulently evading VAT and various other duties. The taxpayers raised a preliminary issue as to whether the imposition of civil penalties for tax evasion gave rise to criminal charges within the meaning of Article 6(1) of the Convention. If so then additional protections such as the right to silence and a privilege against self-incrimination, the presumption of innocence and rights to free legal assistance and a right to an interpreter arose under the Convention.

The Value Added Tax Tribunal found that the taxpayers were charged with criminal offences within Article 6(2) and (3) and that they were entitled to the services of an interpreter. The Commissioners appealed. The Court of Appeal, applying *Engel*, decided that the criteria to apply were:[27]

(i) The classification of the proceedings in domestic law (which was not criminal in these cases). The classification of the offence as civil in domestic law was only a starting point, given that the levying and enforcement of the penalty were designed to punish and deter members of the public in respect of dishonest conduct.

---

[23] There are of course others, such as common law and equity, but these are becoming less distinct.
[24] Or even attracting no Art. 6 protection at all: see discussion of *Ferrazzini v. Italy*, below, 89–93.
[25] *Report of the Committee on Enforcement of Powers of the Revenue Departments* (Cmnd 8822) (HMSO, London 1983).   [26] [2001] STC 1188.
[27] *Ibid.*, paras. 75–78.

(ii) The nature of the offence. It was not the case that dishonest conduct was decriminalized under the 1994 Act, since there was provision for criminal charges to be brought: in other words the nature of the offending activity, fraud/dishonesty, was not intrinsically 'non-criminal'. The difference between prosecution and the imposition of 'civil' penalties was a procedural one only and the jurisprudence of the ECtHR did not permit procedural features to govern or define the nature of the offence under consideration.

(iii) The nature and degree of severity of the penalty the taxpayers risked incurring. The penalty imposed here would be substantial, its purpose was deterrent and punitive, and this attracted the protection of Article 6. The Article might apply where the penalty was not imprisonment.

Each of these criteria pointed to the offence being criminal within Article 6(2). However, the Court stressed, *per curiam*, that the categorization of these cases as criminal was for the purposes of the Convention only, and it did not necessarily engage protections additional to those required by Article 6, such as were provided by the Police and Criminal Evidence Act 1984.[28] Presumably it did not reintroduce the criminal burden of proof. If it did so this would undermine the principal justification in the *Keith Report* for decriminalization.

The *Han* decision thus represents a shift from a procedural to a functional and substantive civil/criminal divide in English law, at least where Convention rights are at issue. As we shall see, functional and substantive divides are also in tension with procedural divides in judicial review, and my argument would be that the procedural requirements ought not to dominate in that area either.[29]

But it is hard to extract firm criteria from the cases. A charge of regulatory misconduct in which the defendant was subject to disciplinary measures by way of exclusion from livelihood and a substantial fine was held not to be a criminal charge.[30] A sex offender order has been held not to be criminal.[31] Nor is an anti-social behaviour order.[32] But penalties imposed on lorry owners for the fact that illegal immigrants have been found on board have been held to be criminal.[33] The autonomous European concept of 'criminal charge' is not taking root easily in English law.

3. CIVIL V PUBLIC LAW?

A particularly uncomfortable distinction for English law is between civil rights and obligations, the term used in Article 6 of the ECHR, and public (non-criminal)

---

[28] See also *Georgiou (trading as Mario's Chippery) v. United Kingdom* [2001] STC 80 (ECtHR); *King v. Walden (Inspector of Taxes)* [2001] STC 822 (Jacob J).

[29] See for instance Oliver, n. 11 above.

[30] *Fleurose v. Securities and Futures Authority* [2001] IRLR 764 (Morison J) and CA 15 January 2002.

[31] *B v. Chief Constable of Avon and Somerset* [2001] 1 WLR 340 (Div Ct).

[32] *McCann v. Crown Court at Manchester* [2001] 4 All ER 264 (CA).

[33] *International Transport Roth GmbH and others v. Secretary of State for the Home Department*, CA, 22 February 2002.

ones. This may be due in part to the fact that our law has, as already noted, been concerned more with wrongs and remedies than with principles and rights. We have noted that Blackstone distinguished between public and private wrongs, i.e. wrongs *against* the Crown or the public, or against private bodies.[34] He did not distinguish between wrongs committed *by* public and private bodies. Nor did he make distinctions between public and private rights, i.e. rights *against* public or private parties, nor between public and private *obligations*, owed respectively to or by public or private parties. The HRA does, however, make a distinction between wrongs committed by public or private bodies, since only public authorities or those performing public functions are under duties to respect the Convention rights of 'victims'. Only non-governmental organizations enjoy Convention rights.[35] The Convention rights are only vertical in their direct effect.

Just as there is no firm divide between English public law and private law,[36] so there is no firm divide between English public law and civil law. Public law includes criminal law, and it is included in civil law, of which judicial review forms a part, as does the extensive case law on the tortious or contractual liability of public authorities or those exercising public functions, which are treated as part of the subject in some major textbooks on public law.[37]

Article 6(1) of the ECHR provides, as already noted, that: '[i]n the determination of his civil rights and obligations . . . everyone is entitled to a fair and public hearing within a reasonable time by an independent and impartial tribunal established by law'. The Article does not explicitly carve out a category of law as not being included in civil (or criminal) law. However, the jurisprudence of the ECtHR on Article 6 does make such a distinction, holding that 'civil rights and obligations' do not include certain public law rights and obligations, which consequently do not attract Article 6 protections.

This distinction between civil rights and obligations and public ones was discussed in the judgment of the ECtHR in the case of *Ferrazzini* v. *Italy*.[38] A taxpayer had applied for supplementary tax assessments in 1988. They had not been heard by 1998. The taxpayer alleged a breach of the reasonable time requirement in Article 6(1). The Italian government submitted that the complaint was inadmissible because the proceedings did not concern a 'civil right', and so Article 6 did not apply. It claimed that the obligation to pay tax belonged exclusively to the realm of public law, which by implication was a separate category from the law relating to civil rights and obligations.

The obligation to pay tax is an interference with property rights.[39] It is enforceable through civil proceedings in the United Kingdom for the recovery

---

[34] Non-criminal public law, broadly what we would expect to see covered in texts on administrative law or judicial review, was covered by Blackstone in vol i of his *Commentaries*, entitled *The Law of Persons*, the persons including the monarch and magistrates, together with husbands and wives, parents and children, and so on.   [35] See Art. 34 of the ECHR and s. 7 HRA.

[36] I agree with Carol Harlow on this. See D. Oliver, *Common Values*, n. 14 above.

[37] The contractual and tortious liability of public bodies is dealt with for instance in De Smith, Woolf, and Jowell, n. 12 above, chap. 19.   [38] [2001] STC 1314.

[39] See Art. 1 of the First Protocol.

of debt. Once assessed, the extent of the liability to pay tax would normally be regarded as a civil obligation in English law.[40] Payment of tax would *also* probably be regarded as a public law obligation in English law, if it were necessary to pigeonhole it, but we would not feel the need to separate public from civil law and to decide that an obligation imposed in public law is not a civil obligation. The two categories are not mutually exclusive in English law.

In *Ferrazzini* the Italian government argued that, although tax enforcement mechanisms were civil, 'taxation matters concerned only public law'.[41] The ECtHR decided by a majority[42] that the duty to pay tax did not raise a civil right, and thus the taxpayer was not entitled to the protection of Article 6(1). All but one of the majority reaffirmed previous case law to the effect that the ECHR concept of civil rights and obligations was 'autonomous';[43] tax matters still form part of 'the hard core of public authority prerogatives, with the public nature of the relationship between the taxpayer and the tax authority remaining predominant'. This 'prerogative', another autonomous concept, appears to derive from French law. It is broadly a state power to take and implement unilateral action without the permission of the court.[44] In relation to tax, prerogative is a 'privilège' deriving from the fact that the imposition of tax is a unilateral act of which only the state is capable and this unilateral character is the criterion for deciding whether something is an administrative or public law decision.[45]

In *Ferrazzini* the court considered that 'tax disputes fall outside the scope of civil rights and obligations, despite the pecuniary effects which they necessarily produce for the taxpayer'.[46] In effect therefore a core state prerogative power need not be exercised in accordance with Article 6. This was despite the fact that other aspects of the relationship between the individual and the state gave rise to civil rights or obligations which might *also* be public. The state is not by any means immune from Article 6 obligations. Instances drawn from the case law of the ECtHR include where decisions affect the sale of land, the running of a private clinic, and authorization of professional practice.[47] But the majority in *Ferrazzini* noted that, for instance, the right to stand for election to a Parliament had been decided not to be civil in nature,[48] and that a number of

---

[40] Tax is also recoverable in Italy through civil, not criminal, proceedings: *Ferrazzini*, n. 38 above, majority opinion, para. 16.   [41] *Ibid.*, para. 16.

[42] Judges Wildhaber, Palm, Ress, Costa, Ridruejo, Bravo, Kuris, Turnen, Greve, Bakan Ugrekhelidze.

[43] *Ferrazzini*, n. 38 above, para. 24.

[44] Other aspects of the state prerogative in France are that the state's debts disappear after four years, powers to expropriate private property, and the principle that the '*domaine public*' is imprescriptible: see G. Braibant and B. Stirn, *Le Droit Administratif Français* (Dalloz, Paris, 4th edn., 1997). I am grateful to Roger Errera for explaining the concept.

[45] See G. Vedel and P. Delvolvé, *Droit Administratif* (Presses Universitaires de France, Paris, 12th edn., 1992), i. I am grateful to John Bell for this explanation and the reference.

[46] *Ferrazzini*, n. 38 above, para. 29.   [47] *Ibid.*, para. 27.

[48] *Ibid.*, para. 28. This may be a contrast with the position in English common law. In *Ashby* v. *White* (1703) 2 Ld Raym 938 it was held that interference with the right to vote was tortious. By analogy with the court's argument in that case that there should be a remedy for any wrong, interference

other aspects of the relationship between citizen and state were still regarded by the court as solely public and not also civil.

The taxpayer urged the court to revisit the categorization of tax as not a civil obligation on the basis of developments in democratic countries over the half-century since the Convention had been written. But the ECtHR felt that those developments had not affected the original position, that tax is a matter of public rather than civil rights and obligations.[49] Developments in fifty years had not entailed a *further* intervention by the state into the 'civil' sphere of the individual's life. In other words, according to the ECtHR the nature of the relationship between the state and the taxpayer as a public law, not a civil law one, had been fixed at the time when the Convention was adopted and should not be reinterpreted or modernized. There is a hermetically sealed category of public rights and obligations apart from the criminal law, which is separate from civil law. But the criteria by which other public law rights and obligations had been recognized also to be civil rights and obligations in the cases mentioned above are not clear.

The concurring opinion[50] and the dissenting opinion[51] in the case take quite different approaches, which are far more in the spirit of Article 6, and closer to what I anticipate would be the English approach in rejecting the idea that civil rights and obligations and public law are in some circumstances mutually exclusive categories so that Article 6 protections do not apply.

The concurring opinion of Judge Ress reaches the same conclusion as the majority in the case but for a reason not alluded to by them, in effect because the taxpayer had suffered no loss.[52] The judge noted that the taxpayers had not paid the tax to which they had been assessed and that the claims had been variously struck out of the list or subject to a stay of enforcement on the basis that serious and irreparable damage might otherwise ensue. Judge Ress's reasoning however supports the taxpayers rather than the tax authorities. In one important respect he differed from the rest of the majority. There had been developments since the Convention was agreed upon. Provisions had been introduced since that time for immediate enforcement of tax liabilities which were similar to penalties and might be even more severe than penalties from an economic point of view. Such provisions, Judge Ress felt, might be covered by Article 6.[53] Taxpayers should have an opportunity to dispute their liability before execution, and a state that denies such an opportunity is imposing an excessive burden on the individual.[54] If a taxpayer is subject to lengthy delays his liability to the tax could not be described as 'part of [the] normal civic duties in a democratic

---

with the right to stand for election may also be tortious at common law. See discussion by C. Harlow, *Compensation and Government Torts* (Sweet & Maxwell, London, 1982), 42–6, 64–5.

[49] *Ferrazzini*, n. 38 above, para. 29.   [50] Judge Ress, *ibid.*, 1321–2.

[51] By Judges Lorenzen, Rozakis, Bonello, Straznicka, Birsan, and Fischbach.

[52] *Ferrazzini*, n. 38 above, 1322, at e–f.   [53] Judge Ress, *ibid.*, 1322.

[54] It is quite a shock to know that there are countries which do not in their domestic legislation give taxpayers a right to challenge the assessment to tax before a tribunal! *Autres pays, autre mœurs!*

society', a reference to *Schouten and Meldrum* v. *Netherlands*.[55] 'This is a factor which might . . . induce the court to review certain aspects of the application of Art. 6 in tax cases.'[56]

The dissenting opinion[57] in *Ferrazzini* notes that the concept of 'civil' does not exist in the English text of Article 14 of the ICCPR (the equivalent of Article 6 ECHR), and that Article 8 of the American Convention on Human Rights expressly covers tax disputes ('rights and obligations of a civil, labour, fiscal, or any other nature'). The *travaux préparatoires* to the Convention should not be a permanent obstacle to a reasonable development of the case law.[58] The implication here is that the ECtHR's jurisprudence establishing a line between some parts of public law and civil law ought to be modified as not being consistent with other international instruments, and that Article 6 protections should apply. Further, the dissent noted, already and rightly a formerly restrictive attitude to the extent of the applicability of Article 6 had been modified. A wide range of disputes between the individual and the state now count as civil (though they may also be public), thus attracting the protection of Article 6. Boldly the dissent went on:[59]

One may raise the question whether it is at all possible to draw any clear and convincing dividing line between 'civil' and 'non-civil' rights and obligation based on the court's recent case law, and, if not, whether the time has come to end that uncertainty by extending the protection under Art. 6(1) to all cases in which a determination by a public authority of the legal position of a private party is at stake.

However, disappointingly the opinion goes on to state that:[60]

This would be rather a far-reaching step that would considerably reduce the independent content of the concept 'civil', which would then become merely a cover for all cases not belonging to the criminal head. The case-law of the court so far does not in my opinion support the conclusion that such a radical step is the only way to overcome uncertainty as to the scope of applicability of Article 6. However, as long as the dividing line between 'civil' and 'non-civil' rights and obligations is maintained in respect of proceedings between individuals and governments, it is important to ensure that the relevant criteria for determining what is 'civil' are applied in a logical and reasonable manner—and that may make it necessary from time to time to adjust the case law in order to make it consistent in the light of recent developments. . . . There can be no doubt that a central factor for the court when ruling on the 'civil' character of rights and obligations has been whether the pecuniary interests of the individual have been at stake in the proceedings. . . .

---

[55] (1994) 19 EHRR 432, 454–5, para. 50.

[56] Judge Ress, n. 38 above, 1322. There is an interesting hint here of a contractual notion of citizenship which requires citizens to pay tax as part of their civic duty in return for which the state must, among other things, provide effective appeal mechanisms.

[57] *Ibid.*, starting at 1322.   [58] *Ibid.*, dissenting opinion, para. 4.

[59] Here the dissent refers to P. van Dijk and G. J. H. van Hoof, *Theory and Practice of the European Convention on Human Rights* (Kluwer Law International, The Hague, 3rd edn., 1998), 406.

[60] *Ferrazzini*, n. 38 above, dissenting opinion, para. 5.

The dissenting opinion found Article 6(1) to be applicable as there were no convincing arguments for maintaining the present case law of the court that proceedings regarding taxation do not determine 'civil rights and obligations' for the purpose of the Article.[61]

The case raises a number of problems for courts and tribunals dealing with tax cases in the United Kingdom. For instance, what would a tax tribunal do if a taxpayer objected to an assessment on the ground that the tax authorities had delayed for many years before dealing with the matter, and the tax authorities argued that there was no requirement in ordinary law, nor under the Human Rights Act, for the taxpayer's liability to be determined within a reasonable time? This was the question in *N Ali and S Begum (Trading as Shapla Tandoori Restaurant)* v. *Commissioners of Customs and Excise*. The VAT Tribunal decided that the *Ferrazzini* decision is not applicable in the UK, at least as far as rights and obligations relating to VAT are concerned, and that obligations imposed by the tax and default surcharge assessments, penalty notices, and notices of requirements to pay security were within the scope of Article 6(1) as being at least 'civil' and not excluded on account of their being obligations of a public law nature.[62]

The concept of 'hard core prerogatives of public authorities' on which the majority relied in *Ferrazzini* is difficult to fit into English law's permeable categories. The concept of the royal prerogative has some resemblance to it, but since the Bill of Rights 1689 tax has no longer been within the royal prerogative. In any event, since the *CCSU* case[63] the prerogative is reviewable unless the matter is non-justiciable. The imposition of taxation is regulated by law, with access to the tax tribunals built into the system. The tax liability of individual taxpayers is clearly justiciable.

It would run right against the development of the tribunal system since the *Franks Report*[64] and the common law rights to procedural propriety where decisions affecting the vital interests of individuals and taxpayers are at stake, to regard decision-making by the tax authorities and tribunals as properly immune from duties of procedural propriety or the rights of access to a fair and independent tribunal which Article 6 requires. The approaches of Judge Ress in the concurring opinion and of the dissenting judges are closer to the British position and the common law. In any event the 'hard core prerogatives of the state' is a judicial gloss on Article 6 in which no reference is made to such prerogatives and the immunities that attach to them.

The approach of the ECtHR in *Ferrazzini* to state prerogatives may be contrasted with the approach in European Community law. One of the emerging

---

[61] *Ibid.*, paras. 7–9.

[62] Value Added Tax Tribunal, 30 May 2002, para. 26. Compare the position in relation to income tax: *Eagerpath* v. *Edwards* [2001] STC 26 (Robert Walker LJ).

[63] *Council of Civil Service Unions* v. *Minister for the Civil Service* [1985] AC 374.

[64] *Report of the Franks Committee on Administrative Tribunals and Inquiries* (Cm.218) (HMSO, London 1957).

principles of EC law is a right given expression under the European Charter of Fundamental Rights, Chapter V, Article 41, to good administration by the institutions and bodies of the Union. Certain taxes are 'European' taxes, VAT and customs duties in particular. The right to good administration under Article 41 of the Charter includes a right to be heard before an adverse decision is taken,[65] a right of access to personal files, a right to reasons for a decision, and a right to compensation for damage caused by Community institutions in the performance of their duties. Article 47 of the Charter provides that: '[e]veryone whose rights and freedoms guaranteed by the law of the Union are violated has the right to an effective remedy before a tribunal . . .'. The law of the Union does not explicitly include 'rights and freedoms' of taxpayers, but Article 17 of the Charter does protect the right to property, and, as we have noted, the obligation to pay tax is an interference with property rights. This may open up the possibility of acknowledgement by the European Court of Justice (ECJ) that respect for property including money to be paid in tax requires access to a court under Article 47.

Although the Charter itself is only declaratory in effect, its provisions are much more in line with English law than some of the ECtHR jurisprudence under Article 6. The anomalous position could be reached that a taxpayer's procedural rights in the UK may depend on whether a European tax or a UK tax is at issue. The same of course will be the case in the other EU Member States, and this anomaly will add to the pressure on the ECtHR to modify its concept of hard core state prerogatives as being outside the sphere of 'civil rights and obligations'. That process in turn will erode the implicit distinction in the jurisprudence under Article 6 between civil and public law rights and obligations.[66]

4. PUBLIC AUTHORITIES AND FUNCTIONS

The next two problematic public/private categories I shall consider are the distinctions between public and private institutions and functions. These problems arise under the Human Rights Act (HRA), which uses a novel statutory concept of 'public authority'[67] to determine which bodies are bound to respect convention rights. This is a parallel to the European law concept of 'vertical effect', by which unimplemented directives may have effect between state bodies and individuals or private corporations, but not between private bodies.[68]

---

[65] See Case 17/74, *Transocean Marine Paint Association* v. *Commission* [1974] ECR 1063.

[66] See also, *Runa Begum* v. *Tower Hamlets LBC* [2002] 2 All ER 668.

[67] But note that under the Public Authorities Protection Act 1893, now repealed, special short limitation periods applied in civil actions against 'public authorities'. In *Gruffiths* v. *Smith* [1941] AC 170, 205–6 Lord Porter focused on the performance of statutory duties and the exercise of public function and the absence of a private or personal profit motive as indicators of public authority status under the Act.

[68] See Case 153/84, *Marshall* v. *Southampton and South-West Hampshire Area Health Authority (Teaching)* [1986] ECR 723, para. 48.

The HRA provides by section 6(1) that: 'It is unlawful for a public authority to act in a way that is incompatible with a Convention right', i.e. with any of the rights in the ECHR Articles 2 to 12 and 14. Section 6(3) and (5) define a public authority to include 'any person certain of whose functions are functions of a public nature' except that 'a person is not a public authority . . . if the nature of the act is private'. It is convenient to refer to section 6(1) authorities as 'standard public authorities' and section 6(3)(b) and (5) bodies as 'functional public authorities'.

Neither the Act nor the jurisprudence of the ECtHR provides developed criteria for determining what institutions are 'public authorities' or what functions are 'of a public nature'. Two important points here are (i) that standard public authorities are bound to respect Convention rights in all that they do, and (ii) that governmental organizations do not have the benefit of Convention rights. This is because governmental institutions cannot be victims of breaches of Convention rights under Article 34 ECHR and section 7(1) of the Human Rights Act. It follows that the implication of finding that a particular body is a public authority, or that a particular function is a public function, is that the body in question will not have the benefit of Convention rights. This would mean that the body was not entitled to free speech, to freedom of association, peaceful enjoyment of its possessions, and so on under the Convention. That might in turn have serious implications for the political process and for pluralism in a democracy. If, for example, universities were considered to be standard or functional public authorities, they would be liable to have their freedoms limited without being able to rely on Convention rights. A government would then be in a strong position to restrict their freedom to publish research, to criticize government policy, and so on.[69]

There are, then, particular problems in determining whether bodies such as privatized utilities, charities, or universities are 'public authorities' for the purposes of the Human Rights Act. Let us focus on universities for a moment. The very different histories and treatment of universities in mainland Europe and in the common law world produce anomalies under the ECHR. Mainland European universities' staff are civil servants.[70] European universities are therefore likely to be regarded as 'governmental organizations' under Article 34 of the ECHR. It follows that they may not be 'victims' of breaches of Convention rights. They appear to be treated as public sector institutions in the European Community, for instance on questions of public access to their research findings.

Universities in the United Kingdom differ in important respects from those in Europe. Their staff are not civil servants. Most of the older universities

[69] See D. Oliver, 'The Frontiers of the State. Public Authorities and Public functions under the Human Rights Act 1998' [2000] *PL* 476.

[70] When those employed by universities are elected to a parliament their jobs as civil servants are suspended, but on leaving Parliament they are entitled to re-enter the civil service in the same or equivalent posts. Does this explain why many politicians in mainland Europe are academics, whereas in the UK academics relatively seldom stand for election and are seldom elected?

were created by Royal Charter, supplemented in due course by legislation. Until the mid-twentieth century they were privately funded, from fees and from endowments.[71] Were they then public authorities or exercising public functions? This is a difficult question to answer, as the concepts did not exist at that time. It could not be said that they were then 'standard' public authorities. Nor in my view were they functional public authorities. They were not exercising a 'core governmental function', a phrase introduced by Burnton J in the *Leonard Cheshire* case,[72] discussed below. When they were founded, facilitating the provision of university education was not regarded as the business of government.

Since the Second World War British universities, old and new, have been largely, but in varying degrees, funded by the state, but public funding cannot be the determinative criterion for 'public authorities' or 'public functions'. They are regulated through the higher education funding councils and various quality assurance measures, but regulation is commonly taken to be an indication that a body is *not* a public authority, nor is it exercising a public function—rather than the reverse.[73]

Given this history, can British universities be said to be exercising a core governmental function now, and if so would it follow that it is a 'public function' within section 6 of the Human Rights Act? My answer to this would be 'no'. But as we shall see the matter is not resolved.

In 1793 the University of Cambridge was subjected to an order of prohibition, which is nowadays regarded (mistakenly in my view[74]) as a public law remedy, when it deprived Dr Bentley[75] of his degrees without a hearing. But in those days there was no real concept of 'public' institutions apart from the Crown and magistrates, nor of public functions. The prerogative writs were available not only against what we would now regard as public authorities and those exercising public functions, but also against bodies and in respect of functions that would now be considered to be private.[76] *Doctor Bentley's case* does not decide that universities are public authorities, nor that they exercise public functions when granting or removing degrees.

However, universities have been subject to judicial review in a number of more modern cases.[77] But it is not clear what the test for amenability for judicial

---

[71] The University of Buckingham is still privately funded.

[72] *R (on the application of Heather)* v. *Leonard Cheshire Foundation* [2001] EWHC Admin 429 (Stanley Burnton J.). See now the Court of Appeal decision *R* v. *Leonard Cheshire Foundation* [2002] EWCA Civ. 366. [73] See, e.g. *Leonard Cheshire* in the Court of Appeal, para. 20(v).

[74] Oliver, n. 11 above. [75] *Dr Bentley's case, R* v. *University of Cambridge* (1723) 1 Str 557.

[76] See my argument in 'Public Law Procedures and Remedies', n. 11 above. Note in particular *R* v. *Barker* (1762) 3 Burr 1265, in which trustees of a Presbyterian chapel were subject to a mandamus to admit the elected pastor to preach. In the USA mandamus is awarded against those in common calling, including the utilities on the ground that they are affected with a public interest: see D. Oliver, 'The Singularity of the English Public–Private Divide', in M. Andenas and D. Fairgrieve (eds.), *Judicial Review in Perspective* (Kluwer Law International, The Hague, 2000), 319.

[77] See for instance *R* v. *Manchester Metropolitan University, ex parte Nolan* [1994] ELR 380 (DC) in which Sedley J. considered that the university was 'a public institution discharging public functions'; see also *Glynn* v. *Keele University* [1971] 1 WLR 487; *R* v. *Aston University, ex parte Roffey*

review has been in such cases, nor whether amenability was conceded. Disputes between staff or students and their universities might be more appropriately dealt with (in the absence of a Visitor[78]) by civil proceedings based on the contractual relations between universities and their students and staff than by judicial review, as was the case in *Herring* v. *Templeman*, for instance.[79]

Moving away from the particular case of universities, let us consider more broadly the concept of 'public functions' within the Human Rights Act, section 6(3) and (5). The phrase was borrowed from the development of the judicial review jurisdiction over private bodies. Its history is relatively short. The *CCSU* case[80] introduced the principle that amenability to judicial review was dependent on the subject matter of a decision and whether it was justiciable, rather than its source. In that case the fact that the respondent was a minister, a standard public authority, was crucial. The principle that emerged from the case was that a public body was amenable to judicial review if the subject matter of the decision was justiciable, whatever the source of the decision-making power, though not if the relationship was governed by contract. No issue arose in that case as to whether the function in question was 'public', although a case could be made that changing the terms and conditions of service of civil servants was no different from the powers exercised by private employers. Nevertheless, it is widely recognized that the decision was rightly subjected to judicial review.

Two years later the *Datafin*[81] case subjected a private body to judicial review, because it was exercising, broadly, a public function, which has been used as shorthand for the fact that it was exercising a public duty affecting the rights of citizens with a statutory underpinning. Thereafter a public function test began to be applied, mistakenly in my view, and in a way which has potentially narrowed judicial review, to the question whether the activities of public bodies are reviewable. For instance, the Civil Procedure Rules, which came into force on the same day as the Human Rights Act, define a 'claim for judicial review' as a claim to review the lawfulness of an enactment or a decision, action, or failure to act in relation to the exercise of a *public function*.[82] This appears to institute a test which was not previously determinative in practice for judicial review.

The pre-*CCSU-Datafin* cases on judicial review of standard public authorities fit more comfortably into a broader, institution-justiciability–no contract pigeonhole than a functional one.[83] There is not the space to develop this argument fully here, but examples will illustrate the point. The decision of the local

---

[1969] 2 QB 538 in which the basis for amenability for judicial review is not clear and in the event the applicant failed.

[78] *R* v. *Hull University, ex parte Page* [1993] AC 682: the visitor is subject to judicial review but the university is not, and the visitor's jurisdiction is exclusive.

[79] [1973] 3 All ER 569.

[80] *Council of Civil Service Unions* v. *Minister for the Civil Service* [1985] AC 374.

[81] *R* v. *Panel on Take-overs and Mergers, ex parte Datafin* [1987] QB 815.

[82] CPR 54.1(2)(a), emphasis added.

[83] Note that C. Lewis, *Judicial Remedies in Public Law* (Sweet & Maxwell, London, 2nd edn., 2000), focuses on the institutional test as the primary one for judicial review.

authority to stop a football club from using the authority's practice ground that was challenged successfully in *Wheeler* v. *Leicester City Council*[84] cannot really be regarded as an exercise of a public or governmental function. A private owner of the practice ground could have taken exactly the same decision. The council's decision in *Wheeler* was subject to judicial review because the institution was a standard public body, and the subject matter was justiciable. The decision was quashed because it was 'a wrong'. It was not legitimate for a public body to punish people who had done no wrong nor to impose illegitimate pressure on the members of the club with the threat of sanctions.[85]

A second example is the distribution of circulars by government. This is not essentially a public or governmental function. But it may be subject to judicial review on the institution-justiciability-no contract test, and it will be quashed if, for instance, it is regarded as a wrong, in that inaccurate or unlawful information or advice is included.[86]

Thirdly, it will be remembered that in *Coughlan*[87] (a pre-HRA case) it was found that the health authority was subject to judicial review for disappointing a legitimate expectation of residents of a home for the disabled. In the *Leonard Cheshire* case, discussed below, on identical material facts it was held that providing a home for disabled persons and deciding to close it is not a 'public function' under the Human Rights Act. If the court was right judicially to review the decision in *Coughlan*, and also right to refuse to do so in *Leonard Cheshire* on the ground that a public function was not at issue, it would seem to follow that *judicial review is available against public authorities in cases other than those where the function in question was a public one*. In *Coughlan* material factors were that the health authority was exercising statutory powers (although, since the *GCHQ* case this is not essential to judicial review), and that health authorities, as public bodies, have no rights or interests of their own.[88] It seems clear that function was not the test for judicial review before the introduction of Part 54 of the CPR. The exceptions on which the courts have often insisted for some, but by no means all, decisions made in the exercise of contracting powers[89] may be regarded as a class of 'non-justiciable' decisions, on the basis that it is inappropriate for the courts to exercise supervisory jurisdictions in certain, but not all,[90]

---

[84] [1985] AC 1054. And see related cases about the use of resources by public authorities, *R* v. *Ealing LBC, ex parte Times Newspapers* [1987] IRLR 129; *R* v. *Lewisham LBC, ex parte Shell UK Ltd* [1988] 1 All ER 938.

[85] See the judgments of Lords Roskill and Templeman in *Wheeler*, n. 84 above.

[86] *Royal College of Nursing* v. *Department of Health and Social Security* [1981] AC 800; *Gillick* v. *West Norfolk AHA* [1986] AC 112.

[87] *R* v. *North and East Devon Health Authority, ex parte Coughlan* [2000] 2 WLR 622 (CA).

[88] See for instance *Derbyshire County Council* v. *Times Newspapers Ltd* [1993] AC 534; in *R* v. *Somerset County Council, ex parte Fewings* [1995] 1 All ER 513, Laws J observed that 'A public body has no heritage of legal rights which it enjoys for its own sake.' See also D. Oliver, *Common Values*, n. 14 above, 112–16.

[89] For instance *R* v. *The Lord Chancellor, ex parte Hibbit and Saunders* [1993] COD 326.

[90] See n. 83 above.

contracts, and that a remedy may be available for breach in a contract action.[91] Assuming however that Part 54 of the CPR remains operative a confusion may arise where a standard public authority is alleged to have acted in breach of a Convention right when *not* exercising a public function, for then judicial review will not be available and the claimant will have to proceed by ordinary action. The claimant will not be entitled to a prerogative order, but will be able to claim an injunction or declaration or, subject to section 8(3)(b) (which provides that they may only be awarded it necessary to afford just satisfaction), damages.

This difficulty about the scope of judicial review under Part 54 was raised in argument in the Court of Appeal in the *Leonard Cheshire*[92] case, and Lord Woolf CJ indicated that Part 54(1) CPR had 'changed the focus of the [previous Order 53 RSC] test so that it is also partly functions based'.[93] The other part of the test is that the claim is for a prerogative order. But if this comment implies that there are other tests for amenability to judicial review, it is hard to reconcile with the actual wording of Part 54. Part 54 may, in this respect, be *ultra vires*.

The European law distinction between horizontal and vertical effects of unimplemented directives provides insights into the criteria for determining whether a body is a standard public authority or a functional one. Broadly, in EC law state bodies and 'emanations of the state' are bound by unimplemented directives whereas 'private' bodies are not. The main authority is *Foster* v. *British Gas*:[94]

[A] body, whatever its legal form, which has been made responsible, pursuant to a measure adopted by the State, for providing a public service under the control of the State and has for that purpose special powers beyond those which result from the normal rules applicable in relations between individuals, is included in any event among the bodies against which the provision of a directive capable of having direct effect may be relied upon.

In that case the privatized British Gas was considered to be an organ bound by an unimplemented directive. Could this test be adopted for the purposes of the HRA public authority or public function tests? In *Foster* the court relied on three particular criteria (providing a public service, being under the control of the state, and possession of special powers) cumulatively to reach the conclusion that British Gas was 'an emanation of the state'. This looks like an institutional principle. But in reality, it is suggested, it was a functional test. British Gas is not a standard public authority. It would not be bound by an unimplemented directive when it was doing acts which do not satisfy the three ECJ criteria. The fact that it is providing a public service should not, on its own, suffice to make a body a standard public authority under section 6(1) of the Act (though the *function* itself might well be 'public' within section 6(3)(d)). Under the contracting-out regime many private firms provide public services, often also providing private services as well, and clearly they are not transformed into

---

[91] *R* v. *Disciplinary Committee of the Jockey Club, ex parte Aga Khan* [1993] 1 WLR 909.
[92] See n. 72 above.   [93] *Ibid.*, para. 37.   [94] [1990] 2 CMLR 833.

standard public authorities for all purposes by the fact that they perform some public functions.[95]

Bearing in mind the *Foster* criteria, what would be the position if, for instance, a charitable housing association or a charity providing accommodation for disabled people, which would normally not be regarded as standard public authorities under section 6(1) of the HRA, were alleged to have acted incompatibly with Convention rights? Suppose such a body had taken on the function of providing housing for people on low incomes or ill or disabled persons from a local authority, or is discharging functions that would have been performed largely by local authorities until the 1980s when many public services were privatized or removed from local authorities? Would the association be regarded as bound in all that it does by the HRA on the basis that it is a standard public authority; or would it be regarded as a functional public authority under section 6(3) and (5), and only bound when exercising public functions; or would it be regarded as outside the section 6 obligation altogether as neither a standard nor a functional public authority? By what criteria is a court to determine either the public authority or the public function test? As we shall see, there has been some case law on this, but before turning to it, let us explore the difficulties briefly.

Many functions exercised by standard public authorities are not public functions. A function does not need to be a public function in order to attract the protection by the HRA of Convention rights. If the body exercising the function is a standard public authority then it is bound to respect Convention rights in all that it does. But where a standard public authority contracts out a non-public function the contractor, as a private body, will not be bound to respect the Convention rights of those affected by its activities, unless or until the courts develop the direct or indirect horizontal effect of Convention rights. This would involve developing private law so as to provide equivalent protections, which the courts have already started to do, for instance, in relation to privacy and confidentiality,[96] and nuisance.[97]

Contracting out may result in anomalous gaps or lacunae in the protection of human rights. A change of control may deprive people of their rights. For instance, privatization of council housing may mean that residents lose their Convention rights or may not be able to enforce them against their private landlords. Problems arise, however, from the fact that the HRA does not supply any criteria for deciding whether a function is a public function. The Act gives the impression that there is a category of functions that are to be regarded as intrinsically 'public', for otherwise subsections (3) and (5) of section 6 would be unnecessary.

Some of these problems fell for decision in the cases of *Poplar Housing and Regeneration Community Association Ltd. v. Donoghue*,[98] and *R v. Leonard*

---

[95] See *Poplar Housing and Regeneration Community Association v. Donoghue* [2001] 3 WLR 183 (CA), para. 58; *R. (on the application of Heather) v. Leonard Cheshire Foundation*, n. 72 above.

[96] See *Douglas and Zeta Jones v. Hello!* [2001] QB 96; *Venables and Thompson v. News Group Newspapers Ltd* [2001] 2 WLR 1038. And/but see *A v. B and C* [2003] QB 195.

[97] *Marcic v. Thames Water Utilities Ltd* [2002] EWCA Civ 65, [2002] 2 All ER 55.

[98] *Donoghue*, n. 95 above.

Cheshire Foundation and HM Attorney-General.[99] A housing association and a charity respectively were providing residential accommodation, but wished to remove residents from the property for managerial reasons. The residents, unwilling to move, claimed that the closures were in breach of their Article 8 rights to respect for their private and family life and their home. The housing associations argued that they were neither standard public authorities nor exercising public functions.

In *Donoghue* Lord Woolf in the Court of Appeal held that: the act of providing accommodation for rent is not without more a 'public function', whoever the accommodation is for.[100] The fact that a body is a charity or a not-for-profit organization does not point to a body being a public authority. These propositions seem relatively straightforward. But then, very puzzlingly, if a private body performs functions which, *if performed by a public body, would be regarded as of a public nature,* such acts may remain private for the purposes of section 6 HRA.[101] One way of reading this would be that, if the particular function or activity were performed by a standard public authority, the person in the street might regard it as 'public' even though it is really 'private'. But Lord Woolf stressed that there was no clear demarcation line between public and private bodies and functions, following the English law tradition that there are no hermetically sealed categories in our law. How can this English approach be reconciled with the distinctions required by the Human Rights Act?

In *Donoghue* the local authority had created the housing association in order to transfer its housing stock to it, and it used the association as the means by which its public duties relating to the provision of housing were performed. The Court of Appeal found that its *role* was 'so closely assimilated to that of [the local authority] that it was performing public and not private functions'.[102] It was therefore bound by Article 8 of the ECHR to respect the private and family life of the residents. This is indeed a puzzling finding, since the court expressly found that providing accommodation for rent was not a public function and that the housing association was not a standard public authority. *Donoghue* then suggests that there is an intermediate category of public function, a function that would be private if done by a purely independent private body, but that becomes public when exercised by a private body if it (i) is a core function of a public authority and (ii) is done on behalf of a public authority by a body that is tightly enmeshed with the authority. On the facts the housing association was held not to be acting in breach of the Convention right.

In the *Leonard Cheshire* case the charity was an independent one, some of whose residents were self-financing and some of whom were paid for out of public funds. Burnton J held at first instance that the charity was not performing a public function and was not therefore bound by Article 8 of the ECHR. On the question of the meaning of 'public functions' Burnton J decided that the mere fact that a particular function is 'a core governmental function' cannot be

---

[99] n. 72 above.   [100] *Donoghue*, n. 95 above, para. 65(iii).   [101] *Ibid.*, para. 65(iv).
[102] *Ibid., per* Lord Woolf, para. 66.

determinative. For instance, the provision of education in schools may be regarded as a core governmental function, but it does not follow that *private* schools are exercising public functions. A function must be 'truly public' for a private body to be regarded as exercising public functions for the purposes of the Act.[103] This means more than that a significant number of people are affected by the function or activity. 'Public' in this context means 'governmental'.[104] However, the criteria for determining whether something is 'governmental' are not clear. In *R v. Chief Rabbi, ex parte Wachmann*,[105] like *Leonard Cheshire* a case on the reviewability of a private body, judicial review was refused because a decision as to the fitness of a rabbi was held not to be 'governmental'. It is not clear what this means. It is clear from the *Aga Khan*[106] case that the 'but for' test does not determine amenability to judicial review of a private body as it is accepted that if the Jockey Club did not exist the state would have to introduce regulation of horse racing.

To return to the *Leonard Cheshire* case, Burnton J held that it differed from *Donoghue* in that in the latter case the housing association was closely assimilated in its role to the local authority and its integration with the functions of the authority,[107] which was not the case with *Leonard Cheshire*.[108] But significantly Burnton J indicated in *Leonard Cheshire* that there was scope either for the common law to develop so as to subject *private* decision-makers exercising private functions to duties of fairness or rationality, or for statute to increase the duties of private bodies exercising private functions to those affected by them.[109] On this question of the development of the law to control private power, we should recall that Harlow has argued that 'just because they fall outside the scope of judicial review, corporate actors should not be immune from legal control',[110] and she suggests that the argument for a principled law of contract which pays proper regard to the obligations of powerful corporations and state alike is a central part of this agenda.[111]

The Court of Appeal in the *Leonard Cheshire* case upheld Burnton J, applying the tests set out in *Donoghue*. The fact of public funding though relevant was not determinative, and the charity was not exercising statutory powers in performing functions for the residents.[112] The *role* that Leonard Cheshire was performing manifestly did not involve the performance of a public function.[113] But the court did raise the possibility that local authorities could include a term in contracts with bodies such as Leonard Cheshire to protect Article 8 rights of

---

[103] *Leonard Cheshire*, n. 72 above, para. 68.   [104] *Ibid.*, para. 86.
[105] [1992] 1 WLR 1036.   [106] N. 91 above.   [107] *Leonard Cheshire*, n. 72 above, para. 89.
[108] It has already been observed that the facts in *Leonard Cheshire* were materially indistinguishable from those in *Coughlan*, from which the inference has been drawn that the test for judicial review before the introduction of Part 54 CPR was not public function.
[109] *Leonard Cheshire*, n. 72 above, para. 106.
[110] C. Harlow, 'Back to Basics: Reinventing Administrative Law' [1997] *PL* 245, 257.
[111] *Ibid.*   [112] *Leonard Cheshire*, n. 72 above, para. 36.   [113] *Ibid.*, para. 35.

residents. Both the local authority and possibly the resident for whose benefit the contract was made could then rely on the contractual term.[114]

This proposed solution to the so-called 'gap' in protection of human rights would however create severe problems, quite apart from the question whether such a contract could indeed be enforced by a resident paid for by a public authority which had contracted with the service provider. Residents paying their own fees would not have the benefit of contracts between public authorities and the service providers. The private providers might be unwilling to accept residents on such terms, as they would interfere with their freedom to manage their homes. These bodies are themselves private and the functions they are performing are, according to *Leonard Cheshire*, private. They therefore have their own rights, freedoms, and interests which they may legitimately pursue. If the contracts were not truly consensual the terms might amount to unjustifiable interference with the property rights of the owners of the enterprises, contrary to Article 1 of the First Protocol to the Convention. Such terms would have serious financial implications if they prevented the owners from moving residents in order to renovate property or modernize their provision. Ultimately the costs could make the enterprise itself non-viable so that it was wound up or went into liquidation. These contractual terms could generate litigation between residents and providers that would consume resources that would otherwise go into the running of the homes and, again, could put them out of business. The providers might seek a premium for accepting residents on these terms. Overall, it is suggested, the imposition of these contractual terms cannot provide a viable solution to the 'gap' in protection of human rights. The system needs to face up to the fact that only public authorities are under vertical obligations to respect human rights, and the horizontal respect for rights will have to be dealt with by incremental developments in the common law.

5. CONCLUSIONS

English law is being pulled in three directions. The pull from Europe is towards establishing a public–private divide with a separate court, separate principles, clear or clearer domestic law concepts of the state, state prerogatives and functions which are compatible with European law and European Convention concepts. The pull from our traditions is against such hermetically sealed categories. The pull from the realities of public and economic life is also against a firm public–private divide. With privatization, outsourcing, franchising, the private finance initiative, public–private partnerships and many other devices of a broadly contractual kind the lines between state bodies and functions and other bodies and functions become harder and harder to draw. And the

---

[114] *Ibid.*, para. 34.

existence of the charitable and voluntary sector, in many respects the precursor of the welfare state in that it provided health care, schooling, university education, and relief from poverty, also undermines a public–private divide. This makes less defensible differences in the substantive law treatment of public and private bodies whose actions can affect the rights of individuals or the public interest according to 'public' or 'private' criteria.

The trend should be towards integrating substantive public and private law rather than trying to construct new hermetically sealed public–private categories. It would chime with developing concepts of citizenship as responsibility to one's fellows if private law were to develop duties of consideration on the part of those in positions of power, including commercial bodies, and voluntary institutions such as charities, housing associations, and universities towards those they deal with on the basis of concepts of wrongs rather than rights.

That is not to argue that private bodies should be treated in all respects in the same way as public bodies, or, to avoid the use of 'private' and 'public', that all bodies should be subject to the same duties towards those they deal with or the public interest. There are degrees of difference between bodies of various kinds: standard public bodies such as the government and local authorities are regarded as not having any interests of their own, and so they must act in the public interest as they conceive it to be[115] and they must take into account and often defer to private interests and rights.[116] Commercial bodies and private individuals on the other hand are entitled, within the law, to act in their own interests as they conceive them to be. Charities and not-for-profit bodies are not entitled to make profits for the benefit of their boards or members, but only for use towards their purposes. But in other respects they act independently, within the law and within limited resources, in accordance with their charter, trust deed, or other constitutive instrument.

The reality is that English law is uncomfortable with self-contained categories and watertight distinctions of almost any kind. The distinction between equity and the common law is disintegrating. So are distinctions between contract and tort, between marriage and cohabitation, even between the genders. Many other public–private divides are proving unsustainable. What civil lawyers commenting on English law regard as the unity of the common law is reasserting itself.

Carol Harlow has argued that the common law should be more confident of itself.[117] The common law tradition has much to offer European law traditions, whether European Community or Convention, in a period of blurring of

---

[115] This principle may be difficult to apply where politicians act on the basis that it is in the public interest that they or their party should win an election: *R* v. *Waltham Forest London Borough Council, ex parte Baxter* [1987] 3 All ER 671; *Porter* v. *Magill* [2002] 2 WLR 37: 'Powers conferred on a local authority might not lawfully be exercised to promote the electoral advantage of a political party': *per* Lord Bingham.   [116] As in the *Coughlan* case, n. 87 above.
[117] 'Export, Import: The Ebb and Flow of English Public Law' [2000] *PL* 240.

boundaries because it is used to operating without hermetically sealed categories on the basis of developing concept of 'wrongs' and flexible remedies. It would be a pity if the preoccupation with 'rights' that are to be respected only by indefinable public authorities were to inhibit the development of responsibilities on the part of those in power and at the same time deprive institutions of civil society like charities and universities of their ability to criticize government and influence the debate that should be encouraged in a deliberative democracy by denying them their freedom of action.

6

'The Peculiarities of the English': Resisting the Public/Private Law Distinction

MICHAEL TAGGART*

One of the most persistent themes in Carol Harlow's oviferous work is the denial of any useful substantive distinction between private law and public law. This view coincides with that of the much maligned but resilient A.V. Dicey. This continuity of resistance to the public/private law distinction is worthy of discussion.

Dicey was an Oxford man of the nineteenth century, distrustful of *droit administratif*.[1] Harlow is a woman of the twentieth and twenty-first centuries, extremely well versed in French administrative law and things Euro. Dicey was a Whig, fearful of the enfranchised masses and collectivism, and a staunch supporter of judge-made law.[2] Harlow is a democrat, wary of judges and a noted proponent of cutting the state a lot of slack.[3] In this, she is a torchbearer for a dissentient, 'left-leaning' public law tradition at the London School of Economics, dating back to the likes of Harold Laski, William Robson, and Ivor Jennings.[4] These scholars defined themselves by opposing Dicey and his prejudices.[5] Harlow herself has crossed swords with Dicey and his followers.[6]

* My thanks go to Bevan Peachey for his research assistance and to the New Zealand law firm of Chapman Tripp that funded that assistance. Thanks go also, with the usual disclaimer, for comments at short notice from John Allison, Mark Aronson, Martin Loughlin, and Janet McLean.

[1] See A.V. Dicey, *Lectures Introductory to the Study of the Law of the Constitution* (Macmillan, London, 1885), Lecture 5. Views have differed as to the depth of Dicey's knowledge of *droit administratif*, but the better view seems to be that it was considerable. See R.A. Cosgrove, *The Rule of Law: Albert Venn Dicey: Victorian Jurist* (Macmillan, London, 1980), 98. I say 'nineteenth century' in the text because, although Dicey lived until 1922, he remained a Victorian in cast of mind.

[2] J. Stapleton, 'Dicey and His Legacy' (1995) 16 *History of Political Thought* 234, 238; B. Hibbitts, 'The Politics of Principle: Albert Venn Dicey and the Rule of Law' (1994) 23 *Anglo-American LR* 1.

[3] See generally C. Harlow and R. Rawlings, *Law and Administration* (Butterworths, London, 2nd edn., 1997) (hereafter *Law and Administration*). [4] *Ibid.*, 27.

[5] See generally R. Rawlings (ed.), *Law, Society and Economy: Centenary Essays for the London School of Economics and Political Science 1895–1995* (Clarendon Press, Oxford, 1997).

[6] See, e.g. C. Harlow, 'Disposing of Dicey: From Legal Autonomy to Constitutional Discourse' (2000) 48 *Political Studies* 356 (hereafter 'Disposing of Dicey'), reprinted in R. Barker (ed.), *Political Ideas and Political Action* (Blackwell, Oxford, 2000), 142; C. Harlow, 'Politics and Principles: Some Rival Theories of Administrative Law' (1981) 44 *MLR* 113.

So what accounts for the seeming similarity of view? My contribution to this well-deserved *Festschrift*, the first one of British origin to honour a female legal scholar,[7] addresses this issue.

1. WHAT'S TORT GOT TO DO WITH IT?

It is significant that Harlow's early research work centred on the tortious liability of the state, comparing *droit administratif* and English law.[8] This was the subject of her doctoral thesis, and that research was spun off into two books and several articles, one of which has become a 'classic'.[9] This deep comparative knowledge of how the French legal system operates led Harlow to appreciate all the more the English refusal to recognize the distinction between public and private law. In this she followed in Dicey's footsteps.

An essential feature of the Rule of Law, according to Dicey, is that any one, no matter how high or low in station, can be personally called into account in the ordinary courts, and that every official is responsible in tort for every action done without legal justification.[10] As the Rule of Law protected life, liberty, and property, the availability of a tort action punishing invasion of those interests against individuals or state actors in equal measure was essential to Dicey's schema. Legions of scholars have pointed out that this did not depict the reality of suing the state in Dicey's own time or subsequently, but as a piece of idealization it was brilliant. A century ahead of the 'level playing field' metaphor, Dicey declared that the citizen and the state were to be on equal footing in the Crown's courts.[11]

Dicey rejected the French system of separate courts to deal with public law matters. Despite support for the French system among prominent public law scholars associated in one way or another with the London School of Economics,[12] twenty years ago the honorand of this book declared the idea 'abandoned by even the most fervent devotees of French administrative law'.[13] It was said that the existence of separate administrative and civil courts made a

---

[7] See M. Taggart, 'Gardens or Graveyards of Scholarship? *Festschriften* in the Literature of the Common Law' (2002) 22 *OJLS* 227, 232.

[8] C. Harlow, 'Administrative Liability: A Comparative Study of French and English Law', Ph.D. thesis, University of London, 1980. See also C. Harlow, 'Fault Liability in French and English Public Law' (1976) 39 *MLR* 516.

[9] See C. Harlow, ' "Public" and "Private" Law: Definition Without Distinction' (1980) 43 *MLR* 241 (hereafter ' "Public" and "Private" Law'). It provoked an equally brilliant response: G. Samuels, 'Public and Private Law: A Private Lawyer's Response' (1983) 46 *MLR* 558.

[10] Harlow said Dicey 'elevated' the idea of tortious liability for personal wrongdoing into 'a sacred constitutional dogma': C. Harlow, *Compensation and Government Torts* (Sweet & Maxwell, London, 1982), 18 (hereafter *Compensation & Government Torts*).

[11] ' "Public" and "Private" Law', n. 9 above, 247: '. . . and most important, . . . [the distinction] offend[s] . . . against the principle of "Equality before the law" which ought to be the paramount consideration'.   [12] I have in mind J.D.B. Mitchell, Ivor Jennings, and W.A. Robson.

[13] *Compensation & Government Torts*, n. 10 above, 30.

wrong choice very expensive, and had given rise to jurisdictional conflicts between the court systems and the creation of different rules of liability.[14]

At bottom, Harlow shares Dicey's belief in the centrality of tort law to holding government officials and the government to account for its actions.[15] Of course, she does not glorify tort law, being acutely aware of its deficiencies, and she emphasizes the role of Parliament and statute, favouring statutory compensation schemes as well as greater use of *ex gratia* payments. Also she is much more realistic in her expectations of judges and courts than Dicey was.[16] Characteristically, Harlow has said:[17]

[W]e must learn not to expect too much from the courts. Dicey's model is an ideal which, like all ideals, often breaks down in practice. The courts cannot be relied on to apply tort law as firmly as they should to punish infringement of individual liberty.

Increasingly, according to Harlow, the judges justify not imposing tortious liability on the government by invoking the 'alien' distinction between public and private law. This cleaving of public law from private law by judicial fiat is designed to give the state the benefit of the doubt, whereas the beauty of Dicey's tort model was that 'the benefit of the doubt has to go to the citizen where civil liberties are at stake'.[18] The judges should strive to uphold the ideal of 'equality before the law' of state and citizen.[19] Generally speaking, the creation of special rules that apply only to the state usually favour the State.[20]

So for Carol Harlow any distinction between public/private law is irrelevant, devoid of intrinsic merit, dysfunctional, outmoded, too rigid, ill-timed bridge-building with Europe, and productive of executive-minded decisions.[21] Her opposition has been unswerving, and all that has happened in the fields of government liability and judicial review law and practice since the mid-1970s has been grist to this mill.

2. PUBLIC/PRIVATE LAW MINDSETS

Of course, in denying the distinction Harlow is not denying that private lawyers and public lawyers view the legal world from different perspectives. This

---

[14] *Ibid.*, 30–1.

[15] *Ibid.*, 80: 'No system of law is perfect and our law of torts is no exception. Nevertheless, at the theoretical level, I believe that Dicey's ideal of equality before the ordinary courts of the land "still provides the basis of a rational, workable and acceptable theory of governmental liability"' (footnote omitted).

[16] That realism is borne out of a deep and abiding scepticism about 'Judge & Co'. 'The Rule of Law is a noble ideal but one which, unrestrained, is capable of degenerating into an ideology of law courts': C. Harlow, 'Francovich and the Problem of the Disobedient State' (1996) 2 *ELJ* 199, 222.

[17] C. Harlow, *Understanding Tort Law* (Fontana, London, 1st edn., 1987), 127 (hereafter *Understanding Tort Law*). This book went into a second edition in 1995. All references are to the first edition.   [18] *Ibid.*, 130.

[19] ' "Public" and "Private" Law', n. 9 above, 250.

[20] *Compensation & Government Torts*, n. 10 above, 78.

[21] ' "Public" and "Private" Law', n. 9 above, 265: 'an attempt by the judiciary to conceal political issues behind a formalist façade and to shield from public criticism some highly executive-minded decisions'.

difference of perspective, or mindset, turns ultimately on the relevance of the common weal or public interest, and its roots can be traced to the very beginnings of the common law.[22] Maitland emphasized the importance of the word 'common' in the Middle Ages:[23]

['Common'] is the word that haunts us in the middle ages. Even in the boroughs the common bell called the commons of the town from the common streets and the green commons to the common hall, and in common hall assembled they set their common seal to a lease of common land, for which a fine is paid into their common chest. All is common; nothing is public; the English for *res publica* is commonwealth; the public house was once a common inn.

By the seventeenth century, the term 'publick' or 'public' was supplanting the older term. In *Table Talk* John Selden wrote this entry under 'Publick Interest': 'All might goe well in the Common Wealth if evert one of the Parliam[ent] would lay downe his own self interest, & aime att the general good. . . . We destroy the Common Wealth, whilst we p[re]scribe our own private Interest & neglect the Publicke'.[24] Selden's younger friend, Sir Matthew Hale, wrote of private interest affected by a 'public interest',[25] in passages that have reverberated down to modern times.[26] By the end of the seventeenth century, as Finn pointed out in an important essay:[27]

The Commonwealth gone, Parliament and not the monarch now occupies the centre of the government stage. With this new polity, changes were occurring in the constitutional vocabulary of lawyers and legislators. . . . Among the new is the 'Publick', a term which quickly assumes a number of roles. In one role, for example, it is merely a substitute for the more ancient term 'common'; in this sense 'public' refers simply to the subjects of the kingdom sometimes as individuals, sometimes as aggregation. . . . In a more complex role 'the public' is used to signify the community at large, the body enjoying the benefits, carrying the burdens of civil government and police. . . . This public is then institutionalised; the Public Debt is born. Government officers, be they the King's officers or those of local corporations, become public officers, the institutionalised representatives and servants of the collective public. And lands vested in the King can now be characterised as being held

---

[22] Cf. M. Shapiro, 'From Public Law to Public Policy, or the "Public" in "Public Law" ' (1972) 5 *Political Science* 410, 411.

[23] F.W. Maitland, *Township and Borough* (Cambridge University Press, Cambridge, 1898), 32.

[24] F. Pollock (ed.), *Table Talk of John Selden* (Selden Society, London, 1927), 58.

[25] The references are found in a collection of manuscripts written by Hale towards the end of his life (*c.* 1670), but not published until a century later. The manuscripts were collected together and published by a prominent barrister, Francis Hargrave (*c.* 1741–1821), under the nondescript title *A Collection of Tracts relative to the Law of England from Manuscripts* (Dublin, 1786). It is common in judicial and academic consideration of Hale's views to isolate one passage only from *De Portibus Maris* about a wharf affected with a public interest (*ibid.*, 77–8), but there are numerous references to private rights tempered by public interest. See *De Jure Maris* (Law of the Sea), *ibid.*, 6, 8, 9–10, 13, 17–18, 22, 33, 36; *De Portibus Maris* (Law of Ports), *ibid.*, 46–7, 50–1, 52–5, 58–60, 72–4, 77–8, 84, 87, 89, 98–9, 100–1.

[26] See generally *Vector Ltd v. Transpower NZ Ltd* [1999] 3 NZLR 646 (CA); *Sky City Auckland Ltd v. Wu* [2002] 3 NZLR 621 (CA); P. Craig, 'Constitutions, Property and Regulation' [1991] *PL* 538; M. Taggart, 'Public Utilities and Public Law', in P. Joseph (ed.), *Essays on the Constitution* (Brookers, Wellington, 1995), 214.

[27] P. Finn, 'Public Function—Private Action: A Common Law Dilemma', in S.I. Benn and G.F. Gaus (eds.), *Public and Private in Social Life* (Croom Helm, London, 1983), 93.

for the public benefit. However, none of these various 'publicks' which appear in the late seventeenth and early eighteenth centuries were to evolve in England . . . into a personification of the monarch. Rather, lawyers were to set 'the public' and its satellites, 'public interest' and 'public policy' to work in lesser roles. . . .

By the end of the nineteenth century the distinction between private law, the primacy of self-interest or self-regarding behaviour, and public law, the primacy of the public interest or public-regarding behaviour, was well and truly in place.[28] The classic modern statement of what divides private and public law remains that of Wade, in successive editions of his textbook:[29]

The powers of public authorities are . . . essentially different from those of private persons. A man making a will may, subject to any rights of his dependants, dispose of his property just as he may wish. He may act out of malice or a spirit of revenge, but in law this does not affect his exercise of his power. In the same way, a private person has an absolute power to allow whom he likes to use his land, release a debtor, or, where the law permits, to evict a tenant, regardless of his motives. This is unfettered discretion. But a public authority may do none of these things unless it acts reasonably and in good faith and upon lawful and relevant grounds of public interest. . . . [U]nfettered discretion is inappropriate to a public authority, which possesses powers solely in order that it may use them for the public good.

I do not understand Harlow to deny this difference of starting point, or mind-set. After all, it is the *raison d'être* of administrative law, the imposition of special (and usually more burdensome) duties and responsibilities on 'public' authorities and the like, because they wield unique powers or distinctly coercive delegated powers.[30]

And when what used to be called the New Right attacked the notion of 'public interest' in order to promote privatization, Harlow and others fought back to protect public law values. But even at the same time as defending the public lawyers' view of the world and attempting to project public law values into the newly privatized and commercialized terrain, Harlow insisted that a public/private distinction would not have been any useful protection against the privatization blitzkrieg.

I will return to public law values and privatization shortly, but for the moment want to concentrate on the relevance of the public/private mindsets to Harlow's view about the centrality of tort law in the English constitutional order.

---

[28] Contrast, e.g., the stance of Lord Macnaghten in *The Mayor, Aldermen and Burgesses of the Borough of Bradford* v. *Pickles* [1895] AC 587, 600–1, and in *Westminster Corporation* v. *London & North Western Railway* [1905] AC 426, 430.

[29] H.W.R. Wade and C.F. Forsyth, *Administrative Law* (Oxford University Press, Oxford, 8th edn., 2000), 357. Almost identical passages appear in earlier editions. The passage has been judicially approved. See, e.g., *R* v. *Tower Hamlets London Borough Council, ex parte Chetnik Developments Ltd* [1988] 1 AC 858, 872, *per* Lord Bridge of Harwich (HL).

[30] See, e.g., N. Bamforth, 'The Public Law–Private Law Distinction: A Comparative and Philosophical Approach', in P. Leyland and T. Woods (eds.), *Administrative Law Facing the Future: Old Constraints and New Horizons* (Blackstone Press, London, 1997), 136, 154–5.

It appears that when the courts enforce public law duties by way of non-pecuniary, mandatory remedies (the old prerogative writs and their modern successors) this does not infringe the common law principle of equality. But if this behaviour gives rise (simultaneously) to distinct public law liability in damages that does raise Harlow's hackles.[31] Similarly, when this 'distinct' administrative law procedure was treated as exclusive, preventing actions for other (private law) remedies in other courts. This is the spectre of *O'Reilly* v. *Mackman*[32] that haunted all English discussions of public/private law in England from the time that case was decided in 1983 until its recent displacement by court rules.[33] Such an exclusive judicial review procedure was anathema to Harlow,[34] and to many others.

As regards the centrality of private law remedies, Harlow's views are at their most developed in commenting on *Malone* v. *Metropolitan Police Commissioner*.[35] There Megarry V-C refused to declare unlawful telephone tapping ordered by the police and carried out by the Post Office, because every act is permitted which is not specifically prohibited. Parliament had not then prohibited telephone tapping, nor was it held to be contrary to the common law, and so it was permissible. In *Law and Administration* Harlow and Rawlings believe that it is paradoxical to give the Commissioner of Police the benefit of a presumption of liberty designed for the protection of private persons.[36] They proffer two means of escaping the paradox.[37]

The *first escape route*, and the obviously preferred one, is to ensure that the common law does provide a remedy for such an obvious 'abuse' of power. In a case note on *Malone*, Harlow criticizes the judge for arguing from precedent rather than policy.[38] It was argued that the *prima facie* tort doctrine provided a legal peg upon which to hang a declaration, and that this would have had the effect of putting the burden of justification on the police. The use of the *prima facie* tort doctrine in this way is ingenious. Any such tort would be available against both officials and individual citizens; and thus would be consistent with the so-called 'private' model of public law,[39] favoured by Harlow.

---

[31] See the discussion of misfeasance in a public office below in the text accompanying nn. 55–56 below.   [32] [1983] 2 AC 237.

[33] See, e.g., J. Beatson, ' "Public" and "Private" in English Administrative Law' (1987) 103 *LQR* 34.

[34] See, e.g., C. Harlow, 'Why Public Law is Private Law: An Invitation to Lord Woolf', in A. Zuckerman and R. Cranston (eds.), *Reform of Civil Procedure: Essays on 'Access to Justice'* (Clarendon Press, Oxford, 1995), 201; C. Harlow, '*Gillick*: A Comedy of Errors?' (1986) 49 *MLR* 768, 770–2.

[35] [1979] Ch 344.

[36] *Law and Administration*, n. 3 above, 43. Cf. *Francome* v. *Mirror Group Newspapers Ltd* [1984] 2 All ER 408 (CA) (illegal wire-tapping by private individual; publication by third party restrained by injunction).

[37] This section draws in part from M. Taggart, 'Reinvented Government, Traffic Lights and the Convergence of Public and Private Law: Review of Harlow and Rawlings: *Law and Administration*' [1999] *PL* 124, 130–3.   [38] C. Harlow, 'Comment' [1980] *PL* 1.

[39] C. Harlow, 'A Special Relationship? American Influences on Judicial Review in England', in I. Loveland (ed.), *A Special Relationship? American Influences on Public Law in the UK* (Clarendon Press, Oxford, 1995), 79, 83 (hereafter 'A Special Relationship?'); *Law and Administration*, n. 3 above, 7, 9, 42; C. Harlow, '*Droit privé*—English Style' (1997) 17 *OJLS* 517, 518 ('Dicey's private law model of public law').

It is worth spending a moment exploring this suggestion. First put forward in Britain by Pollock and supported by Bowen LJ in the *Mogul Steamship* case,[40] the *prima facie* tort was strangled close to birth in the UK.[41] In contrast, underwritten by Holmes' inestimable reputation, the doctrine has thrived in the USA.[42] The pure form of the doctrine is that the intentional infliction of injury without justification is actionable. The act inflicting the injury need not be wrongful or unlawful.[43] This has allowed American courts to get at malicious exercise of legal rights; something the English common law (private law) has not yet been able to do in any systematic way.[44] The English courts at the end of the nineteenth century rejected the civilian doctrine of abuse of rights,[45] and this put paid to the *prima facie* tort doctrine as well.

Harlow has described the absence of a continental-style abuse of rights doctrine, 'for public lawyers, [as] the vital missing principle of tortious liability'.[46] The leading nineteenth century case, *Mayor of Bradford v. Pickles*,[47] is described as a policy decision disguised by the rhetoric of absolute rights.[48] This is far too simplistic. There were many reasons why an abuse of rights doctrine did not develop in England. Many of the reasons overlap, and include: pervasive legal positivism, rapid decline in borrowing from Roman and civil law, unpopularity of things French, misunderstanding of Scots law on the point, domination of *laissez-faire* ideology, Benthamite-inspired drive for certainty, fear and distrust of juries, rapidly rigidifying doctrine of precedent, the wizened state of equity jurisprudence, a focus on remedies rather than rights, and the dominant conception of an English law of torts rather than tort.[49] All of this was tied together with the ribbon of formalism.

Formalism is a catch-all term, given different meanings at various times for various purposes. The characteristics relevant to this discussion are: the outward rejection of policy issues to legal analysis, denial of judicial law-making, a belief

---

[40] *Mogul Steamship Co v. McGregor, Gow & Co* (1889) 23 QBD 598, 613–14 (CA). The case went on appeal: [1892] AC 25.

[41] See *Allen v. Flood* [1898] AC 1. On the intellectual history see K. Vandevelde, 'A History of a General Theory of Intentional Tort' (1990) 19 *Hofstra LR* 447.

[42] See generally K. Vandevelde, 'The Modern Prima Facie Tort Doctrine' (1991) 79 *Kentucky LJ* 519; C. Witting, 'Of Principle and Prima Facie Tort' (1999) 25 *Monash ULR* 295.

[43] In this respect, Holmes parted company with the otherwise influential utilitarianism of Bentham and Austin. See H.L. Pohlman, *Justice Oliver Wendell Holmes & Utilitarian Jurisprudence* (Harvard University Press, Cambridge, Mass., 1984), 44–7.

[44] An impure form of *prima facie* tort doctrine, requiring an unauthorized or unlawful act as a prerequisite, existed in theory in Australia for 30 years (*Beaudesert Shire Council v. Smith* (1966) 120 CLR 145), but after years of misgivings the High Court of Australia finally repudiated the doctrine in 1996 (*Northern Territory of Australia v. Mengel* (1996) 185 CLR 307).

[45] *The Mayor, Aldermen and Burgesses of the Borough of Bradford v. Pickles* [1895] AC 587; *Allen v. Flood* [1898] AC 1. See *Compensation & Government Torts*, n. 10 above, 60.

[46] *Compensation & Government Torts*, n. 10 above, 58.   [47] [1895] AC 597.

[48] *Compensation & Government Torts*, n. 10 above, 62.

[49] See generally M. Taggart, *Private Property and Abuse of Rights in Victorian England: The Story of Edward Pickles and the Bradford Water Supply* (Oxford Studies in Modern Legal History, Oxford University Press, Oxford, 2002) chaps. 5–7.

that law was a deductive science of principles drawn from cases, a hostility to legislation, and an increasing insularity.[50] The citadel of formalism was stormed by the legal realists in the 1930s in the USA. Unlike its common law cousin, the pragmatic and untheoretical English common law has never been systematically accosted by legal realism. Formalism has hung on in England for complex reasons beyond the scope of this essay.[51] But this helps to explain why *Pickles*, accepted on all sides as the product of *laissez-faire* individualism, has never been reconsidered by the courts in the collectivist era which characterized English political thought and action for much of the twentieth century.

Harlow adds her name to an honour-roll of British lawyers criticizing the *Pickles* case.[52] The legal position set out in *Pickles* was described in the 1930s as 'the consecration of the spirit of unrestricted egoism',[53] and many since then have seen it as the 'apogee' of the absolutism of property exploitation.[54] It is commonplace to observe that the tide had turned against *laissez-faire* ideology for much (but not all) of the last century, and that successive waves of regulatory legislation have left little room for such behaviour. It is no doubt time to heed these persistent calls for a reconsideration of the common law position. But the difficulty in doing so at this stage in the history of the common law should not be underestimated. Does one chip away at doctrines here and there by incremental case law development, or does one propose to legislate a remedy across the board, or only in the most egregious instances? How is the tussle between individual autonomy and the public interest to be conducted? I take up this point a little later in speaking about the clash of values.

The *second proffered escape route* from the *Malone* paradox is recognition of the inequality in power between the police and Malone, and the creation of a separate category of public law along continental lines. Predictably, Harlow and Rawlings are not enthusiastic about going down this route.

There is already in public law a distinctive tort, that of misfeasance in a public office. Harlow was sceptical about the historical pedigree of this tort,[55] but it is now firmly anchored in modern case law.[56] This, however, would not provide a remedy on facts such as those in *Malone's case*.

---

[50] I have drawn here mainly on P.S. Atiyah, *The Rise and Fall of Freedom of Contract* (Clarendon Press, Oxford, 1979), 660.

[51] See P.S. Atiyah and R.S. Summers, *Form and Substance in Anglo-American Law: A Comparative Study of Legal Reasoning, Legal Theory and Legal Institutions* (Clarendon Press, Oxford, 1987); P.S. Atiyah, *The Pragmatism and Theory in English Law* (Stevens & Sons, London, 1987); W. Twining, *Blackstone's Tower: The English Law School* (Sweet & Maxwell, London, 1994).

[52] The list includes Lords Denning and Reid, and Professors Roscoe Pound, A.L. Goodhart, Glanville Williams, Wolfgang Friedmann, and C.K. Allen.

[53] H.C. Gutteridge, 'Abuse of Rights' (1933–35) 5 *CLJ* 22.

[54] See, e.g., J. Harris, *Private Lives, Public Spirit: Britain 1870–1914* (Penguin Books, London, 1994), 117.   [55] *Compensation & Government Torts*, n. 10 above, 68.

[56] *Ibid.* See *Three Rivers District Council v. Bank of England (No. 3)* [2000] 3 All ER 1; *Rawlinson v. Rice* [1997] 2 NZLR 651.

Another possibility is the *sui generis* public law action for compensation for breach of constitutional rights. In 1984 the European Court of Human Rights (ECtHR) held that the British system of telephone tapping by administrative order was a violation of the right to privacy under Article 8 of the European Convention on Human Rights (ECHR).[57] As a consequence, remedial legislation was enacted. However, the ECHR was not then part of domestic British law and so it could not support either a declaration or a damages remedy. Harlow observed:[58]

> [*Malone's case*] suggests that Dicey was wrong to put so much trust in the common law and the judges. A Bill of Rights which creates rights may be necessary if tort law is to do an effective job in vindicating civil liberties, particularly when these come in the form of intangible values which do not fit neatly inside the person and property categories of the traditional tort law.

But when, a few years earlier, British judges sought in the Privy Council case of *Maharaj* v. *Attorney-General of Trinidad & Tobago*[59] to fashion remedies against the state for breaches of Commonwealth Constitutions or Bills of Rights, this development was deplored by Harlow for its novelty, and unprecedented use of the public/private divide.[60] And today, when the ECHR has finally been 'incorporated', and provides the ideal vehicle for fashioning monetary remedies in English public law,[61] there is a lack of enthusiasm in some quarters for the judges doing so, due to concern about strengthening further the judiciary's arm.[62]

A *third possible escape route* is suggested by the judgment of Laws J (as he then was) in *R* v. *Somerset County Council, ex parte Fewings*.[63] There Laws J posited an indigenous solution to the paradox, redistributing Diceyan assumptions in reliance on Wade's well-accepted passage about individuals acting as maliciously and self-interestedly as they like, whereas public authorities must pursue the public interest.[64] The principle of liberty, that everyone can do anything that is not prohibited, is for the benefit of citizens only. The rule for public authorities is the opposite: established by Parliament to further the public good, public authorities can only do what they are empowered to do. Now this would deal with the *Malone* case[65] even more directly than an American-style *prima facie* tort doctrine.

---

[57] *Malone* v. *United Kingdom*, ECtHR (1985) 5 EHRR 385.

[58] *Understanding Tort Law*, n. 17 above, 128.

[59] [1979] AC 385 (PC). This case involved deprivation of liberty of the subject and cross-cutting statutory and Constitutional provisions.

[60] ' "Public" and "Private" Law', n. 9 above, 244, 255.

[61] See, e.g. D. Feldman, 'Remedies for Violations of Convention Rights under the Human Rights Act' [1998] *EHRLR* 691.

[62] This is especially so amongst what used to be called the Left. See C. Harlow, 'Refurbishing the Judicial Service', in C. Harlow (ed.), *Public Law and Politics* (Sweet & Maxwell, London, 1986), 182, 205 and C. Harlow, 'Proceduralism in English Administrative Law' in K.-H. Ladeur (ed.) *The Europeanisation of Administrative Law: Transforming National Decision-making Procedures* (Ashgate/Dartmouth, Aldershot, 2002), 46, 65–7. For discussion of the rift between old school and new school 'left-leaning' scholars see Taggart, n. 37 above, 125–9.

[63] [1995] 1 All ER 513 (QBD); aff'd by majority on a narrower point [1995] 3 All ER 20 (CA).

[64] *Ibid.*, 524; the passage is quoted above in the text accompanying n. 27.

[65] D. Oliver, *Common Values and the Public–Private Divide* (Butterworths, London, 1999), 114.

Laws J articulated these different rules for citizen and state under the banner of the Rule of Law. While his reformulation of Dicey's rule of law might solve the *Malone* paradox,[66] it would necessitate cleaving public authorities from private entities, which is inconsistent with the 'private law model of public law', championed by Harlow. Also it entails jettisoning, or at the very least significantly restricting the operation of, what has become known as the 'third source' of governmental power (namely, the power of public authorities as fictious legal persons to contract, to own and use real and personal property, etc).[67] Not surprisingly, given her 'level playing field' disposition, Harlow strongly supports the Crown having all the powers of a natural legal person.

But in a case such as *Malone*, it is precisely that assumption which caused the problem in the first place. As Aronson and Dyer point out, 'it is fundamentally undemocratic and dangerous to allow government all the powers of a natural person. A private person, for example, can snoop on others, but it would be dangerous to allow the Executive the same power'.[68]

These different possible escape routes from the *Malone* paradox permit reflection on the desirability or otherwise of the 'private law model of public law'. The escape route favoured by our honorand seems the least likely to be adopted, and all the others are problematic by her lights.

I want now to place Harlow's resistance to the public/private distinction within the broader framework of administrative law developments.

3. Frying bigger fish

The absence of any substantive distinction between public/private law is one of the key elements of what Harlow describes as the 'classic model' of judicial review that prevailed in the United Kingdom up to the 1970s. The other key elements of the 'classic model' are:[69]

- restricted grounds of review coupled with a strict application of the doctrine of precedent;
- highly individualistic orientation and conspicuously marked by judicial restraint;
- interest-oriented, a fact reflected in the law of *locus standi*;
- remedy-oriented.

[66] See D. Feldman, *Civil Liberties and Human Rights in England and Wales* (Clarendon Press, Oxford, 1993), 386.

[67] This is treated in *Law and Administration*, n. 3 above, 206–17. See generally B.V. Harris, 'The "Third Source" of Authority for Government Action' (1992) 109 *LQR* 626; D. Mathieson, 'Does the Crown have Human Powers?' (1992–93) 15 *NZULR* 117; P. Joseph, 'Crown as a Legal Concept (II)' [1993] *NZLJ* 179.

[68] M. Aronson and B. Dyer, *Judicial Review of Administrative Action* (LBC Information Services, Sydney, 1996), 355. *Accord Committee for the Commonwealth of Canada* v. *Canada* (1991) 77 DLR (4th) 385, 393, *per* Lamer CJ ('inherent dangers'). Recall Oliver Wendell Holmes Jr's description of 'wire-tapping' as 'a dirty business': *Olmstead* v. *US* (1928) 277 US 438, 470.

[69] 'A Special Relationship?', n. 39 above, 83–6. See also C. Harlow, 'Public Law and Popular Justice' (2002) 65 *MLR* 1.

As far as possible, this model purported to keep the judges' noses out of the tent of politics, restricting who could seek judicial review, avoiding 'policy' issues, ensuring the dispute was justiciable and that the remedy matched the wrong. As we have seen, this model is part and parcel of the 'private law model of public law'.

This model has been under attack for some time. At about the same time Harlow was singing the praises of the private law model of public law, Chayes in the pages of the *Harvard Law Review* questioned its suitability to resolve the increasingly complex issues arising in what he called 'public law litigation'.[70] Boiled down to basics, 'public interest litigation' involves bringing political/policy disputes to court, for some sort of resolution there rather than in the legislature. Without going into detail here, suffice it to say that this model rejects many of the constraints of judicial method and procedure of the private law model. Many of the pressures, for example pluralism and the use of the courts strategically by pressure groups, are common to both American and British societies.[71] But, Harlow points out, when public interest law crossed the Atlantic eastwards it was received into a very different, British common law tradition, a tradition where judicial policy-making is viewed as 'alien' and, indeed, dangerous.[72]

What we have here is a clash of political cultures. Often disapproving of easy 'borrowings from the plentiful larder of American public law theory',[73] Harlow has emphasized the importance of indigenous English political culture, aligning herself with the position articulated most famously by Griffith.[74] This resistance is seen also in her objection to the 'transplantation' of doctrines from Europe. So the resistance is on a much wider front than just to the public/private law distinction. Harlow insists that in the United Kingdom political/policy disputes should be settled through the political process, rather than in courts as occurs frequently in the United States and on the continent.

There is a cross-cutting tendency in Harlow's writings. She appears to favour the 'classic model' of judicial review, essentially for its restrained judicial posture, while objecting to the model's 'screen of formalist language' promoting 'the fiction that law is apolitical'.[75] She lays the blame for the latter at the feet of Dicey.[76]

---

[70] A. Chayes, 'The Role of the Judge in Public Law Litigation' (1976) 89 *Harv LR* 1281. This article is described by Harlow as 'seminal' in 'A Special Relationship?', n. 39 above, 87. See also C. Harlow, 'Public Interest Litigation in England: The State of the Art', in J. Cooper and R. Dhavan (eds.), *Public Interest Law* (Blackwell, London, 1986), 90, 105 (hereafter 'Public Interest Litigation'). Cf. R.L. Marcus, 'Public Law Litigation and Legal Scholarship' (1988) 21 *Mich J of Law Reform* 647.

[71] See generally C. Harlow and R. Rawlings, *Pressure Through Law* (Routledge, London, 1992), and M. Shapiro, 'The United States', in C.N. Tate and T. Vallinder (eds.), *The Global Expansion of Judicial Power* (New York University Press, New York, 1995), 43.

[72] 'Public Interest Litigation', n. 70 above, 132–3. *Accord* Lord McCluskey, 'Importing American Rights', in R.C. Simmons (ed.), *The United States Constitution: The First 200 Years* (Manchester University Press, Manchester, 1989), 1, 14.

[73] C. Harlow, 'Changing the Mindset: The Place of Theory in English Administrative Law' (1994) 14 *OJLS* 419, 425 (hereafter 'Changing the Mindset').

[74] J.A.G. Griffith, 'The Political Constitution' (1979) 42 *MLR* 1. Harlow has described this as 'the British tradition' and Griffith's article as a 'classic': C. Harlow, Book review (1998) 18 *Legal Studies* 558, 559, n. 5 and accompanying text.

[75] C. Harlow, 'Back to Basics: Reinventing Administrative Law' [1997] *PL* 245, 247 (hereafter 'Back to Basics'). [76] See 'Disposing of Dicey', n. 6 above.

In *Law and Administration* Harlow and Rawlings quote Griffith's criticism of Lord Greene's judgment in the *Wednesbury* case, and point out that the position of Greene 'strangely echoes Griffith's own views'.[77] A similarly strange echo reverberates around Harlow's critique of Dicey and the formalism of the 'classic model'.

The portrayal of public law as apolitical, Harlow says, is a myth that has 'served the unwritten Constitution well'.[78] The recognition, as Harlow urges, of the close relationship between law and politics would mean the judiciary should no longer pretend to be neutral, independent arbiters, aloof from politics. Nor any longer can they reject 'the idea of constitutional adjudication' as alien.[79] But once the Diceyan scales fall from the judges' eyes and they see that 'public law is simply a sophisticated form of political discourse',[80] it seems unrealistic to think that it will be 'business as usual' at the Royal Courts of Justice. Are the judges likely to continue to respect the shape of 'our traditional constitutional arrangements'?[81] If so, why? What is to stop 'Judge & Co' moving closer to the centre of the political stage? The expansion of judicial power nowadays is remarked upon on all sides. None of this pleases Harlow,[82] but it is not clear what resources are available to stop it happening. How can the genie be put back in the positivist bottle?

Several of the judges were already aboard 'the rights band-wagon',[83] and the others have been given a leg-up by the 'incorporation' of the ECHR. The Convention, by virtue of the Human Rights Act 1998, has attained 'quasi-Constitutional' status.[84] The movement to a ' "rights-based" model of judicial review' appears nigh on unstoppable.[85] Will there be a backlash?

3. PRIVATIZATION, CONTRACTING OUT, AND PUBLIC LAW VALUES

Resistance fighters against a public/private law distinction point to the phenomena of privatization and contracting out, and say that as the state has been transformed any such distinction would be problematic.[86] They point also to

---

[77] *Law and Administration*, n. 3 above, 82.   [78] Harlow, 'Disposing of Dicey', n. 6 above, 360.
[79] *Ibid.*, 364.
[80] *Ibid.*, 358, quoting M. Loughlin, *Public Law and Political Theory* (Clarendon Press, Oxford, 1994), 4.
[81] C. Harlow, 'Export, Import. The Ebb and Flow of English Public Law' [2000] *PL* 240, 253 (hereafter 'Export, Import'); 'A Special Relationship?', n. 39 above, 79, 96.
[82] See 'Back to Basics, n. 75 above.   [83] 'Export, Import', n. 81 above, 251.
[84] See *Thoburn v. Sunderland City Council* [2003] QB 151 (DC); 'Export, Import', n. 81 above, 247. *Contra*, A.V. Dicey, *Introduction to the Study of the Law of the Constitution* (Macmillan, London, 8th edn., 1915), 6.
[85] Cf. M. Loughlin, *Sword and Scales: An Examination of the Relationship between Law and Politics* (Hart Publishing, Oxford, 2000), chaps. 13, 15.
[86] J.W.F. Allison, *A Continental Distinction in the Common Law: A Historical and Comparative Perspective on English Public Law* (Clarendon Press, Oxford, 1996), 101–3. Resistance to the distinction can be overcome only by considerable reform of the legal system, *ibid.*, 237–46, 252.

difficulties European legal systems are having accommodating this phenomenon within the civilian public/private law distinction.[87] But many in this group also oppose the implicit assumption of privatization, the shift from the public to the private sphere, and the corresponding shift in mindset.[88] Carol Harlow is prominent in this group. Harlow points out that:[89]

At the level of deep theory, British public lawyers have made a lesser contribution. . . . In practice, the effect of the ostrich posture [by public lawyers] has been to leave the field clear for economists, already too dominant during the Thatcher regime, and reduce the potential ambit of influence for public law values.

To counterbalance the values of economists and accountants, Harlow rightly insists that 'our own, equally important [public law] values need to be firmly stated if they are to stand a chance of survival'.[90] Not just stated firmly, these values must be fought for.[91] In other words, public lawyers are fighting in the normative trenches along with the law-economists, private lawyers, Euro-lawyers, and so on.

'Public law values' is a term frequently heard nowadays. It is said to be the responsibility of public lawyers to expose the values upon which administration is premissed, as well as to articulate their own values.[92] In large part this self-conscious identification of and emphasis on public law values was a response to Thatcherism and the public choice attack on the 'public-regarding' premiss of administrative law.[93] The response of many administrative lawyers has been to distil the essence of administrative law, its values, for transporting to the newly deregulated and privatized areas.[94] No list of these values is exhaustive, but at various times Harlow has identified openness, fairness, rationality, accountability, participation, independence, transparency, equity, and equality.[95]

In the 'contracting State', command-and-control regulation is replaced by contract as the dominant form of regulation.[96] There are at least four broad responses

---

[87] See C. Harlow, 'European Administrative Law and the Global Challenge', in P.P. Craig and G. de Búrca (eds.), *The Evolution of EU Law* (Oxford University Press, Oxford, 1999), 261, 262, citing F. Dubois, M. Egueleguele, G. Lefevre, and M. Loiselle, 'La contestation du droit administratif dans le champ intellectuel et politique', in J. Chevallier (ed.), *Le Droit Administratif en Mutation* (Presses Universitaires de France, Paris, 1993), 159.

[88] See generally M. Taggart, 'Corporatisation, Privatisation and Public Law' (1991) 2 *PLR* 77, 94.

[89] 'Changing the Mindset', n. 73 above, 433.

[90] C. Harlow, 'The JUSTICE/All Souls Review: Don Quixote to the Rescue?' (1990) 10 *OJLS* 85, 91.

[91] 'Back to Basics', n. 75 above, 261.

[92] *Law and Administration*, n. 3 above, 28; M. Taggart, 'The Impact of Corporatisation and Privatisation on Administrative Law' (1992) 51 *Australian Journal of Public Administration* 368, 371–2.

[93] See especially P. McAuslan, 'Public Choice and Public Law' (1988) 51 *MLR* 687 and P. McAuslan, 'Administrative Law, Collective Consumption and Judicial Policy' (1983) 46 *MLR* 1.

[94] M. Taggart, 'The Province of Administrative Law Determined?', in M. Taggart (ed.), *The Province of Administrative Law* (Hart Publishing, Oxford, 1997), 1, 3

[95] *Law and Administration*, n. 3 above, 133, 230, 251, 271, 313, 318, 528.

[96] *Ibid.*, chap. 8. The words in inverted commas are taken from the brilliant *double entendre* in the title of I. Harden's *The Contracting State* (Open University Press, Buckingham, 1992).

to government contracting.[97] (I will focus here on the law of contract, but recognize that much the same can be said about tort law.) The first response is to apply the private law of contract to government contracting without any modification whatsoever. The second response would be to apply the private law of contract, but modify the rules or the remedies in certain respects to reflect inherent differences between state and citizen. Such modifications as prove necessary or expedient to make would apply only to 'government' contracts, and to that extent 'distinctive' rules may develop for government contracts within the rules of the private law of contract. The remedies awarded, however, will be private law remedies (albeit tempered by public law values). The third response would be to apply administrative law doctrine and remedies to government contracting to prevent unfairness and abuse of power. This would be in addition to any private law remedies. The fourth response would be to apply public law doctrines and remedies to all contracting, and thereby change the law of contract across the board.

Of the four responses to government contracting, all but the first reflect to some degree public law values, although they are given effect by differing techniques and mechanisms.[98] Carol Harlow's preference is to give primacy to private law remedial tools, but to integrate public law values into private law rights and remedies, so that the public interest is protected.[99]

The difficulty with that position, in my view, is that if the contest between private law and public law values takes place on private law terrain, as Harlow's 'private law model of public law' mandates, then it is likely to be an unequal and ultimately unsuccessful struggle. Private law values will likely win hands down. This links with the earlier discussion about underestimating the difficulty of the common law adopting a modern abuse of rights doctrine.[100] As the work of McLean is showing, there is a temptation to underestimate the structural and ideological impediments to the 'interpenetration' of public law values in private law.[101] Championing a private law model of public law may, unintentionally, lead to the continued privileging of a set of values that Dicey was comfortable with.

4. Conclusion

In re-reading Carol Harlow's writings over more than a quarter of a century I have been struck by the importance of tradition, of the importance of holding

---

[97] See generally S. Arrowsmith, *Government Procurement and Judicial Review* (Carswell, Toronto, 1988); M. Allars, 'Administrative Law, Government Contracts and the Level Playing Field' (1989) 12 *UNSWLR* 114; P. Birkinshaw, 'By the Command of Her Britannic Majesty's Government Let There Be Government By Contract', in *Economy, Administration and Self Government* (Poznañ, 1997) 55; J. McLean, 'Contracting in the Corporatised and Privatised Environment' (1996) 7 *PLR* 223.

[98] See, e.g. S. Whittaker, 'Judicial Review in Public Law and in Contract Law: The Example of Student Rules' (2001) 21 *OJLS* 193.   [99] *Law and Administration*, n. 3 above, 42, 241–3.

[100] See the text following n. 53 above.

[101] J. McLean, 'The Ordinary Law of Tort and Contract and the New Public Management' (2001) 30 *Common Law World Review* 387.

on to what is good from the sturdy unwritten constitution, from a time when both politicians and judges supposedly knew their places.[102] Harlow stands up for these virtues in the face of the 'alien' trend towards the legalization of politics and the politicization of law. This resonates with the following passage from an inaugural lecture given at the London School of Economics in the middle of the twentieth century:[103]

A tradition of behaviour is not a fixed or flexible manner of doing things; it is a flow of sympathy. It may be temporarily disrupted by the incursion of a foreign influence, it may be diverted, restricted, arrested, or become dried-up, and it may reveal so deep-seated an incoherence that (even without foreign assistance) a crisis appears.... But ... we have no resources outside the fragments, the vestiges, the relics of its own tradition of behaviour which the crisis has left untouched. For even the help we may get from the traditions of another society (or from the tradition of a vaguer sort which is shared by a number of societies) is conditional upon our being able to assimilate them to our own arrangements and our own manner of attending to arrangements.... In short, political crisis (even when it seems to be imposed upon a society by changes beyond its control) always appears *within* a tradition of political activity; and 'salvation' comes from the unimpaired resources of the tradition itself.

This is not from an inaugural lecture by de Smith or Griffith, but from one by a political philosopher, Oakeshott, the modern oracle of English conservatism.[104] According to Loughlin, Oakeshott's thought underpins the dominant tradition of 'conservative normativism' in British public law that Dicey played such a prominent role in shaping.[105]

It is this emphasis on tradition, their Englishness[106] if you like, that seems to me to link Dicey and Harlow.[107] Their common resistance to a substantive public/private law distinction remains one of 'the peculiarities of the English'.[108]

---

[102] See, e.g., C. Harlow, 'A Community of Interests? Making the Most of European Law' (1992) 55 *MLR* 331, 349.

[103] M.J. Oakeshott, 'Political Education' (Inaugural lecture, London School of Economics, 1951) in M.J. Oakeshott, *Rationalism in Politics* (Methuen & Co Ltd, London, 1962), 126, quoted in J.W.F. Allison, 'Legal Culture in Fuller's Analysis of Adjudication', in W.J. Witteveen and W. van der Burg (eds.), *Rediscovering Fuller: Essays in Implicit Law and Institutional Design* (Amsterdam University Press, Amsterdam, 1999), 346, 361.

[104] Oakeshott succeeded H.J. Laski to the Chair of Political Science at the London School of Economics.

[105] M. Loughlin, *Public Law and Political Theory* (Clarendon Press, Oxford, 1994), 139–40, 156–7 and 159. See also Stapleton, n. 2 above.

[106] See I. Ward, 'A Charmed Spectacle: England and Its Constitutional Imagination' (2000) 22 *Liverpool LR* 235; Stapleton, n. 2 above, 246–55.

[107] Cf. Bamforth, n. 30 above, 154–6; P. Cane, 'Public Law and Private Law: A Study of the Analysis and Use of a Legal Concept', in J. Eekelaar and J. Bell (eds.), *Oxford Essays in Jurisprudence (Third Series)* (Clarendon Press, Oxford, 1987), 57, 61–3.

[108] The quoted words here and in my title derive from the title to an essay by E.P. Thompson, reprinted in E.P. Thompson, *The Poverty of Theory & other essays* (Merlin, London, 1978), 35.

7

Government by Contract Re-examined—Some Functional Issues

MARK FREEDLAND

1. INTRODUCTION

A very important aspect of Carol Harlow's huge contribution to the scholarship of administrative and public law, in the UK and in the European Union more generally, has been the way in which, sometimes in her own sole writings and sometimes in association with Richard Rawlings, she has developed and applied a functional approach to the issues which confront those who make, use, or expound this branch of the law. The second edition of their work on *Law and Administration*[1] articulates this approach at the highest level of sophistication, and brings it to bear not only upon the traditional concerns and preoccupations of administrative lawyers, but also upon the area or type or style of governmental activity, which I among others have seen fit to refer to as 'government by contract',[2] in which governments and public authorities provide or arrange for the provision of services to the public by means of contractual relations with enterprises which form part of the private sector of the political economy. In this essay, I seek to draw attention to some major problems which are beginning to confront the activity of 'government by contract' and the regulation of that activity by administrative law, and which I think can be illuminated by a functional analysis.

Carol Harlow's functional approach to public law consists, above all, in an insistence that, in the regulation of governmental or administrative activity, we should be more concerned with ensuring that the functions of that activity are fulfilled than with maintaining doctrinaire distinctions between the public sphere and the private sphere, or between public law and private law. Hence that approach denies that the central role of administrative or public law is simply to keep government in check and insists, in the terminology which

---

[1] C. Harlow and R. Rawlings, *Law and Administration* (Butterworths, London, 2nd edn., 1997) (hereafter 'H & R').

[2] M. R. Freedland, 'Government by Contract and Public Law' [1994] *PL* 86.

Harlow and Rawlings have made famous,[3] that 'green-light theories' of administrative law may be as valid and important as 'red-light theories': that is to say, theories of the role of administrative law which enable public authorities to 'do their job' are fully as necessary as those which ensure that judges are empowered to monitor executive action for its compliance with objective standards of good and fair administration.

Committed as they are to that functional approach, Harlow and Rawlings are concerned to ensure that 'government by contract' and 'new public management' should not be lightly dismissed as, simply, a commercial adulteration of the purity of the public state. The functional approach demands an open-mindedness to the possibility that these styles or modes of administration may be the optimal ones in the present state of the political economy. On the other hand, it is entirely consistent with that approach to maintain an alertness to the shortcomings or disadvantages of 'government by contract'; indeed, Harlow and Rawlings show themselves to be keenly aware of those hazards.[4] The main purpose of this essay is to draw attention to the very great proportions which those issues may come to assume when 'government by contract' is allowed to become the prevailing ideology and methodology for the provision of public services. It will be argued that an extensive re-conceptualization of the scope and methodology of public law may be necessary in order to maintain an effective functional approach in the face of the challenges which are posed in those circumstances.

We could regard successive British governments, whether Conservative or New Labour, as having made exactly that ideological or methodological commitment at least from the early 1990s onwards, perhaps even from the 1980s. In a broad sense, government by contract has become the dominant paradigm for the provision of public services. From the early 1990s onwards, there has actually been a requirement upon many agencies of government to show good cause why they should provide or arrange for public services on any *other* basis, a requirement introduced under a Conservative government but fully maintained by subsequent governments whether of the same or of a supposedly different political persuasion. In the policy discourse currently employed by the present government, enormous priority is accorded to the 'modernizing' of arrangements for the provision of public services, and this largely means transforming them into the patterns of 'government by contract'.[5]

Against this background, it is important, both generally and for the argument about public law which is being pursued in this essay, to realize how very large and complex the panoply of arrangements for 'government by contract' has become. In order to understand both the magnitude and the complexity of those arrangements, it will be helpful to expound the concept of 'government by

---

[3] See *H & R*, n. 1 above, chaps. 2–3.

[4] For example by developing the critical notion of 'Pseudo-contract' in *ibid.*, chap. 8, section 2.

[5] A very useful account of this evolution is given by P. Craig in *Administrative Law* (Sweet & Maxwell, London, 4th edn., 1999) (hereafter 'Craig'), chap. 5, section 2: 'Towards "Better Government": Contract and Service Provision by Central Government'.

contract' a bit further, in the sense of explaining more fully what arrangements we are describing under that heading, and how those arrangements work and inter-relate to each other. Harlow and Rawlings have recognized,[6] and the present writer strongly asserts, that the notion of 'government by contract' refers to a more extensive and elaborate set of arrangements than those which would fall under the traditional heading of 'government contracting'. Government contracting is essentially the process or practice whereby agencies of government procure goods or services from commercial or private sector providers by making contracts for the purchase of those goods or services.

I now wish to argue that we should understand 'government by contract' to refer not only to government contracting in the above sense, but also to the creation and operation of the institutional structures within which contractual or contract-like arrangements for the provision of public services may take place. This is not put forward as a definition which is particularly rigorous; it may not even be exhaustive of all the activities which we might necessarily regard as 'government by contract'. Thus, when I refer to public services in this context, I mean nothing more precise than services which governments are regarded as responsible for ensuring to their citizens.[7] It is not part of my present purpose to elaborate how that responsibility is or should be specified in any given society at any given time. Nor am I committed to the view that 'government by contract' concerns only the provision of public services. It might usefully also be regarded as extending to carrying out *regulation*, for example environmental regulation, by contract or contract-like mechanisms.

The purpose of putting forward this understanding of 'government by contract' is not, therefore, to de-limit the territory of that concept in any exact way. It is rather to make the point that the notion or activity of 'government by contract' has a very significant structural and institutional dimension. This is true in more than one sense. On the one hand, arrangements for the provision of public services on a contractual or contract-like basis may themselves constitute institutions or structures of government or economic activity. On the other hand, it may be necessary to create new, or fundamentally to adapt existing, institutions or structures of government or economic activity in order to enable contractual provision of public services to take place. The more extensive that the provision of public services on a contractual or contract-like basis becomes, the more it involves structural and institutional adaptation in one or other or both of these senses. It will be useful to elaborate and illustrate this argument.

We may approach this argument by drawing a contrast between the kind of contracts which are actually involved in 'government by contract' and the

---

[6] *H & R*, n. 1 above, chap. 5, 'A Blue Rinse', and chap. 8, 'A Revolution in the Making', and especially chap. 8, section 1, 'Uses and Norms'.

[7] Thus, however, being more inclusive than defining or applying the concept of 'functions of a public nature', as it occurs in s. 6(3) of the Human Rights Act 1998, which was taken by the Court of Appeal in its recent decision in *R (on the application of Heather)* v. *Leonard Cheshire Foundation (A Charity)* [2002] EWCA Civ 366, [2002] HRLR 30; compare Craig, (2002) 118 *LQR* 551. See further below, n. 10.

stereotype of the 'market contract' which we tend unconsciously to draw upon when thinking about this subject. The stereotype of the market contract is essentially that of a purchaser going into a market, that is to say a commercial environment offering multiple opportunities for the transaction in question, and arranging to purchase the goods or services in question in a single transaction or a number of distinct transactions. The contracts or contract-like arrangements of 'government by contract' very rarely correspond to this stereotype. Much more often, they are long-term relational contracts or arrangements which may possibly be formed in a market environment, but which in any event subsist and function in a context which is not a market environment in any ordinary sense. This must be true, for example, of a contract whereby a commercial company contracts with a government department to design and build and to run over a period of years a prison or a school or a hospital.

It must be said that this aspect of 'government by contract' is in a sense acknowledged, even perhaps positively asserted, in the rhetoric with which the New Labour governments which have held office since 1997 describe arrangements of this kind and explain their policy of making such arrangements as extensively as is practically feasible. Where previous governments had made such arrangements, since 1991, under the conceptual umbrella of the 'Private Finance Initiative',[8] governments since 1997 have preferred to regard them as coming under a programme for the making of 'Public/Private Partnerships'.[9] This latter rhetoric positively stresses the continuing relational nature of these transactions or arrangements.

The underlying logic, which is less strongly emphasized because it challenges our constitutional notion of government as an essentially public activity, is that these arrangements constitute, in and of themselves, institutions or structures of government which are partly public and partly private in character. The more extensively that such arrangements cover the territory of public service provision, the more obtrusive this effect becomes. If the Ministry of Defence contracts to buy a million packs of soldiers' rations from a food manufacturer, that does not particularly transform the institutions of government. If the Department for Education contracts with a private enterprise providing educational services for the running of thirty schools for thirty years, a new institution or structure, a particular kind of institution which is at once entrepreneurial and governmental, has been created jointly between the two contracting parties. It is impossible to

---

[8] The development of these arrangements down to 1998 is described in M. Freedland, 'Public Law and Private Finance—Placing the Private Finance Initiative in a Public Law Frame' [1998] *PL* 288; see also Craig, n. 5 above, chap. 5, sections 3 and 5: 'The Private Finance Initiative: Contract and Service Provision by Central and by Local Government'.

[9] The organizational structure and use of the terminology of Public Private Partnerships ('PPP') has become complicated. There is a governmental organization or activity known as the Public Private Partnership Programme ('4Ps'), see www.4ps.co.uk, which encourages and supports the making of PFI contracts by local authorities; but the terminology of PPP is often used to describe the making of PFI and similar contracts by governmental authorities more generally.

classify that institution as a public or a private one; it has both aspects; it is both at once.[10]

If the contracts which form the core of 'government by contract' thus sometimes have the character of transformative governmental structures or institutions in and of themselves, so also do the corporate and regulatory arrangements which governments find it necessary to make in order to enable 'government by contract' to take place. This is a point of the most fundamental importance, all the more so as 'government by contract' becomes the dominant pattern of public service provision. We can already observe a kind of ripple effect, whereby the further that 'government by contract' is developed, the progressively greater is its consequential impact upon the institutions and structures both of government and of the private service provision sector. This essay will continue by attempting to make out that argument in detail, and then to suggest its implications for our system of administrative and public law.

2. PUBLIC AND PRIVATE COMMERCIAL ORDERING

This argument begins by returning to the contrast which was put forward earlier between the market contract stereotype and the contracts or contract-like arrangements through which 'government by contract' takes place. One very important feature of the market contract stereotype is that it assumes or postulates that there are commercial providers of the goods or services in question with which the would-be purchaser of those goods and services may contract, and that the purchasers and providers are and remain independent of each other when forming and performing the contracts which they make between them. That aspect of the market contract stereotype, that is to say the assumption of independent commercial actors on the supply side, may not really apply even to much of the commercial activity which takes place within the purely private sector. In the realm of 'government by contract', very elaborate institutional and structural transformations turn out to be necessary in order to try to make the arrangements in question approximate to the market contract stereotype, and even then that desired effect is often not achieved. Instead, highly complex, mutant, and ultimately unstable combinations occur between public governmental ordering and private commercial ordering, which present very novel and significant new challenges to the legal and constitutional system.

In order to explain and sustain that bold assertion, it may be helpful to envisage 'government by contract' arrangements for public service provision as being of various types which fall at different points along a particular kind of spectrum. At one extreme of that spectrum are situations where arrangements can

---

[10] This conception may be compared with that of the 'hybrid body', with both public and private functions, which is being articulated in the developing case law on the meaning of 'public authority' in s. 6(3) of the Human Rights Act 1998, to which a significant recent contribution was made by the decision of the Court of Appeal in the *Leonard Cheshire* case, see n. 7 above.

be made which correspond fully to the market contract stereotype, in the sense that independent commercial contractors exist and can provide the services in question by means of market contracts on a continuing basis.[11] At the other extreme are situations where such arrangements are regarded as completely unattainable or completely inappropriate, and where the attempt to replicate them in the form of market analogues produce results which are artificial, in the sense that they are really no more than administrative or governmental arrangements presented in contractual form.

Earlier discussion of 'government by contract' has tended to allocate particular kinds of contract or contract-like arrangements to one or other end of this spectrum. On the one hand, discussion of 'government by contract' has hitherto focused to a considerable extent on arrangements which are right at the 'market analogue' end of the spectrum, such as the contract-like arrangements between 'Next Steps' agencies of government and their parent departments of government, or the 'internal market' system within the National Health Service.[12] On the other hand, there has been a tendency, at least on the part of the present writer, to think about PFI or PPP arrangements as being at the 'pure market' end of the spectrum, and to concentrate upon ensuring that their public dimension is recognized and that the public interest in the way that they function is vindicated. By contrast, the next part of this argument will focus attention upon the middle range of the spectrum, into which a large range of 'government by contract' arrangements actually fall. The aim will be to point out certain particular problems in the way that those arrangements work, located as they are in a position on the spectrum at which there is an inherent tension between governmental arrangements and private market orderings.

It is sufficiently clear as to be uncontroversial that British governments since 1979 have been generally concerned to move public service provision towards the 'pure market' end of the spectrum which we have envisaged. However, it should not be imagined that this movement has been a simple or direct one. The technical mechanisms for accomplishing that movement have been privatization, agency separation as in the 'Next Steps' programme, contracting-out, and PFI or PPP arrangements. The degree and the precise nature of movement have varied greatly according to the situation of the public service in question. Many variations and combinations of these mechanisms have been involved. Highly intricate institutional and contractual structures have been devised. Even in the purely private sector of the economy, large development projects have to be mounted within complex structures of that kind. Where major public service provision is concerned, those complexities are multiplied. For example, it is very hard to

---

[11] The making of arrangements for the construction and maintenance of highways provides a good example.

[12] This was the focus, e.g., of I. Harden's seminal work, *The Contracting State* (Open University Press, Milton Keynes, 1992), and is also the subject of A. Davies's very valuable new contribution to this literature, *Accountability—A Public Law Analysis of Government by Contract* (Oxford University Press, Oxford, 2001).

categorize the arrangements which have been made for the railway system, or for the air traffic control system, in terms either of privatization, contracting-out, or PFI/PPP. They represent highly crafted and negotiated combinations of those structural techniques, creating both a network of contractual obligations and a complex set of corporate or institutional vehicles to carry those obligations, and to inter-relate the public and the private interests which are at stake.

The observation that the arrangements for 'government by contract' are institutional and structural as well as purely contractual may serve to alter, in quite radical ways, our understanding of the operation and dynamics of those arrangements. It may also transform our view of what is involved in the appropriate legal regulation of those arrangements, and of whether and how far that regulation should be a matter of public law or of private law. We proceed to develop those two arguments in turn, the latter being consequential upon the former.

3. GOVERNMENT BY CONTRACT: DYNAMICS

We begin by reverting to our argument about the contrast between the market contract stereotype and the actual nature of government by contract arrangements. That contrast is greatly enlarged when we take into account the institutional and structural dimension of government by contract arrangements. The market contract stereotype assumes and depends upon the existence of viable commercial enterprises to operate as parties to market contracts; and the more that those contracts have a long-term relational dimension the more that the market contract stereotype requires the continuing stability of those enterprises.

We have already argued that the making of 'government by contract' arrangements often requires elaborate institutional and structural adaptations in order to create the initial conditions for replicating the market contract stereotype. We now advance the argument that the maintaining of the stability of those conditions often proves very difficult in practice. The institutional and structural arrangements in which 'government by contract' is embodied often come under great stress, and prove in various ways to be less stable and more mutable than their architects had hoped or intended. Uncertainties set in which further undermine the structures, and sometimes appear to threaten the whole set of arrangements in question. Some illustrations will be helpful.

First, experience of electricity supply systems which depend upon a network of contracts between privatized utility corporations in the United States, Australia, and New Zealand already indicates the potential for serious market failure resulting in major breakdowns in electricity supply, necessitating state intervention in the form of re-structuring of the contract system in question.

Secondly, the collapse of the Enron Corporation in 2001,[13] following its transformation from being a fairly localized public utility supplier to being a

---

[13] A useful source of up-to-date information on the litigation which has resulted from this collapse is the US on-line journal Findlaw, the address of which is http://news.findlaw.com.

multi-national venture capital speculator, shows the danger that the private sector contractor may prove to be a financially unstable institution, no doubt again necessitating governmental intervention to maintain or rescue the public service provision in which it was engaged.

Thirdly, we may refer to the experience of the British system, established by legislation and governmental action in the early 1990s, for the provision of employment training by means of contracts between the Department of Education and Science, the Training and Enterprise Councils, and commercial training providers. This system proved to be so unsatisfactory as a way of securing the kind of employment training provision which subsequent governments wished to make that it was decided to close it down and completely to re-constitute it in a different and less contractualized institutional form.[14]

Finally, and most dramatically of all so far as the British practice of 'government by contract' is concerned, the story of the railway system following its re-privatization in 1993 demonstrated the breakdown of a complex set of franchising arrangements which failed to provide the necessary incentives for infrastructural investment, and, again, has required a complete re-constituting by government action of the institutional and structural system for the financing and running of the railway system.[15]

Something new emerges from these examples about the sort of remedial activity which governments have to undertake when systems of 'government by contract' come under extreme stress, and also about the complex and compromised role which governments have to play in such situations. The remedial activity often consists not merely in varying or re-writing contracts, though that may well be included in the remedial activity, but also in elaborate institutional re-structuring. In particular, intermediary institutions between departments of government and private contractors often have to be re-cast or re-constituted, as in the case of the TECs, or, on a grander scale, as with the current exercise of closing down Railtrack, the public limited company established to own and run the railway infrastructure, and replacing it with a non-profit-making company, the capital structure of which is not yet clear at the time of writing this chapter. (It may be appropriate to draw attention in passing to the way in which these institutional adaptations add in no small measure to the already considerable legal and accounting costs of 'government by contract'.)

These examples also tell us important things about the role of governments in making these adaptations. The framework of the post-war welfare state

[14] The TECs were established as a regional network of limited companies, usually by guarantee but sometimes by shares with public authorities as the major or exclusive shareholders. The Learning and Skills Act 2000 replaced them with newly created Non-Departmental Public Bodies, the Learning and Skills Council for England, and the National Council for Education and Training for Wales. The relations between those bodies and the central departments of government were not constituted as contractual ones in the way that the relations with the TECs had been.

[15] Some useful information and comment about the progress, at that date, of this exercise in reconstruction are provided by the Government Statement on Railtrack and subsequent debate in the House of Lords of 25 March 2002; HL Debs, 25 March 2002, cols 64–75.

accustomed us all, more so than previously, to regard governments, both at national and local levels, as providers, indirectly or, more usually, directly of a wide range of public services. The complete or nearly complete privatization of some public services in the 1980s equally accustomed us to regard governments as having a major regulatory role in relation to public services (using that term to cover services previously regarded as public even if now provided through purely commercial mechanisms). The initial experience of 'government by contract' made us aware of an emerging role of government as the creator of market analogues within the structures of public administration. I suggest we should now view recent and current experience of 'government by contract' as alerting us to an emerging new kind of mixed public and private market institutions for the provision of public services, and to the fact that governments have assumed the role of the makers and maintainers of these public/private market institutions. We might perhaps call this the public/private market-making role.

We can begin to perceive that, as the pursuit of 'government by contract' becomes more and more central to the policies of government, and more integral to the running of the political economy as a whole, so this public/private market-making role becomes more elaborate, pervasive, and demanding. It is essentially a role of facilitating, encouraging, and sustaining the process of contracting for public service provision. It has already been argued in this essay that if that is to be done on a grand scale, institutional transformation has to take place and has taken place. The further point is now made that the playing of this role by government also cuts across, and eventually transforms, the way in which governments operate in their more familiar, or better recognized, roles as purchasers or regulators of public service provision. Again, some illustrations will be helpful.

First let us take the example of PFI/PPP. I have sought in earlier writing[16] to show how this initiative or programme of activity has become far more than a simple process of making and implementing a certain kind of public/private contract whereby private corporations make large capital investment in public service provision in return for long-term income for the provision of those services. It has also involved the creation of an institutional apparatus to promote and encourage that contracting process, in other words the provision of market-making institutions. A particular example of that new institutional apparatus is the company called Partnerships UK, which was set up in 1999 as a joint public/private venture to perform the task, which had previously been entrusted to a Taskforce within the Treasury, of developing PPPs. Partnerships UK itself was formally designated a PPP in the course of 2001, and 51 per cent of its equity was put up for sale to private investors. Hence this is a public/private institutional mechanism for carrying out the public/private market-making function on behalf of the government, as such a somewhat 'boot-straps' arrangement according to traditional ideas of public administration.

---

[16] N. 8 above.

There are even more significant examples of the way that parts of the apparatus of government are being in part transformed so that they can serve this market-making role. At the time of writing, a very long-drawn-out battle between the departments of central government and the administration of London, about whether the corporation which owns and runs the London Underground system should serve as a platform for PFI/PPP contracts, seems to have been won by the government; that is to say, the public/private market-making role has emerged as the dominant one. Again, in the recent and current financial and capital re-structuring of the railway system following the government's decision to put Railtrack into administration, a major concern has been to ensure that the new structure will effectively serve the market-making function, both in the immediate sense of providing effective vehicles for the PFI/PPP contracts upon which the improvement of the infrastructure is seen to depend, and in the further sense of retaining the confidence of private investors in the public/private services market more generally.

Consideration of those examples leads to an important general reflection about the tension which may exist or arise when the market-making function becomes very prominent in the functioning of government and the agencies of government, as it has done in those instances. For the demands of the public/private market-making function may be at variance or in outright conflict with the demands of the contracting role or the regulatory role of government. It seems fairly evident that administrators or policy-makers who attach great importance to the making and sustaining of markets for public/private service provision may take a different view of the financial and regulatory terms upon which contracts for that service provision should be made, as compared with those for whom that function does not have priority. I am not suggesting that there are 'right' views or 'wrong' views in this respect; but I am in little doubt that a variance or conflict of views and of outcomes follows inevitably from this underlying difference of approach.

4. Government by contract: legal regulation

That reflection brings us to the central point of this essay. For it poses the following question: what should be the scope, nature, and orientation of the body of law which regulates the activity of 'government by contract'? In the remainder of this essay, I shall put forward some very tentative ideas about that, which I have arrived at by trying to apply what I perceive as Carol Harlow's functionalist approach to the very recent and current experience of 'government by contract' in the United Kingdom. We could possibly think about this as an exercise in sketching, very roughly, the outlines of a body of public/private enterprise law.

In making that sketch, I find myself taking a direction which I at first find to be not merely unfamiliar, but actually rather counter-intuitive. My own earlier writings in this area have been concerned to show that public law, and particularly administrative law, should be applied to regulate the activity of 'government by contract' and even more particularly the PFI/PPP area of activity, and to suggest how that should be done. I continue to admire the symposium of essays which Taggart and his colleagues wrote on the subject of the *Province of Administrative Law*,[17] which seem to me to explore in great depth and to very good effect that same question of how public or administrative law should be applied to the privatized and de-regulated structures of public service provision which post-1980 neo-liberal governmental policies have created in many legal jurisdictions. That inquiry legitimately and usefully in my view includes the search for ways in which the core values of public law can be discovered and vindicated in the private law regulation of much of this area. I have no less of admiration for Davies's recently published study[18] which suggests how we might begin to devise and develop a 'public law of contract', which would maximize the transparency, fairness, and accountability of all aspects of the process of contracting for the provision of public services.

All that said, I am now inclined to suggest that we should build upon all this work not so much by cultivating this area as a garden of public law, but rather by delineating a field of public/private enterprise law in the larger terrain of English law both public and private and including the input from EC law. I hope this is a direction not very significantly different from that taken by MacLachlan in his contribution to *The Province of Administrative Law* in which he very eloquently 'evoke[s] a discipline of public service law *en emergence*'.[19] However, I am conscious that the approach I am now taking may be somewhat less oriented towards public law than his. I hope, equally, that I am doing no injustice to Carol Harlow's functionalist approach by asserting that this approach seems to me to encourage a search for solutions to the question, 'how should we regulate government by contract?' outside as well as inside the domain of public law.

Perhaps, however, that way of describing and drawing upon the functionalist approach puts it too prescriptively. My real reason for sketching out an area of public/private enterprise law, which is not specially oriented towards public law, is not so much the view that 'government by contract' *should* be regulated by a body of law which is not specially oriented towards public law, but rather a prediction that English law *will* on the whole tend to generate a mixed but private law-based body of law for that purpose. On this view, we greatly increase our chances of arriving at a really coherent and persuasive account of this body of law by working on that assumption, and therefore by operating in a number of different legal spheres. In the end, I have come to think the values and goals of public law may best be vindicated in relation to 'government by

[17] M. Taggart (ed.), *The Province of Administrative Law* (Hart Publishing, Oxford, 1997).
[18] N. 12 above.
[19] H. Wade Maclauchlan, 'Public Service and the New Public Management', in M. Taggart (ed.), *Administrative Law*, n. 17 above, 119.

contract' by proceeding in this way. Let me offer some illustrations of ways or areas in which I think this might be the case.

My first illustration is provided by the great 'interest swaps' cases of the early 1990s, those of *Hazell* v. *Hammersmith Borough Council*,[20] *Westdeutsche Landesbank Girozentrale* v. *Islington Borough Council*,[21] and *Kleinwort Benson Ltd* v. *Lincoln City Council*.[22] For local authorities in the late 1980s, interest swap transactions represented a kind of private finance initiative *avant la lettre*, a means by which public authorities could bring in private finance to circumvent limits which had been placed by the rate-capping system upon their capacity to raise funding by (local) public taxation. When the swap transactions began to work adversely for the local authorities, they invoked the public law *ultra vires* doctrine to extricate themselves, and were successful in doing so in the *Hazell* case. However, in the *Westdeutsche Landesbank* and *Kleinwort Benson* cases, the banks were held to have good restitutionary claims against the local authorities for payments made to the local authorities by the banks.

Harlow and Rawlings demonstrate most effectively how all these cases have to be understood in relation to each other.[23] The problem for the courts was, in a sense, whether to give greater priority to the regulatory function of invalidating and deterring unauthorized swap transactions, or the market-making function of maintaining investor confidence in the integrity of public/private dealings. As Harlow and Rawlings' presentation so ably demonstrates, one does not get the answer, and indeed the courts did not give the answer, in the realm of public law alone. In fact, the resolution of that set of issues, admittedly not an especially clear or decisive one, occurred mainly in the private law realm of restitutionary remedies. One does not need to applaud that particular way of addressing the functional problem in order to recognize that it was very typical of the methodology of English law that it should be tackled in that, ultimately private law-based, fashion, and, moreover, that the legal dynamics of this group of cases can only really be understood through the conceptual apparatus of the law of restitution.

I think, rather similarly, that we might expect that the techniques of private law in the areas of contract, tort, and restraint of trade will be the tools mainly used to address issues arising from the tension or conflict between the public contracting role and the public/private market-making function, and that our primary concern should be to ensure that these private law-based instruments are tuned to register the sound of public interest. Let me give some illustrations. The first consists of considering how the English courts might handle the fascinating issues which were addressed by the US Supreme Court in the case of *United States* v. *Winstar Corporation*.[24] In the United States, the savings and

---

[20] [1992] 2 AC 1.   [21] [1996] AC 669.   [22] [1999] AC 349.

[23] *H & R*, n. 1 above, 217–27.

[24] 518 US 839 (1996). See J. Freedman, 'The Contracting State' (2000) 28 *Florida State Law Rev*, 155. I am most grateful to Dr E. Fisher for drawing my attention to the interest and relevance of this material.

loan enterprises, or 'thrifts', which, like building societies and increasingly banks in the UK, provide home loans for individual borrowers have since the 1930s been both regulated and supported by the Federal Government which, in particular, took on the role of insurer to the thrifts. During the 1980s there was a new crisis in the industry, and many thrifts failed or seemed likely to do so. In order to prop up the industry, the Federal Government engaged in some relaxation of regulatory standards.

This case concerned agreements which had been made between the government and some financially sound thrifts which facilitated their acquisition of failing thrifts by relaxing the accounting standards applying to the valuation of the failing thrifts. By acquiring the failing thrifts, the financially sound thrifts relieved the government of potential insurance liabilities. However, Congress subsequently legislated to re-impose stricter accounting standards, and the acquiring thrifts incurred great costs in complying with those stricter standards with respect to the acquired thrifts. In this case, the acquiring thrifts sued the government upon its undertaking to apply the more relaxed regulatory standards. The claim succeeded, and the Supreme Court rejected the government's plea that enforcement of this agreement would treat the government as having conveyed away (the English terminology would be 'fettered') its own sovereign power.

We could view this case as concerned with the conflict between the regulatory role and the market-making role of government in relation to the savings industry. Enforcement of the agreement protected the market-making role but undermined the regulatory one. How might the English courts approach such an issue? It is not very likely that they would address that conflict of roles directly. They might possibly discuss it in terms of the constitutional capacity of government bodies to enter into such agreements, or as a question under the Human Rights Act 1998 of encroachment upon civil or proprietary rights in failing to enforce such agreements. It is equally likely that they might deploy private law techniques of contractual construction, or the essentially private law doctrine of frustration (with questions about self-induced frustration) to attack this problem.

Another illustration might be afforded by considering the legal implications of a problem currently faced by the British government both in its contracting and market-making role with regard to a proposed PFI/PPP arrangement. It was reported at the time of writing that the Inland Revenue and the Department of Social Security were seeking to make such an arrangement for the creation and maintenance of a joint computerized system for their respective operations.[25] They were said to face the problem that the only prospective bidder for this contract was a consortium of the companies who provided and run their present separate computer systems. It was reported that they proposed to create or

---

[25] *Independent on Sunday*, 31 March 2002—Jason Nissé, 'Labour to face row over £7bn tax "farce".'

stimulate competition by agreeing to pay a potential rival bidder the very considerable expenses of preparing a bid from an external position. Suppose that such an agreement were made, and that its enforceability later came into question. Again I suggest that it would be primarily the techniques and reasoning of the private law of contracts which would be used both to define and to resolve the issues.

Moreover, and this seems to me to be a crucial point, such a case would raise profound issues in terms of national and EC competition law. This brings to our attention the way in which the law of public/private enterprise has to be widely multi-disciplinary in character. This means much more than simply straddling the boundary between the public law of judicial review and the private law of contract and tort, an exercise which scholars and teachers and students of administrative law are already well accustomed to performing. It also requires the construction of a body of law capable of regulating an already vast and rapidly expanding area of public/private activity in its economic dimension as well as in its governmental or administrative one.

5. GOVERNMENT BY CONTRACT: THE INSTITUTIONAL DIMENSION

At this point, and as the concluding part of this essay, it will be useful to refer back to the *institutional* aspect of our discussion of 'government by contract'. It will be recalled that one of the crucial steps in the argument was the assertion that the pursuit and practice of government by contract involve both initial and subsequent institutional transformations, as well as merely contractual ones. This requires the creation of new institutions and the re-designing of existing ones so that they may act as participants in public/private activity, whether as the contractors, or as the regulators, or as the market-makers, or in combinations of those roles. These transformations may involve purely public institutions, as where departments of government were reinvented as the combination of a service-procuring parent department and a service-providing agency under the Next Steps programme. On the other hand, these transformations may also involve mixed public/private institutions, such as the various kinds of 'trusts' or foundations or not-for-profit concerns which have been invented or re-worked as participant parties in government by contract in recent years. There is a distinct possibility that the concept of a public interest corporation is starting to concretize, as precisely such a mixed public/private institution, within the framework of EU governmental regulation, with momentous potential consequences for national legal and regulatory systems.[26]

Moreover, last but by no means least, the essential institutional mechanism of private sector economic activity, the company limited by shares, may figure

---

[26] *Proposal for a Council Regulation on the Financial Regulation Applicable to the General Budget of the EC*, COM(2000)461 final; *Amended Proposal for a Council Regulation on the Financial Regulation Applicable to the General Budget of the EC*, COM(2001)691, Art. 54(2)(c).

in government by contract arrangements not just in the classical role of commercial service provider, but also in more complex and mixed roles as both service purchaser and provider and intermediary between government and the private sector as in the case of Railtrack, or even in the role of market-maker as in the curious case of Partnerships UK.

This complex institutional dimension of 'government by contract' arrangements makes further multi-disciplinary demands upon the framework of the law of public/private enterprise as I envisage it. For it means that this legal framework has to refer to the law which determines the structure and governance not just of public bodies, but also of intermediate bodies and fully-fledged private companies. For example, the current saga concerning Railtrack dramatically illustrates how large a part the law of corporate insolvency, not to mention the law of takeovers and mergers, may come to play into the legal regulation of 'government by contract'. As an employment lawyer I cannot forbear to add that the structural aspects of employment law may also have a major role in this discussion. It is already clear that the body of law, partly from domestic and partly from EC sources, which requires the transfer of employment contracts as a consequence of the transfer of ownership of business undertakings, has a crucial effect upon the nature and viability of many actual and potential 'government by contract' arrangements.[27]

As is often the case, the argument of this essay has identified more problems than it has solved. Re-visiting the subject of 'government by contract', I have found in the course of that exploration that the topic requires a more ambitiously constructed legal building to house it than it did when I first visited it, and than I had imagined that it now would. I do not know whether my architectural sketch of a body of public/private enterprise law will turn out to be of sound design, but in any event I have set myself the task for the future of trying to test its engineering and refine its details. I feel sure that I will feel inspired in the task by the example of the acute, perceptive, critical, and non-dogmatic contextual scholarship which Carol Harlow has brought to bear upon the changing world of administrative and public law.

---

[27] The Cabinet Office, clearly concerned about this set of issues, produced in 2001 a Statement of Practice on Staff Transfers in the Public Sector to assist departments and agencies, and the wider public sector, in utilizing the TUPE regulations when planning internal transfers and considering the effect upon employment contracts of PFI proposals and other proposals for contractual arrangements with the private sector—see http://cabinet-office.gov.uk/civilservice/2000/tupe.

8

The Face of Securitas:
Redefining the Relationship of
Security and Foreigners in Europe

ELSPETH GUILD

In 2000, Carol Harlow and I jointly edited a book on the implementation of immigration and asylum powers in European Community law.[1] The book examines the extent of the powers introduced by the Amsterdam Treaty into the EC Treaty in this field and the options for implementation open to the Community. In her analysis of the chapters contributed by experts from various Member States Carol took as her starting point the image of Securitas in Ambrogio Lorenzetti's *Allegory of Good Government* in Siena. She predicted that:[2]

As external borders become more porous 'Securitas' will become an increasingly important actor. It is Securitas who nurtures the 'hard seeds of hate', legitimating reliance on the 'model of aliens' epitomised in the mantra of 'national security', 'general interest' and 'police powers'. The insignia of Securitas today consists of a battery of immigration and police controls, bringing with them division of citizens and non-citizens.

In this essay I will examine the face of Securitas as Carol described it: the expression of state power as national security[3] in the field of immigration and asylum law since the publication of our book in 2001. In particular, the role of Securitas in Europe in dividing citizens and non-citizens by limiting the rights of the latter has become a dominant theme, not least after the terrorist attacks in the USA on 11 September 2001. I will commence by looking at two developments in the UK, first the definition of national security when balanced against security of residence for a foreigner which the House of Lords considered in October 2001 in *Rehman*;[4] secondly the immigration-related measures included in the Anti-terrorism, Crime and Security Act 2001. I will only consider the provisions as introduced not as enacted or their subsequent use. I will then follow the steps of Securitas in the European Court of Human Rights in its

---

[1] E. Guild and C. Harlow, *Implementing Amsterdam: Immigration and Asylum in EC Law* (Hart, Oxford, 2001). [2] *Ibid.*, 318.

[3] My use of the term 'Securitas' is in no way related to any commercial enterprise bearing the same Latin word in its name.

[4] *Secretary of State for the Home Department* v. *Rehman (AP)* [2001] UKHL 47.

decision of 21 November 2001 on the right of an individual to a remedy against torture where that torture has been carried out by a foreign state. The security of legal remedies outside the country of origin in respect of state violence opposes Securitas in the form of state immunity. The balance accepted by the ECtHR was reached specifically in light of the needs of refugees. They are the individuals categorized as the main reason why the borders of legal remedies must be kept sealed. Securitas protects the state both singular and plural.

Securitas has indeed become an increasingly important actor not only in relation to the porousness or otherwise of borders. Its gaze is directed first against foreigners whose interests in respect of security are differently judged from those of citizens. But foreigners are only part of the security question—the presentation of their situation as a threat leads to a diminution of human rights security for all.

1. *REHMAN* AND SECURITAS

On 9 February 1993, Rehman, a national of Pakistan, arrived in the UK having been granted a visa as a minister of religion to work at a mosque in Oldham. His father was also a minister of religion in Halifax and both his father and mother were British citizens. Two of his children were born in the UK. He and his family remained resident in Oldham where he worked. In December 1998 he applied for indefinite leave to remain (a long-stay residence status). This was refused and deportation proceedings were commenced against him. The grounds for the refusal (as quoted in the judgment) are 'the Secretary of State is satisfied, on the basis of information he has received from confidential sources that you are involved with an Islamic terrorist organisation . . . He is satisfied that in the light of your association with the [organization] it is undesirable to permit you to remain and that your continued presence in this country represents a danger to national security.'

The charges against Rehman are chilling in the light of the Autumn 2001 bombing campaign against the Taliban in Afghanistan: recruitment of British Muslims to undergo militant training; fund-raising for a terrorism organization; sponsoring individuals for militant training camps; responsibility for the existence in the UK of British Muslims returned from the militant camps who have been indoctrinated with extremist beliefs or given weapons training.

The interest of the individual foreigner is security of residence. Against this interest is the interest of the state to assure national security. The balance which is found between these interests expresses the division between the foreigner and the citizen. The interest of the citizen is such that his or her security of residence on the territory cannot be brought into play.[5] The right of entry and

---

[5] The limitation on rights of entry and residence for certain types of British nationals, notably British overseas citizens and British nationals (overseas), remains problematic. The European Court

residence on the territory for citizens is established not only in national law but also in numerous human rights conventions, not least the ECHR.[6] The interest of foreigners in security of residence is much more tenuous, a field of negotiation in national law between the benefits of integration of all persons resident on the territory in the interests of social harmony and intolerance and division between those who belong and those who are excludable.[7]

This dividing line between the individual as a foreigner and the state has been the subject of an increasing number of judgments of the European Court of Human Rights from 1993 onwards.[8] The development by that Court of the concept of an integrated alien against whom expulsion can be justified only on very substantial grounds has been resisted by a number of Council of Europe countries as evidenced by the continuing stream of cases pending before the ECtHR. The possibility that the Court may be moving towards a position of prohibition of expulsion of long-resident foreigners as promoted by Schermers in his partly concurring, partly dissenting, opinion in *Lamguindaz*[9] seems to be receding, though the position of enhanced protection remains. The balancing of the interests of the individual and the state even in the light of substantial criminal activity by the foreigner does not, according to the ECtHR, necessarily come down in favour of the state security interest.[10]

What happens when the state's interests are enhanced by reason of national security arguments? How is the balance with regard to the interests of the individual changed? When the label of terrorism is added a number of results flow. Where the charge of terrorism is against a national of the state, it arises in respect of a criminal offence. The offence is specific and regulated by the constitutional settlement between the rulers and the ruled which is contained in

---

of Justice, however, has declined to enter the discussion: Case C–192/99, *R v. Home Secretary, ex p. Kaur* [2001] ECR I–1237.

[6] Protocol 4 ECHR contains the right of admission of nationals to their territory of nationality. The UK has not signed or ratified this protocol. Nonetheless, the European Court of Justice has made specific reference to it in a number of judgments, notably that in Case C–370/90, *R v. Immigration Appeal Tribunal et Singh, ex p. Home Secretary* [1992] ECR I–4265.

[7] B. Nascimbene, *Expulsion and Detention of Aliens in the European Union Countries* (Guiffré, Milan, 2001).

[8] K. Groenendijk, E. Guild, and R. Barzilay, *The Legal Status of Third-Country Nationals who are Long-Residents in a Member State of the European Union* (European Communities, Luxembourg, 2001).

[9] 'I am not so sure, however, whether international law concerning the expulsion of aliens is not changing fundamentally as a result of growing concerns for human rights and of a perceived need for solidarity among States in the face in increasing interstate relations. By admitting aliens to their territories, States inevitably accept at least some measure of responsibility. This responsibility weighs even more heavily in the case of children educated in their territory. For any society, individuals like the present applicant are a burden. Even independent of human rights considerations, I doubt whether modern international law permits a State which has educated children of admitted aliens to expel these children when they become a burden. Shifting this burden to the State of origin of the parent is no longer so clearly acceptable under modern international law. It is at least subject to doubt whether a host country has the right to return those immigrants who prove to be unsatisfactory': (1994) 17 EHRR 213, 218–19.

[10] ECtHR App. No. 54273/00, *Boultif v. Switzerland*, 2 August 2001.

criminal law. The Terrorism Act 2000 was controversial in Parliament not least because of the changes to the balance of the rights of the defence and the rights of the state which flow from the addition of the characteristic of 'terrorism' to what would otherwise be a criminal offence subject to the normal rules.

When the individual subject to the suspicion of terrorism is a foreigner, another option is open to the state: expulsion. Here the proceedings are of an administrative kind and not subject to the need for a criminal charge to which to add the terrorism sobriquet. Being a foreigner is sufficient to allow expulsion measures to be taken. As Lord Slynn put the issue in *Rehman*:[11]

Here the liberty of the person and the practice of his family to remain in this country is at stake and when specific acts which have already occurred are relied on, fairness requires that they should be proved to the civil standard of proof. But this is not the whole exercise. The Secretary of State, in deciding whether it is conducive to the public good that a person should be deported, is entitled to have regard to all the information in his possession about the actual and potential activities and the connections of the person concerned. He is entitled to have regard to the precautionary and preventive principles rather than to wait until directly harmful activities have taken place, the individual in the meantime remaining in this country. In doing so he is not merely finding facts but forming an executive judgement or assessment. There must be material on which proportionately and reasonably he can conclude that there is a real possibility of activities harmful to national security but he does not have to be satisfied, nor on appeal to show, that all the material before him is proved, and his conclusion is justified, to a 'high civil degree of probability'.

The logic at work is that of borders. This is so in two senses, first borders as a protection: once someone is put on the other side of a border, the state or collectivity is safer; secondly, borders are the dividing line of legal orders. Only those fully within the legal order, i.e. citizens, can enjoy the benefits of the legal order for which the border forms the outer limit. Even a 'high civil standard of probability' is rejected in favour of an ordinary civil standard of proof. The safety of borders around legal orders is for those who cannot be expelled. The civil liberties protections of citizens may be diminished where the allegation of terrorism is added to a charge of a criminal offence, but the standard of proof is not similarly diminished. The underlying framework of criminal law provides a resistant structure against which the terrorism label operates. The integrity of borders is also in their effectiveness at providing separation. By placing an individual on the other side of a border, it is not necessarily self-evident that a state or community's security is increased. This is not a lesson which can be learned from the 11 September 2001 terrorist attacks in the USA.

The difference in the level of legal protection of the status of a foreigner as opposed to a national where alleged to be engaging in acts likely to compromise national security is found not least in the standard of proof which the state must satisfy. As Lord Hoffmann points out in *Rehman*, the civil standard of proof

---

[11] *Rehman*, n. 4 above, para. 22.

always means more likely than not: 'the only higher degree of probability required by the law is the criminal standard'.[12] Of course foreigners may be subject to criminal charges involving questions of terrorism, in which case the standard of proof is the same for them and for nationals of the state. In the light of the decision of the first instance court in *Rehman* on the facts, it is evident that the state would have had grave difficulties seeking to satisfy the higher criminal standard of proof even if appropriate charges could have been found for a criminal prosecution of Rehman. The preference for relying on the logic of borders and exclusion lies not least in the dis-application of the civil liberties protections which would otherwise apply.

The UK has some experience with the issue of the borders of the legal order and national security as regards foreigners. In 1996 the ECtHR handed down a judgment against the UK as regards the proposed expulsion of Chahal, an Indian national, to his country of origin on national security grounds.[13] Chahal, who was resident in the UK had sought political asylum in the UK on the ground that if he were returned to India, as a suspect of Kashmiri terrorism, he would be subjected to torture. The Secretary of State rejected his claim and sought to deport him on the basis that this would be conducive to the public good on national security grounds. In domestic law, no appeal, except in an advisory procedure, was permitted against a decision of deportation based on national security.

The ECtHR held that the prohibition on torture contained in Article 3 ECHR was absolute, and in no case could a signatory state return an individual to a country where there was a serious risk that he or she would suffer torture. This absolute prohibition applies when a question of national security is raised. Secondly, as regards the effectiveness of the remedy of an advisory procedure, Lord Slynn pointed out in *Rehman* that:[14]

This [advisory procedure] however, was held by the European Court of Human Rights [...] not to provide an effective remedy within Article 13 of the [ECHR]. Accordingly, the [Special Immigration Appeals] Commission was set up by the 1997 Act and by subsection 2(1)(c) a person was given a right of appeal to the Commission . . .

Lord Hoffmann, commenting on the *Chahal* judgment, noted that the ECtHR had also held that:[15]

If [an individual] was detained pending deportation, he was entitled under article 5(4) [ECHR] to the determination of an independent tribunal as to whether his detention was lawful. The European Court rejected the United Kingdom Government's argument that considerations of national security or international relations made it impossible to accord such a right of appeal. The court . . . commended the procedure established by the Canadian Immigration Act 1976, under which the confidentiality of secret sources could be maintained by disclosing it only to a special security-cleared advocate appointed to represent the deportee who could cross examine witnesses in the absence of the appellant.

---

[12] *Ibid.*, para. 55.   [13] (1996) 23 EHRR 413.   [14] *Rehman*, n. 4 above, para. 9.
[15] *Ibid.*, para. 36.

Such a system was established by the Special Immigration Appeals Commission Act 1997. Rehman appealed to the Special Immigration Appeals Commission against the Secretary of State's intention to deport him on grounds of national security in accordance with the legislation introduced following the ECtHR's decision in *Chahal*. The Commission reviewed the evidence and information provided to it in accordance with its procedural rules (which do not permit sensitive information to be made available to the appellant). It held:[16]

1. Recruitment. We are not satisfied that the appellant has been shown to have recruited British Muslims to undergo militant training as alleged.
2. We are not satisfied that the appellant has been shown to have engaged in fund-raising for the [terrorist organization] as alleged;
3. We are not satisfied that the appellant has been shown to have knowingly sponsored individuals for militant training camps as alleged;
4. We are not satisfied that the evidence demonstrates the existence in the United Kingdom of returnees, originally recruited by the appellant, who during the course of that training overseas have been indoctrinated with extremist beliefs or given weapons training, and who as a result allow them to create a threat to the United Kingdom's national security in the future.

The importance of rights of appeal to a judicial body is evident here. The balancing of security interests between the state and the individual in this most sensitive of areas must be reviewed externally and independently. The assessment by the state of the requirements of national security is not necessarily shared by judicial bodies. In *Rehman* for the first time the issue of the content of national security was addressed. The government argued that the definition of national security and what could constitute a threat to it were matters for the Home Secretary to decide.[17] The Commission rejected this argument, holding that the definition was a question of law which it had jurisdiction to decide. This point was one of the key legal questions on which the state appealed the Commission's decision.

What then is national security? Before determining how it can be protected, its contours must be understood. There is no statutory definition of national security. But, being a danger to national security is a ground for deportation. In *Rehman* counsel for the applicant argued that national security must be understood within the meaning of the job with which the security services have been charged under the Security Services Act 1989. The logic here is that the duties of the security services to protect national security must be coterminous with the state's power to take measures on grounds of national security. The Security Services Act 1989, section 1(2), states that the duties are 'the protection of national security and in particular, its protection against threats from espionage, terrorism and sabotage, from the activities of agents of foreign powers and from actions intended to overthrow or undermine parliamentary democracy by political, industrial or violent means'.[18]

---

[16] *Rehman*, n. 4 above, para. 4.   [17] *Ibid.*, para. 3.   [18] *Ibid.*, para. 14.

While not expressly rejected, this argument was left unanswered. Instead Lord Hoffmann stated 'there is no difficulty about what "national security" means. It is security of the United Kingdom and its people'.[19] Here the fundamental question of interest is posed, albeit never addressed in the judgment: who are the UK's people? When and to what extent can Rehman become or be one of the UK's people? The people are those who are entitled to the protection of the borders including as defined by the legal order. Chahal was deprived of the protection of the legal order in that an allegation of national security risk against him did not give rise even to the rudimentary elements of judicial control of administrative action. This exclusion was held incompatible, *inter alia*, with Article 13 ECHR.

European human rights norms required a transformation by the UK of the concept of 'its people'. The UK was not entitled to exclude entirely from judicial scrutiny, on grounds of national security, a class of persons on the basis of their nationality. The inclusion of even a limited form of judicial scrutiny though the Commission results in a substantially different appreciation of who 'its people' are. The assessment of national security includes, albeit at a limited level, Rehman and his interest in security of residence. He has slipped inside the border of the UK legal order. In the words of Lord Slynn,[20] 'it seems to me that the appellant is entitled to say that "the interests of national security" cannot be used to justify any reason the Secretary of State has for wishing to deport an individual from the United Kingdom'. Rehman has arrived at the edges of the 'UK's people'. Lord Hoffmann went on to state that:[21]

On the other hand, the question of whether something is 'in the interests' of national security is not a question of law. It is a matter of judgment and policy. Under the constitution of the United Kingdom and most other countries, decisions as to whether something is or is not in the interests of national security are not a matter for judicial decision. They are entrusted to the executive.

However, Lord Slynn seems to accept more readily that Rehman is somewhere within the legal borders:[22] 'there must be some possibility of risk or danger to the security or well being of the nation which the Secretary of State considers makes it desirable for the public good that the individual should be deported'.

The next question then is how direct or indirect the threat must be. The Commission adopted a narrow approach to this question:[23]

A person may be said to offend against national security if he engages in, promotes, or encourages violent activity which is targeted at the United Kingdom, its system of government or its people. This includes activities directed against the overthrow or destabilisation of a foreign government if that foreign government is likely to take reprisals against the United Kingdom which affect the security of the United Kingdom or of its nationals. National security extends also to situations where United Kingdom citizens are targeted, wherever they may be.

---

[19] *Ibid.*, para. 50.   [20] *Ibid.*, para. 15.   [21] *Ibid.*, para. 50.   [22] *Ibid.*, para. 15.
[23] *Ibid.*, para. 2.

Here the borders are clearly those of citizenship. The security of Rehman or other integrated foreigners in the UK is not the subject of national security except as a by-product of the more general security of the UK. Abroad, the UK's national security is engaged if British citizens are targeted, though there is no responsibility for integrated foreigners. The assumption is that they remain the responsibility of their state of nationality. The issue of the narrow or wider conception of the risk to national security formed the subject of substantial discussion in the House of Lords' judgment. In the words of Lord Slynn:[24]

> It seems to me that, in contemporary world conditions, action against a foreign state may be capable indirectly of affecting the security of the United Kingdom. The means open to terrorists both in attacking another state and attacking international or global activity by the community of nations, whatever the objectives of the terrorist, may well be capable of reflecting on the safety and well-being of the United Kingdom or its citizens . . . I accept that there must be a real possibility of an adverse effect on the United Kingdom for what is done by the individual under inquiry but I do not accept that it has to be direct or immediate. Whether there is such a real possibility is a matter which has to be weighed up by the Secretary of State and balanced against the possible injustice to that individual if a deportation order is made.

The balance between the state and the individual, where the interests of national security and security of residence conflict, has now been established as a real possibility of an adverse effect on the state. This test much be satisfied even though there is some margin for appreciation of what constitutes an adverse effect in a foreign state. Rehman's interest in security of residence cannot be extinguished at a level lower than a real possibility of an adverse effect even though he is not or perhaps not yet directly an intended subject of the protection of national security. However, the borders within which the security interest may be assessed have been enlarged beyond those of the UK. They now encompass indirect threats, attacks on other states, or the international or global activity of the community of nations.

Two of the judges (Lords Steyn and Hoffmann) in *Rehman* made specific reference to the attacks in the USA of 11 September 2001.[25] Both stated that although they had reached their decisions before the events, those attacks confirmed their opinions. In both cases they indicate that the judiciary must respect the decision of the government regarding the evaluation of threats to national security. Lord Slynn's measured approach to the balance of interests and the role of the judiciary in achieving that balance does not refer to terrorist threats or acts outside the allegations relevant to the case itself.

2. THE UK GOVERNMENT, TERRORISM, AND SECURITAS

Four days after the House of Lords judgment in *Rehman*, the Home Secretary outlined the contents of a legislative package to combat terrorism.[26] According

---

[24] *Rehman*, n. 4 above, para. 17.   [25] *Ibid.*, paras. 29 and 62.
[26] Home Office, *News Release*, 15 October 2001: 'Blunkett outlines further anti-terrorism measures'.

to the press release, the Bill would include robust and streamlined procedures for dealing with those suspected of terrorist acts 'who seek to misuse our asylum and immigration systems'. In this Bill, Securitas is indeed the punitive enforcer: security against the interest of civil liberties. In respect of the measures proposed in the Bill and adopted in the Act against all persons on the territory, a number of non-governmental organizations, notably Justice and Liberty, prepared detailed analyses. Here I will look at only one specific aspect of the measures: that relating to foreigners which is relevant to the increasing division of rights between foreigners and own nationals.

The immigration-related measures in the Bill include removing access to judicial review regarding decisions made by the Special Immigration Appeals Commission. The case of Rehman did not come before the House of Lords on an application for judicial review of the Commission's decision. Rather it arrived there on appeal first to the Court of Appeal on the points of law discussed above, then from there with leave to the House of Lords. Judicial review is the mechanism whereby a decision of the Commission can be attacked as procedurally unsound. It is the watchdog system within the court structure for ensuring the integrity of the judicial decision-making process. It appears that there are too many controls ensuring legality of the decision-making process for the Home Secretary's liking.

Additionally, the Home Secretary announced that his Bill would allow him to detain those who are a terrorist threat but who cannot be removed from the country, whilst retaining a right of appeal. He noted that this would require a limited suspension from Article 5 ECHR, the right to liberty of the person, and based this on Article 15, which allows for suspension in the event of a public emergency. No doubt it will be for the ECtHR at some time in the future to determine whether the UK's use of the Article 15 suspension is lawful in light of a public emergency. The fact that no other Council of Europe state considered the events in the USA and the declaration of war on terrorism sufficiently serious to constitute a public emergency for it in accordance with Article 15 is likely to weigh against the validity of the UK's suspension.

The provision introduced in the Anti-terrorism, Crime and Security Bill (now Act) is that a suspected international terrorist (as defined) may be detained indefinitely even though his or her removal or departure from the UK is prevented wholly or partly by international obligations, for example because of the absolute ban on the return of persons to a country where there is a real risk that they will suffer torture contrary to Article 3 ECHR, or because of practical considerations.[27] The Bill did provide for bail and an appeal to the Commission against designation as a suspected international terrorist. The provisions of this part of the Bill clearly related only to foreigners. Further they were adopted with only minor amendment by Parliament. The consequences for the balance of interests between the individual as regards security of residence and the state

[27] Para. 23, Anti-terrorism, Crime and Security Bill 2001.

as regards national security are substantial. Perhaps the most surprising aspect is the government's perceived need to have a power to detain foreigners indefinitely irrespective of the strength of their residence claims. Such a power is inimical in respect of own nationals.

There is a high cost to seeking to achieve such a power in respect of foreigners. The UK has exposed itself to the risk of substantial international ridicule by other Council of Europe states, which include all the EU Member States, over the assessment of a public emergency. It has weakened its credibility as an upholder of human rights norms by suspending one of the key provisions of the ECHR. It is not entirely clear what the added benefit of these powers will be in the short term in relation to the longer term damage which will follow to the reputation of the UK.

3. SECURITAS AND THE EUROPEAN COURT OF HUMAN RIGHTS

A month and a half after the *Rehman* judgment was handed down and a month after the UK had introduced a new Bill on anti-terrorism measures, the ECtHR gave judgment in the case of *Al-Adsani* v. *UK*.[28] The applicant presents the two faces of belonging and exclusion: Al-Adsani is a dual British/Kuwaiti national. As a foreigner who has been accepted as coming within the strict definition of beneficiaries of national security he was a British citizen. Al-Adsani sought redress for torture which he had suffered at the hands of the Kuwaiti authorities. The facts as presented and accepted by the ECtHR were as follows:[29]

The applicant, who trained as a pilot, went to Kuwait in 1991 to assist in its defence against Iraq. During the Gulf War he served as a member of the Kuwaiti Air Force and, after the Iraqi invasion, he remained behind as a member of the resistance movement. During the period he came into possession of sexual video tapes involving Sheikh Jaber Al-Sabah Al-Saud Al-Sabah . . . who is related to the Emir of Kuwait and is said to have an influential position in Kuwait. By some means these tapes entered general circulation, for which the applicant was held responsible by the Sheikh. After the Iraqi forces were expelled from Kuwait, on or about 2 May 1991, the Sheikh and two others gained entry to the applicant's house, beat him and took him at gun point in a government jeep to the Kuwaiti State Security Prison. The applicant was falsely imprisoned there for several days during which he was repeatedly beaten by security guards. He was released on 5 May 1991, having been forced to sign a false confession. On or about 7 May 1991 the Sheikh took the applicant at gun point in a government car to the palace of the Emir of Kuwait's brother. At first the applicant's head was repeatedly held underwater in a swimming pool containing corpses, and he was then dragged into a small room where the Sheikh set fire to mattresses soaked in petrol, as a result of which the applicant was seriously burnt. Initially the applicant was treated in a Kuwaiti hospital and on 17 May 1991 he returned to England where he spent six weeks in hospital being treated for burns covering 25% of his total body surface area. He also suffered psychological damage and has been

---

[28] App. No. 35763/97, judgment of 21 November 2001.   [29] *Ibid.*, paras. 9–13.

diagnosed as suffering from a severe form of post-traumatic stress disorder, aggravated by the fact that, once in England, he received threats warning him not to take action or give publicity to his plight.

As a British citizen, Al-Adsani is within the group of persons for whose protection national security measures are designed. These include measures to protect his security both within the UK and also wherever else in the world he may find himself according to the *Rehman* principles. Among the most precious of the securities for the individual is the right to legal security. As is apparent from the *Rehman* case, individuals who are excluded by their personal status from the full protection of inclusion for legal purposes too easily become the objects rather than the subjects of national security. In *Al-Adsani* a different assessment of national security raises questions about the reality of the legal protection for the individual, even when a national, when that protection is perceived as unwelcome for foreign states. The UK's national security is to protect its nationals in general, but not necessarily in particular. Thus the interests of state immunity of foreign states may benefit national security in general by denying the individual legal security in the particular.

Al-Adsani began legal proceedings in the UK for compensation against the Sheikh, in respect of whom he obtained a default judgment, two other named individuals, and the Kuwaiti Government. He was refused leave to serve his writ on the Kuwaiti Government, against which decision he appealed. The Court of Appeal granted him leave to serve his writ on the Kuwaiti Government on the grounds of three elements pointing to state involvement: (1) he had been taken to a state prison; (2) government transport had been used on two occasions; and (3) he had been mistreated in prison by government officials. Thus the court held that the Government of Kuwait should not be entitled to immunity under the State Immunity Act 1978, section 1(1), in respect of the acts of torture. However, when the writ was served on the Kuwaiti Government it immediately went back to court and sought to have the proceeding struck out on the basis of state immunity for acts carried out outside the jurisdiction.[30] It succeeded. The Court of Appeal rejected the argument that the prohibition on torture has become so fundamental in international law as to be *jus cogens*, and thus compels the overriding of other principles of international law which conflict with it. Stuart-Smith LJ justified this finding on the ground that if foreigners were allowed to sue in the UK courts for damages relating to torture suffered abroad at the hands of states, then refugees would be able to do so, and the UK courts would find themselves in a difficult position of determining facts which took place abroad. The House of Lords declined to give leave to appeal. Al-Adsani brought a complaint to the ECtHR.

The substance of the complaint to the Strasbourg Court was twofold. First, Article 3 ECHR, the prohibition on torture, entails positive obligations on the

---

[30] The Kuwaiti Government also convinced the court that the applicant had not established on a balance of probabilities that the Kuwaiti Government was responsible for the threats made in the UK.

contracting parties, not only to refrain from engaging in torture or from returning a person to a country where there is a real likelihood that he or she will suffer torture,[31] but also to assist one of its citizens in obtaining an effective remedy for torture against another state. The ECtHR considered its jurisprudence on the positive obligations deriving from Article 3, setting out the cases and its findings. It held unanimously that Article 3 does not go so far as to require a Contracting State to provide for an effective remedy against torture which took place outside its jurisdiction.

Secondly, Al-Adsani argued that there had been a breach of his procedural remedies guaranteed under Article 6(1) ECHR, as he had been denied access to court in determination of his claim against the Government of Kuwait. This claim was also rejected by nine votes to eight, the minority judges providing a particularly important dissenting opinion. The development of the argument is key to understanding the meaning of security, and in particular legal security, in Europe. As Ward LJ in the Court of Appeal noted,[32] 'there may be no international forum (other than the forum of the *locus delicti* to whom a victim of torture will be understandably reluctant to turn) where this terrible, if established, wrong can receive civil redress'. The UK government argued that Article 6(1) was not relevant as it could not oust the internationally recognized principle of state immunity. This claim was rejected by the ECtHR:[33]

It would not be consistent with the rule of law in a democratic society or with the basic principle underlying Article 6(1)—namely, that civil claims must be capable of being submitted to a judge for adjudication—if for example a State could, without restraint or control by the Convention enforcement bodies, remove from the jurisdiction of the courts a whole range of civil claims or confer immunities from civil liability on large groups or categories of persons . . .

The ECtHR did not accept the principle that state immunity has the effect of extinguishing a substantive right. Rather, it is only a procedural bar to the national court's power to determine the right.

Thus the ECtHR arrived at the final two questions: was the restriction imposed on the applicant's right of access to court in pursuit of a legitimate aim and was it proportionate. On the first part of the issue, the legitimacy of the aim, the ECtHR had no difficulty in finding this to be the case in the interests of promoting comity and good relations between states through the respect of another state's sovereignty.[34] However, the Court had more difficulty with the issue of proportionality. Here the central issue was whether the prohibition on torture has acquired the status of *jus cogens*, in other words a norm of international law which takes precedence over treaty law and other rules of international law.

Two legal developments in particular point in this direction: the judgments of the International Criminal Tribunal for the Former Yugoslavia, commencing

---

[31] *Soering* v. *UK*, (1989) 11 EHRR 439 at [86].   [32] *Vilvarajah* v. *UK* (1992) 14 EHRR 248.
[33] *Al-Adsani*, n. 28 above, para. 47.   [34] *Ibid.*, para. 4.

with *Furundzija*,[35] where the Tribunal first developed the argument that 'because of the importance of the values it protects, this principle [proscribing torture] has evolved into a peremptory norm or *jus cogens*, that is, a norm that enjoys a higher rank in the international hierarchy than treaty law and even "ordinary" customary rules'. Secondly, the ECtHR had regard to the House of Lords' assessment of state immunity in the *Pinochet (No 3)*[36] case on the limits of immunity in respect of gross human rights violations by state officials: 'the majority of the House of Lords held that, after the Torture Convention and even before, the international prohibition against official torture had the character of *jus cogens* or a peremptory norm and that no immunity was enjoyed by a torturer from one Torture Convention State from the criminal jurisdiction of another'.[37] The ECtHR found that while there was increasing evidence that the prohibition of torture was *jus cogens*, this applied as regards criminal jurisdiction only, not civil claims for damages for alleged torture committed outside the forum state. Thus by nine votes to eight the ECtHR held that there had been no violation of Article 6(1).

Attached to the judgment are two particularly important opinions, one concurring, the other dissenting. Starting with the concurring opinion, judges Pellonpää and Bratza made an impassioned plea to the Court not to interfere with the principle of state immunity from civil actions for torture. The arguments put forward are practical: the 'chilling effect' on the readiness of Contracting States to accept refugees if they were allowed to use the host state's legal system to seek compensation for torture abroad; the difficulties of enforcement; and the possibility of a further erosion of state immunity as regards public property, relying substantially on US judicial experience. They also argued from the expediencies of diplomacy: international co-operation, including co-operation with a view to eradicating the vice of torture, presupposes the continuing existence of certain elements of a basic framework for the conduct of international relations. The conclusion contained a particularly strong warning to the Court:[38]

I started this opinion by quoting Lord Justice Stuart-Smith. I end it by quoting another eminent jurist, Sir Robert Jennings, who some years ago expressed concern about 'the tendency of particular tribunals to regard themselves as different, as separate little empires which must as far as possible be augmented'. I believe that in this case the Court has avoided the kind of development of which Sir Robert warned.

The dissenting opinion is supported by six judges (followed by a further two dissenting opinions). Their position is diametrically opposed to that of Pellonpää and Bratza. Rather than focusing on what may be the practical consequences in political terms of a finding that the prohibition on torture has

---

[35] Case No IT-95-17/I-T, 10 December 1998, (1999) 38 ILM 317.
[36] *R v. Bow Street Metropolitan Magistrate and Others, ex p. Pinochet Ugarte (No 3)* [2000] AC 147.
[37] *Al-Adsani*, n. 28 above, para. 65.
[38] *Ibid*. Concurring Opinion of Judges Pellonpää and Bratza (unnumbered para.).

become *jus cogens*, they analyse the legal consequences of the failure to apply the reasoning of *jus cogens* to both criminal and civil jurisdictions:[39]

The acceptance therefore of the *jus cogens* nature of the prohibition of torture entails that a State allegedly violating it cannot invoke hierarchically lower rules (in this case, those on State immunity) to avoid the consequences of the illegality of its actions. In the circumstances of this case, Kuwait cannot validly hide behind the rules on State immunity to avoid proceedings for a serious claim of torture made before a foreign jurisdiction, and the courts of the jurisdiction (the United Kingdom) cannot accept a plea of immunity, or to invoke it *ex officio*, to refuse an applicant adjudication of a torture case.

They also criticize the distinction between criminal and civil proceedings as regards the operation of the prohibition on torture:[40]

It is not the nature of the proceedings which determines the effects that a *jus cogens* rule has upon another rule of international law, but the character of the rule as a peremptory norm and its interaction with a hierarchically lower rule.

The face of Securitas which this judgment illuminates is that of state security which protects both itself and other states against claims by individuals. Even in the face of the most widely accepted human rights prohibition, that against torture, state security is permitted to protect officials from the consequences of their acts. State immunity as a form of state security gives legitimacy to the containment of legal orders within borders. The movement of individuals threatens to disrupt that order by seeking redress in respect of international human rights violations in jurisdictions outside that in which the breach occurred. The failure of the legal system of a state to provide redress fuels the attempt to seek a remedy by the movement of the individual to another jurisdiction.

As Stuart-Smith LJ, notes, a threat to the legal system comes from refugees.[41] It is persons with rights to protection against persecution who personify the threat to legal security. Their right to protection in the territory of a foreign state raises the question of their right to legal redress for human rights violations which they are unable to pursue in the country in which the abuses occurred. To permit such redress transforms the nature of legal orders and their inter-relation to the detriment of state security in the form of immunity. However, the failure to do so also carried costs as indicated in the dissenting opinion of the ECtHR. Consistency and coherence are fundamental elements of the legitimacy of judicial decisions. Where individual rights acquire the character of higher principles of international law, this can only occur with the active and voluntary participation of the international community. The ECtHR has accepted that the prohibition on torture has become such a higher principle. The consequence, in particular in relation to immigrants and refugees is the need to find a new balance between state security and the right of the individual

---

[39] *Al-Adsani*, n. 28 above, para. 65. Concurring Opinion of Judges Pellonpää and Bratza (unnumbered paras.).   [40] *Ibid.*

[41] *Al-Adsani v. Government of Kuwait & ors*, 12 March 1996 (CA), 12.

to redress against state torture. It is neither sufficient nor coherent to refuse to acknowledge the consequences of this development of international law. That those consequences demand a reconfiguration of the borders of legal orders must be accepted as a challenge which needs to be met, not an evil to be hidden and denied.

4. CONCLUSION

Securitas takes many forms in seeking to maintain the power of the state. 'National security', 'general interest', and 'police powers' are some of its modern manifestations. There must be control over these forms first by parliaments, and then by the courts. Securitas depends on the triptych of identities, orders, and borders[42] for its rationale. The borders define and are defined by the identity of the people within, the legal orders are circumscribed by the borders, and the borders limit the extent of the legal orders. In a world where borders are becoming increasingly fragmented in the way in which they apply to different categories of objects and persons moving across them, Securitas is also in transformation to adjust to a different understanding of the three.

In the *Rehman* case, the border of the legal order is tentatively reaching out to encompass the foreigner, the person outside the national identity but nonetheless gradually acknowledged as entitled to a claim to security. At the same time, the border of the security interest has widened. It is no longer contained in the border of sovereignty but can include indirect threats, threats to international or global activity by the community of nations. The attempt at closure of the security borders to protect the state against threats as reflected in the Anti-terrorism, Crime and Security Bill, can be achieved, if at all, only at a high cost in terms of international credibility.

In *Al-Adsani* the consequences for Securitas of the redefinition of borders has begun to be played out. The enlargement of the duty of legal orders to admit victims of torture carries with it responsibilities in respect of the acknowledgement of the legal nature of state torture. The legal logic leads only in one direction, the enlargement of the borders of legal orders to accept actions for remedies. The pragmatic arguments about flooding of judicial systems by refugees' claims, the threat to security of international relations, and the practicalities of enforcement counter this movement, but none of them deals with the legal logic.

The nature of Securitas is changing from one circumscribed by identities, borders, and orders into one which encompasses the security interests of the international community, but which is then challenged by the universality of human rights duties.

---

[42] A. Mathias, D. Jacobson, and Y. Lapid (eds.), *Identities, Borders and Orders* (University of Minnesota Press, Minneapolis, Minn., 2001).

PART II

EU LAW

9

Legitimacy, Legitimation, and the European Union: What Crisis?

RODNEY BARKER

1. ALLEGED CRISES

To begin by asking 'crisis? What crisis?' may suggest parallels with the deliberate blindness of Admiral Nelson at the Battle of Copenhagen. So if precise allusions were required, 'The Emperor's New Crisis' might be a more apt title, since I wish to query the existence of an alleged crisis, not ignore a real one. But the second allusion is in fact no better, since it suggests both the absence of any problem and the presence of charlatans, and I wish to suggest neither of those two things. But I do wish to query some of the assumptions which underlie or are implied in much contemporary work on the European Union, and in particular the work which employs the terms 'legitimacy', 'legitimate', and 'legitimation'. A great deal has been written about a legitimacy deficit or legitimacy crisis in the European Union. The body of literature is large, and growing larger, and spans both law and political science.[1] It is not my intention either to add to that

---

[1] A brief but representative selection includes: H. Abromeit, *Democracy in Europe: Legitimising Politics in a Non-State Polity* (Berghahn Books, Oxford, 1998); D. Beetham and C. Lord, *Legitimacy and the European Union* (Longman, London, 1998); J. Blondel, R. Sinnott, and P. Svensson, *People and Parliament in the European Union: Participation, Democracy, and Legitimacy* (Clarendon Press, Oxford, 1998); V. Bufacchi, 'Is European Integration Politically Legitimate?' (1994) 19 *History of European Ideas* 229; G. de Búrca, 'The Quest for Legitimacy in the European Union' (1996) 59 *MLR* 349; C. Carter and A. Scott, 'Legitimacy and Governance Beyond the European Nation State: Conceptualising Governance in the European Union' (1998) 4 *ELJ* 429; D. Chryssochoou, *Democracy in the European Union* (Tauris Academic Studies, London, 1998); B. Einhorn, M. Kaldor, and Z. Kavan (eds.), *Citizenship and Democratic Control in Contemporary Europe* (Edward Elgar, Cheltenham, 1996); J. Gibson and G. Caldeira, 'Changes in the Legitimacy of the European Court of Justice: A Post-Maastricht Analysis' (1998) 28 *British Journal of Political Science* 63; N. Græger, *European Integration and the Legitimation of Supranational Power: Dilemmas, Strategies and New Challenges* (Department of Political Science, Oslo, 1994); S. Hix, 'Executive Selection in the European Union: Does the Commission President Investiture Procedure Reduce the Democratic Deficit?', *European integration on-line papers* (Austria, www.lse.ac.uk/cgi-bin/goto.pl?http://eiop.or.at/eiop/texte/1997–021a.htm, European Community Studies Association, 1 1997); M. Jachtenfuchs, 'Theoretical Perspectives on European Governance' (1995) 1 *ELJ* 115; B. Laffan, 'The Politics of Identity and Political Order in Europe' (1996) 34 *JCMS* 81; J. Mather, 'The Sources of European Union Legitimacy: Political Theories Old and New' (1999) 5 *Contemporary Politics* 277; H. Schmitt and J. Thomassen, *Political Representation and Legitimacy in the European Union* (Oxford University Press, Oxford, 1999); P. Schmitter, *How to Democratize*

literature or to conduct a critical review of it. My purpose here is different. It is to raise, in the most broad and preliminary way, questions about the assumptions on which this literature is grounded, and to suggest another narrative which, without replacing the standard one, may if developed add a further dimension to the understanding of European politics and government. I have therefore drawn on existing literature not in order to conduct a systematic survey, nor to add to the discussion in which it is engaged, but for the purpose of illustration, and tentatively to suggest a complementary narrative. There will therefore be many instances of academic work on the European Union to which I have not referred, and the omission of such reference should not be taken as any kind of judgment on the quality of the omitted work, but as evidence of a different focus and a different narrative. The underlying assumptions of the dominant arguments can be teased out by asking two distinct questions.

First, what understanding or use of 'legitimacy', 'legitimate', and 'legitimation' informs the various accounts of European politics at the close of the twentieth and the beginning of the twenty-first century? (I have used quotation marks to suggest that the three terms identify conceptions of the observer, rather than, necessarily, empirical or historical realities. But to do so for the rest of the chapter would be over fussy, and the words appear hereafter unadorned.) Secondly, what actual historical events, what observable human actions, are being described when 'crises' or 'deficits' are spoken of? When these two questions are pursued, and the answers to the two questions considered together, it will appear that there is within current discussion a strong deductive strand, which is informed both by its normative foundations and its methodological realism. For the answer to the first question is that the terms are normative with built-in empirical expectations, and to the second that the events and actions are expected or hypothesized, rather than observed.

The taken-for-granted starting point of much of the work on legitimacy, legitimation, and the European Union is normative first and empirical or historical only second.[2] That is neither avoidable nor reprehensible. But the unavoidable and desirable normative dimension of any academic enquiry can mask, divert,

---

the European Union . . . and Why Bother? (Rowman and Littlefield, Oxford, 2000); M. Shackleton, The Internal Legitimacy Crisis of the European Union (University of Edinburgh Europa Institute, Occasional Paper 1, Edinburgh, 1994); H. Wallace, 'Deepening and Widening: Problems of Legitimacy for the EC', in S. Garcia (ed.), European Identity and the Search for Legitimacy (Pinter, London, 1993), Chap. 6; A. Weale and M. Nentwich (eds.), Political Theory and the European Union: Legitimacy, Constitutional Choice and Citizenship (Routledge/ECPR, London, 1998); J. Weiler, 'After Maastricht: Community Legitimacy in Post-1992 Europe', in W. Adams (ed.), Singular Europe: Economy and Polity of the European Community after 1992 (University of Michigan Press, Ann Arbor, Mich., 1992), 11–41.

[2] Shore has commented on this aspect of most work on European government: 'Conflating the normative with the empirical—how things ought to be with how they are—is typical both of the way the EU represents itself and of the way it is represented in many textbooks in the burgeoning field of European integration studies': C. Shore, Building Europe: The Cultural Politics of European Integration (Routledge, London, 2000), 126.

or distort discussion if it is not clearly articulated and considered, and both its positive and negative contribution to enquiry taken into account. If a rough articulation of the assumptions shaping the prevailing argument is attempted, it would be somewhat as follows: the EU is a form of government; the governed are the individual citizens of the nations which make up the EU; government both does and should rest on the active consent of the governed; when it does, it can be described, both normatively and actually, as legitimate; and that when it does not it must be suffering, again both normatively and actually, from a deficit; this deficit is both normatively unacceptable and practically disabling or at least encumbering.[3] There is thus an empirical expectation arising from a normative preference. Government, even if it is not conducted by a sovereign nation state, ought to be overtly authorized by public consent. The empirical/ historical claim flows from this. To be so authorized government, and the EU as a form of government, must fulfil certain criteria which those subject to it can be expected to recognize: consent, or efficiency, or correspondence with the values and character of those subject to it. The fulfilment of these criteria can be judged by academic or other observers independently of any statements or actions of subjects. But if that judgment is unfavourable, historical empirical consequences, arising from the perception of subjects, are assumed to follow, even if there is a delay between the judgment of the academic observer and the judgment of the ordinary subject or citizen.

There are two weaknesses in the standard account as thus described. First, the argument is deductive rather than empirical or historical, and the account of the EU is therefore in terms of its distance from a normatively derived model, rather than in terms of its own actual character. The analysis frequently begins with what a government is expected to be, rather than what the EU actually is or does, and with what individual men and women in Europe are presumed to do or not do, or be about to do or not do, rather than what they can actually be observed to be doing or not doing. Such comparison can of course be illuminating, so long as it is recognized as a means of generating understanding by contrast, and not an assessment of a departure from, or failure to reach, a 'natural' form or manner of organization and activity. In so far as it is the latter, it is an instance of a regular feature of enquiry, which casts more light on the thinking of the enquirer than on the nature of the object of enquiry. Questions such as 'why is there no socialism in the United States?', or 'why was there no working class revolution in Britain?' suggest the response 'why do you expect that there would be?'. They can evoke illuminating answers, and may be instances of a fruitful use of counterfactuals. But they can also mislead.

Secondly, by detaching 'legitimacy' from events and practices, much current work on the EU detaches the concept from actual governing relationships.

---

[3] So Weale and Nentwich write that 'The basic principles of political legitimacy in the modern world are democratic in character; the democratic deficit of the EU thus calls into question its political legitimacy': Weale and Nentwich, 'Introduction', in Weale and Nentwich (eds.), n. 1 above, 3.

Legitimacy is a concept which can usefully be applied to rule or challenges to rule. It cannot so usefully be applied to circumstances where rule is absent, hypothetical, or so indirect as to be invisible to the ruled. Whilst the EU may govern, it does not follow that it has subjects in the way that a state has. And yet talk of a 'legitimacy deficit' describes just such a governing relationship or, rather, it decries its absence. It is reasonable to ask whether one can have a deficit or erosion of something which was never there in the first place? The legitimacy crisis of the Stuarts in the twenty-first century is not a realistic phenomenon. But is the legitimacy crisis of the EU significantly different? Whatever the talk of a crisis, the alleged deficit is an absence of something which is desired, but has never yet existed. A crisis is a challenge to an existing constitution, whereas the main weight of the standard argument is not that an achieved or established order is under threat, is in crisis, but that it has not yet been established. That is indeed technically a deficit, but so is the absence of fairies at the bottom of the garden.

That does not mean that useful and important questions cannot be asked about legitimation in Europe and in the European Union. On the contrary, there are questions that could with profit be asked which, on the whole, are not being asked. There are features of government and politics within the European Union which deserve greater attention, which can be illuminated by the concept of legitimation, but which are left out of the account given by standard narratives and by their normative presuppositions. I shall briefly suggest what these are after a short consideration of the current state of work on the EU, and of legitimation, legitimacy, and the EU.

2. WHAT IS LEGITIMACY IN THE 'CRISIS' OR 'DEFICIT' LITERATURE?

The 'common sense' status of the standard argument's normative foundations conceals the fact that not all the commentators are talking about the same thing. So ubiquitous has talk of a legitimacy crisis or democratic deficit become that it is frequently forgotten that 'legitimacy' is a metaphor, not a real phenomenon out there. And as a metaphor, it has no incontestable objective meaning, only the various uses which are made of it. So a great deal of time can be wasted on arguing about what legitimacy 'really is' when often all that is happening is that different, and potentially complementary, narratives of politics and government are being presented.

Existing accounts, and their underlying assumptions, are not as simple or incontestable as they at first seem. And although both 'crisis' and 'deficit' are used to describe the current state of European politics and government, in most cases what is being described is a deficit, in the sense of the absence or minimal presence, of something, rather than a crisis, in the sense of a traumatic moment or turning point in an established condition. The interchangeability of 'crisis' and 'deficit' is indicative of important underlying, and insufficiently articulated, assumptions in the literature: that a necessary element for stability or order is absent, and that the consequences are or must be about to become instability, disorder, and popular dissent. This emerges clearly when it is asked what are these existing accounts describing? Six principal uses of the terms 'legitimacy', 'legitimate', and 'legitimation' can be identified in recent writing about the European Union:

(a) Legitimacy as popular approval, either of policies or institutions.
(b) Legitimacy as the identification by people of themselves as European citizens and, as such, their identification with European government.
(c) Legitimacy as a resource of European government.
(d) Legitimacy as an active relationship, involving the expression of consent by participants.
(e) Legitimacy as the fulfilment of normative criteria.
(f) Legitimacy as a combination of (a), (d), and (e) so that the actions of subjects and citizens express and correspond with the normative values of observers.

(a) Much of what is written under (a) turns out to use legitimacy as a synonym for support or knowledge. Surveys such as the much drawn upon Eurobarometer are cited to indicate either that the inhabitants of Europe are not particularly well informed about, or interested in, the institutions and policy of the EU, or that they do not accord them high levels of approval.[4] In this usage legitimacy is a synonym for favourable or informed responses in surveys of public opinion, and legitimacy deficit a synonym for low levels of measured approval, interest, or information. So deficit can be a matter of three distinct phenomena: hostility or disapproval, lack of information, and lack of interest.

(b) Legitimacy as identification is an aspirational rather than a descriptive account. It envisages a European polity where those who are subjects and citizens of the Member States of the EU see themselves, in addition, as citizens of a European polity, and one whose identity and values are expressed by, or consistent with, those expressed by the governing institutions of the EU.[5]

(c) The description of legitimacy as a resource is the obverse of legitimacy as support. Whereas legitimacy as support sees government as an activity authorized, or not, by subjects and citizens, and views things from below, legitimacy as resource sees government as an initiating activity which employs resources— revenue, staff, popular support, and legitimacy—to pursue its objectives and maintain itself.[6] A problem arises with accounts of type (c) because of a realist

---

[4] See for instance Blondel, Sinnott, and Svensson, n. 1 above; K. Reif, 'Cultural Convergence and Cultural Diversity as Factors in European Identity', in S. Garcia (ed.), *European Identity and the Search for Legitimacy* (Pinter, London, 1993), chap. 8; Schmitt and Thomassen, n. 1 above.

[5] See Reif, n. 4 above.

[6] See for instance H. Drake, 'The European Commission and the Politics of Legitimacy in the European Union' in N. Nugent (ed.), *At the Heart of the Union: Studies of the European Commission* (Macmillan, Basingstoke, 1997), 226.

use of the term 'legitimacy'. The metaphor, which describes an aspect of ruling and being ruled, is treated as a property which can be treated as separate and autonomous. 'Legitimacy' can then be treated as a fuel for the motor of government, in the absence of which a cessation of the motor can be predicted.

(d) Legitimacy as an active relationship has affinities with both support and identification, in that it describes a series of actions, of which elections and voting are the most prominent, whereby citizens of a European polity express their authorization of European government.[7] Such use draws heavily on a comparison, stated or implied, of the EU with the sovereign nation state in more or less modified form.

(e) Legitimacy as normative approval is both a particular account and an underlying perception of all accounts, since the normative conception of legitimacy underlies the discussion of 'deficit' and 'crisis' in all its forms.[8] Whether by extrapolation from existing democratic nation states, or by envisaging a transnational democratic polity, expectations of what normatively European government and politics ought to be, and of what empirically they would need to be are held up against existing conditions, which are deemed thereby to be either deficient or, even worse, in crisis.

(f) The fusing of the normative and the empirical/historical is the characterizing feature of (f), which is both a normative and an empirical/historical expectation about what a good polity must be in terms of the principles which justify it. But justify it to whom, and justify what dimensions of its life? And what are the consequences of either justification or the refusal of justification? Do they have significance other than for the normative observer? The deficit is not anything observable, but the absence of something desired, expected, or recommended. Ordinary people, it is argued or implied, will in due course reach the same conclusions as normative theorists, with destabilizing consequences for government. Under (f) it is too easily assumed or taken as given that there is some phenomenon called legitimate government, in the description of which the empirical observation of normative activity and the normative assessment conducted by an observer are elided. This happens in an otherwise helpful account by Beetham and Lord of a continuum from academic to popular arguments, thinking, and expression.[9] What political theorists do arises out of the particular concerns and arguments of ordinary people in contests over authority. So an analysis of the structure of an argument over legitimation can be at one and the same time an examination of the internal coherence and effectiveness of a normative argument, and an analysis of the actual, observable, events on the ground. This is an attractive argument, but in Beetham's and Lord's use of it, it is insufficiently developed at the 'ground' end, so that its contact with the real business of

---

[7] This is an element in the account given in Beetham and Lord, n. 1 above.

[8] See for instance Weale and Nentwich (eds.), n. 1 above.

[9] Beetham and Lord, n. 1 above, 2.

government and politics is obscure or intangible. It misses the crucial point, too, that what a theorist does is part of a continuum only if what she does is treated as empirical data. The speculations and arguments of the theorists are evidence, in exactly the same way that the opinions of the ordinary voter are. If, on the other hand, they are treated as interpretations OF the data, then the continuum is broken.

All six types of account abstracted above are infused with a heavy dose of deduction when it comes to the historical and empirical engagement with the politics and government of Europe. The deductive approach is sustained by the strong normative presumptions of much of the thinking. This is further sustained by a realist conception of legitimacy, as a property or resource, the absence of which will necessarily lead to crises. The normative dimension of existing narratives has a remarkable continuity with pre-democratic accounts of legitimacy. A discussion of whether or not a particular monarch was invested with divine right, and therefore whether there was a deficit or crisis, could be conducted without any reference to the actual conditions of his or her rule. The same is true of much discussion of the European Union. It thus, despite its empirical conduct, has a strongly un-empirical element. Deficits and crises are imputed or predicted because of the *absence* of events or phenomena, not because of their observable occurrence. In all these accounts, legitimacy is always somewhere else, or some *thing* else, rather than an actually observable phenomenon. A crisis or a deficit, which would be rather different things, is imputed either because the institutions do not meet the criteria which the observer deems necessary to a legitimate order, or because an absence of public information, enthusiasm, or support (which democratic expectations would demand) disqualifies the EU and hence, in the immediate or near future, threatens it with instability or failure.

3. WHO ARE THE PARTICIPANTS? WHO IS BEING LEGITIMATED, AND IN WHOSE EYES?

It will be useful, without contesting existing narratives, to ask some further questions: what is going on? who is involved? what are they doing? The second question is perhaps the most important, because it grounds discussions of legitimacy and legitimation very firmly in the actions of identifiable persons either individually or collectively. That does not bring to an end the study of the normative dimension, but it ensures that it is located within an empirical/historical dimension, and that normative legitimation is the object, not the subject, of enquiry. In asking these questions, I shall use a conception of legitimation which occurs relatively infrequently, and then only fleetingly, in most accounts of the politics and government of the EU. That is of legitimation as an action or series of actions—speech, writing, ritual, display—whereby people justify to themselves or others the actions they are taking and the identities they are expressing or claiming.[10] Such legitimation cannot readily be separated from the other actions with which it is associated, since it functions to justify and explain them, rather than as a facilitating preliminary to their being carried out, or a subsequent or independent authorization.

There are at least three groups of potential participants in any legitimation, or failure of legitimation, or contesting of legitimation, of government within the EU: individual subjects and citizens, subjects and citizens organized in groups, and the governing elites of the EU itself.

(a) Subjects and Citizens

This classification is not without problems, which are immediately identified in much of the deficit and crisis literature. The ostensible subjects of the EU, like Marx's working class, may be subjects objectively, but without any substantial or significance consciousness of the fact. They are subjects by themselves, but not for themselves. People may not have a sense of being governed, or may not have a sense of who it is that governs them. Indeed much of the literature on democratic deficit describes not so much the absence of democracy as the absence of a demos. In response to this difficulty, attempts have been made to construct accounts which take note of the particularity of European government, and of the fact that it is not like the government of a sovereign state, that its rule is indirect, and distant from the lives of those who are described as actually or potentially its citizens. Comparisons have, for instance, been made between the European Union and medieval Europe. What has not been noticed is that in such a set of arrangements, although there are many layers and kinds of rule, the ruler/ruled relationship is always direct. One is not ruled by one's ruler's ruler. What matters is who enforces a command, and what their identity is in the eyes of the person upon whom the command is enforced. Commands and demands, coercion and taxation, are what define a subject, and make her aware that she is a subject. If to be a subject or a citizen is to be in some form of direct contact with a ruler or government, then it may be questioned whether it makes much sense to talk of individual subjects and citizens of the nations of Europe as subjects and citizens of Europe, since most or even all of their experience of government involves their national governments. Even when, as in the United Kingdom with the 'banana affair' in 2000, there is a conflict which is presented as 'Brussels' versus 'the individual', the enforcing officials turn out to be national, not European.[11] The raids by officials of the European Commission's DG4 on the premises of nine mobile phone companies in the UK and Germany on the morning of Thursday, 12 July 2001 were to that extent a

---

[10] I have described this in R. Barker, *Legitimating Identities: The Self-presentations of Rulers and Subjects* (Cambridge University Press, Cambridge, 2001).

[11] http://news.bbc.co.uk/hi/english/uk/newsid_1118000/1118558.stm, Monday, 15 January 2001, 20:55 GMT.

significant departure from the prevailing governed experience which, so far, the inhabitants of the European Union have had of being governed by it.[12]

(b) Groups

A different experience of European government may be found in the actions of citizens organized in various lobbying and campaigning groups. It has been argued by Carol Harlow that at least some pressure groups have begun treating the institutions of the European Union in the same way that they treat those of their national governments.[13] Politics, in other words, has been growing up around government. This suggests another aspect of the medieval model, with alternative jurisdiction and areas of government. The direct involvement of citizens, as members of groups, with European government cultivates the conditions in which a European polity, and hence legitimated rule and compliance, could emerge. In such circumstances it may be reasonable to expect that justificatory accounts, legitimation, would begin to be given by those engaged in such politics within the developing European polis, both of their own actions and identity as embryonic European citizens, and of the European government whose actions, or inactions, they sought to influence.

(c) Ruling Elites

What of the third group, ruling elites? It is amongst the third group, the rulers, whether European civil servants, ministers, commissioners, or parliamentarians, that there is the greatest concern over legitimation, because that is where, and for whom, most legitimation take place. One of the most thorough accounts of 'crisis' and 'deficit', given by de Búrca is of a legitimation crisis which exists predominantly, perhaps solely, for rulers and elites, and not at all for those whom they see, or perhaps are concerned because they fail to see, as either subjects or citizens.[14] The only instance of sustained debate over the legitimacy of European government took place *within* that government, in the form of debates, documents, and discussions amongst the Council, the Parliament, the Commission, and their various associated bodies around the time of the 1996 Intergovernmental Conference.[15] It is similarly noticeable that the evidence of concern over legitimacy used by Jachtenfuchs is drawn largely from documents issued by political parties, and represents the views and worries of politicians and governments, not of subjects or citizens.[16] Most of the evidence in the discussion of deficit and crisis is of rulers' worries, not subjects'. Similarly Beetham and Lord, perhaps against their better or preferred judgment, see the

---

[12] *The Independent*, 12 July 2001, 1.
[13] C. Harlow, 'A Community of Interests? Making the Most of European Law' (1992) 55 *MLR* 331.
[14] de Búrca, n. 1 above.   [15] *Ibid.*
[16] M. Jachtenfuchs, T. Diez, and S. Jung, 'Which Europe? Conflicting Models of a Legitimate European Political Order' (1998) 4 *European Journal of International Relations* 409.

activity of legitimation as one principally conducted by, and of relevance to, rulers. As they put it:[17]

Like any other political body exercising jurisdiction, international institutions require justification in terms of the purposes or ends they serve, which cannot be met by other means, in this case by nation states themselves, or at the individual state level . . . . Yet such justifications rarely percolate out beyond a narrow elite group; nor do they need to, it could be argued, since these institutions are not dependent on the cooperation of a wider public to effect their purposes. It is not the direct cooperation of ordinary citizens that is required to maintain the authority of the UN, of GATT, of NATO, etc., but that of the member states and their officials; and it is for the behaviour of these alone, therefore, that considerations of legitimacy are important.

Shore and Black, anthropologists who have studied the bureaucracy of the European Union, comment that 'if the public at large remain unaware of their "European identity" the same cannot be said of the Commission bureaucrats. Indeed, something of an embryonic European culture does appear to be emerging within the Community institutions'.[18] Shackleton, an official of the European Parliament, is thus well placed to give an account of what he calls a 'crisis' but which is in fact not a crisis at all, but an anticipated difficulty, and one anticipated, moreover, almost exclusively within the governing elite.[19]

It is a foundational assumption in 'crisis' literature that the principal responsibility either for a crisis or for the avoidance of crises lies with the European Union as a governing institution: with the Commission, the Council, and the Parliament. But whilst they may be the principal actors, their actions may not be quite what the crisis literature supposes. The attention paid to legitimacy has obscured the equally important question of legitimation as an activity carried out to a significant degree not for communication to subjects or the world outside the ruling organization, but for the self-identification and legitimation of those within it. The literature on legitimacy starts from the citizens, and seeks to construct or describe government. But it may be fruitful to look at things from the other end. Citizenship can be a response to government, and government can be the precursor of, not the result of, politics. In that case an account of government growing from the centre, from governors, gives a distinctive and different take on the EU. In this case, governors begin by legitimating themselves in their own eyes, then in those of their immediate 'cousins', and only when they actually begin governing, and hence creating, their citizens do they legitimate themselves in the eyes of their subjects.

4. LEGITIMATION AND THE EU

If it is asked not 'is the EU legitimate?' but 'what legitimation is carried out within the EU?', additional dimensions therefore emerge. The account, often

---

[17] Beetham and Lord, n. 1 above, 12.

[18] C. Shore and A. Black, 'The European Communities and the Construction of Europe' (1992) 8 *Anthropology Today* 11.   [19] Shackleton, n. 1 above.

misunderstood, of Max Weber is useful here. Weber's account of legitimation presents it as a claim, an activity, and gives an interesting instance of the legitimation of bureaucrats or, more specifically, of a single fictional bureaucrat. Describing the professional dedication to routine of a bureaucrat, Weber comments that to act otherwise 'would be abhorrent to his sense of duty'.[20] Those engaged in the business of government, in other words, express and act upon a conception of themselves and their role which simultaneously shapes and justifies their actions. Legitimation is an expression of identity, and is in this respect reflexive, rather than, necessarily, published to a wide audience. It is part of saying to oneself who one is. The revisiting of Weber's account suggests another look at the question of what sort of an institution the EU is, and how many of the signs of life of government it displays. For Weber's taxonomy provides an account of events and institutions in terms of actions and characteristics, rather than in terms of their distance from an ideal type. It would not make sense, using legitimation to describe a characteristic activity of government, to talk of a governing institution which did not legitimate itself, since legitimation is one of the characteristics of the institutions to which the label 'government' is attached. But that does not prevent asking how, and with what success, this and various other characteristic activities of government are carried out. Nor, in consequence, does it preclude an historical conception of the growth, and decline, of government. But it begins with the action of governing, or seeking to govern.

The account of legitimation as identification suggests a different set of questions, which arise from a different narrative of legitimation. How do the rulers of the EU legitimate themselves, and to whom? We know, relatively, far less about the legitimation of 'rulers' in the EU than of 'subjects', which is itself significant. There is a brief discussion by Beetham and Lord, and some initial empirical work by Hooghe, Page, Page and Wouters, and Drake. Helen Drake, in an analysis of the use made by Jacques Delors of political language, makes some brief, allusive comments, in particular the observation that:[21]

We can see therefore how in contemporary politics the concept and reality of legitimacy is at least in part bound up with *claims* to legitimacy. Claims to legitimacy are one of the ways in which a leader interacts with the post he or she holds; one of the ways in which he or she interprets the confines and opportunities of the post. In the case of Delors, he was the first Commission President significantly to push outwards the limits of what was a relatively undefined and unscripted role and so create a space within which he could legitimately act. Partly through his discourse, he publicly stamped on his role a defined legitimacy.

The work of Page and Wouters is interesting and important, in that it is one of the relatively few attempts to look at the phenomenon of European government

---

[20] M. Weber, *Economy and Society* (G. Roth and C. Wittich (eds.)) (University of California Press, Berkeley, Calif., 1978), 31.

[21] H. Drake, 'Jacques Delors and the Discourse of Political Legitimacy', in H. Drake and J. Gaffney (eds.), *The Language of Leadership in Contemporary France* (Dartmouth, Aldershot, 1996), 253.

not only in contrast to a desired democratic ideal or in relation to citizen expectations, but also as an activity with its own perceptions, culture, values, and justifications. Page comments that:[22]

[T]he constitutional role of the Commission gives the organization a legitimacy in political controversies rarely given to the permanent administrative organizations of nation states—the legitimate authority to be a major independent actor, and an initiating body, in the policy process.

Whilst Page does not himself go on to draw out the implications of the observation, it can be commented that what is happening here is precisely authority, autonomous self-identification, the claiming, not the granting, of justification by means of a particular form of self-description and self-presentation. The discussion by Page and Wouters of the enclosed culture of EU rulers is illuminating on what they term the 'relatively closed world where the options being discussed and the outcomes of those discussions bear little relationship to publicly expressed preferences'.[23] In such a world, with what Page calls its 'caste-like character',[24] those who are accepted as appropriate participants are as likely to create small extensions of the closed world as to open it up or bring it into accord with the governed world. The discussion by Page and Wouters of the authority or legitimacy of such rulers, European Union bureaucrats and Commissioners, is highly suggestive, both in what it describes and in what it omits. They comment that a 'body of commissioners without any claim to a Europe-wide authority would have little legitimacy within member states'. They write that commissioners need 'the legitimacy of public office', but that this is limited because they are prevented from mobilizing 'public support' and enjoy only 'indirect legitimacy' since they are selected not by the voters, but by the voters' representatives.[25] There is an elision here of the method of selection and the nature of authority. Moreover, more account needs to be taken of the extent to which, particularly in a 'closed world', rulers of all kinds legitimate themselves in their own eyes and for their own confirmation. What makes a public office public in this sense is not that its incumbent has been chosen or approved by the public, but that it entails a public status and the exercise of public power, the occupancy of office and the enjoyment of its rituals. Such legitimation is not dependent on public approval, but is self-generating. Something of this is glimpsed, but not developed, in Page's and Wouters' description of organized groups as being 'acknowledged as legitimate participants in the bureaucratic-political process'.[26] The acknowledgment is from the top down, from within the closed circle. The groups are acknowledged by those who constitute the 'bureaucratic-political

---

[22] E. C. Page, *People Who Run Europe* (Clarendon Press, Oxford,1997), 147–8.

[23] E. Page and L. Wouters, 'Bureaucratic Politics and Political Leadership in Brussels' (1994) 72 *Public Administration* 445, 446.

[24] E. C. Page, 'Administering Europe', in J. Hayward and E. C. Page (eds.), *Governing the New Europe* (Polity Press, Cambridge, 1995), 259.

[25] Page and Wouters, n. 23 above, 456, 457.   [26] *Ibid.*, 447.

process', not vice versa. It is a culture which is very precisely indicated by Page's and Wouters' use of the word 'collegial'.[27]

Hooghe quotes illuminatingly the observation of an EU official that 'what is relevant is the image one has about oneself, and about the policy one is making . . . That is what public interest is. Outside influences do not weigh (very much).'[28] This is what Wallace refers to as 'patrician and technocratic processes'.[29]

Where are the rituals of the EU experienced, and by whom? The evidence is thin and elusive, perhaps unavoidably so. Most of what we know, significantly, comes from anthropologists such as McDonald, Shore, Black, or Bellier and Wilson.[30] The anthropological evidence is some of the most illuminating here, though even to observing anthropologists the nearest Commission officials came to describing such rituals was to complain of the passing of one of them: 'the old Euro plates on cars, once a mark of distinction, are eschewed: "they get vandalised" '.[31] Shore comments that:

[D]espite frequent references to the Commission's *fonction publique européenne*, many Commission *fonctionnaires* clearly do not see themselves as public servants or mere administrators—a sentiment reinforced, according to some officials themselves, by their distances from European taxpayers and the absence of a self-recognising 'European public' to serve. Instead, many preferred to see themselves in grander political terms as 'policy-makers', 'intellectuals' and 'architects' of the new European order whom the Treaties (and 'history' itself) had proclaimed 'custodians of the European interest'.[32]

As one official remarked to Maryon McDonald, 'there could be no Europe without us'.[33] Special privileges are not simply about material advantage. They are a way of marking the privileged off from the rest, like the etiquette of a court or the manners of a caste. To shop at a store to which others are denied access is to enjoy an identity-expressing privilege which functions in the same way as the Royal Enclosure at Ascot or the MPs' exit to the Westminster underground station. There has been little examination of this, though Drake has suggested that:[34]

[I]t seems appropriate that the analysis of politics in the EU contains a reappraisal of the components and ingredients of legitimacy, including a consideration of the degree to which legitimacy is portrayed and mediated through images recognized as quintessentially 'political', such as the protocol and trappings of political office increasingly conferred on Delors over time.

[27] *Ibid.*, 448.
[28] 'Official 058', quoted in L. Hooghe, 'Images of Europe: Orientations to European Integration Among Senior Officials of the Commission' (1999) 29 *British Journal of Political Science* 345, 364.
[29] Wallace, n. 1 above, 97.
[30] Shore and Black, n. 18 above; M. McDonald, 'Accountability, Anthropology and the European Commission', in M. Strathern (ed.), *Audit Cultures: Anthropological Studies in Accountability, Ethics and the Academy* (Routledge, London, 2000), 106; Shore, n. 2 above; I. Bellier and T. M. Wilson (eds.), *An Anthropology of the European Union: Building, Imagining and Experiencing the New Europe* (Berg, Oxford, 2000).
[31] McDonald, n. 30 above, 121.   [32] Shore, n. 2 above, 144–5.
[33] McDonald, n. 30 above, 124.   [34] Drake, n. 6 above, 244.

The relation between manner of legitimation and manner of government lies outside the scope of this essay, but it is a question raised both by the subject and by the narratives that have been given of it. Michelle Cini comments that 'Administrative culture is, of course, only one of many conceptual lenses through which one can understand the workings of the Commission. Although there is no assumption here that this lens will offer a complete and comprehensive explanation of how the institution functions, it is nevertheless a starting-point for developing an awareness of how individuals, collectively, give meaning to what they are, where they are, and what they do.'[35]

5. A EUROPEAN POLITY?

To begin by asking how the governing institutions of the EU legitimate themselves is partially to reverse much current argument. The emphasis there is on two things: the creation of a European polity and the justification or acceptance by that polity of European government. There is a paradox here: the conception of justification is from the bottom up, but that of both the creation of the polity and the achievement of justification from the top down. In the standard account, there is a moral emphasis on citizens, but an expectation that the initiative will come from governors. The normative democratic, and the institutional empirical, perceptions lead in different directions.

The narrative in which governments create citizens, rather than vice versa, draws attention to a feature which marks off the EU from the other form of government within Europe, existing sovereign states. The institutions and personnel of European rule are much more clearly in place than are the subjects and citizens. In this the EU may share some characteristics, not so much with conventional governments, as with governments in exile or rebels. As Bellier and Thomas comment of the European Commission, it is 'an institution whose performance, ideology, and modes of integration are such that it can be considered as the "avant garde" of a new society in the making'.[36] This is so not in respect of their power, but in respect of the account they give of it. They have governmental power, unlike governments in exile, but like governments in exile they do not in general exercise that power directly over those whom they may consider their subjects. But, as with governments in exile, their account of their own identity and authority, their legitimation, precedes the creation of or rule over subjects. Governing institutions have to establish themselves, and they normally do so from the top down.[37] So governments can be legitimating themselves long before, not

[35] M. Cini, 'Administrative Culture in the Commission', in N. Nugent (ed.), *At the Heart of the Union: Studies of the European Commission* (Macmillan, Basingstoke, 1997), 71, 73.

[36] Bellier and Wilson, n. 30 above, 11.

[37] This is a sense of top-down legitimation different from, though related to, that employed by Marcus or di Palma. See G. Di Palma, 'Legitimation from the Top to Civil Society: Politico-Cultural Change in Eastern Europe' (1991) 44 *World Politics*; M. Markus, 'Overt and Covert Modes of

only the state is in legitimate relations with its subjects or citizens of the polity which they aspire to govern, but before that polity has been created or a citizen body been cultivated. And even when the EU does begin to govern, its first 'subjects' are not citizens, but states.

This has implications for theories of deficit and crises, since crises can occur with established governing institutions, but not with governing institutions which have not yet grown to come into effective contact with their citizens. It is governments which create subjects, not vice versa, which is a Tory, rather than a Liberal view: Tories understand government, just as Liberals understand politics, and legitimacy and legitimation are in the first place about government.

6. Citizenship and its consequences

I have spoken frequently of subjects of the European Union. That is not the normal usage. It is more common to refer to the (adult) individuals who are members of the states which make up the Union as 'citizens', and a principal part of the discussion of deficit is concerned with the extent to which such an appellation is accurate. One of the accounts given is of European identity, or lack of it. In other words people do, or do not, see themselves as sharing some common characteristics with those who govern them. But there are two question here, not one, since there may be a common European identity without an identification with the institutions of the EU. In such thinking, one ground for pessimism or apprehension is not considered: a polity does not necessarily identify with or approve of the government around which it forms, and the formation of citizen consciousness does not necessarily lead to enthusiasm for government.

The paradox is that, while European Union government may cultivate or nurture a sense of European citizenship, the resulting or emerging polis may not identify with the regime which has been crucial to its own formation. This is a possibility raised by Drake:[38]

Building images, or worlds, in part through discourse, can of course have both positive and negative effects, and any gap between leaders and the led in the EU can be seen to stem in part from the mismatch between the image/s of European union built by and believed in by elites, and specifically the Commission, and the difficulty for most people of feeling part of (or interested in) that image, or to identify with the European 'project' or ideal that motivates the policy-makers and which they promote.

But whilst the principal initiative may often be from the top, citizenship can develop without direct connection with governing institutions. The growth of citizenship may be associated with aspirations which not only do not connect with or support the aspirations of governing institutions, but conflict with

Legitimation in East European Societies', in T. Rigby and F. Feher (eds.), *Political Legitimation in Communist States* (Macmillan, London, 1982).

[38] H. Drake, *Jacques Delors: Perspectives on a European Leader* (Routledge, London, 2000), 15–16.

them. In its mild version, this may be the distrust which, it has been argued, makes a positive contribution to democracy.[39] In a stronger version, citizen awareness may lead to opposition or disillusion amongst the polity.[40] The history of Eastern Europe in the years around 1989 provides a dramatic illustration of the most negative response, for existing government, of citizen awareness, and the creation of a democratic policy.

7. LOOK BEHIND YOU

It is not necessary to hold a telescope to a blind eye in order to ask 'Crisis? What crisis?' The traditional audience's cry in pantomime, 'look behind you', is provoked by the actor's energy in looking everywhere except at the one place where the menacing villain is actually standing. It is not surprising that, when contemporary commentators scan the European stage for signs of danger save for the one place where it has occurred, they have to predict threats, since few actual threats can be observed.[41] There are few signs which can be presented as symptoms of 'deficit' or 'crisis': little more than some hostile referenda votes, and indifference in response to polling. It is also the case that, at least in the UK, issues relating to the EU are of far greater relative importance to members of the governing elite and its immediate political hinterland, than they are to ordinary subjects and citizens. Even if the UK is exceptional in this respect, as Carol Harlow points out[42] it may be, voting is a different kind of indicator from replies to opinion polls. Legitimation is an observable aspect of politics or it is nothing. It does not occur in a vacuum.

And yet attention has been directed almost entirely at the area where there are few, if any, signs of deficit, let alone crisis, whilst, paradoxically, the one set of events to which the term 'crisis' might be applied has featured hardly at all in the mainstream debate. One crisis *has* occurred, but it does not readily fit into the existing theories. There was an evident disjuncture in the events surrounding the resignation of the entire body of Commissioners in 1999, but it was between members of the administrative apparatus, not between the European Union and individual citizens. The disjuncture was between Parliament's and Commissioners' perceptions of their respective legitimated identities. There were no consequences for the behaviour of citizens, though

---

[39] V. Hart, *Distrust and Democracy* (Cambridge University Press, Cambridge, 1978).

[40] Hall argues that political awareness does not necessarily lead to support of dominant or conventional politics, and can equally lead to support for dissent, oppositional, or radical alternatives to existing policies and institutions. He cites the environmental protestors who used anarchic theatrical direct action against road and runway building plans: P. Hall, 'Social Capital in Britain' (1999) 29 *British Journal of Political Science* 417, 454–5.

[41] An exception to this is McDonald, who comments 'the Commission seemed externally to reach, in the apparently failed reforms, the critical reports and then the resignations of 1999, the acme of its illegitimacy': McDonald, n. 30 above, 109.   [42] Harlow, n. 13 above.

Santer's claims that he was '*blanchi*' did not go down well in the press or with at least some of its readers. The crisis of 1999 was, amongst other things, a clash of legitimations, and of the identifications which went with them, but one which took place, and was principally of consequence, within and amongst the institutions and personnel of government.

It has not been an accident that the language of legitimation, counter-legitimation, and the denial of legitimation has been employed amongst the rulers of the EU rather than between them and their subjects or citizens. Governors who deal with their citizens late, or who have not yet done so, are likely to be more confident of their own authority, and less likely to justify, or to feel the need to justify it in the eyes of a wider constituency.

8. Conclusion

The argument over crisis or deficit is deductive, and states or implies that since the hypothetical conditions for legitimacy are not met, then there must by definition be something called a crisis or a deficit. But legitimation is an enabling, justifying, facilitating aspect of other behaviours, so needs to be looked at as such an aspect. Not, therefore, 'are the conditions in which we would expect legitimacy being met?' but 'what is going on, and how is it best explained?'. I have suggested that if that is the question asked, then there is no crisis. There is legitimation, but it is at a level removed from the experience of individual citizens. A heightened sense of citizenship could in the future, on the other hand, lead to a rejection, not a legitimation, of the institutions of the EU. If the legitimation of the governors of the EU, by themselves and in their own eyes, goes in a direction which does not correspond with that sense of citizenship, then events might develop which could be described as legitimacy deficit or crisis: dissonance rather than distance.

Legitimacy is a metaphor to sum up phenomena, not an essence the phenomenal consequences of which can be presumed. Potential crises therefore are in the future. The single European currency provides the first real direct contact between European government and individual citizens, and that may be a test. On the other hand no decision about compliance is normally involved in using money, even though money has always involved propagandist or legitimizing statements. There is a standard rhetoric for using currency without assenting to its rhetorical claims: 'Render therefore unto Caesar the things which are Caesar's; and unto God the things that are God's'.[43] The EU can be substituted for Caesar, and the nation for God. It is possible to speculate, but only to speculate, about what a legitimacy deficit or crisis might look like. There could be symbolic rejection of the currency in the manner of the Boston Tea parties. But though we may anticipate problems, legitimated government must *precede* a

[43] St. Matthew, chap. 2, verse 21.

crisis, and that has only just begun to happen. That will be a test, though full-scale resistance would be necessary before anything which could be described as a crisis, or even a deficit, would have arrived.

Legitimation is from the centre outwards, and a government which is evolving will have rulers before it has subjects, and will be embroiled in its own self-legitimation long before its subjects are concerned about such matters, or before they even, as subjects, exist. So there may indeed be legitimation problems for the EU, both in the past and the future, but not necessarily where many people thought, and not necessarily raising the problems about which many people have worried. But that does not make them any the less problematic.

10

The Constitutional Foundations of the European Union

TREVOR C. HARTLEY*

Most states were not created by law: their origin lies in a conquest or seizure of power. The European Union is different. It, together with its *alter egos* and earlier incarnations (European Community, EEC, ECSC, etc.),[1] are all creations of the law. They owe their birth and continuing existence to the law: the law came first and the institutions came afterwards.[2] Admittedly, the institutions themselves adopt legislation, but the basic law, the Treaty, was not created by them: they were created by it. This fact is obvious. Some commentators claim that in this respect the Community is no different from those newer states that owe their historical origin and continuing existence to a constitution. The United States is an example. In the United States, the Constitution is the basic provision: the institutions of government, Congress, the Presidency, and the Supreme Court, owe their existence to it. However, the essential difference is that the United States Constitution was not created by another system of law;[3] the basic Treaties of the European Union, on the other hand, owe their existence and validity to international law. Their effect in the Member States depends on the law of those states.

This point is so important that it is worth exploring further. The earliest of the European Communities was the ECSC. It was created by a Treaty signed in

* This essay was originally published in the Law Quarterly Review ((2001) 117 *LQR* 225). It is reprinted here by kind permission of the Editor, Professor F. M. B. Reynolds.

[1] There were originally three Communities (the EEC, now renamed the EC, the ECSC, and Euratom), but since the demise of the ECSC, there are only two. Each has separate legal personality. These Communities, 'supplemented by the policies and forms of co-operation' established by the Treaty on European Union (Maastricht Agreement), make up the European Union: Art. 1 (ex Art. A) TEU.

[2] Looking at the matter from the point of view of his subject, a French international lawyer has written, '*Alors que l'existence de l'Etat s'impose au droit international, celle des Communautés en découle*'. ('While the existence of a state imposes itself on international law, that of the Communities is derived from it.'): A. Pellet, 'Les fondements juridiques internationaux du droit communautaire' (1997) 5 *Collected Courses of the Academy of European Law*, Book 2, 193, 213.

[3] The English common law was in force in the various states before independence and continued in force thereafter. However, the Constitution was not created by the common law. Moreover, any inconsistency would have been resolved in favour of the Constitution.

Paris in 1951 by the six original Member States. There cannot be the slightest doubt that the ECSC Treaty was intended to be a *treaty*: an instrument taking effect under international law. This is clear from its form and wording, and from the procedure for its adoption and ratification. It was regarded by the states party to it as a Treaty, and it was ratified by them according to the requirements laid down in their respective constitutions for the ratification of treaties. Since then, new Communities have been established and new Member States have joined. Each time, a new treaty has been adopted, and each new treaty has been ratified according to the requirements of the national constitutions. Indeed, this is expressly stated in the Treaty on European Union: it provides that any Treaty amending any of the Treaties on which the Union is founded must be 'ratified by all the Member States in accordance with their respective constitutional requirements'.[4]

Thus, Community legislation and the judgments of the European Court owe their validity to the Treaties, and the Treaties owe their validity to international law and the legal systems of the Member States. The Community legal system, and everything built on it, is not, therefore, *self-sustaining*: it is dependent on other legal systems and owes its validity to them. The Treaties constitute the foundation of the Community legal system, but the Treaties themselves have their foundation in international law. To use other terminology, the Treaties do not constitute an independent *Grundnorm*.[5] A *Grundnorm* may be defined as a legal rule on which all other rules in the system depend, but which does not itself depend on any other legal rule.[6] Its validity depends on non-legal considerations. The Constitution of the United States is a *Grundnorm*;[7] the basic Treaties of the European Union are not.

It might be objected that, though this is obviously true as regards the historical origin of the Community, it is no longer true of the Community as it now exists. This view is sometimes called the 'theory of constitutionalization'. It requires careful analysis.

1. CONSTITUTIONALIZATION

Some years ago, the European Court caused a minor stir by referring to the EEC Treaty (now the EC Treaty) as the 'basic constitutional charter' of the Community.[8] This appears to be an assertion that the Treaties are the constitution

---

[4] Art. 48 (ex Art. N) TEU.

[5] The term '*Grundnorm*' is taken from the writings of Hans Kelsen, but it is used here simply as a convenient expression to denote the idea defined above. Its use is not intended to import all Kelsen's ideas into the present discussion.

[6] In this definition, the term 'rule' is to be understood as including all legal propositions.

[7] To be strictly accurate, one should perhaps say that the *Grundnorm* is the rule that the Constitution is valid law and that it can be changed only in accordance with the rules laid down in it.

[8] Case 294/83, *Parti Ecologiste 'Les Verts'* v. *European Parliament* [1986] ECR 1339; [1987] 2 CMLR 343, para. 23.

of the Community. To understand what this might mean, we must confront an ambiguity in the meaning of 'constitution'. In general terms, a constitution may be defined as a set of rules that create a legal entity and define the powers of its organs. A state may have a constitution. This would bring it into being and define the powers of its legislature, executive, and judiciary. In English usage, more humble bodies may also have constitutions: a political party, a trade union, or even a cricket club may have a constitution. In each case, the constitution of the body creates it and defines the powers of its organs. Used in this broad sense, the word 'constitution' clearly applies to the basic Treaties of the European Union: they brought the Union into being and gave its institutions their powers. This is the sense in which the term 'constitution' is used in international law to describe the Treaty setting up an international organization.[9] It emphasizes the special features of such a Treaty;[10] it does not, however, deny that it *is* a Treaty, even less that it owes its validity to international law.[11] If this is all the European Court meant, it was merely stating the obvious.

There is, however, a more restricted meaning, or additional connotation, of the term, which might be more current in some languages than others. This would add to the above definition that a constitution must be legally self-sustaining: its validity must not depend on any other legal principle. In the terminology we introduced earlier, it must constitute a *Grundnorm*. It is only if the word 'constitution' is used in this more restricted sense that the doctrine of constitutionalization has any significance for our discussion.[12]

The Community Treaties undoubtedly owed their creation to other systems of law: no one suggests that they were originally self-sustaining. The question to be considered, therefore, is whether the position changed at some point. Was there some moment at which they changed their character, and ceased to owe their validity to international law?[13] This would have involved a change in the *Grundnorm*.

[9] For example, the treaty setting up the ILO is officially called the 'Constitution of the International Labour Organization' and that setting up the WHO is called the 'Constitution of the World Health Organization'. This usage also applies in French: see the French texts of these two treaties.

[10] On these see S. Rosenne, *Developments in the Law of Treaties 1945–1986* (Cambridge University Press, Cambridge, 1989), 181–258.

[11] Pellet, n. 2 above, 234, writes, with reference to the constituent instruments of international organizations, '*Expression de l'accord des parties, ils sont ancrés dans le droit international et, à ce titre, demeurent des traités; mais, en même temps, à l'origine d'un nouvel ordre juridique, dérivé, ils constituent la norme suprême, la 'constitution', de celui-ci*'. ('An expression of the agreement of the parties, they are founded on international law and, for that reason, remain treaties; but, at the same time, at the origin of a new (derived) legal system, they constitute the supreme norm, the "constitution", of the latter'.).

[12] There is unfortunately a tendency for the proponents of constitutionalization to be vague on this most vital point. This is true not only with regard to the European Court, but also with regard to writers. See E. Stein, 'Lawyers, Judges and the Making of a Transnational Constitution' (1981) 74 *Am Jo Int L* 1; F. Mancini, 'The Making of a Constitution for Europe' (1989) 26 *CMLRev* 595; J. Weiler, 'The Transformation of Europe' (1991) 100 *Yale LJ* 2403; Weiler, 'The Reformation of European Constitutionalism' (1997) 35 *JCMS* 97.

[13] This change is said by some writers to have occurred in the 1960s: see J. Weiler and U. Haltern, 'Response: The Autonomy of the Community Legal Order—Through the Looking Glass' (1996) 37 *Harv Int L Jo* 411, 420 ff.

It is important to be clear what this would mean. If the *Grundnorm* of the legal system of the European Union were to change, things would at first be much the same as before. The man in the street, and the average lawyer, might think that nothing had happened. Community law would continue to be applied by the courts in Member States. The difference, however, would be the reason *why* it was applied. The position before the change would have been as follows: at the first level of analysis, the reason Community law applied would have been that Community law said it was to apply; however, the reason Community law could require its application would have been that the Member States gave it that power. In the case of the United Kingdom, it would have followed from section 2(1) of the European Communities Act 1972. If, on the other hand, the British courts were to recognize a change in the *Grundnorm*, they would take the view that Community law no longer applied by reason of section 2(1), but simply and solely because it declared itself applicable. The practical consequences of this change would not, however, be apparent until some event occurred that put the question in issue, for example, if the British Parliament purported to take back some of the powers conferred on the Union.

(a) How Does the *Grundnorm* Change?

It is generally recognized that the *Grundnorm* can change; in fact, the *Grundnorm* underlying the legal systems of most present-day countries changed at some point in the past: a new constitution came into existence by a means not recognized by the pre-existing constitution.[14] Did this occur in the case of the Community? To answer this, it is useful to examine the ways in which the *Grundnorm* has changed on various occasions in the past.[15]

One way in which the *Grundnorm* can change is through a successful revolution. By 'revolution' is meant some popular upsurge which sweeps away the governmental apparatus of the old regime and replaces it with a new one.[16]

---

[14] In England, this occurred in 1688. Under the *Grundnorm* as it existed prior to the 'Glorious Revolution', James II was King of England. The Bill of Rights declared that William and Mary were King and Queen; however, James did not assent to the Bill of Rights, nor, if one assumes that he had abdicated, was it assented to by his heir; therefore, in terms of the old *Grundnorm*, the Bill of Rights was void; consequently, it could not make William and Mary King and Queen. If one accepts the old *Grundnorm*, every Act of Parliament since 1688 has been a nullity. It is only by positing a change in the *Grundnorm* that one can escape from this conclusion: F. W. Maitland, *Constitutional History of England* (Cambridge University Press, Cambridge, 1908), 283–5; T. P. Taswell-Langmead, *English Constitutional History* (Sweet & Maxwell, London, 11th edn., 1960), 445–9.

[15] The literature on this topic is large. One of the most helpful accounts is to be found in the writing of the late Professor S. A. de Smith: see S. de Smith and R. Brazier, *Constitutional and Administrative Law* (Penguin, Harmondsworth, 7th edn., 1994), 69–73. For further items see n. 17 below.

[16] The French Revolution (1789), the Russian Revolution (1917), and the Iranian Revolution (1979) can be regarded as examples. Similar considerations apply where the new regime gains power only after a prolonged struggle. Examples include the American Revolution (1765–88), the Chinese Revolution (finally successful in 1949), the Cuban Revolution (finally successful in 1959), and the Vietnamese Revolution (finally successful in 1975).

There is a new government, a new army, a new police force, and new courts. A new constitution is adopted and new judges appointed. They swear allegiance to the new regime. If the revolutionary regime successfully maintains its hold on power and its laws are obeyed in practice, it would be reasonable to say that a new *Grundnorm* has come into existence. However, this model is inapplicable to the European Union: no revolution has taken place.

A second example involves a take-over or *coup d'état*. By this is meant that the basic governmental structure remains in place, but a new body of men purport to exercise power. The most common example is a military *coup*: the army marches in, arrests the members of the government, and proclaims a new regime. If the previous judges remain in office, they will sooner or later be confronted with the question whether they should recognize the validity of laws adopted by the new regime. Since those laws will be invalid in terms of the old legal order, they can do this only by expressly or tacitly holding that there has been a change in the *Grundnorm*: what was previously invalid now becomes valid. Sometimes, this is the course they adopt.[17] Again, this model is inapplicable to the European Union.

For our third model we will take the situation where a country grants independence to a former colony or other territory. In the case of Britain, the normal pattern was for Parliament to pass an Act declaring the new country independent. The constitution of the new state, which would have been drawn up in negotiations among the local politicians, would be contained in the Act. The country would then be independent; however, it would have been possible to maintain that its constitution was not self-sustaining since it owed its validity to British law.[18] In some cases, this was not regarded as a problem (because in practice the British Parliament was not going to re-assert its sovereignty), but, in other cases, local leaders sought to make clear that a change in the *Grundnorm* had occurred.

The Republic of Ireland is an example.[19] Originally part of the United Kingdom, it gained independence in 1922. Its first constitution, the Constitution of the Irish Free State, was adopted by a Constituent Assembly in Dublin. The Constituent Assembly considered that it was creating a new *Grundnorm*.

---

[17] See, e.g., *The State* v. *Dosso* PLD 1958 SC 533 (Pakistan), a case subsequently held to have been wrongly decided (*Jilani* v. *State of Punjab* PLD 1972 SC 139; *Uganda* v. *Prison Commissioner, ex p. Matovu* [1966] EA 514 (Uganda); *R* v. *Ndhlovu* 1968 (4) SA 515 (Rhodesia, now Zimbabwe). For analysis of the issues raised in these cases see: J. Harris, 'When and Why Does the Grundnorm Change?' [1971] *CLJ* 103; J. Eekelaar, 'Splitting the Grundnorm' (1967) 30 *MLR* 156 and 'Rhodesia: The Abdication of Constitutionalism' (1969) 32 *MLR* 19; T. Honoré, 'Reflections on Revolutions' [1967] *Irish Jurist* 268; S. de Smith, 'Constitutional Lawyers in Revolutionary Situations' (1968) 7 *Western Ontario L Rev* 93; R. Dias, 'Legal Politics: Norms behind the Grundnorm' (1968) 26 *CLJ* 233; F. Brookfield, 'The Courts, Kelsen, and the Rhodesian Revolution' (1969) 19 *U of Toronto LJ* 326. One way in which the new regime can avoid these problems is to require all the judges to swear allegiance to it: those who refuse can be dismissed and, if they cause trouble, arrested.

[18] In the terminology of the 1960s, it could be said that it was not 'autochthonous', a word which means 'sprung from the land itself'.

[19] See K. C. Wheare, *The Constitutional Structure of the Commonwealth* (Clarendon Press, Oxford, 1960), 90–4.

The British Parliament, however, took a different view: it adopted a statute, the Irish Free State Constitution Act 1922, which purported to give legal validity to the Irish Constitution (which was appended to the Act). The British view was that the Irish Constitution derived its validity from British law.[20]

This ambiguity was resolved only with the adoption of the Constitution of Eire in 1937. When this occurred, great care was taken to ensure that there was a clear gap in legal continuity: the *Dáil* approved the Constitution, but did not *adopt* it; it was then submitted to a referendum and its acceptance by the people of Ireland was regarded as constituting its enactment. There was then no way in which the Constitution could be regarded as dependent on British law. This model is again inapplicable to the European Union because the successive Treaties on which it is based have all been concluded and ratified in a manner that makes clear that no break in legal continuity has occurred.

Our final example is Canada. In a sense, this is hypothetical, since one cannot be absolutely sure that a change in the *Grundnorm* has occurred. Canada was originally a British colony and its various constitutions derived their validity from British Acts of Parliament. The current Constitution was given legal force by a British statute, the Canada Act 1982, section 2 of which provides that no future British statute will apply in Canada. Does this mean that the Canadian Constitution is now self-sustaining? Has a new *Grundnorm* been created?

It might be thought that even if the old (British) *Grundnorm* continues to apply, its sting has been drawn because the British Parliament is no longer able to legislate for Canada. However, it is a basic principle of British constitutional law that, though Parliament can pass any statute it pleases, it cannot limit its future powers. Therefore, under the existing *Grundnorm*, the provision in section 2 of the Canada Act (which purports to deprive Parliament of the power to legislate for Canada) is without effect. On this view, the Canadian constitution is just as dependent as it ever was.

However, even if this view were to prevail in the United Kingdom, it is unlikely that it would be accepted in Canada. If the British Parliament purported to legislate for Canada, the Canadian courts would almost certainly hold that legislation invalid. They would hold (expressly or by implication) that a change in the *Grundnorm* had occurred.

(b) The Search for a Principle

In order to apply these models to the European Union, we must first derive a principle from them. In doing this, we shall put revolutions on one side, and assume that the same judges remain in office. If they were appointed before the

---

[20] This difference in attitudes is reflected in the differing views expressed by courts in the two countries: compare the judgment of the Supreme Court of the Irish Free State in *The State (Ryan)* v. *Lennon* [1935] IR 170, 203 with that of the Privy Council in *Moore* v. *The Attorney-General for the Irish Free State* [1935] AC 484, 497.

purported change in the *Grundnorm*, their judicial oath would, expressly or by implication, have bound them to the old *Grundnorm*. Given this, when would it be justifiable for them to change their allegiance and support the new *Grundnorm*? Clearly, this would be a serious step. It is not something a judge should do simply because he thinks a change would be a good idea. It is a step he should take only on the basis of some objective criterion that does not depend on his personal opinion. It is suggested, therefore, that it would be justifiable in only two situations, where there is overwhelming force or overwhelming acceptance.

In the first situation, if the new regime so clearly has might on its side that all resistance is useless, a judge might feel that rejection of the new *Grundnorm* would result in his removal from office and replacement by a more pliant individual. In such circumstances, he might consider he had no option but to comply.[21] In the second, if virtually the entire population supports a proposition that requires a change of *Grundnorm*, the judge ought to accept this. Let us take the example of Canada. Assume that the British Parliament were to pass a statute repealing the Canada Act 1982, and returning Canada to colonial rule. This would conflict with a proposition accepted by virtually the whole population of Canada: the proposition that Canada is an independent state. Since that proposition is sustainable only on the basis that there has been a change in the *Grundnorm*, Canadian judges would be justified in ruling that such a change had occurred.[22]

(c) Application to the European Union

Since the EC Commission has not staged a *coup d'état*, and the proposed European military force does not yet exist, there can be no question of overwhelming force. It is equally clear that there can be no question of overwhelming acceptance. If the European *Grundnorm* were to change so as to transform the Community Treaties into a self-sustaining constitution, the result would be that Community law would no longer apply in the Member States because the Member States accepted it: it would apply whether they liked it or not. Their continuing membership of the European Union would no longer depend on their consent: they would be members whether they liked it or not.[23] Moreover, since the European Court has ruled in numerous cases that Community law prevails over Member-State law, the national law of each Member State would apply in that state only to the extent permitted by Community law. Finally, since the European Court considers that it has the final say on the powers of the Community, the area over which the Community has jurisdiction, and

---

[21] Not everyone would accept this.

[22] More difficult issues would arise if the question came before a court in the UK. It could, however, be argued that virtually the entire population in the UK also accepts the proposition that Canada is an independent state; therefore, a UK judge might be justified in ruling that a change in the *Grundnorm* has occurred.

[23] The Community Treaties contain no provision permitting a Member State to leave the Union.

hence the area over which the Member States have jurisdiction, would be outside the control of the Member States. If a change in the *Grundnorm* occurred, one could legitimately say that sovereignty had been transferred to the Union.[24] In a very real sense, the Member States would no longer be independent. Would these propositions command overwhelming acceptance by the peoples of Europe? Clearly not. In most, if not all, Member States, they would be overwhelmingly *rejected*. There is, therefore, no legitimate basis on which a judge could hold that a change of *Grundnorm* has occurred. The theory of constitutionalization, if understood in the more restricted sense explained above, is wrong. The Community Treaties are not a constitution in that sense.[25]

Though the European Court might feel tempted to adopt that theory if it thought it could get away with it, any such action would be illegitimate.[26] Moreover, it is clear that the Member-State courts would reject it. The highest courts in two Member States, Germany and Denmark, have already done so in express terms. In Germany, the Federal Constitutional Court (*Bundesverfassungsgericht*) ruled in 1993, in *Brunner* v. *European Union Treaty*,[27] that Community law applies in Germany only because laws passed by the German Parliament say it does.[28] It also said that Germany has preserved its status as a sovereign state.[29] In Denmark, the Supreme Court held in *Carlsen* v. *Rasmussen*[30] that Community law applies in Denmark only by reason of, and to the extent permitted by, the Danish Constitution:[31] if the Community tried to legislate beyond those limits, the law in question would have no effect in Denmark;[32] the same would apply to judgments of the European Court.[33] The Supreme Court affirmed that, despite EU membership, Denmark remains an independent state.[34] Although the issue does

---

[24] As long ago as 1964, the European Court said that the Member States have limited their sovereign rights: Case 6/64, *Costa* v. *ENEL* [1964] ECR 585, 593.

[25] For this reason, the 'constitutional charter' *dictum* of the European Court should not be interpreted as questioning the international nature of the Treaties. This view is strengthened by the fact that, when the *dictum* was repeated five years later in Opinion 1/91, *EEA Case* [1991] ECR 6079, para. 21, the Court expressly acknowledged that the Treaty was concluded in the form of an international agreement.

[26] Since the European Court has jurisdiction only to give rulings on questions of Community law, and since this question is by definition one that lies outside Community law, any ruling it gave would be outside its jurisdiction and not, therefore, binding on the courts of the Member States.

[27] Decision of 12 October 1993 [1994] 1 CMLR 57; (1994) 33 ILM 388; 89 BVerfGE 155; 20 EuGRZ 429; [1993] NJW 3047. For a full discussion and analysis see U. Everling, 'The *Maastricht* Judgment of the German Federal Constitutional Court and its Significance for the Development of the European Union' (1994) 14 *YBEL* 1; N. Foster, 'The German Constitution and EC Membership' [1994] *PL* 392; M. Herdegen, 'Maastricht and the German Constitutional Court: Constitutional Restraints for an "Ever Closer Union"' (1994) 31 *CMLRev* 233; J. Kokott, 'Report on Germany', in A.-M. Slaughter, A. Stone Sweet, and J.H.H. Weiler, *The European Courts and National Courts—Doctrine and Jurisprudence* (Hart, Oxford, 1998), 77; N. MacCormick, 'The *Maastricht-Urteil*: Sovereignty Now' (1995) 1 *ELJ* 259.

[28] [1994] 1 CMLR 57, para. 55.   [29] *Ibid.*

[30] Danish Supreme Court (*Højesteret*), judgment of 6 April 1998, *Carlsen* v. *Rasmussen* [1999] 3 CMLR 854. For further discussion see K. Høegh, 'The Danish Maastricht Judgment' (1999) 24 *ELRev* 80.

[31] *Ibid.*, section 9.2 of the judgment.   [32] Section 9.6 of the judgment.   [33] *Ibid.*

[34] Section 9.8 of the judgment.

not appear to have been expressly considered by a court in any other Member State, there are a number of judgments that take it for granted that the original *Grundnorm* remains in force.[35]

2. COMMUNITY LAW: A SEPARATE LEGAL SYSTEM?

What we have done so far is to establish that there has been no change of *Grundnorm*: Community law continues to owe its validity to the Treaties, which in turn owe their validity to international law. Before we discuss the consequences of this dependent relationship, however, we must consider whether Community law is a separate legal system from international law.[36] This is a different question from that of dependency: a legal system may be separate from

[35] See, e.g., the decisions of the French *Conseil Constitutionnel* in *Maastricht I*, Decision 92–308 DC, 9 April 1992, *Recueil*, 55; [1993] 3 CMLR 345 and *Amsterdam*, Decision 97–394 DC, 31 December 1997, JORF No. 2 of 3 January 1998; comment by S. Mouthaan (1998) 23 *ELRev* 592. (In *Sarran et Levacher*, *Conseil d'Etat*, 30 October 1998, *Revue française de droit administratif*, 1998, n. 14, 1081; *L'Actualité juridique, Droit Administratif*, 1998, 1039, the French *Conseil d'Etat* held that international treaties are subordinate to the French Constitution; the case did not, however, concern the EU: see C. Richards, 'Sarran et Levacher: Ranking Legal Norms in the French Republic' (2000) 25 *ELRev* 192.) In *R v. Secretary of State, ex p. Factortame (No. 2)* [1991] AC 603, 659, Lord Bridge said that the duty of a UK court to allow directly applicable Community provisions to override rules of national law follows from the European Communities Act 1972. See now also *Thoburn v. Sunderland District Council* [2002] 3 WLR 247, 278–9 (DC). The Italian Constitutional Court (*Corte Costituzionale*) has held that Community law cannot prevail over the basic principles of the Italian Constitution, a position which seems incompatible with a change of *Grundnorm*: see *Frontini, Corte Costituzionale*, Decision No. 183 of 27 December 1973 [1974] 2 CMLR 372, para. 21; [1974] RDI 154; *Fragd, Corte Costituzionale*, Decision No. 168 of 21 April 1989, English translation in A. Oppenheimer (ed.), *The Relationship between European Community Law and National Law—The Cases* (Cambridge University Press, Cambridge, 1994), 653; [1990] I *Foro Italiano* 1855. See, further, M. Cartabia, 'The Italian Constitutional Court and the Relationship between the Italian Legal System and the European Union', in *The European Courts and National Courts*, n. 27 above, 138–9; B. de Witte, 'Sovereignty and European Integration: The Weight of European Legal Tradition', *ibid.*, 288–9. In Greece, the Sixth Chamber of the Council of State held in *Vagias v. DI KATSA*, Decision No. 2808/1997 of 8 July 1997, that, though Community law prevails over Greek statutes, it is subordinate to the Greek Constitution: see E. Maganaris, 'The Principle of Supremacy of Community Law—The Greek Challenge' (1998) 23 *ELRev* 179. When the matter was reconsidered by a plenary session of the Council of State (29 judges), a majority side-stepped the issue through a dubious interpretation of the relevant provisions of Community law: see E. Maganaris, 'The Principle of Supremacy of Community Law in Greece—From Direct Challenge to Non-Application' (1999) 24 *ELRev* 426.

[36] This question has given rise to a significant body of literature over the years. The first phase was in the 1970s and 1980s: see, e.g., P. Pescatore, 'International Law and Community Law—A Comparative Analysis' (1970) 7 *CMLRev* 167 (further citations, *ibid.*, 168, n. 5); D. Wyatt, 'New Legal Order, or Old?' (1982) 7 *ELRev* 147; R. Plender, 'The European Court as an International Tribunal' [1983] *CLJ* 279; F. G. Jacobs, *European Community Law and Public International Law—Two Different Legal Orders?* (Institut für Internationales Recht an der Universität Kiel: Schücking Lecture, Kiel, 1983). The second phase began in the late 1990s and is still continuing: see A. Pellet, 'Les fondements juridiques internationaux du droit communautaire' (1997) 5 *Collected Courses of the Academy of European Law*, Book 2, 193; G. Lysén, 'The European Community as a Self-Contained Regime' (1999) 2 *Europarättslig Tidskrift* 128; E. Denza, 'Two Legal Orders: Divergent or Convergent?' (1999) 48 *ICLQ* 257; O. Spiermann, 'The Other Side of the Story: An Unpopular Essay on the Making of the European Community Legal Order' (1999) 10 *EJIL* 763.

another even though it derives its validity from it.[37] This is apparent if one takes the example of a British colony which has been granted internal self-government. A British statute may give it a constitution providing for a legislature, an executive, and a judiciary: the legal system of that colony would owe its validity to the statute, but it would nevertheless be a separate system from United Kingdom law.

If a group of states conclude a Treaty in order to create an international organization with law-making powers, the question whether the law created by that organization is a separate legal system must depend on the intention of those states. Since no express statement of intention appears in the Community Treaties, the intention of the Member States must be inferred from the terms of the Treaties. These have been analysed elsewhere,[38] and it was concluded that, though the Community Treaties contain many novel features, there is nothing in them inconsistent with an intention that Community law should be part of international law. Even their most unusual features, the power of the European Court to hear preliminary references from national courts[39] and the direct effect of Community law,[40] would not be inappropriate in an international organization governed by international law; indeed, most international lawyers would regard them as highly desirable. Consequently, notwithstanding the impressive advance displayed by Community law over traditional international-law regimes, the terms of the Treaties do not indicate an intention to create a separate legal system.

Despite this, the European Court has taken the position that Community law is separate from international law. In 1963, it stated, somewhat ambiguously, that the Community constitutes a 'new legal order of international law'.[41] A year later, in *Costa* v. *ENEL*[42] it came out more clearly in favour of separation when it said, 'By contrast with ordinary international treaties, the EEC Treaty

---

[37] We are thus using the term 'legal system' in a fairly broad and flexible sense, the sense in which most lawyers would use it. All we mean by it is a set of legal rules (broadly defined) that are consistent (non-contradictory) and are generally applied together. Legal philosophers such as Austin and Kelsen used it in a stricter sense: see, e.g., J. Raz, *The Concept of a Legal System* (Oxford University Press, Oxford, 2nd edn., 1980), 95 ff.

[38] T.C. Hartley, *Constitutional Problems of the European Union* (Hart, Oxford, 1999), 128 ff.

[39] At present, there are at least three other international courts with jurisdiction to give preliminary rulings on a reference from a national court: the Benelux Court, the Andean Court of Justice, and the EFTA Court, the last having jurisdiction only to give advisory opinions. On the Benelux Court see Art. 6 of the Treaty establishing the Benelux Court, 1965 (in force on 1 January 1974); on the Andean Court, see Arts. 28–31 of the Treaty creating the Court of Justice of the Cartagena Agreement, 1979 (1979) 18 ILM 1203; on the EFTA Court, see Art. 34 of the Agreement between the EFTA States on the establishment of a Surveillance Authority and a Court of Justice [1994] OJ L344 (see, further, P. Christiansen, 'The EFTA Court' (1997) 22 *ELRev* 539, 542–3). These courts were all established after the European Court; however, in 1907 it was suggested that the proposed International Prize Court (which, in the end, was never set up) should have the power to hear appeals from national courts. Other international courts may well come to have some such a power in the future. In fact, one author has written, 'From the perspective of public international law, the novelty of the Community's system of references for preliminary ruling lies less in the conception than in the achievement', Plender, n. 36 above, 284.   [40] Discussed below.

[41] Case 26/62, [1963] ECR 1, 12.   [42] Case 6/64, [1964] ECR 585, 593.

has created its own legal system'. More recently, in 1991, it simply said that the Communities' Treaties have established a 'new legal order'.[43] This view has been accepted by the Constitutional Courts of both Germany and Italy.[44] It would take us too far from our main theme to consider whether this is correct: for present purposes, we will assume that it is. Even if it is correct, however, it in no way detracts from the dependent position of Community law.[45]

3. Dissolving the union

One of the consequences of the dependent character of Community law is that the Member States, provided they act unanimously, could dissolve the European Union if they wished. All that is needed is a new Treaty terminating the existing ones. The fact that the Community Treaties make no provision for the dissolution of the Union is irrelevant.[46] The existence of the Union does not depend on Community law: it depends on the Treaties, which in turn depend on international law. Consequently, international law decides whether the Treaties can be terminated. Under international law this is possible if all the parties agree: it is not necessary that the Treaties should themselves make provision for their termination.[47] The position would be the same even if the Treaties expressly provided that they could not be terminated. Such a provision cannot be binding.[48] Take the analogy of a provision in a contract that the contract cannot be terminated even if all the parties agree. That cannot prevent the

---

[43] *Opinion 1/91, First EEA Opinion* [1991] ECR 6079, para. 21.

[44] *Bundesverfassungsgericht, Internationale Handelsgesellschaft* case, 29 May 1974 [1974] 2 CMLR 540, para. 19; *Corte Costituzionale, Frontini* case, 27 December 1973 [1973] CMLR 372, para. 12.

[45] The European Court's decision to declare Community law a separate system has had important consequences for the relationship between Community law and international law. For example, in Case C–280/93, *Germany* v. *Council* [1994] ECR I–4973 ('Banana Case'), the Court held that a Community regulation could be valid even though its adoption was contrary to the GATT, a Treaty binding on both the Community and the Member States. It is hard to imagine that it could have reached this decision if it had regarded Community law as part of international law. Interestingly enough, the example usually quoted of the consequence of declaring Community law separate from international law, Cases 90, 91/63, *Commission* v. *Luxembourg and Belgium* [1964] ECR 625, would probably have been decided the same way under international law: see Wyatt, n. 36 above, 160.

[46] Art. 97 of the ECSC Treaty states that it is concluded for a period of fifty years from its entry into force, a provision which might be regarded as implying that it cannot be terminated before then; the other Treaties contain no such provision, which could be regarded as implying that they can be terminated at the will of the parties, or that they can never be terminated, or neither.

[47] To the extent that the Community Treaties contain no contrary provision, this follows from Art. 54 of the Vienna Convention on the Law of Treaties 1969, which provides that a treaty may be terminated *either* in conformity with the provisions of the Treaty *or* by consent of all the parties. If, however, the Treaties were regarded as containing some provision impliedly preventing their termination, the Vienna Convention would be inapplicable by reason of Art. 5 of the Vienna Convention, which states that the Convention applies to the constituent treaty of an international organization 'without prejudice to any rules of the organization'. In such a case, the matter would be outside the scope of the Vienna Convention and would have to be resolved on the basis of customary international law, under which termination by unanimous consent is (it is suggested) possible.

[48] It is assumed that no question arises regarding the rights of third parties.

parties from subsequently agreeing to terminate the contract. One cannot believe that the position is different in the case of a Treaty. How could international law decree that an international organization lives on if all its members want it dissolved? Such a result would be unrealistic and impractical.

4. AMENDING THE TREATIES

If nothing in Community law can prevent the total repeal of the Treaties, nothing can prevent their partial repeal; so nothing in Community law can prevent the repeal of any particular provision in the Treaties. Moreover, just as a provision in a contract or Treaty stating that the parties will not rescind that contract or Treaty (in whole or in part) is of no effect, so too is a provision that the parties will not add a particular provision to their contract or Treaty. That also cannot be binding on them. It cannot prevent them from subsequently agreeing to add the provision. It follows that the Treaties cannot prevent their amendment.[49]

As is well known, the Treaties contain procedural rules governing their amendment. Today, these are contained in Article 48 (ex N) of the Treaty on European Union. This provides that the Council must deliver an opinion (after consulting the European Parliament and, where appropriate, the Commission) in favour of calling a conference of the representatives of the governments of the Member States. The conference is then convened and must determine unanimously what amendments are to be made. Though not specified by Article 48 (ex N), the amendments take the form of a new Treaty amending the existing Treaties. However, for the reasons explained above, Article 48 (ex N) cannot deprive the Member States, acting unanimously, of the power to amend the Treaties without complying with its requirements.[50] Those requirements must,

---

[49] For the opposite position, see J.-L. Cruz Vilaça and N. Piçarra, 'Y a-t-il des limites matérielles à la révision des traités instituant les Communautés européennes?' [1993] *CDE* 3, a position which draws support from a cryptic statement by the European Court in *Opinion 1/91* [1991] ECR 6079, para. 72. However, it is accepted by most authors, including Cruz Vilaça and Piçarra, that this view is tenable only under the theory of constitutionalization (in the form rejected earlier in this essay): see in particular [1993] *CDE* 3, 10–13.

[50] All the arguments are collected and analysed with lucidity and thoughtfulness in M. Deliège-Sequaris, 'Révision des traités européens en dehors des procédures prévues' [1980] *CDE* 539. At the time this article was written, the author was a junior lecturer (*assistant*) at the University of Liège. For a rather clumsy attempt by a professor at the same university to refute her conclusions, see J.-V. Louis, 'Quelques considérations sur la révision des traités instituant les Communautés', *ibid.*, 553. A more sophisticated case for the view that the procedural requirements in the Treaty are binding on the Member States is to be found in Weiler and Haltern, n. 13 above, 417–23. The authors of this latter article accept that their argument stands up only if one accepts the theory of constitutionalization (in the form rejected in the earlier part of this essay). In international law, it is generally agreed that if a treaty lays down special procedures for its amendment, the states party to it may follow those procedures if they wish, but are not bound to do so: see B. de Witte, 'Rules of Change in International Law: How Special is the European Community?' (1994) 25 *Neth Yb Int L* 299, 312 ff. Weiler and Haltern accept this: see 417–18 of their article. For the opposite view see Pellet, n. 36 above, 214–17. Pellet bases his view on Art. 5 of the Vienna Convention on the Law of Treaties (explained above, n. 47). However, Art. 5 merely excludes the application of the Vienna Convention

therefore, be regarded as not mandatory but merely directory: failure to comply with them is an infringement of Community law,[51] but does not affect the validity of the amendment.[52] This is borne out by the fact that on two occasions in the past the ECSC Treaty has been amended without following the procedure laid down in it.[53] No one has ever questioned the validity of these amendments.

5. DIRECT EFFECT

Direct effect (defined below)[54] is concerned with the way in which a provision of one legal system is applied in another. It thus involves the transfer of a provision between systems. The way in which this is determined depends on the relationship between the two systems. If one is dependent on the other (in the sense that it derives its validity from it), the question of transfer must be determined by the primary system. It can decide whether provisions of the one system can apply in the other and, if they do, in what circumstances this will occur. If, on the other hand, neither system is dependent on the other, each system decides for itself whether provisions of the other can be transferred to it.

This will be clear from two examples. Assume, first, that the United Kingdom decides to give home rule to a territory under its jurisdiction. It sets up a regional assembly with law-making powers and creates a system of courts for that territory. Clearly, United Kingdom law determines whether provisions of United Kingdom law apply in the dependent legal system or whether provisions of the dependent system apply in the United Kingdom system. This is because United Kingdom law is the primary system.

Now contrast the position where each system is independent of the other. Let us take the relationship between English and French law. English law may have one provision dealing with a particular matter, say, the validity of a marriage, and French law may have another. The question whether an English court will apply the French provision with regard to a particular marriage must depend on English law, the English rules of conflict of laws.[55] Whether a French court

---

where its terms conflict with the provisions of the constituent treaty of an international organization: it does not give those provisions any greater effect than they would have had apart from the Convention. The matter therefore falls to be determined by customary international law, under which amendment by unanimous consent with any special procedure is always possible.

[51] In theory, proceedings could be brought against the Member States (all of them!) under Art. 226 (ex 169) EC.

[52] If the dictum of the European Court in Case 43/75, *Defrenne* v. *Sabena* [1976] ECR 455, para. 58 was intended to deny this, it cannot be right.

[53] The first was the Treaty of 27 October 1956, which brought about certain amendments consequent on the return of the Saar to Germany, and the second was the Convention on Certain Institutions Common to the European Communities, which was signed at the same time as the EEC and Euratom Treaties: see P. Pescatore, *L'ordre juridique des Communautés européennes* (Presses Universitaires de Liège, Liège, 1975), 62–3.   [54] See text to n. 58, below.

[55] Some would say that an English court never applies foreign law as such, but merely applies a provision of English law modelled on the foreign provision: see W. W. Cook, *Logical and Legal Bases*

would apply the French or the English provision to the marriage would, however, depend on French law. The result is that the same marriage might be valid in English eyes and invalid in French eyes. This is unfortunate, but inescapable, in view of the relationship between the two legal systems.

These principles also govern the relationship between international law and national law. Since these two systems are independent of each other,[56] the question whether a provision of international law applies in national law must depend on the latter. This is indeed the case. The law of each country decides to what extent international law has effect as part of the legal system of that country.[57]

The important issue for our purposes is the application of a treaty in the domestic law of the states that are parties to it. If a treaty (or a provision in it) applies in the legal system of such a state without that state having to adopt any legislation specifically providing for the application of that treaty, the treaty is said to be 'directly effective' or 'directly applicable'.[58] A treaty that is directly effective is automatically part of the legal system of the state in question. If, on the other hand, it is not directly effective, it cannot be applied in the domestic law of the state without the adoption of legislation to make provision for this.

When states sign a treaty, they normally agree to achieve a certain result, but reserve to themselves the right to determine the means by which this will be brought about. If the desired result involves an alteration of their law, their law decides whether this will follow automatically from the treaty (direct effect) or whether legislation will be necessary. In certain states (sometimes called 'monist'), direct effect is possible;[59] in others (sometimes called 'dualist') it is not.[60] In both cases, however, it is by virtue of the law of the state in question that the treaty

---

of the Conflict of Laws (Harvard University Press, Cambridge, Mass., 1942), 20–1. It is true that the English court may not apply the foreign provision in precisely the same way as the foreign court would; nevertheless, it is hardly justified to say that the foreign provision is not applied. For further discussion see J. H. C. Morris, *The Conflict of Laws* (Sweet & Maxwell, London, 4th edn., 1993, by D. McClean), 446–7.

[56] This may be rejected by theorists who follow the monist view of international law, but it accords with the actual, real-life relationship between the two systems.

[57] See F. G. Jacobs and S. Roberts (eds.), *The Effect of Treaties in Domestic Law* (Sweet & Maxwell, London, 1987), p. xxiv (introduction by Jacobs, based on studies of individual countries in later parts of the book). For the United States see the thoughtful analysis by J.H. Jackson, *ibid.*, 153–5.

[58] It is not necessary to consider the arguments that raged at one time on a possible distinction between direct effect and direct applicability: the differences, if they exist, are of no consequence for our discussion.

[59] This does not mean that every treaty will be directly effective: the law of the state in question specifies the requirements for direct effect. Frequently, it must be shown that the treaty is self-executing. This concept was explained as long ago as 1829 by the United States Supreme Court in *Foster and Elam* v. *Neilson* 2 Pet 253, 314, where it distinguished a Treaty provision which 'operates of itself, without the aid of any legislative provision' from a provision in which one of the parties 'engages to perform a particular act'. In the former case, the treaty provision is self-executing; in the latter, it is not.

[60] The distinction between the 'monist' and 'dualist' approaches is actually more complex and far-reaching than this, since it concerns the over-all relationship between international and domestic law: I. Brownlie, *Principles of Public International Law* (Oxford University Press, Oxford, 5th edn., 1998), 31 ff. In adopting these terms, we are not, however, raising these wider questions: we are simply using the terms as handy tags to denote the two approaches set out in the text above. Even if the terms are used in this limited sense, however, the statements in the text are still something of an over-simplification: see F. Jacobs in Jacobs and Roberts, n. 57 above, pp. xxiv–xxvi.

is applied: in a 'monist' country, it is the rule permitting the direct application of treaties (a rule that may be anything from a judge-made principle to a constitutional provision); in a 'dualist' country, it is the legislation passed to give effect to the particular treaty in question. In this latter case, the legislation may take various forms. At one end of the spectrum, it may simply amend national law to bring it into line with the treaty, possibly without even referring to it.[61] At the other end, it may provide that the treaty (contained in a Schedule to the legislation) will have the force of law in the country concerned.[62] In this last situation, the only real difference between a 'dualist' and a 'monist' country is that in the former there is a separate legislative measure each time a treaty has to be applied in the domestic legal system, while in the latter there is one measure providing for the application of all future treaties.[63]

Since Member-State law is not dependent on Community law, it follows that Community law cannot apply in the legal systems of the Member States unless Member-State law says so: no rule of Community law can itself bring this about.[64] In Article 249 (ex 189), the Member States agreed that EC (originally, EEC) regulations would be directly applicable in all Member States. This meant that, unlike the position in most treaties, the parties to the EC Treaty not only agreed to achieve a certain result, but also agreed on the means by which this would be brought about (direct effect). In other words, all the Member States undertook to adopt the 'monist' position in this particular case.[65] Though unusual, such a provision is in no way contrary to international law.[66]

[61] In such a case, there might be some justification in saying that the treaty is not applied as such, but rather that a rule of national law is modelled on the treaty: see n. 55 above.

[62] For an example of this latter method see s. 2(1) of the Carriage of Goods by Sea Act 1971, which provides that the Hague-Visby Rules (an international agreement) will have the force of law in the UK. For a more detailed discussion of the position in the UK, see R. Higgins in Jacobs and Roberts, n. 57 above, 126–9.

[63] Even though the UK is a 'dualist' country, legislation adopted to give effect to a treaty will, if possible, be interpreted in such a way as to conform to the treaty: *James Buchanan & Co Ltd* v. *Babco Forwarding and Shipping (UK) Ltd* [1978] AC 141; *Fothergill* v. *Monarch Airlines Ltd* [1981] AC 251; see, further, A. Dicey and J. Morris *The Conflict of Laws* (L. Collins (ed.), Sweet & Maxwell, London, 13th edn., 2000), 9–16. This rule can apply even if the UK legislation does not refer to the treaty, provided it is shown that the legislation was passed to give effect to it.

[64] See, e.g., *Brunner* v. *European Union Treaty, Bundesverfassungsgericht*, decision of 12 October 1993 [1994] 1 CMLR 57, para. 55; (1994) 33 ILM 388; 89 BverfGE 155, in which the German Constitutional Court stated that Community law applies in Germany only because the German laws ratifying the Community Treaties said that it would.

[65] Art. 249 (ex 189) also states that directives are binding as to the result to be achieved, but they leave to each Member State the choice of form and methods, thereby making the effect of a directive in the legal systems of Member States dependent on national legislation. Thus, provision was made both for instruments of a 'monist' character and for those of a 'dualist' character, each to be used where appropriate. The novelty of this was not the recognition of these two approaches, but the fact that all the parties to the Treaty agreed to adopt the same approach in any given case. The advantage of this is that each Community measure applies in the same way in every Member State. Unfortunately, the European Court has distorted this scheme by holding that directives can have a limited direct effect: see Case 41/74, *Van Duyn* v. *Home Office* [1974] ECR 1337. It has also ruled that Treaty provisions can be directly effective: Case 26/62, *Van Gend en Loos* [1963] ECR 1. For further discussion see Hartley, n. 38 above, 24–30.

[66] See Jackson, n. 57 above, 154; see also Plender, n. 36 above, 287–8; cf. the Advisory Opinion of the Permanent Court of International Justice in the *Danzig Railway Officials* case (1928) PCIJ Ser. B No. 15.

Having undertaken this, the Member States then had to carry it out. In the case of the 'monist' countries, the rule of national law making general provision for direct effect, the rule making that country 'monist', was sufficient; in the case of 'dualist' countries, on the other hand, a special rule had to be adopted for the purpose. In the United Kingdom, this was section 2(1) of the European Communities Act 1972, which states that all provisions of Community law (including those to be adopted in the future) that under Community law are to be given legal effect without further enactment (direct effect) will be directly effective in the United Kingdom. It is only by virtue of this provision that Community law is directly effective in the United Kingdom. Thus, while the obligation to give direct effect to certain provisions of Community law stems from the treaties, the *carrying out* of that obligation is a matter for national law.

6. SUPREMACY

If a provision of one legal system is applied in another, it may conflict with a provision of the latter. When this occurs, the principles discussed above must determine which prevails. Thus, where an international treaty is applied in the legal system of one of the parties to it, the question whether the treaty overrides national law must be determined by the law of that state. In the case of a 'monist' country, the rule providing for the direct effect of treaties may also indicate their position in the legal hierarchy; otherwise, there will usually be a judge-made rule. In the United States, for example, a treaty that is directly effective[67] has the same position in the legal hierarchy as a federal statute: it prevails over earlier federal statutes but is subordinate to later ones.[68] This is a judge-made rule, though it is partly derived from Article VI, section 2, of the United States Constitution.[69] In the Netherlands, on the other hand, the Constitution provides that directly effective treaties prevail over both prior and subsequent legislation.[70]

In the case of a 'dualist' country (such as the United Kingdom), the status of a treaty depends on the instrument by which it was given legal effect. If words from a treaty are incorporated into a statute (either with, or without, a reference to the treaty), they take effect as part of that statute: it is the statute, not the treaty, that is applied. If there is a conflict with another legal provision, the conflict is not between the treaty and the other provision, but between the

---

[67] Not all international agreements count as 'Treaties' in the United States, and not all 'Treaties' are directly effective. For the details see Jackson, n. 57 above, 142–59.

[68] *Ibid.*, 162. For further details, see *ibid.*, 159–64.

[69] Art. VI, section 2, reads: 'This Constitution, and the Laws of the United States which shall be made in Pursuance thereof; and all Treaties made, or which shall be made, under the Authority of the United States, shall be the supreme Law of the Land; and the Judges in every State shall be bound thereby, any Thing in the Constitution or Laws of any State to the Contrary notwithstanding.' This establishes that treaties prevail over state legislation, but does not clearly determine their position with regard to federal legislation.

[70] See H. Schermers in Jacobs and Roberts, n. 57 above, 112–14.

statute and the other provision. The normal rules determine which prevails. If, on the other hand, the statute says that the treaty has the force of law, it makes sense to say that the treaty itself is being applied. Nevertheless, it is applied only because the statute says so; consequently, the status of the treaty is the same as that of the statute. In both cases, therefore, the position of the treaty in the legal hierarchy depends on that of the legislation by which it was given effect. If this was a statute, it will prevail over earlier statutes, but not over later ones. If it was subordinate legislation, it will have the same status as that legislation.[71] These rules can, however, be changed if the legislation which gave effect to the treaty so provides. The Human Rights Act 1998 is an example: though it gives (limited) effect to the European Convention on Human Rights in the domestic law of the United Kingdom, it provides that the Convention does not prevail over *any* United Kingdom legislation, either subsequent or prior.[72]

These rules do not normally prevent states from carrying out their treaty obligations. Since most treaties merely require the parties to achieve a given result, the status of the treaty in their domestic law does not matter as long as the result is achieved. The fact that the treaty could be overridden by later legislation is not a breach of the obligations under it, if this does not in fact occur. If it occurs inadvertently, the matter can be put right as soon as the conflict is evident. For example, the United Kingdom was a party to the European Convention on Human Rights for many years before the Human Rights Act 1998 came into force. Whenever it appeared, perhaps in a judgment of the European Court of Human Rights, that United Kingdom law conflicted with a provision of the Convention, the position was rectified by the amendment of the offending legislation.[73]

The European Court has never expressly rejected these principles, but it has been loath to give express acceptance to them. The first time the question came before it, in *Van Gend en Loos*,[74] the Court took great care to avoid considering it. The case arose when a Dutch tribunal[75] asked the European Court to give a ruling on the direct effect of Article 12 of the EEC Treaty (as it then stood), and it was argued by the Dutch and Belgian governments that the question whether the Community provision prevailed over a conflicting provision of Dutch law depended on Dutch law, and therefore fell within the exclusive jurisdiction of the Dutch courts. The European Court did not deny this, but said it had not been asked to rule on Dutch law, but merely to interpret the Treaty.[76] When the Belgian government insisted that no answer the European Court might give could possibly have any bearing on the proceedings before the Dutch

---

[71] The status of subordinate legislation normally depends on that of the statute under which it was adopted.

[72] See ss. 3 and 4. This is said to have caused some bemusement in the House of Lords: see K. Ewing, 'The Human Rights Act and Parliamentary Democracy' (1999) 62 *MLR* 79, 88, n. 57.

[73] In this respect, the position will not be greatly changed by the Human Rights Act, UK.

[74] Case 26/62, [1963] ECR 1.

[75] The *Tariefcommissie*, a tribunal concerned with customs duties.   [76] [1963] ECR 1, 10–11.

tribunal, it replied that it was none of its business why the Dutch tribunal had chosen to ask the questions it had or whether its answer would be relevant to the proceedings before it: all that mattered was that the questions concerned Community law.[77]

There is no provision in the Treaties stating that Community law prevails over Member-State law. It could, however, be argued that Article 249 (ex 189), which as we have seen provides that regulations are directly applicable, implies that they should be given at least a certain degree of supremacy.[78] The numerous statements by the European Court that directly effective Community law prevails over Member-State law, both prior and subsequent, are based on the proposition that this is what the Member States (implicitly) agreed when they signed the Treaties:[79] there is no other source from which such a principle could be derived.

Have the Member States carried out this agreement? Here we have a problem. As we have seen, Community provisions can have effect in Member States only by virtue of Member-State law, and the extent to which they prevail over domestic law also depends on a rule of Member-State law. However, all rules of Member-State law derive their validity from the national constitution: consequently, they cannot be valid if the constitution declares them invalid. Since the rule providing for the supremacy of Community law is itself a rule of Member-State law, its validity too depends on the national constitution. This means that the supremacy of Community law in a country always depends, in the last analysis, on the constitution of that country. If the constitution imposes limits on such supremacy, there is no way those limits can be avoided—unless the constitution itself is amended.

This is most obvious in those countries with written constitutions. In Germany, for example, the Constitutional Court has stated expressly that Community law applies in Germany only because the Treaties were approved by the German Parliament. Since the German Parliament is subject to the Constitution, it could not grant the Community any powers that conflicted with the Constitution. Although the Constitution permits Germany to confer powers on an international organization like the Community, those powers

---

[77] [1963] ECR 1, 10–11. Since the Netherlands is a 'monist' country and the Dutch Constitution provides that treaties prevail over Dutch legislation, the Dutch tribunal would have been willing to give primacy to a provision of the EEC Treaty, provided it was self-executing (see n. 59 above). The Dutch government considered that this was a question for Dutch law to decide. The Dutch tribunal, however, referred it to the European Court, perhaps because it thought that the correct interpretation of the Community provision would assist it in reaching a decision. In these circumstances, it was not unreasonable for the European Court to say that the Dutch tribunal's reasons for making the reference were none of its concern. However, once it had surmounted the jurisdictional hurdle, the European Court went on to consider not only whether the Community provision was self-executing (it held that it was), but also whether the Member States had implicitly agreed to give self-executing Treaty provisions direct effect (it held that they had). This last point was not relevant in the case of the Netherlands, but the Court was obviously preparing its position for future battles against 'dualist' states.

[78] Case 6/64, *Costa v. ENEL* [1963] ECR 585, 594.   [79] *Ibid.*

must not be open-ended: they have to be defined in advance. This means that the Community cannot be given the power to extend its powers, what the Germans call *Kompetenz-Kompetenz.* The German Constitutional Court has, therefore, ruled that any Community measure that contravenes this principle would be inapplicable in Germany.[80] The Danish Supreme Court has reached a similar conclusion.[81] Section 20 of the Danish Constitution permits the delegation of powers to an international organization, but this too requires that they be defined in advance. The Supreme Court, therefore, held that if a Community measure went beyond the powers conferred on the Community, the Danish courts would declare it inapplicable in Denmark. In both Germany and Denmark, the national courts would be the ones to decide.

Similar views have been expressed by courts in other Member States (though they have not always been so clearly formulated).[82] So far, however, there has been no case in which a Community provision has actually been held to infringe the constitution of a Member State. If this were to happen, the European Court would presumably declare that the state in question had infringed the Treaty.[83] That state would then have to amend its constitution, if this were possible.[84] If not, all the Member States would have to work together to find a solution, possibly by amending Community law.

An example of the way in which Community law can be changed to accommodate national constitutional problems is to be found in the series of cases in which the European Court has developed the Community doctrine of fundamental human rights. Once it became clear that the German Constitutional Court would not permit the application of Community law in Germany if it infringed fundamental human rights as defined in the German Constitution, the European Court declared that fundamental human rights, in which it had previously shown little interest,[85] were 'enshrined in the general principles of Community law and protected by the Court'.[86] In later cases, it has said that it will strike down Community measures that are incompatible with fundamental human rights as recognized in the constitutions of the Member States.[87] At the same time, however, it has insisted that the validity of a Community measure or

---

[80] *Brunner*, n. 64 above (see n. 27 above).

[81] *Carlsen* v. *Rasmussen*, Danish Supreme Court (*Højesteret*), judgment of 6 April 1998 [1999] 3 CMLR 854 (see further n. 30 above).   [82] See n. 35 above.

[83] The European Court claims that Community law must always prevail over national constitutions: see, e.g., Case 106/77, *Amministrazione delle Finanze dello Stato* v. *Simmenthal SpA* [1978] ECR 629. For the more lenient rule under international law see the Vienna Convention on the Law of Treaties, Art. 46. In view of its theory that Community law is separate from international law (discussed above), the European Court would almost certainly regard international law as inapplicable in this case.

[84] Certain provisions of the German Constitution cannot be amended: *Grundgesetz*, Art. 79(3); moreover, in both Germany and other Member States, it might be politically impossible to obtain the necessary majority to amend the Constitution.

[85] Case 1/58, *Stork* v. *High Authority* [1959] ECR 17, 26 (rights under *Grundgesetz*, Arts. 2 and 12); Cases 36–8, 40/59, *Geitling* v. *High Authority* [1960] ECR 423, 438 (rights under *Grundgesetz* Art. 14).

[86] Case 29/69, *Stauder* v. *Ulm* [1969] ECR 419, para. 7.

[87] Case 4/73, *Nold* v. *Commission* [1974] ECR 491, para. 13.

its effect within a Member State cannot be affected by allegations that it is contrary to fundamental human rights as formulated by the constitution of a Member State.[88] These two statements do not seem entirely consistent; nevertheless, the general message is clear: Member States must accept that Community law prevails over their constitutions, while the European Court will ensure that, at least as far as human rights are concerned, any Community provision that conflicts with the constitution of a Member State will be declared invalid. As a result, the German Constitutional Court, which had originally said it would examine Community measures to ensure that they complied with German notions of fundamental human rights (and refuse to permit their application in Germany if they did not),[89] eventually decided to let the European Court perform this task,[90] though it has not resiled from its position that the German Constitution prevails over Community law in Germany.

The United Kingdom's minimalist Constitution is less likely to produce conflicts of this kind; however, there is one situation in which such a clash could occur. This concerns one of the fundamental provisions of the British Constitution, the rule that Parliament cannot limit its future powers. Since there is no way (short of a change in the *Grundnorm*) in which this rule can be altered, it is not constitutionally possible for Parliament to disable itself from legislating contrary to Community law in the future. If the European Court demanded this (as distinct from demanding that Parliament should not exercise its power), the United Kingdom could not comply.

When the United Kingdom joined the Community, Parliament gave Community law the maximum degree of supremacy that was constitutionally possible. This was done in the European Communities Act 1972. Section 2(1) of this provides for the direct effect of Community law, and section 2(4) provides that all past and future Acts of Parliament must be 'construed and have effect' subject to section 2(1). This might appear to limit the power of Parliament to pass legislation that conflicts with directly effective Community law, but all it can be regarded as doing, since this is all Parliament is constitutionally capable of doing, is laying down a rule of interpretation to the effect that, since Parliament had no intention when it passed the European Communities Act of legislating contrary to Community law and, since it did not believe that it would have such an intention in the future, subsequent Acts of Parliament should be interpreted as not being intended to apply to the extent that they conflicted with directly effective Community law. Such a rule of interpretation would prevent

---

[88] Case 11/70, *Internationale Handelsgesellschaft* v. *Einfuhr- und Vorratsstelle für Getreide und Futtermittel* [1970] ECR 1125, para. 3. Interestingly, this statement is absent from the *Nold* case, n. 87 above, but it reappears in later cases: see, e.g., *Hauer* v. *Land Rheinland-Pfalz* [1979] ECR 3727, para. 14.

[89] *Internationale Handelsgesellschaft* case, *Bundesverfassungsgericht*, 29 May 1974 [1974] 2 CMLR 540.

[90] *Wünsche Handelsgesellschaft* case, *Bundesverfassungsgericht*, 22 October 1986 [1987] 3 CMLR 225.

unintended conflicts. However, if Parliament made clear that the legislation was intended to apply notwithstanding any contrary provision of Community law, the courts would have to give effect to that.

7. CONCLUSION

It will be seen that everything in this essay follows from its initial premiss that the Community Treaties are what they appear to be: treaties under international law. Once this is accepted, it is possible to rebuild the bridge between Community law and international law, a bridge that once existed but was deliberately destroyed in the early days of the Community by over-zealous judges and lawyers who believed they were laying the foundations of a new superstate, a United States of Europe. If this misconception is abandoned, many apparent problems are revealed as normal and acceptable; moreover, the concepts and solutions of Community law can then be used to develop the legal systems of other international organizations of a similar kind.[91]

---

[91] For further discussion of some of the issues considered in this essay see T. Schilling, 'The Autonomy of the Community Legal Order: An Analysis of Possible Foundations' (1996) 37 *Harv Int Law J* 389; Pellet, n. 2 above; D. R. Phelan, *Revolt or Revolution—The Constitutional Boundaries of the European Community* (Round Hall Sweet & Maxwell, Dublin, 1997); Spiermann, n. 36 above; Hartley, n. 38 above, chaps. 7–10 (on sovereignty).

11

Integration and the Europeanization of the Law

ALEC STONE SWEET

Carol Harlow blends the concerns of the lawyer and the social scientist as well as anyone in the world. Given the focus of her research, how legal systems actually operate, with what social consequences, one might see blending as an obvious or natural move. Yet, traditional legal scholarship prefers determining what the law is, rather than tracing how actors make it work; it typically defends obsolete distinctions between 'law' and 'politics'; and it still shies from adopting perspectives considered somehow 'external' to the law. Providing a counterpoint to these tendencies has been an important purpose of Harlow's work.[1] Harlow sees the myriad ways in which a greater environment, comprised of markets and corporations, interest groups and organizations, elected officials, administrators, and networks of knowledge-based elites, shapes and is, in turn, shaped by what litigators and judges do.[2] Litigation and judicial rule-making breathe life into the law, permitting it to evolve in unforeseen and, at times, problematic ways. Further, because the law both enables and constrains actors and activity, courts can exert an irresistible attraction to those who would seek to use the law instrumentally.[3] Harlow not only cares about how and why the law evolves; she always attends to who wins and loses as a result. To my mind, these orientations are basic, even pre-requisite, to a legal scholarship that seeks to understand or change the law in modern European polities.

One overarching theme of Harlow's work has been the broad and progressive expansion of the power of judges to monitor policy processes and to control outcomes through their decisions. In recent years, Harlow has turned her sights on

---

[1] In addition to the publications cited in the notes below see C. Harlow, 'Disposing of Dicey: From Legal Autonomy to Constitutional Discourse' (2000) 48 *Political Studies* 356.

[2] C. Harlow, 'Public Service, Market Ideology, and Citizenship', in M. Freedland and S. Sciarra (eds.), *Public Service and Citizenship in European Law: Public and Labour Law Perspectives* (Clarendon, Oxford, 1998), 49; C. Harlow, 'European Administrative Law and the Global Challenge', in P. Craig and G. de Búrca (eds.), *The Evolution of EU Law* (Oxford University Press, Oxford, 1999), 261.

[3] C. Harlow, 'A Community of Interests?: Making the Most of European Law' (1992) 55 *MLR* 331; C. Harlow and R. Rawlings, *Pressure Through Law* (Routledge, London, 1992).

the emerging EU legal system. Among other things, she argues that integration and the accompanying development of European law accentuate the effects of trends already underway in (at least some) national legal systems. In Harlow's view, public law is being transformed, especially in the UK, by a set of linked practices and ideologies. These include sustained privatization, the rise of economistic models of competition and regulation, the gathering influence of transnational business, the retreat of the interventionist state, and the decline of trade union power. European integration, a highly organized microcosm of globalization, entails a 'shift of power' to private actors and especially transnational ones, to business and other pressure groups effectively organized at the European level, and to technocrats, regulatory officials, and courts.[4] Further, Harlow shows that integration has rapidly subverted conceptual categories that many in her field take for granted (though she seems never to have accepted these categories uncritically). She notices and draws important consequences from the fact that in European law and *Europeanized* national law, the boundaries between the public and the private quickly break down, that constitutional and administrative law are not separate domains but, rather, are co-constitutive, and that 'remedies, rights, procedure, and substantive law can converge'.[5] She advocates, and indeed provides, a relatively synthetic, holistic, open, and systemic approach to the study of a world where judicial authority is a significant political fact.

This essay provides support for these propositions and orientations. It also constitutes a report on a research project now coming to an end. The project began as an effort to test a theory about how a particular type of social system, a rule of law polity, emerges and evolves, with what political consequences. The theory was developed without reference to the European Community (EC).[6] In the first stage of research, I identified key variables and deduced causal relationships among them; and the theory was illustrated with regard to the *judicialization* of the GATT–WTO and of the French Fifth Republic.[7] I then derived a series of hypotheses about how new legal systems evolve, and began searching for an appropriate empirical setting in which to test them.

The EC provided an attractive case, as a new, and indeed novel, legal system. The system had a clear beginning point; data were, in principle, available; and

---

[4] Harlow, 'European Administrative Law and the Global Challenge', n. 2 above, 261–2.

[5] C. Harlow, 'A Common European Law of Remedies?', in C. Kilpatrick, T. Novitz, and P. Stidmore (eds.), *The Future of Remedies in Europe* (Hart, Oxford, 2000), 73.

[6] Because the focus of this essay is on the evolution of the legal and political system constituted by the Treaty of Rome, I use EC throughout.

[7] A. Stone Sweet, 'Judicialization and the Construction of Governance' (1999) 31 *Comparative Political Studies* 147; A. Stone Sweet, 'The New GATT: Dispute Resolution and the Judicialization of the Trade Regime', in M. Volcansek (ed.), *Law Above Nations: Supranational Courts and the Legalization of Politics* (University of Florida Press, Gainesville, Fla., 1997), 118–41. The basic model was also adapted to help explain the impact of constitutional adjudiciation on legislating and judging in Western Europe: A. Stone Sweet, 'Constitutional Politics: The Reciprocal Impact of Lawmaking and Constitutional Adjudication', in P. Craig and C. Harlow (eds.), *Lawmaking in the European Union* (Kluwer Law International, London, 1998), chap. 5; A. Stone Sweet, *Governing with Judges: Constitutional Politics in Europe* (Oxford University Press, Oxford, 2000).

no systematic social science on how it had developed and operates existed. With the support of the US National Science Foundation[8] and the European Court of Justice (ECJ), three graduate assistants,[9] Neil Fligstein,[10] and I collected comprehensive data on trading, litigating, lobbying, and legislating in the EC, most of which had never been compiled or analysed before. We tested our propositions, using both quantitative and qualitative methods; and we considered our findings in the light of current scholarly debates about European integration more generally.[11] This second part of the project served as the basis for the development of a more explicitly argued theory of integration.[12] Finally, in a third part of this research, we examined the relationship between the European Court and the national courts in the making of the EC's legal system.[13]

This essay summarizes this project's arguments and findings, and relates them to Harlow's own research on related questions. The first part of the essay examines the relationship between market forces, lobbying in the Commission, EC legislation, and the legal system. We find that the development of causal connections between these four processes produced a self-reinforcing system that has largely determined the pace and scope of integration. We also show that the construction and operation of the EC's legal system has been a crucial component of integration, which we conceive broadly as a joint market-building and polity-building project. The second part of the essay explores how litigants, national judges, and the European Court have interacted. Some important puzzles have been, at least partly, solved, but others deserve the full attention of lawyers and social scientists. Many of these relate to the complex, multidimensional impact of the development of European law on national legal systems.

---

[8] Law and Social Science Grants SBR 9412531 (1994–7), and SBR 9710963 (1997–2000).

[9] Thomas Brunell (now Assistant Professor of Political Science, SUNY-Binghampton), Rachel Cichowski (now Assistant Professor of Political Science, University of Washington), and Margaret McCown (Ph.D candidate at Oxford).

[10] Professor of Sociology, University of California, Berkeley, Calif.

[11] A. Stone Sweet and J. Caporaso, 'From Free Trade to Supranational Polity: The European Court and Integration', in W. Sandholtz and A. Stone Sweet (eds.), *European Integration and Supranational Governance* (Oxford University Press, Oxford, 1998), 92; A. Stone Sweet and T. Brunell, 'Constructing a Supranational Constitution: Dispute Resolution and Governance in the European Community' (1998) 92 *American Political Science Review* 63.

[12] N. Fligstein and A. Stone Sweet, 'Of Polities and Markets: An Institutionalist Account of European Integration', *American Journal of Sociology*, forthcoming; A. Stone Sweet and N. Fligstein, 'Institutionalizing the Treaty of Rome', in A. Stone Sweet, W. Sandholtz, and N. Fligstein (eds.), *The Institutionalization of Europe* (Oxford University Press, Oxford, 2001), 29.

[13] R. Cichowski, 'Integrating the Environment: The European Court and the Construction of Supranational Policy' (1998) 5 *JEPP* 387; R. Cichowski, 'Judicial Rulemaking and the Institutionalization of Sex Equality Policy', in *The Institutionalization of Europe*, n. 12 above, chap. 6; A. Stone Sweet and T. Brunell, 'The European Courts and the National Courts: A Statistical Analysis of Preliminary References, 1961–95' (1998) 5 *JEPP* 66; A. Stone Sweet and T. Brunell, 'The European Court, National Judges and Legal Integration: A Researcher's Guide to the Data Base on Preliminary References in European Law, 1958–98' (2000) 6 *ELJ* 117.

1. EUROPEAN INTEGRATION

We have developed and tested a theory of European integration that focuses on the development of specific causal relationships between three factors: social exchange (i.e. society), organizational capacity to respond to such exchange (i.e. governmental organs), and rule structures (i.e. law).[14] It bears mention in advance that, compared with virtually any other contemporary approach to integration, our theory is pitched at a higher level of abstraction, and the data analysed are more comprehensive and more highly aggregated. Our approach is both macro and dynamic, directing attention to how big processes interact, across multiple dimensions, over time. The approach allows us to 'see', and to make sense of, the main features and patterns exhibited by the integration process, as it proceeds. The theory is relevant to, but cannot itself explain, many discrete economic, legislative, or judicial events or decisions, at least without being supplemented by detailed case studies and process tracing. Our findings bear directly upon several long-standing, general concerns of EC studies. Two of these deserve emphasis upfront.

First, our main finding is that, over time, the activities of the EC's organizations mixed with the activities of traders and other transnational actors to produce a self-reinforcing system whereby evolving rule structures, modes of governance, and market integration became linked. We interpret these results as providing broad support for some of the core claims of 'neofunctionalist', regional integration theory, developed by Haas forty years ago,[15] as modified more recently.[16] We read Haas as arguing that integration would develop an 'expansive logic', serving to link the activities of an increasing number of actors operating in otherwise separate arenas of action. Haas labelled this logic: 'spillover'. We argue that (1) rules, organizational capacity to respond to social exchange, and effective procedures to process disputes, and (2) the behaviour and dispositions of political and economic actors, could evolve symbiotically. They would do so through positive feedback loops that would push steadily for deeper integration.

Secondly, it is commonly asserted[17] that 'negative integration' and 'positive integration' are governed by separate social logics. Negative integration,

---

[14] This part of the essay is based on Fligstein and Stone Sweet, 'Of Polities and Markets', n. 12 above; and Stone Sweet and Brunell, 'Constructing a Supranational Constitution', n. 11 above.

[15] E. Haas, *The Uniting of Europe: Political, Social, and Economic Forces, 1950–57* (Stanford University Press, Stanford, Calif., 1958); E. Haas, 'International Integration: The European and the Universal Process' (1961) 15 *International Organization* 366.

[16] A. Stone Sweet and W. Sandholtz, 'European Integration and Supranational Governance Revisited' (1999) 6 *JEPP* 144.

[17] E.g., F. Scharpf, *Governing in Europe: Effective and Democratic?* (Oxford University Press, Oxford, 1999), chap. 2; F. Scharpf, 'Negative and Positive Integration in the Political Economy of European Welfare States', in G. Marks, F. Scharpf, P. Schmitter, and W. Streeck (eds.), *Governance in the European Union* (Sage, London, 1996).

because it enables the Member States to reap large and diffuse joint gains, moves forward relatively smoothly. Positive integration, in contrast, regularly pits these same governments against one another, to the extent that deciding on one form of regulation or intervention as opposed to another will have distributive consequences for identifiable national constituencies, given restrictive decision rules. It is further argued that, as a result, the 'market' has been constituted without corresponding governmental capacity to regulate it, or to counter its excesses. In contrast, we find evidence for the view that negative and positive integration, far from being distinct processes, are in fact connected in important ways (they are meaningfully endogenous to one another).

We began by taking up four different, but well-known, stories that scholars have told about European integration. We used these narratives, in conjunction with other theoretical materials, to derive specific, testable hypotheses.

The first story focuses attention on the consequences of rising economic transactions across borders. The flow of goods, services, investment, and labour across national boundaries not only generated economic growth that states came to rely upon, but created or accentuated a host of transnational governance problems (the negative externalities of interdependence). Those who transacted across borders actively pressured governments and the EC's organizations to remove national barriers to further economic exchange (negative integration), and to regulate, in the form of European legislation (positive integration), the emerging Common Market.[18] Some scholars, including Harlow,[19] noted the fact that certain kinds of economic actors, especially big producers and importers, have benefited more from market integration than have non-exporting firms, while national systems of social welfare, labor relations, and interest representation have been eroded.

The second narrative traces the causes and effects of the 'constitutionalization' of the Treaty of Rome: the transformation of the EC from an international regime to a quasi-federal polity through the consolidation of the doctrines of direct effect and supremacy.[20] Constitutionalization profoundly altered, within domains governed by EC law, how individuals and firms pursue their interests, how national judiciaries operate, and how policy is made.[21] The doctrine of direct effect enabled private actors to plead rights found in EC law against their own governments in national courts, and the doctrine of supremacy meant that national judges had to resolve such litigation with reference to EC law. Two

---

[18] A. Moravscik, *The Choice for Europe: Social Purpose and State Power from Massina to Maastricht* (Cornell University Press, Ithaca, NY, 1999); F. Scharpf, 'Negative and Positive Integration', n. 17 above; A. Stone Sweet and T. Brunell, 'Constructing a Supranational Constitution', n. 11 above.

[19] Harlow, 'A Community of Interests?', n. 3 above, 337; P. Schmitter and W. Streeck, 'From National Corporatism to Transnational Pluralism' (1991) 19 *Politics and Society* 133.

[20] E. Stein, 'Lawyers, Judges, and the Making of a Transnational Constitution' (1981) 75 *American Journal of International Law* 1; J. H. H. Weiler, *The Constitution of Europe* (Cambridge University Press, Cambridge, 1999).

[21] A.-M. Burley and W. Mattli, 'Europe Before the Court: A Political Theory of Legal Integration', (1993) 47 *International Organization* 41.

dynamics were quickly established. First, transnational economic actors litigated to remove national hindrances to their activities; and, secondly, private actors not directly engaged in cross-border activity (e.g. those who seek to enhance women's rights or environmental protection) sought to use the EC legal system to destabilize or reform national rules and practices. In many legal domains, the operation of the legal system pushed the integration project a great deal further than Member State governments, operating under existing legislative rules, would have been prepared to go on their own.[22]

Our third integration narrative traces the myriad causes and consequences of the growth of interest group representation at the supranational level. Early on, the Commission worked hard to co-opt technical experts and directly affected parties into the policy process, to help draft new and assess existing market rules, and to help legitimize new proposals proposed. As the scope and density of EC rules increased, more and more groups, including those representing 'diffuse', public interests, discovered that it was in their interest to set up shop in Brussels.[23] Over the past two decades, complex symbiotic relationships have develop between lobby groups and the Commission, as Brussels became, in Harlow's terms, 'a lobbyist's town'.[24] Today, a wide range of policy outcomes can only be understood by taking into account the influence of these groups[25] within increasingly institutionalized procedures for consultation and participation.[26]

A fourth stream of scholarship seeks to explain the sources and consequences of permutations in the regimes that govern the EC's legislative process on policy-making efficiency.[27] Most important, of course, has been the move away from unanimity voting and the enhancement of the role of the European Parliament. Generally, we see intergovernmental bargaining (i.e. the decision-making of governments) and the evolution of legislative procedures as being embedded in the overall process of integration.

We had good *a priori* reasons to think that the activities of market actors, lobbyists, legislators, litigators, and judges were in fact connected to one another, both directly and through feedback loops. For the sake of brevity, I will

---

[22] Literature cited in nn. 11, 12.

[23] S. Mazey and J. Richardson (eds.), *Lobbying in the European Union* (Oxford University Press, Oxford, 1993); M. Pollack, 'Representing Diffuse Interests in EC Policy-Making' (1997) 4 *JEPP* 572.

[24] Harlow, 'A Community of Interests?', n. 3 above, 335.

[25] S. Anderson and K. Eliasson, 'European Community Lobbying' (1991) 20 *European Journal of Political Research* 173; J. Greenwood and M. Aspinwall (eds.), *Collective Action in the European Union: Interests and the New Politics of Associability* (Routledge, London and New York, 1998); Harlow, 'A Community of Interests?', n. 3 above, 339.

[26] R. Dogan, 'Comitology: Little Processes with Big Implications' (1997) 20 *West European Politics* 31; C. Joerges and J. Neyer, 'From Intergovernmental Bargaining to Deliberative Political Processes: The Constitutionalisation of Comitology' (1997) 3 *ELJ* 272; S. Mazey and J. Richardson, 'Institutionalizing Promiscuity: Commission-Interest Group Relations in the EU', in *The Institutionalization of Europe*, n. 12 above, 71.

[27] Moravscik, n. 18 above; G. Tsebelis, 'The Power of the European Parliament as a Conditional Agenda Setter' (1994) 88 *American Political Science Review* 128; G. Tsebelis and G. Garrett, 'The Institutional Determinants of Intergovernmentalism and Supranationalism' (2001) 55 *International Organization* 357.

provide stylized examples of such linkages, without fully developing the theoretical foundations for these expectations. Given certain necessary causal conditions, for example the acceptance of supremacy and direct effect by national judges, and the implementation of trading 'rights'[28] actors could find in Articles 28–30, we expected that intra-EC would provoke litigation, as traders found their activities hampered by national law and administrative practices. Further (a more stringent hypothesis), relatively more trade would produce relatively more litigation, and thus relatively more references to the Court. The hypotheses is testable, both cross-nationally and across time. Further, to the extent that the legal system actually does remove unlawful hindrances to trade, more trade will be stimulated. A feedback loop is thereby constituted, one that connects trading to litigating, and the cycle will begin anew. We also hypothesized that as EC secondary legislation is produced, in more and more domains, an increasing number of lobby groups would choose to invest in the Brussels complex; and we expected—the feedback loop again—that lobbyists would help produce more legislation in the arenas in which they operated. A third example: we expected that legislating and litigating could also become connected, since new regulations and directives (if directly effective) give private actors new grounds on which to vindicate their rights under EC law, through litigation. These latter two logics could be formalized as testable hypotheses, not only across time, but across policy domains: new legislation in specific areas of EC law (e.g. agriculture, consumer protection, sex equality, etc) would stimulate more lobbying and more litigating, which might then generate the attendant feedback effects.

We collected the data, the indicators of our variables, measures of the 'outputs' of each of our four process, for most of the life of the EC.[29] We then used econometric and other statistical means to describe, quantitatively, the integration process, and to test our various hypotheses. Figures 11.1–11.4 report, as time series, the outputs of each of our four processes. For reasons that will become apparent, we found it useful to think of European integration as being sequenced in three periods (and we later showed that there were significant period effects in the way that our variables interacted with one another over time). We think of these changes as 'parameter shifts' in the evolution of the EC, whereby important qualitative events generate quantitatively significant transformations. In the first period, roughly 1958–69, actors were engaged in the process of building the EC's main organizations and figuring out how to make the Treaty of Rome work; and they succeeded in establishing the common agricultural policy and important competition rules. The pivotal event during this period was the Court's constitutionalization of the Treaty through the doctrines of supremacy and direct effect. During the second period, 1970–85, the Commission and ECJ worked to dismantle barriers to intra-EC trade and other

---

[28] M. Poiares Maduro, *We, the Court: The European Court of Justice and the European Economic Constitution* (Hart, Oxford, 1998).

[29] Some of the data end in 1994, others extend to mid-1998.

kinds of transnational exchange (negative integration). At the same time, the Commission and the Council sought to replace the disparate regulatory regimes in place at the national level with harmonized, EC regulatory frameworks (positive integration). Although the data show that positive integration proceeded more steadily than is often appreciated, many important harmonization projects stalled in the Council, not least because more ambitious initiatives required the unanimous vote of national ministers. The unanimity rule, a product of the Luxembourg compromise in the 1960s, made it very difficult to forge agreements at a time when the cumulative impact of negative integration was to raise the costs of intergovernmental deadlock for an increasing number of social and economic actors who wanted wider and deeper integration. This period ended with the passage of the Single European Act 1986, which altered the voting rules for adopting legislation pertaining to the Single Market Programme, from unanimity to qualified majority voting in most cases. Our final period, from 1986 to the present, can be characterized as the most active from the perspective of institutionalizing European market and governance structures through positive integration.

This periodization can help us to make sense of the broad patterns of growth in trade, legislation, litigation, and lobbying in the EC. Figure 11.1 presents the growth in intra-EC exports for the period 1958–94. One observes a slow increase, but relatively low level of exports during the 1960s. In 1970 as EC rules start to bite, exports rise more steeply. Following 1985 with the announcement of the Single European Act, this rise accelerates. Changes in patterns of intra-European trade coincide with important events within the EC. The rules governing free movement of goods, such as the prohibition of maintaining national quotas and other measures of equivalent effect, entered into force in 1970, and thereby became directly effective for traders. In 1985, the EC agreed to the completion of the Single Market and to important changes in the voting rules just discussed.

Changes in trade are mirrored in changes in litigating and legislating. Figure 11.2 tracks increases in the use of Article 234 EC. Article 234 allows national judges to send cases involved in disputes over the EC rules to the European Court of Justice. This measure is the best indicator now available of the degree to which litigants have claimed rights issuing from EC law in national courts. The figure shows that levels of references were very low during the 1960s, and then began pick up in 1970 as EC rules entered into effect and as national judges accepted the doctrines of supremacy and direct effect. References doubled by 1980, then levelled off until 1985. After the Single European Act, they shot up once again.

Figure 11.3 indexes the annual production of regulations and directives in the EC. The passage of secondary legislation is a rough indicator of the growth of rules producing positive integration of the market. Most of the legislation during the first two periods was oriented towards producing collective market rules that would apply across Member States, and most required the unanimous vote of the Council to be adopted. But, even here, the pattern that emerges resembles

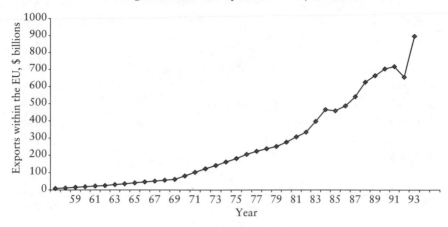

Figure 11.1: Exports within the EU, in $ billions (1990 dollars)
Source: Eurostat, 1997.

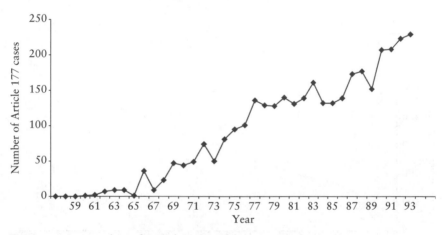

Figure 11.2: Number of Article 234 references, 1958–94
Source: Stone Sweet and Brunell, 1999.

those that appear in the prior two figures. Legislative production during the 1960s was relatively low, if rising. It picks up during the 1970s, and peaks in 1978. Between 1978 and 1985, legislating stabilizes, but takes off again after the passage of the Single European Act.

Figure 11.4 presents data on the cumulative number of lobbying groups in Brussels, over time. We were able to compile data on almost 600 significant lobbying groups. The beginning of the EC witnessed a flurry of foundings. Foundings decreased during the mid-1960s, and then bounced around during the 1970s and early 1980s. Following the passage of the Single European Act,

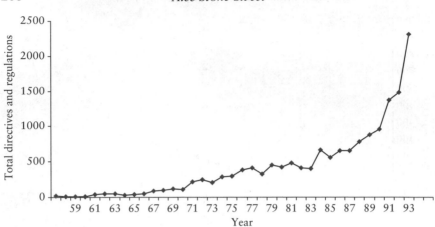

Figure 11.3: Legislation in the EU, 1958–94
Source: EU, Directory of Legislation in Force, 1996.

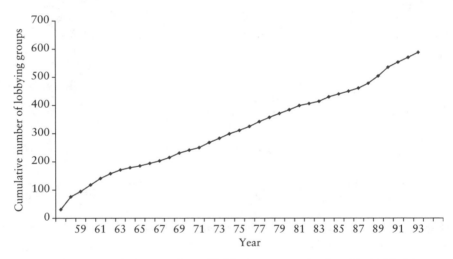

Figure 11.4: Cumulative number of lobbying groups in the EU, 1958–94
Source: Philips and Gray, 1997.

the establishment of new lobbying groups shot upward, to their highest levels since the early 1960s. Clearly, the Single European Act convinced groups that being in Brussels mattered, and that new legislative initiatives further stimulated the formation of new lobbying groups.

Taken together, these figures depict much of what we are trying to explain. They show that trading, litigating, legislating, and lobbying, which we take to be key indicators of European integration, grew over time, and that this growth roughly follows similar patterns that broadly conform to our periodization of EC activity. We are not arguing that in 1970, and again in 1986, everything that matters suddenly changed. On the contrary, each period contains, and passes forward to the next, institutional materials that structure what takes place thereafter. To take just one pertinent example, the doctrines of supremacy and direct effect, established in the first period, constitute necessary conditions for the expansion of litigation and the development of the Court's famous doctrine of mutual recognition during the second period. In the second period, the Commission, in alliance with transnational business coalitions, built on the Court's work, successfully converting Member State governments to the idea that mutual recognition could constitute a general strategy for moving integration market integration forward. Member State governments were not the key movers in this story.[30] Governments ratified the basic solutions had already emerged, out of the structured interactions between transnational actors, the Court, and the Commission. And the push to deepen integration was given urgency by a sense of crisis, brought on by globalization, the failure of go-it-alone policies to sustain economic growth, and an accumulation of rulings and legal precedents that empowered traders and the Commission in legal disputes with national administrations (legal outcomes are surveyed in Part II).[31] I now turn to some of our findings.

2. ANALYSIS AND RESULTS

(a) Litigating

First, we found that cross-border economic exchange, like trade, has been a fundamental determinant of litigating EC law. The underlying logic of this relationship should be obvious. Those who most engage in, or profit from, economic transactions across borders are the most likely benefactors and users of the EC Treaty, at least in the beginning, and the most likely to attack national rules and practices as violations of EC law. They have the most to gain from removing national barriers to exchange (negative integration), and from shaping the progressive development of EC regulations and standards (positive integration). As important, they will possess the resources and expertise required using litigation as a means of evolving EC rules in pro-integrative directions.

---

[30] K. Alter and S. Meunier-Aitshalia, 'Judicial Politics in the European Community: European Integration and the Pathbreaking Cassis de Dijon Decision' (1994) 26 *Comparative Political Studies* 535; W. Sandholtz and J. Zysman, '1992: Recasting the European Bargain' (1989) 42 *World Politics* 95; but A. Moravscik disagrees, 'Liberal Intergovernmentalism and Integration: A Rejoinder' (1995) 33 *JCMS* 611.

[31] If it makes sense to analyse the dynamics of institutionalization of the Community in terms of three periods that comprise a single overall process, we also recognize that this process has always been messy and complex. Much of importance will not be captured by schema that aggregate complex phenomena across time and policy space.

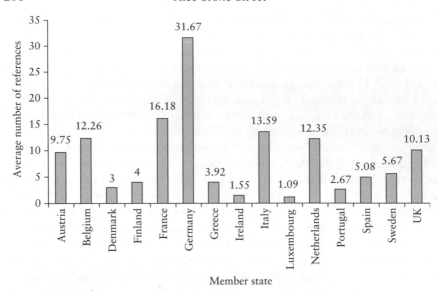

Figure 11.5: Average annual number of references by Member States

Note: For each Member State the total number of Article 234 references was divided by the number of years in which that Member State has been making references to the ECJ.

Source: Alec Stone Sweet and Thomas L. Brunell, *Data Set on Preliminary References in EC Law, 1958–98* (Robert Schuman Centre for Advanced Studies, European University Institute, San Domenico di Fiesole, 1999).

We tested the relationship between economic exchange and litigating EC law in diverse ways, only some of which are reported here.[32] Figure 11.5 shows the average number of references per year since 1961 (or a subsequent date of entry into the Community for new members). What accounts for the wide variance in preliminary references? We employed data on a range of variables plausibly associated with levels of references, including population, GNP, intra-EC trade, and indicators or 'pro v. anti' EC sentiment, and regressed these data (the independent variable) on Article 234 activity (the dependent variable). Given our theoretical priorities, we expected to find a high correlation between levels of transnational exchange and references. Unfortunately, systematic data on a number of factors that are associated with transnational activity, such as labour flows, mergers, and investment, and so on, do not exist or are incomplete. We therefore used intra-EC trade as a proxy for transnational exchange. The choice is defensible given the primary importance of trade and the common market to the European integration as a whole; further, the EEC Treaty required the abolition of national measures restricting trade as of 31 December 1969.

---

[32] See Stone Sweet and Brunell, 'Constructing a Supranational Constitution', n. 11 above.

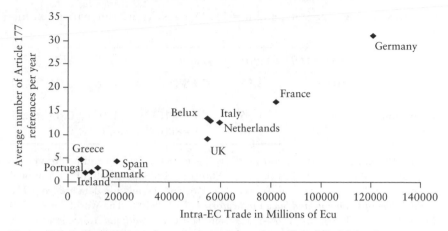

Figure 11.6: Intra-EC trade and average number of Article 234 references

Figure 11.6 depicts the linear relationship between average annual levels of intra-EC trade and average annual levels of Article 234 activity across the EC–12, with no time element.[33] This relationship is nearly perfect (the adjusted R2 is 0.92), indicating that almost all of the cross-national variance in preliminary references is accounted for by one independent variable. As the notes attached to the figure show, this model widely outperforms rivals in every meaningful measure.

For each Member State, the total number of Article 234 references was divided by the number of years in which that Member State has been making references to the ECJ. Belux is Belgium and Luxembourg combined. Trade figures are the annual average of intra-EC imports and exports for each Member State measured in Ecu (European currency unit), 1960–93. Trade data are from *Eurostat: External Trade 1958–93* (EC Publications, Brussels, 1995). The source for Article 234 references is data collected by the authors and the ECJ. The regression equation is $y = 0.2105 + 0.0002247(\text{Trade}) + e$. Adjusted $R^2 = 0.92, n = 11$, and the SEE = 2.46. The t-statistics are: 0.178 for the constant; and 10.8 for intra-EC trade.

We tested whether, respectively, (a) higher levels of diffuse support for the European legal system (measures developed by Caldeira and Gibson, 1995), (b) larger populations (aggregated as the average population for each Member State, 1961–93), and (c) larger economies (aggregated as the average GDP for each Member State, 1961–93) generate higher levels of references per Member State. The dependent variable for each model is the average number of Article 234

---

[33] Unfortunately the trade data end in 1994, and have not been updated by *Eurostat*.

references per Member State, and n = 11. Our results are summarized as follows:

	Interceptt-stat	Coefficient	t-stat	Adj. R^2	SEE	
Diffuse support	10.08	3.92	19.88	1.18	0.04	8.54
Population	6.4	1.55	$9.43(10^{-8})$	1.16	0.03	8.55
GDP	3.33	1.48	$1.48(10^{-11})$	4.3	0.63	5.27

Sources: The index of diffuse support for the ECJ is from Cr. Caldeira and J. Gibson 'The Legitimacy of the Court of Justice in the European Union: Models of Institutional Support' (1995) 89 *American Pol. Science Rev.* 356, 364. Population data are from *The World Tables of Economic and Social Indicators* (ICPSR #9300), The World Bank, 1990 (2nd Release). GDP data for 1960–9 are from *The Cross-National Time-Series Study* (ICPSR #7412, Arthur Banks, 1976); and GDP data for 1970–94 are from *The World Tables* (The World Bank, 1995).

We then analysed the relationship between annual levels of intra-EC trade and preliminary references for the EC as a whole, with no cross-national element. A dummy variable is included in this regression model to account for the linked effects of the constitutionalization of the Treaty system and the entry into force of common market provisions of the EEC Treaty. We coded the dummy variable as '0' for the years 1961–9, and '1' thereafter. Figure 11.7 presents our

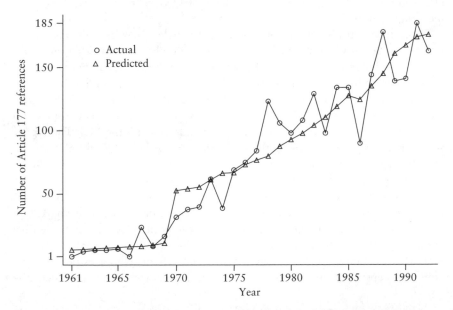

Figure 11.7: Actual and predicted annual levels of Article 234 references from intra-EC trade

results. The Predicted line—generated by a regression model in which the dependent variable is the number of preliminary references per year, and the independent variables are intra-EC trade and the post-1969 dummy—plots the annual number of references predicted by our two independent variables; the Actual line plots the actual number of references registered per year. The connections between our independent and dependent variable remain enormously powerful; the adjusted R^2 is 0.91, indicating that the model explains more than 90 per cent of the variance in annual Article 234 activity.

The Actual line plots the yearly number of Article 234 references by national courts to the ECJ, 1961–92. The Predicted line plots the number of annual references predicted by the regression analysis in which intra-EC trade and a post-1969 dummy variable (coded '0' from 1961–9, and '1' from 1970–92) are the independent variables, and the annual number of Article 234 references for the EC as a whole is the dependent variable. Levels of aggregate trade begin with the original six Member States (Belgium, France, Germany, Italy, Luxembourg, and the Netherlands), and as new Member States join the EC, their trade figures are included. Trade data are from *Eurostat: External Trade 1958–93* (EC Publications, Brussels, 1995). The source for Article 234 references is data collected by the authors and the ECJ. The regression equation is y = 3.56 + 0.0000938(intra-EC Trade) + 39.93(post-1969 Dummy) + e. The adjusted R^2 = 0.91, $n = 32$, SEE = 17.92, and the Durbin-Waston statistic for the regression equation = 1.85. The *t*-statistics are: 0.59 for the constant; 10.59 for intra-EC Trade; and 4.52 for the post-1969 Dummy.

We cross-checked these results in a series of 'pooled' regression models. In this type of analysis, cross-national data are combined with time-series data to increase the number of observations being examined, providing a more rigorous test of hypothesized relationships among variables.[34] What is being examined in our pooled model is the causal relationship between intra-EC trade and references, for each Member State, for each year. Table 11.1 summarizes the results. The correlation between our variables remains remarkably robust, and both the trade variable and the post-1969 dummy remain highly statistically significant.

We also hypothesized that the legislation would provoke litigation. Here we present only our analysis of the statistical relationship between annual levels of intra-EC trade (a proxy for transnational activity), European secondary legislation adopted (a proxy for European rules), and Article 234 activity (a proxy for litigating EC law). Figure 11.8 plots the actual and predicted levels of Article 234 references. The Predicted line—generated by a regression model in which the dependent variable is the number of preliminary references per year, and the independent variables are intra-EC trade, EC secondary legislation, and the post-1969 dummy—plots the annual number of references predicted by our

---

[34] N. Beck and J. Katz, 'What to Do (and Not to Do) with Time Series Cross-Section Data' (1995) 89 *American Political Science Review* 634.

Table 11.1: The impact of intra-EC trade on Article 234 references: pooled, cross-sectional, time series models

	Model 1	Model 2
Intra-EC Trade	0.000126***	0.0000995***
	(18.89)	(13.29)
Post-1969 Dummy		7.64***
		(6.25)
Adjusted R^2	0.73	0.77
SEE	6.19	5.74
N	246	246

*** $p < .001$.

Entries are unstandardized regression coefficients, with t-statistics reported in parentheses. The dependent variable is annual Article 234 references for each Member State, per year. The independent variable for model 1 is intra-EC trade, the value of both imports and exports for each Member State (Belgium and Luxembourg combined) with all other Member States, for each year. The independent variables for model 2 are intra-EC trade and a dummy variable coded '0' from 1961–9, and '1' from 1970–92. The model consists of 246 observations: Belgium-Luxembourg 1961–92; Denmark 1973–92; France 1961–92; Germany 1961–92; Greece 1981–92; Ireland 1973–92; Italy 1961–92; Netherlands 1961–92; Portugal 1986–92; Spain 1986–92; UK 1973–92. The source for the trade data is *Eurostat* (1995). The source for Article 234 references is data collected by the authors and the ECJ. Econometric Views 2.0 was used to estimate a fixed effects model. See J. Stimson 'Regression Across Time and Space' (1985) 29 *American Pol. Science Rev.* 914, and L. Sayrs, *Pooled Time Series Analysis* (Sage Newbury Park, Calif., 1989) for a discussion of pooled models.

two independent variables; the Actual line plots the actual number of references registered throughout the EC per year. The adjusted R^2 is 0.92, and the coefficients for all three variables are positive and significant.

The Actual line plots the yearly number of Article 234 references by national courts to the ECJ, 1961–92. The Predicted line plots the number of annual references predicted by the regression analysis in which intra-EC trade, Euro-rules, and a post-1969 Dummy variable (coded '0' from 1961–9, and '1' from 1970–92) are the independent variables, and the annual number of Article 234 references for the EC as a whole is the dependent variable. Levels of aggregate trade begin with the original six Member States (Belgium, France, Germany, Italy, Luxembourg, and the Netherlands), and as new Member States join the EC, their trade figures are included. Trade data are from *Eurostat: External Trade 1958–93*: (EC Publications, Brussels, 1995). Euro-rules are the annual number of directives and regulations promulgated by the EC. The source for Article 234 references is data collected by the authors and the ECJ. The regression equation is

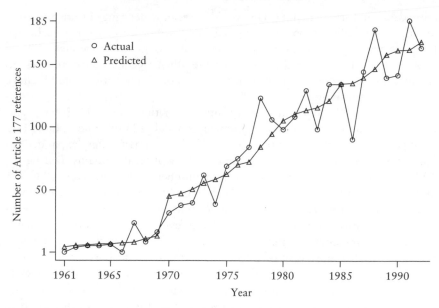

Figure 11.8: Actual and predicted annual levels of Article 234 references from intra-EC trade and Euro-rules

$y = 2.84 + 0.0000731$(intra-EC Trade) $+ 2.04$(Euro-rules) $+ 31.35$(post-1969 Dummy) $+ e$. The adjusted $R^2 = 0.92$, $n = 32$, SEE $= 17.01$, and the Durbin-Watson for the regression equation $= 2.18$. The t-statistics are: 0.50 for the constant, 5.55 for intra-EC Trade, 2.04 for Euro-rules, and 3.34 for the post-1969 Dummy.

We claimed that negative and positive integration would be intertwined in myriad ways, notably through the construction of feedback loops. As the most obvious hindrances to transnational exchange are removed (e.g. border inspections, fees and duties, and so on), new obstacles to integration are revealed and become salient (e.g. national regulations designed to protect consumers, the environment, public safety, and so on). These national rules and practices will then be targeted by traders in subsequent rounds of litigation. In fact, by the late 1970s governments had discovered that litigation in the area of free movement of goods was punching large 'holes' in national regulatory frameworks, exposing to possible attack virtually any national rule that might have an adverse effect on intra-EC trade.[35] As this process proceeded, governments experienced mounting pressure to replace national regulatory regimes, designed to pursue perfectly legitimate public policy purposes, with supranational ones. To the extent that the EC legislator responded to these pressures in pro-integrative ways, that is, as the structure of supranational norms and governance became

---

[35] Maduro, *We, the Court*, n. 28 above.

more dense and articulated, EC law would attract a wider range of private actors to litigate, including those not engaged in cross-border economic exchange. Litigants would seek to Europeanize national law in order to subvert local regimes, to replace national rules with more advantageous European ones, to enhance the role of the judiciary as an arena for policy innovation, and to reduce that of the national government and parliament.

The data provide some preliminary support for these ideas. First, we examined the evolution of the substantive content of Article 234 references. Table 11.2 vividly records the extent to which reference activity has expanded in scope and intensity, across an increasing number of legal domains. During the 1970–4 period, over 50 per cent of the total number of areas invoked fell within just two domains, agriculture and the free movement of goods, while these areas today are the source of barely 20 per cent of total activity. In the meantime, we see an important expansion of reference activity in other domains, such as environmental protection, taxation, commercial policy and competition, and the free movement of workers. Strikingly, in the 1990s nearly one in twelve references concerned sex discrimination law (which the Court codes as 'social provisions'). As the scope of EU rules expand, the legal system becomes a vehicle not simply for economic interests, but also for more diffuse, 'public' interests. That is, litigants will not only be those engaged in transnational exchange, but will include those who seek to impose or make more effective European law within national legal orders.

We also found, using various measures, that the impact of trade on litigating is declining over time, and that the impact of the EC rule structure is increasing. Put differently, the relative importance of negative integration, compared to positive integration, is gradually being reweighted in favour of the latter—and this change is partly endogenous to the relationship between the two processes.

(b) Legislating, Lobbying, Trading

In addition to the analysis already reported, we used econometric methods to test a series of hypotheses concerning the causal relationships among our four variables. On various measures, we found that litigating and legislating were mutually reinforcing. Similarly, we found that legislating and lobbying were co-constitutive. The other intriguing result concerned the growth of lobbying groups and their effects. It was the density of lobbying groups in a domain that produced legislation and similarly encouraged other organizations to set up shop in Brussels. This is a relatively pure measure of the political success of the EC. As some groups achieved influence over legislation, others perceived the necessity of joining them in Brussels or suffer being left out of processes that would impact them. The positive integration project was pushed, in part, by this 'bandwagon' effect. Put differently, as with litigating the impact of big export or trading concerns has declined, as more diffuse, public interests become better organized in Brussels. These results support some of Harlow's

Table 11.2: Distribution of references by legal subject matter (Article 234 EEC)

Subject Matter	1958–98*	58–69	70–74	75–79	80–84	85–89	90–94	95–98*
Agriculture	%	13.4	41.5	35.8	26.9	21.4	15.3	9.5
	n = 1,008	13	129	232	202	170	163	99
Free Movement of Goods		17.5	18.7	19.4	21.6	21.3	16.2	12.3
	832	17	58	126	162	169	172	128
Social Security		26.8	10.3	12.2	7.9	8.9	10.2	6.5
	444	26	32	79	59	71	109	68
Taxation		14.4	3.2	4.2	6.1	7.4	8.1	9.8
	344	14	10	27	46	59	86	102
Competition		12.4	7.1	4.3	4.9	5.5	10.5	6.1
	318	12	22	28	37	44	112	63
Approximation of Laws		1.0	1.0	1.5	4.9	4.2	3.9	8.9
	217	1	3	10	37	33	41	92
Transportation		0	1.6	1.5	1.2	1.1	2.6	1.5
	77	0	5	10	9	9	28	16
Establishment		1.0	1.9	3.7	2.1	6.4	8.4	9.8
	289	1	6	24	16	51	89	102
Social Provisions		0	0.3	1.2	2.8	3.9	8.5	8.2
	236	0	1	8	21	31	90	85
External		1.0	2.6	2.3	3.1	1.8	1.6	3.0
	109	1	8	15	23	14	17	31
Free Movement of Workers and Persons		1.0	2.9	2.9	2.9	5.2	3.7	6.8
	202	1	9	19	22	41	39	71
Environment		0	0	0.2	1.7	1.0	1.0	4.1
	75	0	0	1	13	8	10	43
Commercial Policy		0	1.3	1.2	1.3	1.4	2.4	1.4
	72	0	4	8	10	11	25	14
Other Domains		11.3	7.7	9.6	12.5	10.5	7.9	12.3
	483	11	24	62	94	83	84	125
Total Claims	4,706	97	311	649	751	794	1065	1039
% of Total Claims by Period	100**	2.1	6.6	13.8	16.0	16.9	22.6	22.1

* The table contains information from the complete data set. The data for 1998 are incomplete, ending, for most countries, in May or June 1998.

** 'Joined references' are excluded from these calculations. Due to rounding, percentages of total claims by period add to 100.1%.

Source: Alec Stone Sweet and Thomas L. Brunell, *Data Set on Preliminary References in EC Law, 1958–98* (Robert Schuman Centre for Advanced Studies, European University Institute, San Domenico di Fiesole, 1999).

hunches about interest-group politics in the EC.[36] Although trading is linked to litigating and legislating (by far the strongest determinant of trading was the growth of EC secondary legislating), we found no significant linkages between lobbying and trading, and none between lobbying and litigating.

3. THE EUROPEANIZATION OF THE LAW

Most theories of European integration seek to explain, among other things, the expansion of supranational governance, that is, the relative competence of EC actors and organizations to make, interpret, and apply rules authoritatively in the territory comprised by the EU Member States. The research project can then be defined through specification of the dependent variable: supranational governance varies across time and policy domain, and one major task of the analyst is to explain that variance. One can, of course, conceptualize *Europeanization* (like *integration*) in different ways. Here, I define *Europeanization* as the impact of market integration (i.e. cross-border economic exchange) and supranational governance (i.e. EU rules, procedures, actors, and organizations) on processes and outcomes at the national level. The research is thereby defined through specifying the dependent variable: this impact will vary across time, policy domains, national organizations (or arenas), and across Member States. Conceptualizing the research question in these ways constitutes an assertion that the dependent variable of integration studies becomes the independent variable of Europeanization studies. Surely the more the EC possesses and exercises its authority to make, apply, and interpret EC law, at any given time in any given policy domain, the more pressure has been exerted on national legal systems to adapt, other things equal.

In this section, I address some aspects of Europeanization in light of how litigants, national judges, and the ECJ have interacted. These relationships are organized and sustained by the preliminary reference procedure established by Article 177 (now 234). This Article combines with the development of the doctrines of supremacy and direct effect to constitute a decentralized means of enforcing EC law. It provides a mechanism of incorporating EC law into national law, and of diffusing, within national legal orders, modes of reasoning and decision-making developed by the Court. And because Member State governments are often the *de facto* defendants in these proceedings, such interactions possess the capacity to generate policy outcomes and to structure future policy processes, at both the national and supranational levels. For these reasons, a good deal of what would fall under the label, *the Europeanization of national law*, has been determined, or at least meaningfully conditioned by, processes and outcomes generated through Article 177. It is crucial to emphasize

---

[36] In 'A Community of Interests?', n. 3 above, 337–46.

that national courts are not simply moulded by integration and supranational governance, they actively participate in both. Had national judges refused to accept the ECJ's various constitutional doctrines, had they refused to file pre-liminary references, the legal system would have been stillborn. Yet, as Part 1 of this essay shows, the development of the EC's legal system constituted a nec-essary causal element of the inherently expansionary system that generates the effects that one might call Europeanization.

(a) The Constitutional Politics of Supremacy

The Court's supremacy doctrine was constitutional in that it sought to organ-ize the juridical relationship between otherwise distinct legal orders, the national and supranational. The gradual acceptance of the doctrine by national judges was political, because it involved a choice, and because that choice would impact on politics (the decision-making of legislators, administrators, and judges).

These politics of supremacy have been the subject of a great deal of scholarly debate. Some focused on the sources and logics of co-operation between the ECJ and national courts, others on the logics of conflict, although everyone recog-nized that the relationship has been extremely complex and fluid. Co-operation received the most early attention, as a puzzle to be explained. In some national jurisdictions, supremacy required judges to abandon certain deeply-entrenched, constitutive principles, such as the prohibition against judicial review of legis-lation; and direct effect required some judges to set aside traditional rules of standing and recognition, and to evolve new ones. Further, supremacy forbids the use of traditional, dualist solutions to conflicts between national and inter-national law (such as the *lex posteriori* doctrine), and direct effect enables private actors to sue Member State governments for non-compliance with EC law, including failure to implement EC secondary legislation. Because accepting supremacy entailed significant adaptation, it could not simply be presumed to follow automatically from the Court's pronouncements.

Joseph Weiler's ingenious solution to the puzzle has become dominant.[37] Weiler argued that the protective shelter of Article 234 enabled the ECJ and national judges to develop a partnership that both empowered one another (*vis-à-vis* other governmental authorities) and increased the effectiveness of EC law for private actors. In a seminal article that focused on the needs of a grow-ing transnational society, Burley and Mattli translated much of Weiler's argu-ment into the language of regional integration theory, and emphasized the EC legal system's capacity to expand its purview over time, as more and more actors found it in their interest to orient themselves to EC law.[38]

---

[37] J. H. H. Weiler, 'A Quiet Revolution: The European Court and Its Interlocutors' (1994) 26 *Comparative Political Studies* 510; J. H. H. Weiler, 'The Transformation of Europe' (1991) 100 *Yale LJ* 2403.   [38] Burley and Mattli, n. 21 above.

We have proposed a more mundane interpretation of national judicial behaviour: judges who handle relatively more litigation in which EC law is material will be more active consumers of EC law, and more active producers of preliminary rulings, than judges who are asked to resolve such disputes less frequently.[39] (I do not deny the logic of empowerment, but only that it supplements other forces.) This formulation assumes that national judges seek to do their jobs well and effectively, that is, they would like to leave their courts at the end of their week having resolved more, rather than fewer, work-related problems. As the percentage of cases involving EC law rises, so do judicial incentives to master the tools that are most appropriate for the job, and those tools have been supplied by the ECJ. Judges that do not need these tools will be slower or more reticent to master them, and have less reason to be concerned with the overall effectiveness of EC law. The approach helps us to explain some of the variation we find within Member States, between autonomous court systems. We know, for example, that across the EC civil law jurisdictions typically accepted supremacy more quickly and with fewer reservations than did, say, administrative law courts, and they produced far more references.

In any event, those who have focused on intra-judicial co-operation and empowerment did not ignore intra-judicial friction, but took friction for granted as the *expected* state of affairs. The trick, then, was to explain why the legal system had nonetheless taken off. After all, the logics of empowerment, and integration and spillover, clearly did not apply to all judges, constitutional ones, for example. Other judges would see that the Court's case law could evolve in ways that would undermine their own carefully-curated jurisprudence, autonomy, or relations with other governmental authorities. Still others might see that the development of EC law would, in effect, expand the 'menu of policy choices' available to them, and they would exploit this development creatively, but not always in pro-integrative directions.[40] Alter, in her recent book on the reception of supremacy by French and German judges, pays full attention to the dynamics of conflict between national judges and the ECJ.[41] She shows that there were multiple, overlapping, and ever-changing reasons for how national judges chose to make use of EC law, or to resist the ECJ's bid to Europeanize their work.

This area remains fertile ground for ongoing research. There exists virtually no systematic research on national standing rules and remedies, as they relate to EC law, and the same can be said of the study of the growth of law firms that

[39] Stone Sweet and Brunell, 'The European Courts and the National Courts', n. 13 above.

[40] A. Stone Sweet, 'Constitutional Dialogues in the European Community', in A-M. Slaughter, A. Stone Sweet, and J. Weiler (eds.), *The European Court and the National Courts* (Hart, Oxford, 1998), 303; Stone Sweet, *Governing with Judges*, n. 7 above, chap. 6.

[41] K. Alter, *Establishing the Supremacy of European Law* (Oxford University Press, Oxford, 2001). Although I would argue that Alter has built on the main literature, she attacks all extant approaches for having failed to address the questions she has posed (but see Slaughter, Stone Sweet, and Weiler (eds.), *The European Court and the National Courts*, n. 40 above, which also explores the acceptance of supremacy).

specialize in litigating EC law. Yet each of these three factors, as they vary across court systems, would very likely explain some of the variation in Europeanization (levels of litigation in the EC, Article 234 references, and the feedback of the Court's case law on policy and subsequent litigation). Further, as Alter's work shows, we need much more comparative research on what Europeanization actually means, in context, even on the purely doctrinal front. The basic issues have been defined, but not settled. Harlow, for example, argues that 'the EC legal order is a parasitic construction; it fastens itself on the branches of the national legal orders'.[42] The claim, at least implicitly, seems to deny co-empowerment logics, whose imagery is one of symbiosis between judges in the two systems. But the formulation may also provide another interpretation: Article 234 activities and the case law of the ECJ have forced national judges and legal systems to adjust, far more than the other way around, even if national judges have, on average, increased their capacity to control policy outcomes.[43] My own view is that as the European legal order has gathered in strength, the traditional precepts of national legal orders have in fact been eroded, to the overall advantage of judges at both levels.

(b) Outcomes

Who wins through litigating EC law in national courts? Obviously, the more the EC legal system produces the kinds of outcomes desired by those who have activated it, the more subsequent litigation will be stimulated. Put differently, to the extent that Article 234 increases the effectiveness of EC law within national legal orders, private actors will be encouraged to use litigation to pursue their own goals and policy objectives. Positive outcomes attract litigation, whereas negatives ones deter it.

To assess some of these dynamics, Cichowski (whose recent dissertation focuses on litigating and lobbying in sex equality and environmental protection),[44] McCown, and I compiled comprehensive data sets on certain types of outcomes in three different areas of the law: free movement of goods, social provisions (including sex equality), and environmental protection. First, we examined all ECJ decisions pursuant to references in each of these three legal domains, noting, for each case, whether the Court ruled that the national law or practice in question was, or was not, in conformity with EC law. We sought an answer to the question: what has been the success rate for those who have litigated EC law in national courts? Secondly, we examined the relationships between the arguments contained in the observations filed by the Commission and the Member States, for each case, and the Court's ultimate decisions. We sought an answer

---

[42] Harlow, 'Common European Law of Remedies?', n. 5, 76.

[43] Harlow, 'European Administrative Law and the Global Challenge' n. 2 above, 267–71.

[44] R. Cichowski, *Litigation, Mobilization, and Governance: The European Court and Transnational Activists*, Doctoral Dissertation, Department of Political Science, University of California-Irvine, 2002.

to the question: to what extent do observations presage (or influence) the Court's ruling? Given our theory and earlier findings, we assumed that the Commission and the Court would exhibit a joint interest in enhancing the effectiveness of EC law within national legal orders, and in expanding the scope of supranational governance.[45] We also expected to find that private litigants would win enough to attract subsequent litigation, given its cost, and that the preferences revealed by Member State governments in their briefs would not have a significant impact on outcomes.

In the free movement of goods domain, the ECJ ruled in favour of those who attacked national rules or practices as being an unlawful hindrance on trade in slightly more than half of all decisions. The Commission's position, as laid out in observations, 'predicted' the Court's ruling more than 80 per cent of the time, while the observations of the Member State governments, especially Germany's, were largely ineffectual. In the area of social provisions and sex equality, private litigants had a success rate of 55 per cent, which rises to 60 per cent when the 'defendant state' is one of the big three, France, Germany, and the UK. The Commission's observations tracked the Court's ultimate ruling in nearly 90 per cent of the cases. Last, in the domain of environmental protection, the Court found no violation of EC law in 53 per cent, while private actors prevailed in only 47 per cent of the cases. Thus, we found that the preferences of Member State governments do not constrain the Court in any systematic way. As important, these data tells us a great deal about why litigating EC law is so attractive to private actors.

Judicial power is a brute fact of political life in the EC. Much of what is most important in European law is judge-made. Judges possess meaningful discretion over the legal norms they interpret and apply, and they have exercised that discretion in ways that have expanded the supranational aspects of the EC, reduced the intergovernmental aspects, and transformed the nature of national law and judging. If such discretion did not exist, the Europeanization of the law would be a pre-ordained, mechanical process, rather than the fluid and dynamic one that we see.

There are two basic sources of judicial discretion in the EC. First, as in all legal systems, norms are always at least partly indeterminate, and constitutional norms are often the least determinant, or open-ended, of norms. The EC Treaty, read as a constitutional text, leaves much vague, which constitutes a wide grant of discretion to judges. The Rome Treaty did not lay down a clear blueprint for how the national and supranational legal orders were to interact. In Harlow's terms, the EC legal system 'lacked both culture and constitutional context', a gap that was filled in, gradually, through inter-court dialogue and judicial law-making.[46] The fact that the legal system now treats important parts of EC law in rights terms has only increased judicial discretion. Secondly, the decision rule

---

[45] Harlow, 'European Administrative Law and the Global Challenge', n. 2 above, 267, has argued that 'both the Commission and the Court were infused with the dominant ideology of integrationism'.

[46] Harlow, 'European Administrative Law and the Global Challenge', n. 2 above, 266.

that governs reversal of the Court's interpretations of the Treaty (unanimity of the Member States plus ratification) favours the ongoing dominance of judges over the evolution of the system.

The exercise of judicial discretion, in any effective legal system, constitutes a functional response to normative indeterminacy.[47] If discretion is basic to law-making, law-making tends to destroy the notion that the judge is a neutral entity, *vis-à-vis* the litigating parties, one who resolves legal disputes by applying pre-existing, and known, rules.[48] The production of doctrine and precedent constitutes a functional response to the legitimacy 'crisis' provoked by judicial law-making, that is, precedent seeks to justify the exercise of discretion, through showing how it is constrained by previously-developed legal principles and reasoning. McCown and I have compiled comprehensive data on self-citation by the ECJ, data that we are using to identify and to chart the evolution of specific doctrinal structures in the various domains of EC law.

These data show that precedent in EC law developed slowly, but is now a robust, even taken-for-granted practice. The Court has, in complicity with litigants and national judges, propagated increasingly nuanced doctrinal frameworks, and these have helped to structure the evolution of the legal system. Doctrinal structures typically render the law less indeterminate for those who are networked by and participate in the system, drawing more and more actors into a specific kind of discursive politics. Perhaps most important, practices associated with precedent have become primary mechanisms of Europeanization, powerfully conditioning, among other things, how actors make use of Article 177: whether or not to litigate; how to pose preliminary questions to the Court; how to respond to such questions; and how to implement preliminary rulings. If we are right, then the Europeanization of the law must be understood, at least partly, in light of legal doctrine, as it moves down certain paths, closes down others, and as it branches and becomes more specialized.[49]

Finally, although any given ECJ decision may be usefully understood as the end of one story, it is also embedded in a longer story, and at times is the beginning of new ones. Not enough attention has been paid to compliance (judicial and political) with the Court's rulings, or with the impact of the Court's interactions with national judges on national politics. Two recent studies, however, deserve mention. Nyikos, in her doctoral dissertation,[50] analysed all of the

---

[47] A. Stone Sweet, *On Law, Politics, and Judicialization* (Oxford University Press, Oxford, 2002), chap. 2.

[48] M. Shapiro, *Courts: A Comparative and Political Analysis* (Chicago University Press, Chicago, Ill., 1981).

[49] A. Stone Sweet and M. McCown, 'Path Dependence, Precedent, and Judicial Power in Europe', paper presented at the Annual Meeting of the American Political Science Association, San Francisco, Calif., 2002.

[50] S. Nyikos, *The European Court of Justice and the National Courts: Strategic Interaction within the EU Judicial Process*, Doctoral Dissertation, Department of Government and Foreign Affairs, University of Virginia, 2000.

preliminary questions raised in multiple legal domains, and traced their various effects on latter stages of the process. She found overwhelming evidence to the effect that when national judges have 'signalled' to the Court a preferred outcome, the Court has responded favourably. She argues, convincingly in my view, that these interactions have been key to facilitating compliance with the ECJ's preliminary rulings. Conant, in yet another recent dissertation (now a book[51]), argues rightly that the field's concern for the Court's decision-making, and for the operation of the EC legal system, is simply not enough. EC law and litigation must find agency in national environments that are full of obstacles and complexities. She demonstrates that the effectiveness of EC law varies widely, across various national polities and policy domains, as a function of myriad factors that operate with different effects at different places and times. When observed in this way, the scope and effectiveness of EC law looks quite 'patchwork' and 'fragmented', not least because quasi-federal governance is constantly being 'negotiated' by organized groups and officials, operating different levels of government, and possessed of different amounts and kinds of resources to shape outcomes.

4. CONCLUSION

When we look at the overall sweep of European integration, we see that trading, litigating, legislating, and lobbying did not take place in isolation from but, in fact, were deeply embedded in one another. Private actors activated the Commission and the legal system, seeking to remove barriers to economic exchange. As an ever-widening range of national regulation and administrative practices were placed in the shadow of EC law, and as actors advantaged by EC institutions pushed for more political integration through lobbying and litigation, EC legislators found that the search for Euro-wide solutions to the problems posed by the expansion of transnational society and economic interdependence were the only feasible response. As the EC's rule structure became more dense and differentiated, so have the grounds for legal action, and actors moved to push the Commission and the Court to establish or interpret new rules in their favour, whether or not they engaged in cross-border economic exchange. From the point of view of the present volume, the essay shows that the construction and operation of the legal system have been crucial to the overall course of integration.

When we begin to examine the consequences of integration for national judging, we do indeed observe significant Europeanization, especially through Article 177. This Article has developed in such a way as to bind together the activities of litigants, national judges, and the ECJ. The system has produced

---

[51] L. Conant, *Justice Contained: Law and Politics in the EU* (Cornell University Press, Ithaca, NY, 2002).

positive outcomes for litigants of EC law and for national judges who make references, encouraging more of the same. On the other side, litigation and references provide the ECJ with opportunities to build EC law, and to enhance its effectiveness. It is undeniable that the expansive dynamics of this virtuous circle have determined the broad course of legal integration. Still, the Europeanization of the law is a far more complex and messy phenomenon than even the most elegantly-specified theory, or the most rigorous statistical tests, could ever capture. We desperately need comparative, contextually-rich case studies that blend the lawyer's concern with the 'doctrinal' and the social scientist's concern with explanation in a sustained, coherent way. I have noted four recent doctoral dissertations here, completed by younger women political scientists, all important contributions.[52] One can only hope that this kind of research will beget more.

---

[52] Carol Harlow has inspired and encouraged several generations of younger scholars, both through example and mentoring. This group includes the authors of some of the new work mentioned and, of course, myself.

12

Trans-Atlantic: Harlow Revisited

MARTIN SHAPIRO

In a series of articles Carol Harlow has examined the general condition of administrative law in the USA, UK, and EU.[1] Ever conscious of crucial differences between them, nonetheless she develops a set of basic themes common to them all. Her efforts point the way to a growing potential for a kind of trans-Atlantic studies that grounds itself in discovering a set of common causes, values, and ideas working their way down differing institutional pathways and established policy patterns from which emerge comparable, if not identical, legal and political outcomes. Harlow's assessment of these trans-Atlantic developments is informed, how could it be otherwise, by an essentially English sensitivity. She hopes that a non-dogmatic, pragmatic, public administration seeking the common good, but sensitive to individual interests and rights, will emerge and will do so with a minimum of contention and coercion. Here I shall seek to take precisely the same themes she so cogently offers and develop them from quite a different sensitivity, one that might or might not be called American, but one that prefers hard edges to soft, and contention to sweet reason. I am not at all sure that I am more correct than she, but the clash of sensitivities may prove useful.

1. RULES AND REGULATION

Central to Harlow's analysis is regulatory politics. It has become a commonplace that in the last four or five decades there has been a general loss of faith in the potential for productivity of the public sector, a renewed faith in private sector markets as the most efficient route to plenty and a consequent emphasis on

---

[1] 'Back to Basics: Reinventing Administrative Law' [1997] *PL* 245; 'Codification of EC Administrative Procedure? Fitting the Foot to the Shoe or the Shoe to the Foot' (1996) 2 *ELJ* 3; 'A Special Relationship? The American Influence on English Public Law', in I. Loveland (ed.), *Lessons from America* (Clarendon Press, Oxford, 1995), chap. 3; 'European Administrative Law', in P. Craig and G. de Búrca (eds.), *The Evolution of EU Law* (Oxford University Press, Oxford, 1999), chap. 7.

regulation as the nexus between the two sectors. All of us are familiar with the paradox that, while initially accompanied by enthusiasm for deregulation, eventually the new reliance on markets led to more regulation, not less. Increased regulation occurred because more markets necessarily meant more potential for market failure and market abuse with stakes so high that only the external coercions of law seemed sufficient to ensure acceptable market outcomes.

If regulation is the central activity of government, then a number of things automatically follow in the contemporary world. One is that technical specialization and expertise will be the central characteristics of the regulators because what must be regulated is a high-tech economy. A second is that most of the regulatory norms will not be statutory but embodied in what are variously called rules, regulations, supplementary or delegated legislation, or even less statute-like pronouncements made not by parliaments but by administrative bureaucracies. All this necessarily occurs because what is to be regulated is too complex, too rapidly changing, and too quick to respond strategically to norms imposed upon it, to be regulated successfully by statutes alone or even primarily. And it follows from all this, I would argue, that the central concern of administrative law ought to be what Americans call the rule-making process as opposed to the particular applications of those rules to particular persons.

Either as a corollary or independently, at the same time that regulatory rule-making comes to be of central concern throughout the industrialized world, we experience increasingly pressing demands for transparency and wider participation in government. No doubt there are grand causes of these yearnings which seem to pervade western societies and are most dramatically illustrated by the fall of the Soviet Empire. In a very immediate way, however, if law-making moves from parliaments that have long-established if often illusory practices of openness and representation to technocratic bureaucracies that do not, we should expect heightened concern for transparency and participation in rule-making from any citizenry that values democratic law-making processes.

Seeming to pull in a somewhat different direction are the widespread demands for regulatory rationality. We all recognize that in part such demands have been disguises worn by deregulators who simply hope to encumber as much as possible those regulatory efforts they cannot block completely. Nevertheless, if we love markets because they are efficient, and regulate markets in order to make them even more efficient, demands that the regulations themselves be efficient are bound to follow. Thus the vogue in regulatory analysis, regulatory impact statements, regulatory costs, and so on. And thus concern for whether greater regulatory transparency and participation lead to more or less rational or efficient regulation.

Finally we come to the two great religious movements of the twentieth century. One of these is environmentalism. The other, of direct concern to us here, is rights. According to the normal logic of pluralist, representative democracy neither religion ought to have much political clout. Both are diffuse interests, of some general concern to everyone but confronting highly concentrated, organized, specific, and immediate interests seeking to protect very tangible, immediate material benefits. In such confrontations diffuse, general interests are supposed to lose. And indeed on particular measures at particular times, in particular law-making processes they often do. But overall environmentalism has won an awful lot. And so have demands for individual or constitutional or human rights.

It may be wrong for many purposes to conflate rights with judicial review. Nevertheless the remarkable spread of the institution of constitutional judicial review across Europe has been one of the clearest signs of the strength of rights sentiments. As we all know this movement has occurred not only in individual states but on a Europe-wide basis in the European Court of Human Rights (ECtHR) and the European Court of Justice (ECJ) with the customary quibbles, of course, over whether their review is quite constitutional review. And also, as we all know, by fits and starts the UK joins in the rights judicial review movement. Two aspects of this movement seem to me particularly important for administrative law.

First as courts are supposed to do and are seen to do more and more rights reviewing, whether as a matter of constitutional law, domesticated treaty law, or 'direct effect' EU law, there is bound to be a spill-over effect. If courts do rights in those parts of law, why not in administrative law? Or, to put the matter differently, if judges gain confidence in doing some rights business, they gain confidence in doing other rights business. This is all the more true because administrative law did a certain amount of rights business even before the current enthusiasm for rights.

Secondly, in the contemporary world, individual rights business always turns into group rights business. Once courts accept individual rights claims, larger interests inevitably learn to repackage their group preferences as individual rights. The story of affirmative or positive action is, of course, the most dramatic example. What begin as claims by individuals to the right to be treated without discrimination end up as the claim of a whole race or gender to be given legal preference over other races and genders. The earlier transposition of property rights into judicial defence of business interests is an equally well known, but less applauded, example. If the religion of rights is judicially transported into administrative law, we may reasonably expect that it will come in group, as well as individual, packages. Moreover, where regulatory rule-making is involved, those complaining of rights violations are likely to be large corporations, often parts of multinational conglomerates. In such a setting the individual is so big that the distinction between individual and group rights is meaningless.

My American perspectives are no doubt already too clear. The American manifestations of each of the four phenomena I have described, the prominence of rule-making, increased participation and transparency, the desire for regulatory rationality, and the fascination with judicially enforced rights, are too obvious to require elaboration here. Further attention to the UK and the EU, however, might be in order.

Harlow grounds her analysis in two traditions of administrative law, one which sees law and judicial review as a means of controlling the administration, the other emphasizing law and review as internal disciplinary devices. As they have played out in Europe, however, neither of these traditions appears to be coping adequately with the four developments we have just examined.

If regulatory rule-making, or supplementary or delegated legislation, is a central feature of the new legal regime, then Europe is in deep, deep trouble. Until very recently English courts have exercised no control over this administrative activity at all. There is now one leading case,[2] which will no doubt join the thin litany of the half dozen or so other leading cases of judicial control over central government administrative action that the English sing to reassure themselves that the courts are alive. Like the others it will almost certainly be an isolated and peculiar incident. For the UK political system, characterized by two highly disciplined parties and resulting cabinet dictatorship, places courts in a peculiarly weak position in reviewing rules. Should a court find a rule unlawful, that is in violation of a Parliamentary statute, the government need not bring the rule into conformity with the statute. It need only order Parliament to amend the statute to bring it into conformity with the rule. The judges know this and avoid exercises in futility and judicial humiliation.

Of course to say what I have just said shows a failure to understand the nuanced relationship between government and Parliament that supposedly robs the three line whip of at least some of its sting. The bottom line, however, remains that when push comes to shove rules declared judicially unlawful can be maintained and rendered lawful with ease in disciplined, two-party, parliamentary systems. US courts have been the most active in the world in controlling rule-making precisely because presidential systems with weak party discipline provide very lean opportunities for the administration to save its unlawful rules by changing the laws rather than changing the rules.

On the continent the Germanic tradition of administrative law cannot directly reach rule-making at all, but only the particular application of rules to particular, regulated parties. It is true that a very bold administrative court may indeed quash a particular application of a rule on the ground that the rule itself is unlawful. If the highest administrative court in the land were prepared repeatedly to take such a stance toward a particular rule, and regulated parties were prepared repeatedly to mount litigation pressing it to do so, then eventually the rule itself effectively might be quashed. Such a scenario is likely to be a relatively rare one.

The French tradition is, as is well known, quite different. The Council of State insists that it does have the power to invalidate delegated legislation as unlawful.

---

[2] *R* v. *Secretary of State for Social Security, ex parte Joint Council for the Welfare of Immigrants* [1997] 1 WLR 275.

In reality, however, like their British counterparts, French judges may frequently declare local government rules unlawful, but almost never those of the central government. Much of what might be done by parliamentary delegation in other countries is done in France by the massive constitutional delegation of decree-law powers to the President. Unlike normal delegated legislation such decree-laws cannot easily be challenged as unlawful in the administrative courts. Moreover Council of State intervention either in regard to these decree-laws or supplementary legislation based on parliamentary, statutory delegation is likely to be most intense at the drafting stage. Having voiced and had satisfied its legal concerns at the drafting stage, there will be almost no occasion for the Council to strike down a rule as unlawful in subsequent litigation. Thus there is little visible Council of State jurisprudence on rules and rule-making by the central government.

The European Union is now engaged in a lot of delegated legislation. As Harlow has pointed out, some sort of European administrative law of rule-making seems desirable. Yet the traditions of national administrative law in Europe provide only scanty resources for developing such an administrative law.

At the two borders of trans-Atlantic politics lie the USA and the lands of the former Soviet Empire. Beginning in the 1960s the USA experienced a virtual revolution in administrative law, a revolution fuelled by concerns for creating greater transparency and participation in government policy-making.[3] At the very centre of these concerns was the regulatory rule-making process. While currently experiencing some reaction and retrenchment, judicial review of rule-making in the USA has become the most intrusive in the world, particularly in its insistence on hyper-transparency and private sector participation in the rule-making process. At the other border, in the lands of *perestroika*, the revolution was more than virtual. Certainly the fall of the Soviet Union was the result, not of yearnings for democracy, but of yearnings for western levels of material prosperity. But those yearnings at least marched under the banners of participation and transparency.

I think that it can be argued that these yearnings for transparency and participation have been much in evidence, between the antipodes as well. For the most part, however, they have been turned into channels quite different from those of the administrative law of rule-making.

In the UK a great deal of dissatisfaction with government secrecy has been voiced and a certain increase in transparency may have been achieved. But much of the discontent has been manifested in somewhat indirect ways. There is, of course, the whole push toward privatization which Harlow treats as central. That push is, I suppose, more directed at efficiency than participation and transparency, but no doubt initially there was probably also a belief that getting things out of Whitehall would make them more open. We have since learned

---

[3] See R. Stewart, 'The Reformation of American Administrative Law' (1975) 88 *Harv L Rev* 1667; M. Shapiro, *Who Guards the Guardians* (University of Georgia Press, Athens, Georgia, 1988).

that the private sector can beat the public any day at opaqueness and impenetrability. Perhaps more successful has been a more traditional path of seeking to revitalize Parliamentary oversight of administration through the select committee system and other such devices. This remains, however, transparency and participation not directly but by representation. Finally the movement for a written constitution, charter of rights, and extended judicial protection of rights has a transparency and participation component. For in practice those pushing rights will quickly come to see that proactive efforts to secure rights, facilitated by transparency and participation requirements, are actually preferable to litigational counterattack after rights have been violated. Whatever the success of all these efforts, however, it can hardly be said that the Whitehall corridors have become an arcade. And it certainly can be said, and is by Harlow rather thankfully, that nothing comparable to the American administrative law of rule-making has emerged.

On the continent concerns about the opaqueness of government have taken their most dramatic form in scandals over government corruption, or more often party corruption that in turn corrupts government. Here there is judicial activism, but in that peculiar sense that so often confounds those of common law background. For continentals, prosecutors are judges, and indeed the most independent of judges. It is these judges who have been letting some sunshine into the dark passages of government. Thus judicial strivings for transparency occur, not in administrative law and administrative courts, but in criminal law and criminal courts. The very last thing anyone wants is that such criminal prosecutions should become a regular, normal institutionalized mode of achieving transparency and participation in the administrative process.

The EU has experienced its own corruption scandal, and certainly hopes it will have been a unique black spot, not a continuing mode of administrative oversight. I have argued at length elsewhere that some signs of transparency and participation forcing judicial review are emerging in European jurisprudence.[4] Interestingly, echoing the UK experience, however, is that it is not transparency for and participation by the public that has been most at issue, but transparency for and participation by the Parliament. The Parliament has achieved major gains in participation in the Council-centred law-making process, both in terms of formal 'constitutional' arrangements and in terms of its internal committee and party group resources. In the area of delegated legislation exercised by the 'Comitology' system, the Parliament has waged an increasingly successful battle for access. Yet the Comitology mode of law-making, which we shall return to in a moment, remains among the most opaque and closed of rule-making processes.

---

[4] 'The Giving Reasons Requirement in European Community Law' [1992] *University of Chicago Legal Forum* 179; 'The Institutionalization of European Administrative Space', in W. Sandholtz, A. Stone Sweet, and N. Fligstein (eds.), *The Institutionalization of Europe* (Oxford University Press, Oxford, 2001), chap. 5.

While demands for access and transparency look toward democratic government, at least in the pluralist or group version of democracy, demands for rational regulation seem to look toward technocratic government. In a high-tech environment rationality involves major technical components, specialized expert knowledge, much of it in the realm of science and engineering. Most fundamentally of course the call for rational regulation sounds in economics. The ultimate questions become questions about economic efficiency. Does a particular regulation, taking all costs and benefits into account, contribute to the economic efficiency of the market?

It is usual to focus on the anti-regulatory component of this rationality movement. The regulator is forbidden to seek more than efficient levels of health or safety or consumer protection. The technocratic or anti-democratic component is, however, just as important for administrative law. Rationality requires knowledge. If those with knowledge should regulate, then the theme of judicial deference to technical expertise tends to come to the fore. It is not necessarily so. It can be, and often is, argued that maximum participation and transparency for the regulated and the putative beneficiaries of regulation will increase the rationality of regulation by bringing far more information to the table than the technocratic regulators could acquire on their own. Yet participation and transparency also threaten the pluralist downside, that regulations will be merely the aggregation of special-interest preferences and, worse yet, not even a fair aggregation, given that some interests have far greater participatory resources than others.

As part of the reaction to the supposed excesses of US adversarial legalism,[5] there is today much talk of deliberation which is supposed to give us the benefits of transparency and participation without the costs. Like pluralists, deliberators emphasize transparency and participation, but the multiple players brought to the table are supposed to arrive at good regulations, not simply aggregate the preferences they originally brought to the table. Looked at in this way, the call for regulatory deliberation is a call for rational democracy. However ultimately illusory, this is the hope of most American proponents of a deliberative administrative law.

The banner of deliberation can, however, be flown over quite a different parade. If transparency and participation bring group preferences to the fore in regulation, then regulatory efficiency will give way to those selfish interests. Regulation will be political rather than efficient. *And* regulation will be aggregative rather than deliberative. If, however, group preferences, a.k.a. politics, are kept away from the table, all the seats at which are then filled with technocrats, then true deliberation may take place. By virtue of their expertise, the technical experts bring to the table the knowledge necessary for true deliberation unencumbered by the self-interest that turns the table from deliberation to interest-group bargaining. Thus freed, the deliberating regulators will

---

[5] See R. Kagan, *Adversarial Legalism* (Harvard University Press, Cambridge, Mass., 2001).

arrive at rational, efficient regulations. In this guise deliberation becomes a hymn to technocratic government. Or at least it becomes a hymn to technocratic regulation. For this style of deliberation may have untoward distributional consequences, for instance leaving geographic pockets of unemployment or rendering certain categories of persons unemployable. 'Politics', having been shoved out of regulation, may be permitted to run along afterwards cleaning up these consequences of technocratic, efficient, deliberatory regulation by various compensatory schemes.

It is no accident that the call for this kind of deliberatory regulation has been loudest in the context of the EU rather than the individual Member States.[6] The general push toward participation and transparency is more forceful and more dangerous at the EU level than in the Member States. The Member States have practised a more or less corporate style of regulation, with close co-operation between the regulators and the regulated. These close connections have been somewhat attenuated by the movement of regulatory decision-making from national capitals to the EU. So long as the regulated were insiders in national, corporatist, regulatory decision-making, they had no reason to support greater transparency and participation for outsiders. To the extent the regulated have become less insiders as regulation moves from their home towns to Brussels, they become proponents of transparency and participation. Thus the danger arises that the administrative law of the EU will go the same route that American administrative law went when it sought more transparency and participation. The dreaded adversarial legalism may become an EU, as well as an American, disease. If the corporatist element of European regulation is to be reduced by the movement of regulation to EU levels, then at least technocratic regulation can be substituted for friendly national regulation and the deadly American, arm's length, adversarial, political regulation can be avoided. Or at least that is the hope of many of the European proponents of deliberation.

2. CONSTITUTIONAL LAW, ADMINISTRATIVE LAW, AND RIGHTS

Finally Harlow, and the rest of us, have had to confront the rights revolution and what it means for administrative law in Europe. An English observer may be particularly sensitive to the rights-administrative law connection. Continental observers are likely to translate rights into constitutional rights and become preoccupied with the dramatic rise of constitutional judicial review in Europe. That review is practised by constitutional courts isolated from regular and administrative courts. Thus the rising preoccupation with rights may be

---

[6] G. Majone, *Regulating Europe* (Routledge, London, 1996); C. Joerges and J. Neyer, 'From Intergovernmental Bargaining to Deliberative Political Process: The Constitutionalization of Comitology' (1997) 3 *ELJ* 273.

more or less channelled away from administrative law. Without formal constitutional judicial review, with the same courts hearing all legal questions, and
with the administrative law doctrines of *ultra vires* and natural justice doing
duty for what in many other countries would be constitutionally based
challenges to government action, English preoccupation with rights brings us
directly to administrative law.

In the crudest, but probably accurate, line of reasoning, it might be said that
a judge who one day vetoes a whole statute by declaring it unconstitutional will
have little trouble the next doing the far less bold thing of declaring an administrative act unlawful. That American courts so often feel their constitutional
oats might alone account for their boldness in administrative judicial review.
Where a litigator simultaneously may present a constitutional rights and an
administrative law procedural challenge to a particular government act, judges
may easily persuade themselves that they are taking the less bold path by striking down government action on merely administrative law grounds. The
American constitutional due process clauses, in any event, point toward a
conflation of constitutional and administrative law, and thus a conflation of
judicial activism in the two realms.

UK courts, of course, do not enjoy, or suffer from, these constitutional prods.
Precisely because UK courts do not engage in constitutional review, but do exercise general jurisdiction over all legal matters including administrative law,
those in the UK concerned with rights must direct their pleas to the regular
courts and administrative law if they are to resort to any existing body of law
and courts at all. Indeed it is by extending what are essentially the administrative judicial review powers of their regular courts that the British have most
concretely expressed their rights concerns. UK courts cannot become bolder in
administrative law because they wield the great club of constitutional veto over
statutes, but they may become bolder as demands are made that they use their
administrative law review powers as a surrogate for that club in the protection
of rights.

As already noted, the continental situation is different. The separate administrative courts need not feel the heat of constitutional rights demands. The
European Convention on Human Rights, once domesticated by national
statutes, does inject higher law, if not constitutional law rights, into the administrative courts. But precisely because it is foreign, treaty-based, in a sense international law, national administrative courts are unlikely to be particularly
emboldened by it, although they may certainly use it if they wish to be bold.

The situation of the ECJ is most strikingly different from that of continental
administrative courts, and even of English courts enjoying general jurisdiction
but no clear constitutional judicial review powers. Indeed the position of the
ECJ is most comparable to that of the US Supreme Court. It is a court of general jurisdiction exercising a constitutional judicial review power, as well as
engaging in judicial review of administrative action including delegated law-
making. Indeed as with the American due process clauses, the 'giving reasons'

clause of the Treaties provides a constitutional foundation for administrative law review, particularly for transparency demanding review. Legitimacy and judicial self-confidence built up in the realm of constitutional review are easily transferred to administrative review. Indeed a court of general jurisdiction, exercising constitutional judicial review and acting within a strong environment of rights, is very likely to constitutionalize administrative law rights such as the right to be heard or receive reasons. The ECJ has now committed itself to the protection of individual rights to be imputed to the Treaties. The new Union Charter of Rights gives more substance to that commitment. So the Court becomes a beneficiary of the religion of rights and a target for interest-group lit-igation presenting itself as rights litigation. Its extensive gender equality jurisprudence clearly shows the move from individual to group rights. And it was chastized for not giving sufficient homage to group rights in its positive or affirmative action decisions. If an enthusiastic discourse of rights develops in the Court's constitutional business, it can hardly fail to spill over into its admin-istrative review.

If regulation has become the central concern of EU law, and rights discourse has become central to judicial review, then why should rights discourse not become prominent in the administrative review of regulatory rules by a court of complete judicial review jurisdiction, particularly when rights talk may be used to enhance transparency and participation? Moreover, quite unlike in the UK situation and like in the American, the ECJ confronts a very sticky law-making process that cannot easily retrofit the statutes to overcome adverse administrat-ive review. And unlike in France, the ECJ is not going to be able directly to intervene in the rule-drafting process and so will have to intervene visibly by court decision if it is to intervene at all.

3. REGULATION, RULES, AND JUDICIAL REVIEW

Currently the EU is engaging in a great deal of delegated legislation through the Comitology process and the proliferating 'independent' agencies.[7] In these arenas transparency to the general public is very low and participation may be high for those within the relevant epistemic community or network, but non-existent for everybody else. Indeed it is precisely because the democratic deficit is so high in these delegated decision processes that a whole wardrobe of deliberative and rationality veils has been trotted out to clothe them.[8] Technical or scientific legitimacy is to serve as a substitute for democratic legitimacy.

The key question for the administrative law of the Union is the relationship between this deliberative move and judicial review. If we are to praise technocracy

---

[7] C. Joerges and E. Vos, *EU Committees: Social Regulation, Law and Politics* (Hart, Oxford, 1999); A. Kreher (ed.), *New European Agencies* (European University Institute, Florence, 1996).

[8] See Joerges and Neyer, n. 6 above.

to fend off democratic doubts, it seems to follow that reviewing courts ought to be very deferent to administrative expertise. For if judges question that expertise, the clothes fall off and the democratic doubts march back in. If the democratic doubts march back in, an activist judicial review demanding transparency and participation may assuage those doubts.

To oversimplify Harlow's view and our disagreement, we share a deep suspicion of the deliberative talents of technocrats, but she wants transparency and participation without activist review, and I welcome such review as the one feasible route to such transparency and participation. We are certainly in agreement that it is delegated rule-making by committees and agencies that poses the crucial challenge. Given the problem, one obvious solution is for the European Union to borrow the American activist style of judicial review of rule-making that has made US rule-making the most open and transparent in the world. The difficulty with this solution is the widespread perception that American judicial activism has spawned an adversarial legalism that seriously undercuts the effectiveness of the American rule-making process which is now marked by great delay and high expense.

Indeed, as Harlow notes, there had been a strong reaction in the USA itself reflected not only in scholarly writing[9] but such Supreme Court decisions as *Vermont Yankee*[10] and *Chevron*.[11] I believe, however, that the US experience may have been read wrongly in Europe, and indeed often in the United States as well. The key to understanding the US experience is to view it as an evolutionary development over time rather than simply a dialectic of judicial activism versus judicial self-restraint. From the 1960s and through the 1980s the US Courts of Appeal rapidly escalated transparency and participation requirements for rule-making and were consistently backed by Congress, many of whose new statutes explicitly incorporated the new judicial standards. It is true that these new requirements made rule-making more time-consuming and expensive, but the costs seemed worthwhile not only in terms of the democratic benefits but in terms of improving the rationality of outcomes. An administrator faced with meeting judicial demands for transparency and participation will almost automatically end up doing the regulatory cost-benefit analysis demanded by the rationality school. There were, however, two ghosts at the feast.

One was strategic behaviour by regulated parties. If the regulatory rule-maker had to consider and adequately respond to each and every point raised by every interested party, then regulation could be slowed by generating an endless blizzard of points to be responded to. The other ghost held hands with the first. Judges who were really motivated by policy disagreements with the rule-makers could search through the great drifts of rule-making record left by the

---

[9] W. Jordan, 'Ossification Revisited: Does Arbitrary and Capricious Review Significantly Interfere with Agency Ability to Achieve Regulatory Goals Through Informal Rulemaking?' (2000) 94 *Northwestern Univ L Rev* 393.

[10] *Vermont Yankee Nuclear Power Corp v. Natural Resources Defense Council, Inc* (1978) 435 US 519.

[11] *Chevron USA v. Natural Resources Defense Council* (1984) 467 US 837.

blizzard and pick up some arguably inadequate response by the agency to serve as the basis for striking down the rule finally made. It was these ghosts that the Supreme Court attempted to lay in *Vermont Yankee*. In fact that decision accepts and endorses every new transparency and participation requirement that had been introduced. It only cautions the Courts of Appeal not to disguise their policy disagreements with the agencies as findings of procedural error.

The full transparency and participation requirements that had been developed before *Vermont Yankee* survived it nicely not because the US Courts of Appeal have a considerable capacity to resist the Supreme Court, but because the Supreme Court had approved the requirements. *And so has everyone else ever since*. None of the turn of the century reaction has called for a reduction in transparency and participation. What is denounced is the strategic behaviour of the regulated and the disguised judicial policy-making.

The same story can be told of *Chevron*. In fact the Supreme Court has long maintained two equal and opposite lines of precedent, one deferring to agency statutory interpretation and the other asserting that ultimately it is the courts that must have the final say on what a law means until legislators choose to amend it. It can hardly be otherwise. No court that takes judicial review, or more broadly the judicial function itself, seriously can give up its authority decisively to decide questions of law. To allow an agency exercising delegated rule-making powers to be the sole and final interpreter of the delegating statute would render every such delegation unlimited until recalled. On the other hand, no court engaged in administrative review can deny that the agency to which rule-making authority is delegated must interpret the delegating statute in order to make rules under it. Again the problem is one of disguised judicial policy-making, in which a court pretends that there is only one true interpretation of the statute when what it means is that it dislikes the one of several plausible interpretations chosen by the agency, or rather the policy results that follow from that interpretation. Indeed that is precisely what *Chevron* says, that the Courts must acknowledge agency interpretative discretion but not allow an agency to disobey the law. The final rule in *Chevron* is that courts must defer to the interpretations of administrative rule-makers when the statutory language is ambiguous and the agency interpretation reasonable. The courts continue to have the final say on whether the statute is ambiguous and the interpretation reasonable. This is hardly judicial surrender.

The Supreme Court has chided the Courts of Appeal for covertly substituting their own policy judgments for those of the rule-makers, but it has not substantially cut back on judicially imposed transparency and participation requirements. Rule-making still takes far more time and agency resources than it did in the 1950s.

US courts today may be less activist than they were some years ago in the sense of striking down fewer rules. In some part that may be because of chiding by the Supreme Court and the commentators. For the most part, however, it is because the agencies have learned to meet high transparency and participation requirements. And in part it is because, in the long haul, technocrats are more powerful than judges in societies that heavily depend on technology. Once judges have demanded a full and complete record of decision-making that is in fact highly technical, they find they cannot understand the record they have demanded. That a judge bereft of technical training can make correct decisions because the adversary process presents contending technical arguments is an illusion, and no one is more aware of this illusionary quality than are the judges. During an initial period judges may impose their policy hunches on technical specialists by transposing policy disagreement into procedural demands or statutory interpretations. Over the longer haul the technocrats can learn to deal with legal demands far better than the judges can learn to deal with technical contentions. Judicial review of high-tech regulation is self-limiting over time. Its very demands for fuller explanation lead to a situation in which judges are compelled to admit their limited understanding, and thus their limited competence to intervene. In this process, however, there is likely to occur a real increase in transparency and participation, and even an increase in technical rationality. These increases come at a cost in time and administrative resources, but they may well be worth the costs.

If judicial activism is ultimately self-limiting in US administrative judicial review of rule-making, in Europe it is likely to be more self-limiting and to rise to lower peaks along the way. The education, selection, in-service training, and career patterns of European judges, and what Harlow calls the instrumental vision of administrative judicial review fostered by these factors, are likely to dampen judicial activism in Europe. European corporatist traditions of regulation, although enervated by the move to Brussels, are not likely to die. They encourage regulatory players to stay away from courts. And finally the very rise and recession of judicial activism in the USA is likely to teach the courts of the EU valuable lessons in steering a mid-course between technocracy and adversarial legalism.

We need not rely entirely on case law to initiate greater transparency and participation in Union rule-making nor on a detailed administrative code. A broadly written notice and comment Union regulation for Comitology and agency rule-making would put the Council imprint of legitimacy on greater judicial supervision. But it also would serve to restrain independent judicial procedural law-making by announcing that transparency and participation requirements were statutory, not constitutional, in character so that judicial excesses might be cured by relatively easy legislative amendment.

Harlow repeatedly announces her distaste for a juridified, adversarial governance while noting the movement of Europe in that direction. She sees judicial activism as simply adding judges to the neo-corporatist network of actors-regulators—international businessmen, bureaucrats and politicians—who dominate post-modern governance. But is this network better with the judges out than the judges in? I prefer the judges in, for a number of reasons. To the extent that judges demand participation and transparency they reduce the neo-corporatism. It is true that the strongest repeat players in administrative review litigation will be corporations and government itself. It is also true, however, that non-corporate and often anti-corporate interest groups, the same groups that pushed for regulation in the first place, will become repeat players. Indeed the potential for litigation may help in the constituting and self-definition of such groups. Judicial review also acts to ameliorate technocracy. The judge may be the sole lay player in a process otherwise completely in the hands of experts. If we must have a chicken regulation, I would prefer it to be made by ten poultry scientists and one judge than by ten poultry scientists. The judge's view of chickens is likely to be closer to that of the demos than is the collective view of the ten chicken experts. The formal requirements of litigation, that parties be treated as equal and that they explain themselves, provide a useful interlude in a rule-making process in which different players bring very different levels of resources to the table.

Finally while Harlow is undoubtedly correct in viewing judicial review as a poor surrogate for real democratic accountability, it may be useful to see the two not as alternatives but as complements. Litigation is a way of arousing public attention. It shapes on-going policy issues which are not news into particular events which are. It provides both journalists and readers with examples or stories that are more interesting and comprehensible than are general problems. No doubt litigation is more in tune with pluralist or group oriented than with popular democracy. Group democracy is, however, better than none. And more public attention is better than less. Again my viewpoint may be too American, but regulation with activist review would appear to me to promise at least a little more tilt toward democracy and away from technocracy and corporatism than regulation without such review. I believe that would be true even under a relatively more successful regime of democratic accountability than actually is likely to occur in the Union.

There are now a number of comparative studies suggesting that corporatist regulatory implementation is more efficient than legalistic rule enforcement.[12] However that may be, fostering a litigation market for rule-making as opposed to rule-implementation offers substantial advantages. The exercise of delegated rule-making power by technically expert administrative agents typically is difficult for legislative principles to police. Even acknowledging the successes of the UK Parliament's committee on statutory instruments, legislatures usually lack both the technical back-up to conduct full and independent evaluations and the capacity to monitor rules as they manifest themselves over time in thousands of detailed applications. Given the complex, awkwardly divided legislative delegator of the EU, the difficulties of delegator monitoring of delegatee are multiplied. It is precisely the technically sophisticated, pervasive monitoring of

---

[12] See e.g. M. Verweij, 'Why is the River Rhine Cleaner than the Great Lakes (Despite Looser Regulation)?' (2000) 34 *Law and Society Review* 1007.

delegated legislation as its meaning becomes clear over time that a litigation market fostered by activist judicial review provides. It is the regulated parties who are in the best position to observe and have the highest incentives to point out the rule-maker's deviations from the parent statute if a suitable forum exists for pointing out and achieving a correction of the deviations. A sufficient level of judicial activism may assure not only greater transparency of and participation in rule-making, but a litigational market of thousands of continuous, self-interested decisions by regulated parties, themselves possessed of the very technical knowledge at issue, or capable of hiring it, to test or not test each rule in court. Such a market will add up to precisely that detailed, technically sophisticated surveillance of delegated legislation that the delegators find it hard to provide themselves. While the government will bear part of the costs of false positives in this system, that is it will have to defend against incorrect allegations that a particular delegated rule is unlawful, most of the surveillance costs will be born by the regulated parties.

Harlow has cogently argued against a detailed administrative code of the German kind. She has evidenced her antipathy, widely shared, to excessive judicial activism. Can we get sufficiently transparent, participatory, or even rational, let alone deliberative, rule-making without passing through a period of judicial activism, excessive to some. Harlow hopes so. And surely she is right that we ought to try, through the enunciation of general principles of European administrative law by courts and commentators, through internal structuring conducted by administrators themselves prodded by scholarly commentary, perhaps through some appropriately specific statutory rules for committee and agency proceedings, and perhaps through some limited direct intervention by courts beyond the 'jawboning' of general judicial homilies on good government.

I myself believe that these channels will be insufficient against the great pressures for technocratic government generated by transnational regulatory regimes. I believe that precisely because such regimes weaken corporatist regulation, powerful regulated parties will themselves press for more judicial activism favourable to 'outsiders'. The result, I think, will be that Union courts will expand the more activist judicial review they are now exercising over quasi-judicial administrative proceedings to rule-making proceedings as well. And while, in the medium run, the result may be slightly more disguised judicial policy-making than one might like, and a good deal more strategic behaviour by the regulated and their lawyers, in the longer term Union rule-making processes will be more improved with this judicial activism than without it.

13

Cymru yn Ewrop: Wales in Europe

RICHARD RAWLINGS*

'A pluralist Europe is not inconsistent with a commitment to international-
ism. Cultural diversity is valuable in its own right and is a basic strength of
the European enterprise ... Systems and processes which work in one
Member State may be largely ineffectual in others and effectiveness in the
real, grass roots, sense provides the strongest of arguments for pluralism.'

(Carol Harlow[1])

'Wales is a microcosm of Europe's diversity. It has many lessons to learn and
much to offer.'

(Wales European Centre—homepage[2])

1. INTRODUCTION

The topic of *Cymru yn Ewrop*—'Wales in Europe'—is an appropriate one for
this *Festschrift*. On a personal note, it marks Professor Harlow's strong Welsh
ancestry through her father, the distinguished medieval and Tudor historian and
sometime Vice-Principal of King's College London, Professor C. H. Williams. As
for the substance, the topic neatly bridges the two main streams in this book of
domestic and European public law. A watershed in the history of the territory,
the novel constitutional development that is Welsh devolution is constructed in
terms of the historical unity of the English and Welsh legal system and is
strongly oriented to the growth of European integration.

As the opening quotation makes clear, the topic also bears on a major theme
in Professor Harlow's writings, the preference not for one Europe, or even for several, but for strong forms of pluralism and diversity in the legal and political con-
struction(s). Rightly in my view, she has thus stressed the contribution of the

---

* I am grateful for their co-operation to Gary Davies, Head of the European and External Affairs
Directorate, Welsh Assembly Government; Desmond Clifford, Head of the Assembly Government's
Representation in Brussels; and Joseph Gallagher, former Director of the Wales European Centre.
The usual disclaimer applies.
    [1] C. Harlow, *Voices of Difference in a Plural Community*, Harvard Jean Monnet Working Paper
3/2000 (Cambridge, Mass., 2000), 2, 12. See also C. Harlow, *European Administrative Law and the
Global Challenge*, EUI Working Paper RSC No. 9823 (EUI, Florence, 1998).
    [2] http://ewrop.com/wales.

different constitutional, legal, and administrative traditions in the Member States. In her words, 'even if globalisation is bringing European societies closer together, there remains a considerable cultural divergence. National and sub-national culture is still strongly reflected in modes of government and in public administration.'[3] More especially, and no doubt reflecting in part British constitutional traditions, Professor Harlow has set about re-emphasizing the important role and place of the national (and sub-national) parliaments.[4]

Like many of Professor Harlow's interventions, the chosen topic could scarcely be more topical. The current debate on 'European governance' was initiated by a Commission White Paper[5] notably warm to the regional dimension, while 'the future of Europe' debate, begun in Nice and promoted at Laeken,[6] inevitably raises (indirectly or otherwise) the vexed question of regional competencies and representation in the EU. 'Wales in Europe' is a useful touchstone.

Carved in the light of local experience, this essay establishes a novel conceptual framework, a five-fold model of engagement at the regional level, which can be used as a tool for comparative analysis and evaluation. First, however, a word is in order about the nature of the Welsh devolutionary development.

2. WELSH DEVOLUTION: DIVERGENCE AND CONVERGENCE

As constituted in the Government of Wales Act 1998 (GWA), and instituted since mid-1999 in the powers and proceedings of the National Assembly for Wales, the territory now has its own first democratically elected and accountable form of government. Viewed in comparative perspective however, it represents a weak form of legal autonomy, a model of executive devolution involving the transfer of certain subordinate and not primary law-making powers, and allowing for the ordering of local expenditure but with no power of taxation. History speaks volumes in this context, most obviously that of close integration with a powerful neighbour, 'England's first colony', or of internal territorial fragmentation and limited consensus for change. Such anyway is the logic of the large-scale asymmetry in the UK devolutionary development, with Wales as the junior partner among the Celtic lands.[7]

'Distinctively Welsh': such is a charitable interpretation of the original design of the new representative body. As a corporate body, it is to the National

---

[3] C. Harlow, *Voices of Difference*, n. 1 above, 10–11.

[4] C. Harlow, *Accountability in the European Union* (Oxford University Press, Oxford, 2002).

[5] European Commission, *White Paper on Governance*, COM(2001)428.

[6] Treaty of Nice, Declaration No. 23 on The Future of the Union; Laeken Declaration, *The Future of the European Union*, SN 273/01.

[7] See, further, R. Rawlings, 'The Shock of the New. Devolution in the United Kingdom', in E. Riedl (ed.), *Aufgabenverteilung und Finanzregimes im Verhältnis zwischem dem Zentralstaat und seinen Untereinheiten* (Nomos, Baden-Baden, 2000).

Assembly as a whole that power is devolved. A legislature but not a parliament, an executive and a presiding officer but no formal legal separation of functions, an umbilical cord joining ministers and members constituted by a comprehensive system of subject committees; certain key features reflect and reinforce the sense of a strange anatomy.[8] That is, local divergence, or a style of internal architecture outside the mainstream of comparative constitutional development both in Europe and the Commonwealth.

The 'background theory' of the British Constitution, in the sense of the mindset or deep values associated with an exceptionally strong tradition of parliamentary government, is not so easily subjugated. One of the most fascinating features of this devolutionary development is how quickly countervailing forces have set in.[9] *De facto* separation of functions, conventions of cabinet government, establishment of the self-styled 'Welsh Assembly Government': subsequent developments represent in comparative perspective a flattening of differences.[10] A different but related point: there is increased pressure, including from inside the Assembly, for a more generous allocation of functions, which currently finds expression in an Independent Commission on the powers and electoral arrangements of the Assembly.[11] Complex and confused: the existing division of functions within the fields of devolved competence is singularly hard to defend.[12] Perhaps hopefully, expanding on the original design of the devolution statute as a framework for organic change,[13] Wales is well on the road to a form of legislative devolution.

Again, the devolutionary development in Wales may look different, but it also stands for an underlying process of convergence. Overload of the central government apparatus, demands for democratization and participation, minority nationalism: explanatory features commonly associated with the rise of regional or meso-government in Europe[14] are clearly identifiable in the local phenomenon. So also, the UK Government's devolution White Paper, *A Voice*

---

[8] See generally, R. Rawling, *Delineating Wales. Constitutional, Legal and Administrative Aspects of National Devolution* (University of Wales Press, Swansea, 2003).

[9] Events are chronicled in J. Barry Jones and J. Osmond (eds.), *Building a Civic Culture* (Institute of Welsh Affairs, Cardiff, 2002); J. Barry Jones and J. Osmond (eds.), *Birth of Welsh Democracy* (Institute of Welsh Affairs, Cardiff, 2003).

[10] R. Rawlings, *Towards a Parliament: Three Faces of the National Assembly for Wales* (University of Wales Press, 2002).

[11] The (Richard) Commission is expected to report in late 2003 (after the second set of Assembly elections). See for details Assembly proceedings, 18 April 2002.

[12] The Assembly has adopted the idea of a set of governing principles: see National Assembly, *Assembly Review of Procedure* (February 2002), chap. 4; and, for the original proposal, R. Rawlings, 'Quasi-Legislative Devolution: Powers and Principles' (2001) 52 *Northern Ireland Legal Quarterly* 54. See also, Welsh Affairs Select Committee, *The Primary Legislative Process as it affects Wales* (HC 79, Session 2002–03).

[13] R. Davies, *Devolution: A Process not an Event* (Institute of Welsh Affairs, Cardiff, 1999).

[14] See for leading examples of a voluminous literature L. Sharpe (ed.), *The Rise of Meso Government in Europe* (Sage, London, 1992); and M. Keating, *The New Regionalism in Western Europe* (Edward Elgar, London, 1998).

for Wales, underscored the European influences. 'Experience elsewhere shows that effective regional government can bring additional gains both for member states and for areas such as Wales.'[15] The territory was thus to be reinvented as a 'Euro-region'.

As a motor of constitutional change, considerations of economic development are highlighted here. Providing clear leadership and a strategic direction to improve the Welsh economy was stipulated as one of the Assembly's most important tasks.[16] To explicate, although the territory has a creditable record in attracting inward investment, it has continued to struggle in the wake of the decline of heavy industry, as also now of the rural economy. A low GDP in Wales is typically a product both of low economic participation rates and low levels of productivity.[17] Again, looking forwards, the economy of the region clearly faces formidable challenges, not least in terms of the intensifying competitive pressures that mark the trajectory of the European construction. By which is meant not only the creation of the Euro-zone (from which—at least for the moment—the territory is excluded), but also the geographical tilt eastwards that now constitutes EU enlargement. For many years a low wage economy inside the continental trading regime, the territory must now contend with the labour pool of the Accession States, and do so as a peripheral region.

To quote Wales' first chief minister, 'the progressive response to globalisation must be to reach out, to work with others, to pool our talents, so that we are stronger and fitter and better equipped to meet the challenges of tomorrow'.[18] Of course the autonomy of sub-state government is liable to be eroded by the peculiarly intense growth of 'relations across borders' represented by European integration, together with the more diffuse forms of integration into global arrangements.[19] But equally it does not follow that regions and localities have no scope for policy initiative and response, better to harness the economic and other opportunities.[20] For a territory like Wales, necessity is the mother of invention.

The local devolutionary development may thus be seen to exemplify the simultaneous processes of integration and fragmentation in Europe. Including, that is, in terms of the interaction or the way in which a re-emphasis on territoriality reflects the competing stresses and strains generated by a widened and deepened market economy.[21] The important role of regions in achieving an

---

[15] *A Voice for Wales* (Cm. 3718, The Stationery Office, London, 1997) para. 2.25.

[16] *Ibid.*, para. 2.1.

[17] See for details the Welsh Assembly Government's strategic plan, *A Winning Wales* (2002).

[18] A. Michael, 'The Dragon on our Doorstep: New Politics for a New Millennium in Wales' (Institute of Welsh Politics, Aberystwyth, November 1999). See for a useful general discussion M. Telr (ed.), *European Union and New Regionalism: Regional Actors and Global Governance in a Post-Hegemonic Era* (Ashgate, Aldershot, 2001).

[19] A. Giddens, *Runaway World* (Profile, London, 1999).

[20] See for a valuable corrective J. Loughlin (ed.), *Sub-national Democracy in the European Union: Challenges and Opportunities* (Oxford University Press, Oxford, 2001); also, J. Hopkins, *Devolution in Context: Regional, Federal and Devolved Government in the European Union* (Cavendish, London, 2002).

[21] A familiar theme in the literature: see R. Rawlings, 'Law, Territory and Integration. A View from the Atlantic Shore' (2001) 67 *International Review of Administrative Sciences* 479.

effective mix of economic and social policies is a message officially taken to heart in Wales: 'a necessary complement to the macro-economic and structural reforms which are applied at Member State and European levels'.[22]

Much has been heard of the 'hollowing out of the State'[23] and even of 'a Europe of the Regions'.[24] It is, however, one thing to recognize the increased force of models of multi-layered governance,[25] the relocation of decision-making powers from the central state to supranational institutions and to territories and localities ('internal subsidiarity'), and quite another to subscribe to the thesis that the nation-state is somehow withering away. Expressed slightly differently, it is a mistake to see the rise of sub-state government in terms of a zero-sum game in which the central tier of administration necessarily loses out.[26] Mixtures of law and administration, which notably include more interdependence across hier-archical state structures and co-operative systems of negotiation, form a key ingredient of the twin processes of (EU) integration and fragmentation.

3. ENGAGING EUROPE: A FIVE-FOLD MODEL

Territorial, functional, political spaces: Euro-regions, it is commonly observed, come in all shapes and sizes. As indicated, however, Wales is a good showcase of the opportunities for, as well as the constraints on, sub-state creativity in a contemporary era characterized by the broad currents of market liberalization and supranational modes of ordering.

Easily recognizable by the lawyer, the first concept in the analytical framework is that of 'the implementing region'. Reference is here being made to the legislat-ive space available to the region in the implementation of EU requirements. EC directives obviously provide the litmus test, according to the classic Treaty for-mula of choice of forms and methods.[27] How substantial is this space, or to what extent is the region allowed—and equipped—to go it alone? The question is sharply posed in the case of Wales, in view, first, of limited domestic experience or lack of constitutional tradition in such matters of divided competencies, and, secondly, of the retarded administrative, legal, and political development of the territory in historical terms. From civil service outpost of London to creative and major user of European legislative space is a quantum leap.

---

[22] Welsh European Task Force, *The National Assembly for Wales and the European Union* (1998), 3. See also in the UK context E. Balls and J. Healey, *Towards a New Regional Policy: Delivering Growth and Full Employment* (Smith Institute, London, 2000).

[23] R. Rhodes, 'The Hollowing Out of the State: The Changing Nature of the Public Service in Britain' (1994) 65 *Political Quarterly* 138.

[24] For example A. Adonis and S. Jones, *Subsidiarity and the Community's Constitutional Future* (Nuffield, Oxford, 1991).

[25] G. Marks, 'An Actor-Centred Approach to Multi-Level Governance' (1996) 6 *Regional and Federal Studies* 20.

[26] T. Christiansen, 'Territorial Politics in the European Union' (1999) 6 *JEPP* 349; C. Jeffery, 'Sub-National Mobilization and European Integration: Does it Make Any Difference?' (2000) 38 *JCMS* 1.

[27] Art. 249 EC.

The second concept, 'the partnering region', relates to novel forms of local democratic governance, including in terms of appropriate models of regional economic development, as well as to the tools and practices of administrative and political co-operation across the various layers of government. Such is the quality of the change in the local administrative structures that Wales may be considered something of a laboratory in the contemporary search for collaborative or mutually beneficial solutions, one which places special emphasis on inclusiveness.[28] Notably, much was made of the concept of partnership in the devolution White Paper, *A Voice for Wales*. Ambitiously, the Assembly's partners were said to include local authorities and other public bodies in Wales, the voluntary sector, central government in Whitehall, and European institutions.[29]

The particular twist involves EU regional policy in the guise of the structural funds. Designated as a lagging region, much of Wales is a major beneficiary in the current programming period (2000–6). This feature sits comfortably with the strong economic orientation of the Welsh devolutionary development, not least given the particular challenges to the region posed by the Euro and EU enlargement. But further, it brings into play the newly strengthened 'partnership principle' of the EU policy. That is the legal requirement of shared responsibility between the different layers of government and the public and private sectors in the name of solidarity and democratization, efficiency, and self-government or non-hierarchical forms of co-ordination.[30] Wales is once again a key testing ground; and all the more so, it may be said, by reason of the synergy involving the domestic or devolutionary aspect of 'the partnering region'.

The concept of 'the national region' serves to illuminate the multifaceted nature of the legal and constitutional position of a territory like Wales. That it is conceptualized in terms of a nation, while remaining—as a region for EU purposes—firmly anchored inside the Union/Member State, is of the essence of the devolutionary development. The new 'National Assembly' thus provides a focus for Welsh identity and democratic culture, which in turn highlights particular cultural and political sensitivities and capital.[31] A feature, it may be observed, that is all the more significant in view of the comparative weakness of the formal powers, and one which the devolved administration has been notably keen to exploit in the European context.

Central government has to learn to live with a new dispensation of shared roles and responsibilities. Moving beyond the comparative experience of constitutional systems of divided competencies this general issue is given a whole new lease of life by the rise of meso-government in an environment of intensifying supra-national ordering and global forces. Attention is thus drawn in the

---

[28] Themes familiarly associated with A. Giddens, *The Third Way* (Polity, London, 1998). And see for general discussion in the Welsh context P. Chaney and R. Fevre (eds.), *New Governance: New Democracy?* (University of Wales Press, Cardiff, 2001).   [29] N. 15 above, para. 3.1.

[30] Council Reg. 1260/1999 [1999] OJ L161/1, Art. 8.

[31] See further B. Taylor and K. Thompson (eds.), *Scotland and Wales: Nations Again?* (University of Wales Press, Cardiff, 1999).

UK context to a novel instrument of intergovernmental relations, the *Concordat on Co-ordination of European Union Policy Issues.*[32] Notably, this choice of soft-law technique is seen to fit with the idea of expanding patterns of interdependence and collaborative forms of decision-making across state structures, as well as illustrating the administrative and political values of flexibility and responsiveness. Proper accommodation and co-ordination of state and substate interests in EU affairs: such are the concerns of 'the national region'.

'The lobbying and networking region' is another closely related concept. It involves so-called 'paradiplomacy', the international activities of sub-state governments, a strong growth of which in recent years is typically associated with the effects of globalization and in particular the rise of continental trading regimes like the EU Single Market.[33] To this effect, a critical test of sub-state mobilization is the responsiveness of paradiplomacy to change in the opportunity structure or policy-making environment. This is not to overlook formal scrutiny, consideration by the regional representative body of draft European legislation. It hardly needs saying, however, that the multifaceted nature of the EU process, let alone its sheer scale, raises formidable obstacles to a sustained and effective input of this type.[34]

The case of Wales is especially noteworthy for illustrating a diverse range of contacts, dedicated first to raising the international profile, and second to grasping the competitive opportunities.[35] The identity of a 'national region' may be used to great advantage here. Regional associational networking at the pan-European level, a familiar feature in paradiplomacy, is one aspect. Another one is the establishing of close bilateral relationships targeted especially on the (more dynamic) economies in the Accession States. Neatly illustrating the broad knock-on effects of EU enlargement, this development exemplifies the potential for regional initiative in the harsh light of intensifying market forces, and thus the concept of 'the lobbying and networking region'.

The concept of 'the constitutional region' is the fifth one. Recently, the term has been used in the EU context to denote entities such as internal or stateless nations and (federal) lands or provinces with substantial (constitutionally) guaranteed legislative powers.[36] Politically speaking, it stands for the demand of certain significant and clearly delineated territories, such as Cataluña in Spain and Scotland in the UK, for closer parity with Member States inside the EU umbrella or supranational framework. A demand, it is observed, which is felt all the more keenly in view of enlargement, the imminent prospect of

---

[32] See *Memorandum of Understanding and Supplementary Agreements* (Cm. 5240, 2001).

[33] F. Aldecoa and M. Keating (eds.), *Paradiplomacy in Action: The Foreign Relations of Sub-national Governments* (Frank Cass, London, 1999).

[34] C. Carter, 'Democratic Governance Beyond the Nation State: Third-Level Assemblies and Scrutiny of European Legislation' (2000) 6 *EPL* 429.

[35] Reference may further be made to the special networking arrangements involving Wales that have begun to emerge in the context of Northern Ireland (Strand Three of the Belfast Agreement (Cm. 3883, 1998)). See Rawlings, n. 21 above.

[36] See, for example, N. MacCormick, *Democracy at Many Levels: European Constitutional Reform* (Convention paper 298/02, 2002).

privileged status for more small states, and one which further implies a process of differentiation from other EU regions. Or as one could say, not so much 'the third level'[37] as 'two-and-a-half'. And a venture, it is immediately apparent, in which Wales is somewhat awkwardly placed by reason of the limited scheme of executive devolution.

In this essay, the concept is afforded a wider meaning: the region as an actor in the general debate on constitutional and administrative change in the EU. 'European governance', 'the future of Europe': the new Welsh polity has thus become engaged with major reform processes that are currently taking shape. The approach, it will be seen, is founded on but not confined to co-operation with central government in the role of Member State. It is also, given the territorial history, the more remarkable for happening. Constitutionally, as well as administratively and economically,[38] post-devolutionary Wales is learning by doing.

4. THE IMPLEMENTING REGION

Whisper it gently: as an instrument of territorial autonomy, the current devolutionary scheme is in some ways more limited than the design model of executive devolution that was first established for Wales a generation ago.[39] Such is the knock-on effect of the widening and deepening of EU competencies in the intervening period, on such major fields of devolved activity as agriculture and environment, as also of the burgeoning EU rules and regulations in matters like public procurement. Power devolved may in the famous phrase be power retained, but much in the substance is no longer in the gift of the national parliament.[40]

The extent to which the new devolved polity is constrained has evidently come as a shock to many Assembly Members.[41] In contrast, that is, to the determinedly upbeat message about 'Wales in Europe' retailed in the White Paper, *A Voice for Wales*. In particular, a ministerial emphasis on the margin of appreciation, implementation (of EU directives) 'in a way that [the Assembly] considers best takes account of Welsh interests',[42] has so far borne little fruit in the policy and practice of Assembly law-making.

---

[37] A familiar theme in the literature, linked most obviously to the Germanic tradition: see, e.g., U. Bullmann, 'The Politics of the Third Level' (1996) 6 *Regional and Federal Studies* 3.

[38] K. Morgan and G. Rees, 'Learning by Doing: Devolution and the Governance of Economic Development in Wales', in P. Chaney and R. Fevre (eds.), *New Governance: New Democracy?* (University of Wales Press, Cardiff, 2001).

[39] In the ill-fated Wales Act 1978, aborted after a referendum.

[40] Space precludes discussion of the impact on the devolved territory of the (partial) incorporation of the European Convention on Human Rights in the Human Rights Act 1998. See R. Rawlings, 'Taking Wales Seriously: Devolution, Human Rights and Legal System', in T. Campbell, C. Gearty, and A. Tomkins (eds.), *Sceptical Approaches to Human Rights* (Hart, Oxford, 2001).

[41] Most obviously in such important fields in Wales as rural policy: see, e.g., J. Barry Jones, 'Driven by Events', in J. Barry Jones and J. Osmond (eds.), *Inclusive Government and Party Management* (Institute of Welsh Affairs, Cardiff, 2001).

[42] Welsh Office press release, 20 February 1998.

(a) Transmission Belt

A generous and principled allocation of legislative implementing powers, it is not. To explicate, under the scheme of the devolution statute, the power to designate a Minister of the Crown under section 2(2) of the European Communities Act 1972, so allowing the Minister to make regulations 'for the purpose of implementing any Community obligation', may be exercised to designate the Assembly.[43] By April 2003 nine such Orders in Council had been made, but far from dealing in a generic way with such subjects as the environment, they constituted a ragbag of specifications. In one of them, for example, the Assembly gained certain powers of implementing directives in relation to such diverse activities as keeping wild animals in zoos, the management of hazardous waste, and the deliberate release of genetically modified organisms.[44] On the one hand, this lack of pattern, especially striking from the viewpoint of federal systems of divided competencies, is all at one with the particularistic or highly pragmatic approach to the allocation of domestic law-making powers that is the hallmark of the particular Welsh model of executive devolution.[45] On the other hand, such cautious use of the designation power is indicative of a concern in central government to maintain a dominant position in this important legal field of Member State responsibility, at least, that is, on an England and Wales basis.

The Assembly had made seventy Orders under designated powers by April 2003.[46] Reflecting the substance of the designations, the vast majority of these statutory instruments were in the fields of agriculture, fisheries and food. Further, much of the output was driven by events, with a good third of the Orders being directed to the handling of foot and mouth disease, and another ten Orders stemming from the earlier BSE crisis in Britain. Other instruments again were largely technical in character or were part of EU-wide forms of (disease) control allowing for no local discretion. Turning the argument round, only a small group of Orders (for example, to do with financial support for organic farmers[47]) demonstrates any real creativity at the territorial level.

The devolved administration, a transmission belt: such then is the dominant model. Procedurally speaking, a notable feature of EU-inspired legislation in the Assembly is the recourse to executive or urgency procedure, a Westminster-type form of secondary legislative process involving little formal scrutiny. In contrast,

---

[43] GWA sec. 29. Central government retains concurrent powers to make subordinate legislation for the purpose of implementing Community obligations: GWA Sched. 3, para. 5.

[44] European Communities (Designation) (No. 3) Order, SI No. 3495, 2001.

[45] D. Lambert, 'A Voice for Wales: The National Assembly for Wales', in T. Watkin (ed.), *Legal Wales: Its Past, Its Future* (Welsh Legal History Society, Cardiff, 2001).

[46] See www.wales-legislation.org.uk.

[47] Tir Gofal (Amendment) (Wales) Regulations 2001, SI No. 423 (W.17), 2001; Organic Farming Scheme (Wales) Regulations 2001, SI No. 424 (W.18), 2001.

that is, to alternative and much-vaunted Assembly procedures which allow for close and detailed discussion of draft orders including in plenary session. The practice reflects and reinforces the fact that there is little substantive difference from the parallel orders produced for England by the UK central government departments. Constitutional change—political, administrative, and legal continuity: the product of devolution, one is reminded, need not be diversity; and all the more so, under the long shadow of supranational ordering.

A battery of explanatory factors can be adduced: not only 'European' considerations, a subject matter which frequently does not lend itself to different regulatory regimes, or the evident incentive 'to play safe' in view of state liability;[48] but also domestic ones, over and above the national style of designation. Thus the historical legacy of the previous territorial department, the essentially administrative apparatus that was the Welsh Office, cannot simply be wished away: most notably, a perceived lack of policy-making capacity in Wales and—a classic tale of leaning on England—little hands-on experience of legislative drafting.[49] Careful prioritization or strong focus on flagship policies; exploration of the EU 'margin of appreciation' is apt in these conditions to appear an unnecessary luxury for a new governing entity which is concerned to (be seen to) make a difference.[50]

A long tradition of legislation on a joint England and Wales basis is effectively underscored in this context by the provisions of the EU Concordat. Reflecting the close interest of central government in its role as the responsible Member State, the Concordat thus builds in a raft of notification, consultation, and liaison requirements in the case of the devolved administration minded to implement differently.[51] A case, one could say, of the use of administrative disincentive; that is, over and above the standard considerations of official convenience and limitation of legislative complexity which favour matching drafts. Reference should also be made to the initial fact post-devolution of Labour Party hegemony at the central and territorial levels.[52] The close (inter-)dependency that is entailed in the scheme of executive devolution gives this a special administrative as well as political significance in the case of Wales. In short, *pace* the Minister's apparent optimism, it would have been remarkable if the Assembly had departed immediately and radically from the English/UK EU template.[53]

[48] Cases C–6/90 and C–9/90, *Francovich and Bonifaci* v. *Italy* [1991] ECR I–5357. And see below on EU penal competence and the domestic transfer of sanction.

[49] Only now are these constraints being tackled in a serious way, including in a rapid expansion of Assembly legal services. See National Assembly, *The Role of the Office of the Counsel General* (2001).

[50] Welsh Labour Party and Welsh Liberal Democrats, *Putting Wales First: A Partnership for the People of Wales* (October 2000).   [51] *EU Concordat*, n. 32 above, para. B4.17.

[52] A 'partnership government' of Labour and Liberal Democrats has held sway in the Assembly, following two minority Labour administrations. Meanwhile the 'regional' nationalist opposition that is Plaid Cymru seeks after a Parliament for Wales, initially at least on the Scottish model: I. Wyn Jones, *From Assembly To Parliament* (Institute of Welsh Politics, Aberystwyth, 2001).

[53] See further, for instructive parallels in the context of primary legislation for Scotland, A. Page and A. Batey, 'Scotland's Other Parliament: Westminster Legislation Affecting Scotland Since Devolution' [2002] *PL*, 501.

Nevertheless, the Assembly legislation looks different. As the title of the chapter testifies, a central tenet of this new territorial polity is bilingualism: equal respect for English and the (minority) Welsh language, especially (subject to exceptions) in matters of legislative drafting.[54] Parallel texts is a phenomenon not unknown in the European construction! The strength of the local policy is demonstrated by its general application to EU-inspired orders. At one and the same time, this is very proper in view of the distinctive cultural heritage of Wales, and absorbs scarce resources, not least because Welsh has to be reinvented as a living language of the law.[55]

All this takes on additional relevance by virtue of the contemporary preference for framework directives, at least as articulated by the Commission White Paper on European Governance. The Commission, as part of a less top-down approach, thus aims to 'bring greater flexibility into how Community legislation can be implemented in a way which takes account of regional and local conditions'.[56] Perhaps it comes as no surprise to learn that the assembled Welsh polity has declared itself in favour of this proposal.[57] Enough has been said, however, to demonstrate the distance between local aspiration and current realities. Put simply, putting framework directives to distinctive use for Wales *qua* Wales would require something of a revolution in the making of EU-inspired Assembly legislation. Such change may happen, and of course is liable to be prompted in part by new opportunities, but at this stage of the post-devolutionary development of the territory the prevailing domestic forces point firmly in the opposite direction. Here as in other places, the constitutional, political, and administrative 'glue' of the Union State is not about to come unstuck.

(b) Against the Commission

What, it may be asked, of the statutory provisions on compliance? The devolution legislation solemnly records that the Assembly has no power to act in a way incompatible with Community law. It is further stated that any relevant Community obligation of the UK is an obligation of the Assembly.[58] Given the general dictates of EC law, by which is meant especially the duty of loyal co-operation, this is aptly described as having 'a quality of belt and braces'.[59]

---

[54] See GWA 1998, ss. 66, 122; and see for practical discussion National Assembly, *Bilingual Lawmaking and Justice* (2001).

[55] Part of the historical legacy of legal assimilation with England: see further Sir John Thomas, 'Legal Wales: Its Modern Origins and Its Role After Devolution: National Identity, The Welsh Language and Parochialism', in T. Watkin (ed.), *Legal Wales: Its Past, Its Future* (Welsh Legal History Society, Cardiff, 2001).   [56] Commission White Paper, n. 5 above, 4.

[57] Assembly proceedings, 17 January 2001. The Assembly's detailed response to the White Paper is discussed below.

[58] GWA, s. 106. See, on the special court machinery established for dealing with 'devolution issues', P. Craig and M. Walters, 'The Courts, Devolution and Judicial Review' [1999] *PL* 274.

[59] Art. 10 EC: A. Dashwood, 'The European Union and the National Assembly', in D. Miers (ed.), *Devolution in Wales* (Wales Public Law and Human Rights Association, Cardiff, 1999), 60.

One affair stands out, seeing the Assembly at odds with the Commission in its familiar role as 'the Guardian of the Treaties'.[60] The policy context is Welsh opposition to the development of genetically modified plant varieties, as encapsulated in an all-party preference for a 'GM-free territory'. Contrary, that is, to the tide of EU legislation, seen (at least in the Assembly) as successfully influenced by the biotech companies through the United States.

In the event, an Assembly debate in late 2001 saw the Minister seeking approval of secondary legislation designed to secure compliance with the EU regulatory framework. Infringement proceedings had by now been launched against the UK for failure, by reason of Welsh obduracy, to transpose the relevant directive. And the Commission had threatened the Assembly with the prospect of penalty proceedings under Article 228 in the case of non-compliance. To quote the Minister, 'the wolves are at the door'.[61]

To the lawyer, this was a case of clear and manifest breach: the Assembly had already delayed for some eighteen months beyond the due date for implementation. Whereas under the scheme of the Treaties the penal jurisdiction involves sanction on the Member State *qua* Member State, the true 'bite' or dissuasive effect largely depends on the domestic arrangements for transfer (or otherwise) of the sanction. Attention is thus drawn to the words of the EU Concordat: 'to the extent that financial costs and penalties imposed on the UK arise from the failure of implementation or enforcement by a devolved administration . . . responsibility for meeting these will be borne by the devolved administration'.[62]

The region against the Commission: typically it was no contest. For the local opposition politician, it was a painful lesson in the powerful constraints on territorial government under the long shadow of supranational ordering. In her words, 'why vote . . . if we cannot reject?'[63] Nor is it surprising to learn that the UK government was in these conditions prepared to stand back and allow the Assembly to make its 'own' decision.

One aspect of the affair merits special attention, namely the scale of the threat. To explicate, in the only case so far decided by the Court of Justice under Article 228, Greece was fined some €20,000 per day from the date of judgment for continuing failure by the regional authority in Crete adequately to deal with a problem of toxic waste.[64] While the Welsh case is appropriately labelled a more serious breach, the failure to transpose directives being a chief target for Commission enforcement action, this should not obscure the stark differential in the approach to sanction. By the time of the Assembly debate, Commission representatives were indicating a fine of up to £300 million; that is, a potential

---

[60] Arts. 211, 226 EC; and see for discussion of the competing modalities R. Rawlings, 'Engaged Elites. Citizen Action and Institutional Attitudes in Commission Enforcement' (2000) 6 *ELJ* 4.

[61] Assembly proceedings, 23 October 2001.

[62] *EU Concordat*, n. 32 above, para. B4.25.

[63] Plaid Cymru AM Jocelyn Davies, Assembly Proceedings, 23 October 2001. See now, Genetically Modified Organisms (Deliberate Release) (Wales) Regulations 2002, SI No. 3188 (W. 304), 2002.

[64] Case C–387/97, *Commission* v. *Greece* [2000] ECR I–5047. In accordance with its responsibility under Art. 228 to propose a sanction, the Commission had suggested a daily rate of some €25,000.

daily charge, levied from the due date for transposition, some twenty-five times the rate eventually imposed on Greece. So much, from the viewpoint of this little country, for equality of treatment!

To pursue the point, the scale of the threat was wholly disproportionate or, as an English (and Welsh) administrative lawyer might prefer to say, is indicative of abuse of discretion. That is, from the regional or 'bottom up' perspective. Put another way, the affair illustrates once again the lack of 'fit' in the European construction between, on the one hand, the unitary conception of Member States as found in major elements of EC law, and, on the other hand, the domestic political realities of divided competencies, federal or otherwise.[65] To this effect, the current penalty system as devised by the Commission is explicitly predicated on the ability to pay of the Member State,[66] as against, in the case of the Assembly, a juvenile delinquent.

5. The partnering region

Much has been heard in this context of so-called 'Team Wales'. There are significant elements here of a neo-corporatist strategy of economic development, predicated upon close linkages between the public and private sectors, as well as the assertion, bound up with the concept of national devolution, of a common territorial interest.[67] It has thus been seen as 'imperative that the opportunities and needs of Wales are tackled from an all-Wales perspective, through a strong commitment by the Assembly to mobilise the range of organisations'.[68] Together with the strong economic element in the territorial constitutional construction, the idea of the region as a player in the competitive (single and global) market struggle is powerfully demonstrated here.

One of the growth industries of Welsh devolution is strategic planning. Originally it was *An Economic Strategy for Wales* and the happy sounding *Pathway to Prosperity*. Then it was a *National Economic Development Strategy* and—an Assembly corporate plan—*A Better Wales*.[69] Today it is the vision of *A Winning Wales*, which, as the title suggests, establishes (some remarkably) ambitious targets for transforming the economy of this peripheral Euro-region. Both the scale and trajectory of the planning process are all at one with the strong collaborative theme. 'If the people, businesses and communities of Wales can work together, within an integrated framework agreed by the Government of the National Assembly, the job can be done.'[70] It is worth adding that the

[65] See, e.g., A. Dashwood, 'The Limits of European Community Powers' (1996) 21 *ELRev* 113.
[66] See for discussion M. Theodossiou, 'An Analysis of the Recent Response of the Community to Non-Compliance with Court of Justice Judgments' (2002) 27 *ELRev* 25.
[67] See further on this type of approach, which is epitomized by so-called 'Quebec Inc.', M. Keating, 'Stateless Nation Building. Quebec, Catalonia and Scotland in the Changing State System' (1997) 3 *Nations and Nationalism* 689.   [68] Welsh European Task Force, n. 22 above, 1.
[69] Available at: www.betterwales.com.
[70] Welsh Assembly Government, *A Winning Wales*, n. 17 above, 1.

Government of Wales Act mandates the fostering of Assembly relationships with local government, business, and the voluntary sector.[71] Incorporation of the value of inclusiveness was thus made an original design feature.

Turning to the substance, the designation of 'West Wales and the Valleys' for the purpose of concentrated support under Objective 1 of the European Regional Development Fund (ERDF) is the key development. Funding for the Programme totals some €3,950 million, of which the structural funds will provide EUR 1,850 million. The action priorities include developing and expanding the SME base, developing innovation and the knowledge-based economy, community economic regeneration, and rural development and the sustainable use of natural resources.[72] All this is sorely needed in light of the low GDP of an especially deprived region inside Wales. 'The resulting combination of poor housing, ill health, low educational achievement and skills levels, and low disposable incomes has led to some areas experiencing social exclusion.'[73] Whether this Programme can (begin to) generate effective 'compensation' as the EU moves east remains to be seen of course.

The Programme has achieved extraordinary political salience in the first years of the Assembly. On the one hand, it has offered the devolved administration an unrivalled opportunity to be seen to make a difference, and thus to shore up the fragile legitimacy inside the territory of the new representative institution.[74] On the other hand, by reason of the requirements in the ERDF for match funding etc, the Programme has brutally exposed the high dependency of the Assembly on the UK Government, and has even served as the pretext for the overthrow of its first chief minister (Alun Michael).[75] From the comparative perspective, the Programme further illustrates the elasticity of the concept of a 'region' in the European construction, and in European regional policy in particular. 'West Wales and the Valleys': this peripheral 'region' of the peripheral region is a local invention designed solely for the purpose of qualifying under the Objective 1 threshold.[76] As an example of sub-state mobilization in the face of supranational ordering and intensifying market forces, this kind of 'creative geography' could scarcely be bettered.

In this classic field for theories of multi-layered governance, including, from the viewpoint of the lawyer, in terms of Community provisions and precepts that are formally addressed to the regions,[77] the partnership principle takes on

---

[71] Government of Wales Act 1998, ss. 113–115.

[72] National Assembly for Wales, *Single Programming Document: The Economic and Social Regeneration of West Wales and the Valleys* (April 2000).   [73] *Ibid.*, 2.

[74] As demonstrated most obviously in a wafer-thin majority in the Welsh devolution referendum.

[75] Ostensibly for failure to secure HM Treasury guarantees of support: see Assembly proceedings, 9 February 2000. See for discussion M. Marinetto, 'The Settlement and Process of Devolution: Territorial Politics and Governance Under the Welsh Assembly' (2001) 49 *Political Studies* 306.

[76] *Per capita* GDP less than 75% of the Community average: see K. Morgan and A. Price, *The Other Wales* (Institute of Welsh Affairs, Cardiff, 1998).

[77] See, on this form of categorization, B. Hessel and K. Mortelmans, 'Decentralised Government and Community Law: Conflicting Institutional Developments?' (1993) 30 *CMLRev* 905.

a special prominence. Especially, that is, in the view of the Commission: 'a powerful means of increasing the effectiveness, visibility and democratic acceptance of the Structural Funds', even, with a hint of desperation, 'an excellent way of making Europe better known to Europeans'.[78] However, the provisions of the Council Regulation are wonderfully ambiguous, wearing all the characteristics of the intergovernmental bargaining and compromise that took place as part of the general reform of the structural funds ahead of EU enlargement.[79] On the one hand, a widening and deepening of the obligation is in part a response to the mediating of EU policy by national constitutional and administrative traditions, such that prior observance of the partnership principle has been patchy, to say the least.[80] On the other hand, the individual Member States retain considerable discretion or room for manoeuvre in the ordering of arrangements. Partnership is to take place for example 'within the framework of . . . national rules and current practices'.[81]

So it is all the more striking that the partnership principle has been taken extremely seriously in Wales. Once again, there is good fit, since particular EU requirements concerning respect for gender equality and the importance of sustainable development echo general provisions in the devolution statute.[82] The obvious touchstone, however, is that major local instrument of structural funds administration and implementation, the Programme Monitoring Committee.[83] The Regulation may be silent about composition, but the Assembly in close dialogue with the Commission has established a strict tripartite framework, consisting of equal representation from the public sector, the 'private/social sector' (business, farmers, and the trade unions), and the voluntary/community sector. It is in turn this key partnership that gives strategic direction to the Welsh European Funding Office (WEFO), an executive agency of the Assembly which performs the day-to-day functions of managing authority and paying authority.[84]

This is the proverbial 'tip of the iceberg'. The Objective 1 Programme in Wales is now being implemented through partnerships operating at three further levels: local, regional, and strategic.[85] To explicate, the first level is geo-politically structured: fifteen local partnerships each covering one local authority area. The second level is thematic in character, ten regional partnerships each covering

---

[78] Commissioner Michel Barnier, *Inforegio Newsletter* (October 1999).

[79] J. Sutcliffe, 'The 1999 Reform of the Structural Funds Regulations: Multi-level Governance or Renationalization?' (2000) 7 *JEPP* 290.

[80] L. Hooghe (ed.), *Cohesion Policy and European Integration: Building Multi-Level Governance* (Oxford University Press, Oxford, 1996). See also J. Scott, 'Law, Legitimacy and EC Governance: Prospects for "Partnership" ' (1998) 36 *JCMS* 175.

[81] Art. 8(1) of Council Reg. 1260/1999 [1999] OJ L161/1. See for critical analysis, M. Bauer, 'The EU's "Partnership Principle" ' (2002) 80 *Public Administration* 769.

[82] Government of Wales Act 1998 ss. 120–121.

[83] Council Reg. 1260/1999, n. 81 above, Art. 35.

[84] As elaborated in Commission Reg. 438/2001 [2001] OJ L63/21.

[85] See for details Welsh European Funding Office, *Making European Funds Work in Wales* (Cardiff, 2001); also, J. Bachtler, 'Objective One: A Comparative Assessment' (2002) 15 *Contemporary Wales* 30.

individual topics, from infrastructure to human resources, and on through countryside and forestry to tourism. Typically, the main role of these two levels is to identify, support, and assist the development of projects. The third level consists of four strategy partnerships, designed to provide an overview of activity in the different parts of the Programme, specifically so-called 'business assets' and 'human assets', and 'rural assets' and 'community assets'. Naturally, all these various bodies must have 'an agreed strategy framework' for their area of responsibility and also 'a lead body' to provide logistical support. In a word, partnership is piled on partnership.

It is obviously too soon for proper empirical assessment.[86] Enough has been said however to identify the Objective 1 Programme in Wales as a flagship enterprise for contemporary canons of European regional policy. Put simply, if structural funding cannot be made to work efficiently and effectively in Wales, in conditions of happy juxtaposition with the domestic devolutionary development of the national region, then where can it be?

For the avoidance of doubt, there is clearly much to be said for the types of involvement, especially at grassroots level, that the partnership principle is designed to encourage and promote. The energizing element of committed and innovative partnerships between the public, private, and voluntary sectors at the local level, not least in releasing untapped potentials, is rightly seen as of the very essence of this regenerative Programme. Nor for example, from the legal perspective, would one wish to downplay the potential benefit in the techniques of co-ordination and collaboration of formal dispute avoidance.[87] However, it is not surprising to learn of complaints from the 'coalface' not only of cumbersome process and lengthy delays, an elongated decision-making chain, but also of elements of incoherence and duplication of activity across the range or different levels of partnerships.[88] There is, too, evident tension between, on the one hand, a Programme objective of 'developing the skills and attitudes to allow the region to compete as a modern advanced economy'[89] and, on the other hand, limited or small minority representation of business in the formal structures of partnership. Whither, it may be asked, the entrepreneurial spirit in a body like the Assembly's Monitoring Committee? Politically incorrect this may be, but it can plausibly be argued that in the case of Wales the partnership principle has been taken too seriously.

---

[86] There were significant early difficulties in the policy implementation and delivery, unsurprisingly so, given the size of the Programme and the novelty of the Welsh constitutional dispensation. For discussion see L. McAllister, 'Devolution and the New Context for Public Policy-Making: Lessons from the EU Structural Funds in Wales' (2000) 14 *Public Policy and Administration* 38.

[87] That well-known 'saga' of the structural funds—Mullaghmore—springs to mind: Case T–105/95, *WWF* v. *Commission* [1997] ECR II–313. See especially J. Scott, 'Regional Policy: An Evolutionary Perspective', in P. Craig and G. de Búrca (eds.), *The Evolution of EU Law* (Oxford University Press, Oxford, 1999).

[88] A. Thomas, 'Sharpening the Cutting Edge of Economic Governance' (2001) 4 *Journal of the Institute of Welsh Affairs* 24.   [89] Welsh European Funding Office, n. 85 above, 4.

6. THE NATIONAL REGION

In the words of Rhodri Morgan, the Assembly First Minister, 'it makes sense for Wales to work with the UK so that we can punch above our weight' in EU matters.[90] In the event, the institutional arrangements in the Member State for accommodating territorial interests present a dual character. On the one hand, in contrast to certain advanced federal systems, there is no element of constitutional guarantee and veto power: a weak formulation. On the other hand, many of the individual provisions are generous. At least, that is, when viewed in terms of the insubstantial history of Wales in the counsels of the Union state. To this effect, Welsh representatives were successful in achieving broad parity of process with Scotland, an important example of the counter-vailing pressures for symmetry in the UK devolutionary development.[91]

Once again to quote the First Minister, 'it is difficult to measure objectively how effective [the] mechanisms are for influencing policy'.[92] The situation in terms of 'the national region' is in fact very fluid. Co-ordination and collaboration across state forms: the difficulty of such matters is compounded in the UK precisely because of the hitherto highly centralist form and culture of government that has found expression in the doctrine of Parliamentary Sovereignty, as also the strong asymmetrical element in the general devolutionary development.[93] Officials from a devolved administration like the Assembly have now actively to explore the boundaries. Informal alliances between what are sometimes referred to in Whitehall as 'the Celtic Cousins'—Scotland, Wales, and Northern Ireland—is but one way forward.[94]

The EU Concordat cannot be understood separately from the raft of soft-law instruments, 'concordatry',[95] that now frame the new modalities of intergovernmental relations in the UK. Good communication and especially prior consultation; co-operation on matters of mutual interest; exchange of information: the statement of post-devolutionary principles that is set out in the general *Memorandum of Understanding* may be seen as a watered down version of the

---

[90] R. Morgan, *Memorandum* to the House of Lords Select Committee on the Constitution, *Devolution: Inter-Institutional Relations in the UK* (Evidence: HL 147, Session 2001–027), at para. 25.
[91] See for further details Rawlings, n. 8 above.   [92] Morgan, n. 90 above, at para. 25.
[93] N. Walker, 'Beyond the Unitary Conception of the United Kingdom Constitution?' [2000] *PL* 384; P. Hogwood, M. Burch, and A. Scott, 'Devolution and EU Policy Making: The Territorial Challenge' (2000) 15 *Public Policy and Administration* 81.
[94] As already illustrated in the saga of 'beef on the bone': see R. Hazell, 'Intergovernmental Relations: Whitehall Rules OK?', in R. Hazell (ed.), *The State and the Nations* (Imprint Academic, Thorverton, 2000).
[95] R. Rawlings, 'Concordats of the Constitution' (2000) 116 *LQR* 257; J. Poirier, 'The Functions of Intergovernmental Agreements: Post-Devolution Concordats in a Comparative Perspective' [2000] *PL* 134. And see generally, House of Lords Select Committee on the Constitution, *Devolution: Inter-Institutional Relations in the UK* (HL 28, Session 2002–03).

(legal) concept of comity familiar in certain federal systems.[96] Typically, the system also prioritizes confidentiality, thereby establishing an administrative model of free flows of policy ideas and information.[97]

The EU Concordat may be read as the principles of concordatry writ large. So it is that the provisions on implementation by the devolved administrations constitute a thick wedge of consultation requirements, etc. Nowhere, however, is this aspect better illustrated than in the detailed provisions on the formulation of the UK policy line. These have elsewhere been analysed in terms of a bargain.[98] At one and the same time, a national region like Wales has broad access in terms of policy inputs and is effectively constrained from operating outside agreed channels. To this effect, 'the UK Government will involve the devolved administrations as fully as possible in discussions . . . on all EU issues which touch on devolved matters' but 'subject to mutual respect for the confidentiality of those discussions' and—crucially—to 'adherence to the resultant UK line'.[99] Holding the whip hand in the role of Member State, the UK government can threaten withdrawal of collaboration in a situation of non-compliance.

In the case of the national region, the related issue of (Member State) representation in the EU Council of Ministers wears a special symbolism. The EU Concordat itself carefully preserves the UK government's position. As well as no formal legal guarantees of national regional representation, the composition and negotiating tactics of the UK team are presented as essentially being for the lead UK Minister.[100] Participants from the devolved administrations have the constricted role of supporting and advancing the UK line in the formal EU process. Yet this is not the whole story. After a slow beginning, Assembly Cabinet Ministers now frequently appear on the UK team, and have even led from the front. The development is all at one with a local policy of raising Wales' profile. The domestic arrangements have in this respect proved sufficiently responsive.

As soft law the UK system of concordatry is expressly designed to limit the role of the courts in intergovernmental relations to the greatest extent possible. Procedural co-operation is also, as indicated, the chief focus of the system, while being apt to facilitate the related function of policy co-ordination in such vital matters as the implementation of EU obligations. Especially noteworthy are the speed and intensity of the in-fill, by which is meant the complex and variegated forms of interlocking arrangements inside government that are so familiar in constitutional systems of divided competence and (as exemplified in EU matters) of concurrent powers. To say, as Rhodri Morgan has, that 'the formal

[96] Most notably in Germany—'*bundestreue*'. See for an introduction P. Blair and P. Cullen, 'Federalism, Legalism and Political Reality: The Record of the Federal Constitutional Court', in C. Jeffery (ed.), *Recasting German Federalism* (Pinter, London, 1999).

[97] S. 28 of the Freedom of Information Act 2000 provides that information is 'exempt information if its disclosure . . . would, or would be likely to, prejudice relations between any administration in the United Kingdom and any other such administration'.   [98] Rawlings, n. 95 above.

[99] *Memorandum of Understanding*, n. 32 above, para. 20.

[100] *EU Concordat*, n. 32 above, paras. B4.13–14.

machinery would struggle to work without effective and informal relationships across the UK' is something of an understatement.[101]

The twin themes of continuity and change in the UK devolutionary development are brilliantly illustrated in this context. Pre-existing machinery, more particularly in the case of executive devolution by the Office of the Secretary of State for Wales (territorial representation in the UK Cabinet), and most importantly in EU matters the United Kingdom Permanent Representation (UKRep), has a vital role to play. At the same time, the special need for efficient and effective means of domestic co-ordination and compromise in EU matters—or as one could say, for a system of 'co-operative devolution'—is recognized in particular use of another product of concordatry, the Joint Ministerial Committee (JMC).[102] Operating in sectoral as well as plenary format, this ministerial machinery has thus been adapted to allow for simultaneous consultation on EU issues affecting devolved matters. In the event, the practice has quickly emerged of JMC meetings ahead of the major European Summits.

Via London: the indirect route to Brussels will surely remain of chief importance to Wales for the foreseeable future. As Rhodri Morgan says, size matters. 'The European Union is large and Wales is small. The UK is a large and influential Member State'.[103] Closer to home, it makes good practical sense for the Assembly Administration to lean on the powerful and well-oiled UK central government machine in the specialist areas of EU policy-making. How could it be otherwise, given on the one hand the limited resources available to the Assembly both at the political and civil service levels, and on the other hand the nature of the European agenda: diffuse and complex, or voluminous and elongated? The trick obviously is to identify the critical issues for Welsh interests and to deploy the local political and administrative capital accordingly, using the Whitehall networks. This may be far more easily said than done, but it nonetheless represents the essential fact of life for the national region. Such are the ties that bind.

Given the need for mutual trust and respect for difference across administrations, it is perhaps reassuring to be told that the arrangements have worked tolerably well. 'Inevitably', in the words of the official communique, 'there had been differences of view', but these 'had been handled amicably in a way which respected the legitimate interests of each administration'. So also 'the extent of joint working at all levels of government had been remarkable', which was 'a tribute to the robustness of the [devolution] settlements'.[104] It is important to bear in mind, however, the favourable political conditions for these new modalities of intergovernmental relations of Labour hegemony. Let us hope that by the time the pendulum swings, and administrations of different political hues

---

[101] Morgan, n. 90 above, para. 4. See further, for competing views, House of Lords Select Committee, n. 95 above; (UK) Government *Response* (Cm. 5780, 2003).

[102] Composed of representatives of the UK Government (also representing England) and the three devolved administrations: see *Memorandum of Understanding*, n. 32 above.

[103] Morgan, n. 90 above, para. 25. Mr Morgan is a former Commission representative in Wales, a fact which no doubt helps to explain the strong Euro-centric orientation of the Welsh Assembly government. [104] Joint Ministerial Committee, 'Devolution One Year On' (September 2000).

are installed in London and Cardiff, that sufficient understandings have been forged to ameliorate any destructive tendencies. A history of close integration with England including in EU matters is not simply to be wished away.

Speaking more generally, the famed flexibility of the British Constitution can operate to advantage in this realm. It is thus appropriate to stress the fit of these political and administrative arrangements with a fast-changing environment, in terms not only of the evolutionary character of the UK devolutionary development, as highlighted in the case of Wales, but also of the ongoing process that is the European construction. We leave the point here, to pick it up in the context of the debate on 'the future of Europe'.

7. The lobbying and networking region

The new devolved administration has naturally been keen to explore the potential of direct links with EU institutions, so as to supplement and reinforce territorial inputs into Member State policy formation, and with other official actors in the European political and economic space, most obviously at the same regional level. In fact, so rapid is the development in this field that it is already possible to speak of two main phases.

The first phase sees the Assembly overwhelmingly focused on the Objective 1 Programme, and seeking to make good a history of little engagement by the old territorial department in EU affairs. Further reflecting the sense of a 'Team Wales' approach, the wider effort is strongly focused on the Wales European Centre (WEC), a pre-existing partnership (which the Assembly quickly joins) involving the local authorities, the many Welsh quangos, and elements of civil society. A sensible and pragmatic approach at this initial stage, the infant body is thus seen tapping into an established pool of experience and contacts in Brussels. In conjunction, that is, with establishing a small Assembly Office at the heart of the Union, with direct links into the diplomacy via UKRep.

WEC's mission has been 'to give Wales an edge in Europe'. To this end, four main objectives have been pursued: to provide information and intelligence on funding opportunities and relevant policy developments; to present Welsh needs and proposals to the EU institutions; to raise the profile of Wales in Brussels; and to encourage and assist in creating strategic transnational partnerships.[105] At one and the same time, the work echoes much in the growth industry that is regional representation,[106] and—promoting the policies of the different member organizations—represents a distinctive format for regional activity in Brussels.

---

[105] See for details Wales European Centre, *Annual Report 2001/2002*; and see, for comparison in terms of the pre-devolutionary development, D. Hughes, *Wales European Centre 1991–1999: A Retrospective* (Wales European Centre, Brussels, 1999).

[106] See J. Goodburn, *A Representative Office for the Scottish Executive in Brussels* (Scottish Office, 1998). As Goodburn observes (at 13), the success of regional offices in Brussels is 'almost impossible to quantify in any objective manner', not least because of the range and diversity of contacts.

EU enlargement brings a fresh impetus to inter-regional activity. In the case of Wales, better to grasp the opportunities or, more bleakly, to mitigate the adverse consequences, the aim has been to make the territory a valued player in Central and Eastern Europe, thus realizing mutual economic benefits via inter-regional co-operation and trading links.[107] An obvious peg has been the Community Phare programme for Eastern Europe, as also the accession instruments ISPA (environment and transport) and SAPARD (agriculture and rural development). Welsh actors have thus been involved in a range of contacts from technical exchanges to consultancy and twinning. Pride of place goes to the Welsh Development Agency (WDA), which has a proven track record in terms both of attracting inward investment and of encouraging an 'info-structure' of business services, skills, and social capital.[108] Self-proclaimed in fact as 'Europe's most successful economic development agency', it thus has a wealth of experience and expertise to offer prospective regional partners.

Such activity further illustrates what the first chief minister called 'the progressive response to globalization'. Especially that is with a view to achieving concentration or multiplier effects, or, as the lawyer might say, to a form of 'relational contracting' predicated on careful selection of priority countries and regions. In this way, 'scarce resources in Wales can be optimised, the impact in the countries will be maximised and the added value from synergies created'.[109] Latterly, these ideas have been taken forward under the direct political guidance of the all-party Assembly Committee on European and External Affairs.[110] In turn, the establishment of a special working group on enlargement, chaired by Rhodri Morgan, underlines the seriousness with which the devolved administration now takes this kind of activity. In the event, certain regions, most notably Silesia in Poland, have now been identified as suitable partners for Wales.[111] Such, it may be said, is the regional beauty contest in today's Single Market.

Wales of course must flaunt its own attractions. The territory has cultural capital in abundance and the local policy has been to exploit this with a view to promoting and cementing new official and economic linkages, while at the same time striving to update the image of Wales in Europe (and the World).[112] As a region, that is, which is diverse and innovative, not simply interested in handouts, and which is willing and able to engage with partners, even to play

---

[107] Wales European Centre, *Moving East. What Enlargement Means for Wales* (Brussels, 1999) and, *EU Enlargement and the Implications for Wales* (Brussels, 2000).

[108] K. Morgan, 'The Regional Animateur: Taking Stock of the Welsh Development Agency' (1997) 7 *Regional and Federal Studies* 70.

[109] Wales European Centre, *Engaging Wales. A Draft Strategy for Wales in the Enlarged European Union* (Brussels, 2001), 10.

[110] J. Barry Jones, 'Wales in Europe', in Barry Jones & Osmond (eds.), n. 9 above.

[111] As well, that is, as some of the small Baltic States. See for details proceedings of the Assembly's European and External Affairs Committee, February–March 2002.

[112] So, as one could say, from the famous male voice choirs to so-called 'Cool Cymru' and beyond. The fact of various 'national' institutions and bodies in Wales—from sports to opera—is an obvious marketing advantage.

a part (however small) in the progress of Europe.[113] In summary, as a lobbying and networking region, a territory like Wales is, and takes care to be, much better placed than, say in the UK context, a 'non-national region' such as the North East of England.

This is not to underestimate the many obstacles that the territory faces, not least in Central and Eastern Europe. Apart from the evident lack of contiguity, the basic duality of inter-regional relations—competition as well as co-operation or collaboration—is illuminated here. Thus the difficulty arises of balancing the benefits from productive partnerships with a concern to protect the position of the territory as an attractive destination for direct foreign investment.[114] There is also the problem for a fragile local economy of securing and then focusing resources for the purpose of engagement. In the event, however, the devolved administration has not been dissuaded from also developing the broader 'diplomatic' dimension: quite the reverse. The local preference in dealings with the Accession States has thus been to establish relationships early or ahead of enlargement, such that economic partnership serves to lay the groundwork for future political co-operation inside the EU.[115] After all, at this precise moment in time, who knows where the 'constitution' of Europe is going?

What, it may be asked, of the constraints imposed by the formal UK system of concordatry? In practice the type of activity that is increasingly standard in the case of Wales, work related to economic development or regeneration in a European context, is unlikely to be hindered. It is thus open to the devolved administration, in co-operation with the UK Foreign and Commonwealth Office (FCO), to make arrangements or agreements with foreign sub-national governments, etc in order to facilitate co-operation between them on devolved matters.[116] Put another way, the constitutional and political idea of reinventing a territory like Wales as a 'Euro-region' is given ample expression here, with specific provisions allowing for regional offices overseas and for the separate promotion of trade and inward investment.[117] For its part, the Assembly Representation in Brussels is formally obliged to 'work closely with, and in a manner complementary to, UKRep', which 'remains responsible for representing the view of the United Kingdom to the European Institutions'.[118] Once again, however, there is little to suggest other than positive encouragement on the part of the FCO.

The beginnings of a second main phase of activity are made apparent. The devolved administration is seen taking an increasingly multi-focused approach, engaging both with the main institutions and other actors in the Community,

---

[113] Reference may further be made to the fact of individual Welsh 'assets' in Brussels. Besides the region's MEPs, the obvious example is Neil Kinnock as Vice-President of the Commission.

[114] Wales European Centre, *Moving East*, n. 107, above, Annex 1.

[115] Wales European Centre, *EU Enlargement*, n. 107 above.

[116] Provided, that is, the arrangements do not affect the conduct of international relations or prejudice UK interests: *Concordat on International Relations* (Cm. 5240, 2001), at para. D4.7.

[117] *Ibid.*, para. D4.16.   [118] *EU Concordat*, n. 32 above, para. B4.27.

and one that is expressly geared towards securing access and influence. To this effect, the changing opportunity structure, including in terms of the constitutional architecture of the EU, cannot be overlooked.

Perhaps hopefully, much is made of the synergy of the different types of initiative. The hard-nosed business perspective—the region as competitive entity—is thus coupled with the general aspiration of Wales being more visible;[119] as also the constitutional dimension of a Welsh voice in Europe. At the same time, the development is predicated on a strong leadership role for the Welsh Assembly Government. This reflects the internal dynamic of the devolutionary scheme, the emergence of a separate government machine inside the legal framework of the corporate body, as well as the increased confidence of Assembly politicians and officials in treating with Europe. Put another way, the trajectory of Wales as a lobbying and networking region is in part a product of an autochthonous process of constitution building that has quickly gathered pace.

Reflecting the broader linkages and in particular the disciplines of the competitive struggle for inward investment in an era of globalization, the reach both of the specialist committee and of the relevant policy directorate has now been expanded from 'European' to 'European and External Affairs'. In turn, a five-fold branch structure for the Division is indicative of the increasing range and scale of activity: from European Policy, Enlargement, and the Euro to Interreg[120] and State Aids, and on through the Assembly Representation in Brussels to Wales Trade International and International Relations. As with much of the rest of the Assembly, the level of staffing is considerably increased from the minimalist base that was the Welsh Office.[121]

An important clue is official questioning of the design and orientation of WEC. Constitutionally speaking, the strong partnership model of this body, whereby the Assembly as one of a number of 'clients' lacks effective control of the machinery, has appeared increasingly at odds with the political and administrative position inside Wales. It is to this effect an obvious source of frustration for a newly delineated Welsh Assembly Government concerned to exercise strategic political direction at the territorial level: so much so that the devolved administration has now withdrawn from the partnership.[122] Likewise, the preexisting local authority partners have decided to have their own direct representation in Brussels.[123] All this is in fact a mark of the gradual maturation of the new Welsh polity: acceptance of the view that a single body serves too many masters, growing experience in the Assembly of EU matters.

---

[119] European Affairs Committee, 'International Relations and the Profile of Wales' (March 2000). See further K. Morgan, *The Multi-Level Polity: Subsidiarity in the European Union* (Wilton Park, 2000).

[120] Wales has had a series of collaborative programmes with Ireland under this cross-border rubric. Details are available from WEFO, the current Managing Authority.

[121] Rawlings, *Delineating Wales*, n. 8 above.

[122] See Assembly proceedings, 4 March 2003.

[123] Leaving WEC to reconstitute itself on a much reduced basis, with a few core members (quangos, etc) and offering services to a number of other bodies.

The touchstone is the upsizing of the Assembly Representation in Brussels. At one and the same time, this is a natural progression, expansion of official support beyond occasional attendance at the Council of Ministers to the conduct of (Welsh) government business in Brussels, and reflects and reinforces the distinctive trajectory of the Welsh Assembly government. In turn, the advantage to the devolved administration of the linkage into and through UKRep is prioritized. To this effect, the Assembly's Representation may be considered part of UKRep's 'extended family', whereby its officials have diplomatic status, and easy access to all the official documentation, while at the same time working unambiguously for the Assembly. It is after all these parts that WEC could not reach. Looking forwards, specialist Assembly representation across the chief fields of devolved powers, better to generate information flows and early inputs into the decisional processes of the Union, is readily anticipated. The process has already begun with agriculture, targeted in particular on Comitology procedure. In other words, the Welsh presence in Brussels should quickly emerge now as more akin to the Scottish model of functionally separate representation for the Executive and for other actors.[124] As so often in the history of the Union State, Wales is playing catch-up.

Another strand is introduced, in the form of inter-regional networking at the pan-European level. So as well as the formal linkages, Assembly representation on the Committee of the Regions (CoR) and (under the aegis of the Council of Europe) the Congress of Local and Regional Authorities, the territory has been actively engaged in forging new multilateral alliances. Better that is, in the words of the First Minister, 'to exchange ideas on policies and, where relevant, to develop common approaches'.[125] To which might be added—over and above more profile raising—the prospective gain in access and influence from associational inputs in the decisional processes of the EU. Delegations, the Assembly government has quickly learned, are apt to open doors, including in the Commission.

In fact Wales was involved pre-devolution in an association with the four so-called 'motor' regions of Europe (Baden Württemberg, Cataluña, Lombardy, and Rhônes-Alpes). Significantly, however, this arrangement, big on 'hands across Europe' or less hard-edged, is now largely overshadowed. Wales has, for example, recently joined the large and well-established association that is the Conference of Peripheral Maritime Regions (CPMR). As the name suggests, this represents a good fit in terms of the policy orientation. CPMR thus offers the new devolved administration valuable connections and considerable representational experience in such important matters to Wales as Interreg and the structural funds, coastal issues and transport policy.

It is worth adding that the Assembly is somewhat spoiled for choice. Such is the attractiveness of the national region, and such is the growth of this paradigmatic form of paradiplomacy across Europe.[126] The trick for this small country is

---

[124] See generally now A. Sloat, *Scotland in Europe: A Study of Multi-Level Governance* (Peter Lang, Bern, 2002).   [125] Morgan, n. 90 above, para. 24.
[126] The devolved administration has chosen for example not to join the Assembly of European Regions. See for a useful overview F. Sodupe, 'The European Union and Inter-regional Co-operation', in Aldecoa and Keating (eds.), n. 33 above.

once again to be highly selective, not dissipating too much effort in multitudinous places.

8. THE CONSTITUTIONAL REGION

It is, then, all the more striking that Wales has become involved in two further inter-regional networks, which are explicitly focused on constitutional and administrative reform in the EU. The development is at one and the same a mark of the seriousness with which the territorial entity now takes itself, and a natural extension of its situation as a national and lobbying and networking region. Including, lest one forget, in terms of the devolutionary coda: 'our relationship with the UK Government as our Member State is crucial'.[127]

The first such network is the large and diverse grouping which is the Regions with Legislative Power (RegLeg). Perhaps hopefully, the Welsh Assembly Government has concluded not only that 'Wales fits comfortably into the group', but also that, measured in terms of powers, the Assembly features in 'the top half'.[128] First established ahead of the Nice IGC, and now targeted on the Constitutional Convention on 'the future of Europe', this network has a convoluted history, as befits a 'bottom-up' or even 'grassroots' initiative. Essentially, however, RegLeg serves to underscore as a political phenomenon, and seeks to make good, the evident tension between the classical conception of the EU as a constitutional order of states and the rise of meso-government across Europe.[129] More especially, the perceived inadequacies of the Committee of the Regions (CoR) as an instrument of representation—most obviously for the so-called 'Constitutional Regions' (in the narrow sense of the term)—is a clear prompt.[130] The Welsh Assembly Government is once again pleased to be involved, and further, it may be said, to exercise a moderating influence in this most sensitive area of constitution building for Europe.

The 'Flanders Declaration', promulgated in May 2001, was the product of a self-selecting working group or inner core, comprised of seven of the most important 'Constitutional Regions'.[131] 'In order to ensure due compliance with

---

[127] Welsh Assembly Government, *European Commission White Paper on Governance: Response from the First Minister on behalf of the National Assembly for Wales* (March 2002), para. 1.

[128] European and External Affairs Committee, *European Regions with Legislative Powers* (March 2002). Despite its name, the network includes (directly elected) regional governments with power to legislate or 'to take significant executive decisions'; see for details, Co-ordination Committee of RegLeg, *The Regions with Legislative Power in the Framework of the Next Institutional Reform of the EU* (2002).

[129] See for a general overview J. Kottman, 'Europe and the Regions: Sub-national Entity Representation at Community Level' (2001) 26 *ELRev* 159.

[130] J. Jones, 'The Committee of the Regions, Subsidiarity and a Warning' (1997) 22 *ELRev* 313.

[131] *Political Declaration by the constitutional regions of Bavaria, Catalonia, North-Rhine Westphalia, Salzburg, Scotland, Wallonia and Flanders* (Flanders, May 2001). And see Colloquium of the Constitutional Regions, *Reinforcing the role of the constitutional regions in Europe* (Flanders, February 2001).

the principle of subsidiarity and therefore guarantee full respect for the constitutional regions' own areas of competence, the political role of these regions has to be strengthened within the European Union.' Other demands included direct participation in the current Constitutional Convention[132] and privileged access to the Court of Justice.[133] Successively, however, the networking process has been broadened, in the form of a RegLeg steering group now sufficiently large to include Wales; and (some of) the language tempered, as in the 'Liège Resolution' of November 2001.[134] 'The application of the principle of subsidiarity should not be restricted to relations between the European Union and its member states, but should be affirmed at every level, including relations between states and regions in particular, but not only with regions that have legislative power.'[135] It suffices to add that the Assembly administration has been actively engaged in the working group on the political declaration from RegLeg to the Constitutional Convention. Such, it may be said, is the early success of its paradiplomatic effort.

Latterly, and once again reflecting and reinforcing the visibility of Wales in Europe, the territory has been invited to join a highly selective inter-regional grouping, the so-called Emilia-Romagna network. Expressly targeted on issues of European governance, this grouping is the more notable for benefiting from the personal interest of Commission President Romano Prodi. A fact, one could say, which in the finest traditions of paradiplomacy has not gone unnoticed in Wales.[136] In the event, the network has produced one of the few inter-regional responses to the Commission White Paper.[137] Not, it should be said, that the content is anything other than bland, being indicative like so many such common declarations of the lowest common denominator. The White Paper, it is solemnly stated, is welcome as 'an important basis for discussion'. The usual pleas are made for a more inclusive model of EU policy-making as well as for the greater use of framework legislation.

The new Welsh polity has also been keen to engage on its own account in the governance debate. Indeed the range of territorial involvement, from committee hearings in Cardiff and in Brussels to an Assembly plenary debate, and on through discussions with leading Commission officials to an all-Wales forum incorporating elements of civil society, has been described by the chief author

---

[132] In the event, there is regional representation through CoR and (indirectly) via a Contact Group of Regional and Local Authorities: http://europa.eu.int/futurum.

[133] Under Art. 230 TEC; and see for jurisprudence Case T–214/95, *Het Vlaamse Gewest (Flemish Region) v. Commission* [1998] ECR II–717; Case T–609/97, *Regione Puglia v. Commission* [1998] ECR II–4051.

[134] Second Presidential Conference of the Regions with Legislative Power, *Towards the reinforced role of the Regions with legislative power within the European Union* (Liège, November 2001)

[135] For his part, the Assembly First Minister has recorded his 'broad agreement and enthusiasm' for the general approach and aspirations expressed at Liège: *Response from the First Minister of the Welsh Assembly Government to the Liege Resolution* (November 2001).

[136] Welsh Assembly Government Cabinet Paper, *The Regional Dimension of European Governance* (January 2002).

[137] Emilia-Romagna *et al.*, *Common Declaration on European Governance* (Brussels, March 2002).

of the White Paper as almost unique.[138] A case, one could say, of the new devolved authority wishing to be (seen to be) 'good Europeans'. The process is part of the story in another respect, since the White Paper has offered a route into dialogue inside the territory on 'Wales in Europe'—aspirations, expectations, options. In the event, the response from the Assembly represents a consensual position, as well as being notably free from direct UK government interference.

The White Paper has elsewhere attracted severe criticism:[139] not least for being high on sentiment and low on practical proposals, and for prioritizing Commission-dominated processes of public 'involvement' in EU decision-making at the expense of more concrete forms of national political and administrative representation. More particularly, whereas the White Paper correctly points up the positive role that meso-government can play in bringing the EU closer to its citizens, it was singularly lacking in detail or specific ideas for charting a way forward.[140] So, for example, a suggestion of 'target-based, tripartite contracts' involving the Commission, Member States, and sub-national governments, one that in the process of consultation on the White Paper provoked more questions than answers is only now coming to fruition. Meanwhile, other proposals to enhance the role of the Committee of the Regions and to underpin processes of 'involvement' via a code of consultation, are seen to gloss over the heterogeneity and lack of democratic legitimacy of CoR, and application and differentiation in the case of the regions, respectively.[141]

However, the official response from Wales skipped lightly over such concerns. The tone was unremittingly positive. The devolved administration 'welcomes the spirit of the Commission's initiative' and would encourage the exercise 'as a way of bringing about early improvement'. There was support for increased involvement by CoR, keenness to explore the 'intriguing idea' of tripartite contracts, strong support for a code of consultation, and so on. The Assembly was once again an active partner.

Would one expect much else? Far from an academic discursus this obviously is a political response, and one that is naturally imbued with the institutional self-interest of the Assembly. Not only are local actors still feeling their way, but also—a point to bear in mind when assessing the value of the consultation exercise—why offend the ultimate 'repeat player' that is the Commission? Similarly, while there may be scratching of heads over the meaning of 'target-based,

---

[138] See Assembly proceedings, 17 January 2002.

[139] Including from Carol Harlow and the author: see LSE Study Group on European Administrative Law, *Taking Governance Seriously* (2002); available at www.europa.eu.int/comm/governance/contributions/index_en.htm. And see especially European Parliament, Constitutional Affairs Committee, *Report on the Commission White Paper on European Governance*, Rapporteur S-Y Kaufmann, Doc A5-0399/2001 final (PE 304.289).

[140] See Commission White Paper, n. 5 above, 12–14. The fact that the document proceeded on the basis of the Treaties (and thus assumed a lack of constitutional 'fit' with the rise of the regions) is only a partial explanation.

[141] See generally, Commission, *Report on European Governance* (2003).

tripartite contracts', there is good reason to become engaged at an early stage, better to fashion the initiative in a way that suits British administrative traditions and Welsh interests, even to curry favour.

What, then, it may be asked, of the individual Welsh perspective on 'the future of Europe' debate? The full territorial position will no doubt prove elastic in light of the deliberations of the Constitutional Convention. Notably, however, the Welsh Assembly Government has been an enthusiastic participant in discussions on the UK policy line that have been taking place in the JMC machinery and elsewhere. At such a moment, the non-occurrence of political 'cohabitation', as the French like to call it, comes sharply into focus. Indeed, a point that will not be lost in Europe, we are a long way here from past patterns of UK Conservative Euro-scepticism, especially, it may now be said, in the case of Wales.

Some preliminary observations are in order. First, along with colleagues in Scotland, the Assembly Cabinet has been successful in persuading the UK Government to promote a series of pro-regional initiatives in the Constitutional Convention.[142] From a Treaty reference acknowledging the role of regions in the EU to mandatory consultation by the Commission of regional authorities on matters for which they have responsibility for implementation, and on through institutional reform of the Committee of the Regions: in the words of the first Minister, this UK intiative represents 'a major achievement for Wales in taking forward our European agenda'.[143]

Secondly, with regard to the idea that is sometimes floated of delineating regional (as well as Member State and EU) competencies in a 'Constitution of Europe',[144] the type of concern familiarly expressed in other constitutional systems through the concept of 'the open flank' still lacks salience in this domestic context. A tendency to (internal) centralization via the force of (supranational) integration, as constituted by Member State responsibility for EU affairs, is apt to appear less of a problem when the region is newly constituted. At least that is in the case of Wales, only now awakening from a history of exceptional dependence on England and the powerful UK central government machine.

Thirdly but relatedly, the First Minister has notably stressed the advantages accruing to Wales from the unwritten British Constitution. Its innate flexibility is thus seen as facilitating the growth of territorial activity on the European stage, including by reference to the comparable position in certain federal states. In Rhodri Morgan's words, 'in terms of expanding Wales' role and what we can contribute, we have already achieved a great deal in ensuring that our

---

[142] See P. Hain, *Europe and the Regions* (Convention paper 526/03, 2003). At the time of writing, the discussions in the Convention are too fluid for a proper analysis. Suffice it to say that the general sense of an incremental approach to the regional dimension sits comfortably with the official Welsh perspective.

[143] Welsh Assembly Government, *Cabinet Statement* 6 February 2003.

[144] The heterogeneity of Euro-regions obviously is a formidable obstacle, as illustrated now in the proceedings of the Convention. See, for example, Praesidium, *The regional and local dimension in Europe* (Convention paper 518/03, 2003).

voice is heard'.[145] To this effect, in terms of the current constitutional endeavour in Europe, Wales may prove a useful ally in the pursuit of greater recognition for regions in formal legal terms, but the Welsh Assembly Government will happily leave it to the likes of Cataluña to lead the charge.

At the same time, bringing the discussion full circle, there is evident potential here for linkage with the autochthonous process of constitution building now taking place in Wales. Increased recognition of the role of the regions in bringing the EU closer to its citizens, internal movement at territorial level towards parliamentary government and legislative devolution: it would be a case of mutually reinforcing pressures on central government for greater constitutional generosity to Wales. For his part, the First Minister has made this precise calculation.[146] That is, a novel form of convergence.

9. Conclusion—Wales in the United Kingdom in Europe

Cultural diversity in the European enterprise, cross-fertilization of ideas and techniques, critical elements of decentralization: from the comparative viewpoint there is already much to be gleaned from the experience of this national region, not least in view of its own sharp learning curve. Unnaturally weak the formal constitutional dispensation may be, but this should not be allowed to obscure the expanding patterns of the territorial engagement with Europe. That it is pre-eminently a case of mixed results is only to be expected. It could hardly be otherwise in an increasingly complex and dynamic world of multi-layered governance.

The infant has far to go. The effort that will be required to ensure the 'mainstreaming' of Community policies and opportunity structures in the new Welsh administrative process should not be underestimated. A specialist division and committee, the horizontal effects of the EU integrative process: it is a familiar but formidable challenge of dissemination. The struggle to have 'a voice for Wales' heard amid the cacophony of voices in Europe is an unremitting one, and will no doubt intensify in the light of enlargement. The need for a careful prioritization, or the importance of the search for 'added value' when engaging with Europe, is a recurring theme. Local enthusiasm has to be tempered, in favour of a tight quality threshold.

Many useful steps have been taken. The sub-national response in the light of supra-national ordering and (global) forces of market liberalization is thus clearly illustrated as multi-faceted in nature, including in the guise of overlapping and

---

[145] Rhodri Morgan, Assembly proceedings, 17 January 2002. The touchstone typically is attendance at the Council of Ministers.

[146] Directly in terms of the Independent Commission on the powers and electoral arrangements of the Assembly: see Assembly proceedings, 19 December 2000.

mutually reinforcing functions. The five-fold classification introduced in this chapter serves to place in comparative perspective the terms of engagement. Constraint and opportunity, and in particular the forms of territorial initiative, the cross-currents (in constitutional reform) of continuity and change: once again matters are writ large in the case of Wales, including by reason of its situation as a national region, in the big player that is the United Kingdom.

The formal legal weakness of the devolutionary scheme is powerfully illustrated in the lack of EU-oriented legislative space made available to the Assembly. The approach of central government appears overly cautious, in view of the many good reasons for substantive domestic uniformity irrespective of the local source of legislative power, more especially in the case of England and Wales. Again, the territorial experience illuminates a tension in the European Commission's approach to implementation at the meso-government level, between encouragement of a spirit of adventure—in the White Paper on Governance—and a peculiarly depressive or heavy-handed approach in the calculation of sanction. What, it may be asked, of the risk-averse region?

Partnering is seen as something of a fetish in the new territorial polity. Exemplifying the strong economic orientation of the devolutionary development, and exemplified in the Objective 1 Programme for West Wales and the Valleys, the phenomenon has taken on a momentum of its own, above and beyond the formal legal requirements. Wales will thus be a significant test of the capacity for regeneration using the structural funds, or of more energizing at local level as against the dangers of administrative overload and fragmentation. In this respect the auguries are not all good.

The concept of the national region is an especially valuable one in the case of Wales. Conveying a suitably contemporary sense of multiple identities, it serves to highlight the strong measure of interdependency between the territorial and central tiers of government in the light of expanded modalities of supranational ordering. Concurrency and complexity of EU responsibilities and obligations; political and administrative liaison, co-operation and co-ordination; crosscurrents of decentralization and re-centralization: far from withering away, the Union state is (once again) in the process of being reinvented. In the event, the devolved administration has reason to be encouraged, with constitutional practice under the UK system of concordatry proving generous to Wales in such matters as attendance at the Council of Ministers. A different but related point: the special advantages of (cultural) identity available to the national region in the territorial competitive struggle are splendidly shown in the case of Wales. The Single Market—a level playing field: dream on!

In fact, the speedy emergence of Wales as a lobbying and networking region demonstrates a major channel of opportunity for the new territorial polity. Once again, the local phenomenon epitomizes a powerful contemporary trend in comparative public administration in the guise of paradiplomacy. An expanded web of both bilateral and multilateral connections now ranges beyond the more obvious economic and cultural linkages to the articulation of a regional voice in EU constitutional and administrative affairs. A window on Europe, as well as a window on Wales, this aspect of the territorial engagement is distinctly liberating.

Howsoever defined, the pressures will surely persist for the 'constitutional regions' in particular to play a less submerged role in the formal European construction, most obviously in the context of enlargement. Wales, it may be noted however, is not a Flanders! A moderate stance on regional constitutional advancement sits well with the strong and continuing dependency on Whitehall encapsulated in the scheme of executive devolution. So also, a distinct local preference for flexibility in relevant political and administrative arrangements has special resonance in the context of the debate on 'the future of Europe'. Values of pluralism and diversity, an EU constitutional framework for organic change, a mix and match of codification and convention: Europe it should hardly need saying has many futures.

Wales in the United Kingdom in Europe: there is in the terms of devolution no going back. A fitting conclusion, since the last word surely belongs to Professor Harlow:[147]

In the Community . . . integrationism was once seen as something of a loyalty test; today pluralism is squarely on the political agenda . . . If the Community is to embrace within its boundaries a new swathe of entrants . . . acceptance of diversity will become a necessity. It will be essential to treat the Community as . . . weighted to the bottom level. Co-operative political activity will be based on strong existing national and sub-national structures which legitimate it.

[147] Harlow, *Voices of Difference*, n. 1 above, 24.

14

Of Institutions and Individuals: The Enforcement of EC Law

ADAM TOMKINS*

1. ADMINISTRATIVE LAW AND ENFORCEMENT

One of Carol Harlow's principal contributions to English administrative law was the famous metaphor she and Richard Rawlings adopted to explain to generations of students the two essential schools of thought which dominated English administrative law scholarship throughout the twentieth century. I am referring, of course, to the 'red-light' and 'green-light' theories of administrative law, which are compared and contrasted across the opening chapters of what remains one of the most challenging and original texts in contemporary British public law, *Law and Administration*.[1] The question addressed by these theories is, 'What is administrative law for?' or 'What is it supposed to do?'. The answers, to express it at the crudest level, are that traditionally, following such leaders as Dicey and Wade, lawyers have seen administrative law as something which stops unlawful administration, as a constraining control mechanism. The alternative position, adopted as a response by such critics as Robson and Griffith, is to view administrative law as something which should first identify and then facilitate and encourage good administrative practices, as a positive channelling of good administration rather than merely as a negative restraint. As courts are poorly placed to perform this ambitious task, green-light theorists have championed the roles of alternative institutional actors, such as inquiries, regulators, and ombudsmen.[2]

For the English administrative lawyer brought up on this basic division, EC administrative law looks a strange beast indeed. Neither red- nor green-light

---

* It is a particular honour to be able to contribute to this collection of essays for Carol Harlow. Professor Harlow was the supervisor of my LLM dissertation in the University of London in 1990–1, and since that time I have constantly learnt from and been inspired by her scholarship and leadership, both as a friend and as a colleague. I owe her a great deal.

[1] C. Harlow and R. Rawlings, *Law and Administration* (Butterworths, London, 2nd edn., 1997).

[2] For a fuller summary of red- and green-light theories, and of the newer arrival, amber-light theories, see A. Tomkins, 'In Defence of the Political Constitution' (2002) 22 *OJLS* 157, 158–61.

theories seem particularly helpful or appropriate in explaining the functions or the functioning of EC administrative law.[3] As far as red-light theory is concerned, while it might be argued that when the defendant in an action under EC administrative law is a Member State or some other national administrative unit (e.g. under Article 226 or Article 234) the ECJ is frequently concerned with stopping unlawful national administrative (or legislative) implementation of Community law, the same argument would be far more difficult to apply in the context (e.g. under Article 230) where the defendant is an institution of the Community. It is a well-known feature of EC administrative law that as regards both procedure and substance, there is a great difference in the approach of the ECJ as between actions against national authorities on the one hand and the institutions of the Community on the other. Any comparison of the extension of direct effect, with its seemingly relentless promotion of the private enforcement of Community law as against national authorities, with the Court's continuing reluctance to extend any sort of advanced or sophisticated individual standing under Article 230(4) is surely sufficiently clear testimony to that as far as procedure is concerned. As for substance, the painfully slow way in which the ECJ (and more recently the Court of First Instance) has struggled to develop even the most basic principles of good administrative practice further indicates the limitations of red-light theory as an explanation of EC administrative law.[4]

If red-light theory struggles to make sense of EC administrative law, green-light theory wholly fails. Not only have the Courts not exhibited any significant green-light tendencies, but more worryingly for those sympathetic to the ambitions of green-light theory, neither have the other European institutions of administrative regulation, such as the auditors and the European Ombudsman. The latter, indeed, has been a big disappointment, displaying extreme caution, minimalism, and narrow legalism throughout at least his early work.[5]

If red- and green-light theories seem at least for the time being incapable of explaining EC administrative law, is there an analytical framework which we can instead adopt? Do the respective limitations of red- and green-light theories mean that no theory could explain EC administrative law, or only that these theories cannot do so? The argument in this essay will be that EC administrative law can be explained, that while frequently imperfect in execution, an overall

---

[3] This observation is not to be taken as a criticism: neither red-light nor green-light theories present themselves as being general theories of administrative law. They are expressly concerned only with seeking to explain the peculiarities of English administrative law.

[4] See among many such cases, Case 17/74, *Transocean Marine Paint* v. *Commission* [1974] ECR 1063; Case 64/82, *Tradax* v. *Commission* [1984] ECR 1359; Case C–269/90, *Hauptzollamt München-Mitte* v. *Technische Universität München* [1991] ECR I–5469. See generally H. Nehl, *Principles of Administrative Procedure in EC Law* (Hart, Oxford, 1999). One exception to this general picture appears to be transparency, an area where in particular the CFI has been notably proactive: see A. Tomkins, 'Transparency and the Emergence of a European Administrative Law' (1999–2000) 19 *YBEL* 217, 224–34.

[5] For an account of this see *ibid.*, at 235–44. For an account of the limitations of audit in Community law see I. Harden, F. White, and K. Donnelly, 'The Court of Auditors and Financial Control and Accountability in the EC' (1995) 1 *EPL* 599.

objective can be identified from which, as Community jurisprudence continues to develop, a fully-fledged theory of administrative law may emerge. That objective, I suggest, is the *enforcement* of Community law. That is to say, the purpose of EC administrative law is to secure the enforcement of Community law, particularly as against national authorities. Harlow and Rawlings state, following Laski, that 'behind every theory of administrative law there lies a theory of the state'.[6] The constitutional underpinnings of the enforcement model of EC administrative law can be found in the doctrine of supremacy, a doctrine which concerns, of course, the relationship between national and Community law. Perhaps this helps to explain some of the differences in intensity between judicial review of Community institutions under Article 230 and judicial review of national bodies under Articles 226 and 234.[7] To suggest that the purpose of EC administrative law is to secure the enforcement of Community law may sound somewhat banal, and maybe it is, but that should not blind us to the fact that this purpose is quite different from anything experienced in English administrative law.[8] To suggest that the purpose of EC administrative law is to secure the enforcement of Community law raises two questions: what is meant by 'enforcement', and what is meant by 'Community law'? The answers to both of these questions are liable to change; neither is, nor should be seen as, in any sense static. Neither of these claims is particularly novel, and both may be relatively quickly dealt with.

As for 'enforcement', the path from Commission-led enforcement through Article 226 to individual-led enforcement through the extraordinary development of the judicially created doctrines of direct effect, indirect effect, the *Francovich* remedy in damages, the relaxation of the presumption of procedural autonomy, and so forth is a familiar one to all Community lawyers.[9] Over the course of the past four decades the ECJ has consistently expanded the means whereby norms of Community law, whether they find their sources in the Treaties themselves, in secondary legislation, or in judge-made principle, may be enforced, both by national courts and by the ECJ itself, as against executive and administrative actors of all varieties. Aspects of these developments are re-visited in the next section of this essay.

As for 'Community law', the meaning and scope (as well as the mere content) of this phrase has likewise expanded, is expanding, and is likely to continue to expand. As well as Treaty-based and legislative norms, and in addition to the well-established general principles of Community law (such as proportionality)

---

[6] Harlow and Rawlings, n. 1 above, at 1.

[7] On the supremacy point it will noted below (see n. 35) that *Simmenthal*, a leading authority on the doctrine of supremacy, was one of the principal authorities relied on by the ECJ in *Factortame*, which, as will be shown below, is one of the ground-breaking cases in the development by the Court of EC administrative law.

[8] Although there may well be other national legal systems in the EC which EC administrative law more closely resembles.

[9] For an interesting treatment of the meaning of 'enforcement' in the context of Art. 226 see A. Gil Ibanez, *The Administrative Supervision and Enforcement of EC Law* (Hart, Oxford, 1999), chap. 1.

Community law is growing in at least three areas in ways which will impact significantly on administrative law. The first is in the relatively recent case law of the Court of First Instance (CFI) concerning the cautious expansion of principles of administrative procedure;[10] the second is the doctrine (both judicial and legislative) of transparency;[11] and the third, of course, is the unknown potential of the Charter of Fundamental Rights.[12]

2. 'INSTITUTIONAL' AND 'INDIVIDUAL' ENFORCEMENT

How does the EC Treaty envisage that Community law is to be enforced? For a Treaty usually regarded by lawyers as being curiously reticent on questions of its enforcement, there is actually a perfectly clear answer: it lies with Articles 226–228 EC (formerly Articles 169–171 of the EC Treaty). Easily the most important of these provisions is Article 226. It has been there since the Community's inception, and remains unamended from its original form. It empowers the Commission to bring an action in the ECJ against a Member State in respect of a failure on the part of the Member State to fulfil any of its obligations under the Treaty. Article 227 enables Member States to bring each other before the Court in similar circumstances.[13] Articles 228 is a relative newcomer, having been added only at Maastricht. It provides that the Court may impose a penalty payment in respect of a Member State which persistently breaches Community law following a finding under Articles 226 or 227. The procedures outlined in Articles 226–228 will be referred to in this essay as mechanisms of the *institutional enforcement* of Community law. We shall return to consider in more detail the operation of Articles 226–228 below, in the final sections of this essay.

The Court of Justice, however, has never accepted that this Treaty-based scheme of institutional enforcement should be the only, nor even the principal, means by which Community law may be enforced. To this end, the Court has gone out of its way in numerous high-profile cases to develop new means by which Community law may be enforced. Four such means may be identified: direct effect, indirect effect, the dilution of the principle of national procedural autonomy in *Factortame*,[14] and the remedy in damages established in

---

[10] See, e.g., Case T–450/93, *Lisrestal* v. *Commission* [1994] ECR II–1177 and Case T–260/94, *Air Inter* v. *Commission* [1997] ECR II–997. See generally Nehl, n. 4 above.

[11] See Tomkins, n. 4 above.

[12] See, e.g., Case C–173/99, *BECTU* v. *Secretary of State for Trade and Industry* [2001] ECR I–4881, Tizzano AG paras. 27–82, in which it was suggested that 'the Charter . . . includes statements which appear in large measure to reaffirm rights which are enshrined in other instruments', and that 'in proceedings concerned with the nature and scope of a fundamental right, the relevant statements of the Charter cannot be ignored'. In its judgment in the *BECTU* case, however, the ECJ did not refer to the Charter.

[13] Use of Art. 227 is rare, but see Case 141/78, *France* v. *United Kingdom* [1979] ECR 2923 and Case C–388/95, *Belgium* v. *Spain* [2000] ECR I–3213.

[14] Case C–213/89, *R* v. *Secretary of State for Transport, ex p. Factortame Ltd.* [1990] ECR I–2433.

Francovich.[15] These means are referred to in this essay as mechanisms of the *individual enforcement* of Community law. I recognize that these terms are not perfect. It is frequently the case, for example, that the Commission's institutional enforcement of Community law will be triggered by a complaint from an individual: individuals are not wholly excluded from the processes of institutional enforcement (although, as we shall see, it is an argument of this essay that the ECJ ought to have done considerably more to have recognized this). Equally, many of the individuals who have benefited most from the Court's development of what I am referring to as mechanisms of individual enforcement are multinational corporations rather than individual citizens. While there may be infelicities in the language, however, the distinction is nonetheless apposite, as the argument as it is developed in this essay will show.

The fame of the cases in which the Court has developed its jurisprudence of individual enforcement should not blind us to their radicalism. They may be relatively familiar to us, but they are far from unexceptional. Throughout the history and development of Community law the ECJ has constantly sought to supplement the means of enforcement laid down in Article 226.[16] The question posed in this essay, however, is whether the remedies created by the Court's jurisprudence have been designed not so much to supplement, as to supplant, the Article 226 procedure. Have direct effect and its progeny damaged the prospects for institutional enforcement? Has the Court's extension of the notion of the 'rights' of individuals to invoke Community law in national courts, rights which while not spelled out in the Treaty have been deemed by the Court to lie implicitly within its 'spirit' and 'general scheme', so over-promoted the role of individual enforcement within the Community legal order that insufficient room has been left for its institutions? If so, has anything valuable been lost in the process, and how might we go about the task of recovering it if it has? Before moving on to explore these issues in more depth, let us first revisit the seminal decisions which have contributed to the corpus of law on individual enforcement, taking each of the principal developments in turn.

(a) Direct Effect

The first, of course, was the Court's invention of direct effect in *Van Gend en Loos*.[17] The question in this case was whether as a matter of Community law an importer (Van Gend en Loos) could plead before a Dutch national court (the Tariefcommissie) that Article 12 of the EC Treaty (now Article 25) had been

---

[15] Cases C–6/90 and C–9/90, *Francovich & Bonifaci v. Italy* [1991] ECR I–5357.

[16] As the Court stated in *Van Gend en Loos*, n. 17 below, 'the vigilance of individuals concerned to protect their rights amounts to an effective supervision in addition to the supervision entrusted by Articles 169 and 170 to the diligence of the Commission and of the Member States'.

[17] Case 26/62, *Van Gend en Loos v. Nederlandse Administratie der Belastingen* [1963] ECR 1.

infringed, and more specifically whether the importer could as a matter of Community law claim the protection of rights conferred on it by Community law, rights which the national court was under a duty to protect. Article 12 (25) provided that 'customs duties on imports and exports and charges having equivalent effect shall be prohibited between Member States'. The Tariefcommissie referred these questions to the ECJ under Article 177 (now 234). What is important about the decision for present purposes is the consideration given in it to Article 226 (or 169 as it then was).

It is important to remember that in this case, which was decided when the Community comprised only six Member States, three of those Member States intervened in the proceedings, all of them submitting arguments against the importer (Van Gend en Loos). The Dutch and Belgian governments argued that the ECJ did not have the jurisdiction to answer the questions referred to it. They submitted that the solution to the problem posed by the importer fell within the exclusive jurisdiction of the national court, 'subject to an application in accordance with the provisions laid down by Articles 169 and 170 of the Treaty'. In other words, in the view of the Dutch and Belgian governments, the enforcement of Article 12 was as a matter of Community law governed by Article 226 (as it now is)—it was a question for the Commission. If the Commission considered that the (in this instance) Dutch authorities had failed adequately or properly to implement the aspects of the free movement of goods which were required by Article 12, then it could bring infringement proceedings before the European Court of Justice. If an importer such as Van Gend en Loos was unhappy with the Dutch authorities' compliance with Article 12, then its remedy in Community law was not to sue in the national courts, but was to take the much cheaper route of complaining to the Commission, so that the Commission could take the necessary legal action under Article 226. It is important to note here that it was not the view of the Dutch and Belgian governments that this would necessarily be the only remedy available to the importer. This would be the remedy available as a matter of Community law, but there may in addition be a domestic or national legal remedy open to the importer, but if there were that would be a question for the national legal authorities (in this instance for the Tariefcommissie), and not for the ECJ to determine. What role provisions of Community law could play in national legal proceedings was in their view a national issue, not one for the ECJ to decide.

While Advocate General Roemer agreed with the tenor of these submissions, the Court, of course, chose not to follow his advice. It rejected out of hand the submission that it lacked jurisdiction, stating that the Dutch and Belgian governments' argument had 'no legal foundation'. The Court's reasoning in support of this ruling was terse and cryptic. The Court stated that it was not being asked to adjudicate on the application of the Treaty according to the principles of national law, a matter which it conceded remained a question for national courts. Rather, in the Court's view, it was being asked 'to interpret the scope of Article 12 . . . within the context of Community law and with reference to its effect on individuals'.[18] For the Court, it followed immediately from this observation that the argument of the Dutch and Belgian governments was without legal foundation. With respect, however, this reasoning does not address the issue at the heart of the Dutch and Belgian objections: that objection was that the question of the individual enforcement of Community law was a question for the national court to determine, and not for the Court of Justice. Just because the provision of Community law has an effect on 'individuals' (i.e. on multi-national corporations) does not justify the claim, which the Court makes, that the issue is therefore necessarily one for the ECJ to determine. The conclusion simply does not follow from the reasoning.

What happened next is well known. The Court found that while the Treaty contained no specific textual authority in support of the view that provisions of Community law could be directly effective, authority for such a view could nonetheless be gleaned from 'the spirit, the general scheme and the wording' of the Treaty. Having established that the notion of direct effect was recognized in Community law, the Court then proceeded to find that Article 12 was sufficiently 'clear and unconditional' to be capable of bearing direct effect. We need not here dwell any further on this.

(b) Indirect Effect

It is not the case that all provisions of Community law are capable of bearing direct effect: whether they do or not depends upon their content, and is a question to be determined by the Court of Justice. The law of direct effect was introduced, as we have seen, in the context of the interpretation of a Treaty provision. Since *Van Gend en Loos*, the law of direct effect has been extended to apply also to regulations[19] and to directives, but to the latter only in limited circumstances. In the case of directives, even where a provision of a directive is deemed sufficiently clear and unconditional to bear direct effect (which is relatively rare in itself) it may be invoked by a litigant before national courts only when the litigant is taking action against the state, and not when the litigant is taking action against a private party. Thus, in the jargon of Community law, directives may have vertical direct effect, but not horizontal direct effect.[20] Many lawyers have argued that the distinction between vertical and horizontal direct effect should be abolished, and that directives should be capable of bearing horizontal as well as vertical direct effect. Advocates General van Gerven,[21]

---

[18] Describing Van Gend en Loos as an individual is rather odd. It is a company which was founded in 1796 and which by 2002 employed over 4,100 people in 27 offices located in three states.

[19] See Case 39/72, *Commission* v. *Italy* [1973] ECR 101.

[20] Case law on this point includes Case 152/84, *Marshall* v. *Southampton & South-West Hampshire Area Health Authority (Teaching)* [1986] ECR 723 and Case C–91/92, *Dori (Faccini)* v. *Recreb Srl* [1994] ECR I–3325. On the meaning of the state in this context see Case C–188/89, *Foster* v. *British Gas* [1990] ECR I–3313.

[21] See Case C–271/91, *Marshall* v. *Southampton & South–West Hampshire Area Health Authority (Marshall II)* [1993] ECR I–4367.

Jacobs,[22] and Lenz[23] have each made such an argument to the Court, but to its credit the Court has resisted this temptation, and gave a striking constitutional defence of its position in the important case of *Faccini Dori*, decided by the full Court.[24]

This is not to say, however, that the Court has not found other ways of seeking to give effect to directives. Two such methods have been developed by the Court, each of which significantly contributes to the ability of individuals to seek the enforcement of Community law. These means are: the doctrine of indirect effect and the *Francovich* remedy in damages. We shall come to *Francovich* a little later. First, we must consider the law of indirect effect. Indirect effect came less suddenly, and more cautiously, than did direct effect. The first case to consider is *Von Colson*.[25] Two female social workers, Von Colson and Kamann, had sought employment in a German prison which was administered by the *Land* Nordrhein-Westfalen (i.e. by the regional government). The prison catered exclusively for male prisoners. Von Colson and Kamann were refused employment on the ground, it appears, of their sex. They sued in the German labour court relying on the German law which had purported to implement the terms of Directive 76/207, a directive which concerns the implementation of the principle of equal treatment for men and women as regards access to employment. Under that national law the German court could order by way of remedy that Von Colson and Kamann be compensated only for such losses as they had suffered as a result of applying for the positions which had been denied them. No broader compensation or damages for discrimination were permitted. The national court referred to the ECJ the question whether such a restriction in the availability of compensation was compatible with Community law. Von Colson and Kamann could not rely on the Directive itself in their proceedings before the German labour court, as the terms of the Directive were insufficiently precise and unconditional to satisfy the test for direct effect.[26] However, the Court went on to rule that this did not necessarily mean that the Directive could be of no assistance to the plaintiffs. Having regard to Article 10 EC (ex Article 5)[27] the Court ruled that 'in applying the national law and in particular the provision of a national law specifically introduced in order to implement Directive 76/207, national courts are required to interpret their national law in the light of the wording and the purpose of the directive'.[28]

---

[22] See Case C–316/93, *Vaneetveld v. Le Foyer SA* [1994] ECR I–763.

[23] See Case C–91/92, *Dori*, n. 20 above.

[24] See in particular para. 24 of the judgment, in which it proclaimed that the effect of allowing directives to bear horizontal direct effect 'would be to recognise a power in the Community to enact obligations for individuals with immediate effect, whereas it had competence to do so only where it is empowered to adopt regulations'.

[25] Case 14/83, *Von Colson & Kamann v. Land Nordrhein-Westfalen* [1984] ECR 1891.

[26] *Ibid.*, para. 27.

[27] Art. 10 EC provides that 'Member States shall take all appropriate measures, whether general or particular, to ensure fulfilment of the obligations arising out of this Treaty or resulting from action taken by the institutions of the Community'.

[28] Case 14/83, n. 25 above, para. 26. The precise ambit of the ruling in *Von Colson* was not clear. The Court expressed itself slightly differently in para. 28 of its judgment where it stated that: 'It is

At first, this ruling could sensibly be interpreted as being limited to the specific context of the interpretation by a national court of national law whose explicit purpose was the transposition of Community law (and in particular of directives) into national law. However, any such limited an interpretation was scotched by the Court in the follow-up case, *Marleasing*,[29] in which the Court ruled that 'in applying national law, whether the provisions in question were adopted before or after the directive, the national court called upon to interpret it is required to do so, as far as possible, in the light of the wording and purpose of the directive'.[30] Even the qualification 'as far as possible' does not lessen the degree to which this ruling represented a vast extension to the Court's earlier ruling in *Von Colson*. Nowhere in either *Von Colson* or *Marleasing* is Article 226 even mentioned. Whereas the law of direct effect was developed notwithstanding the Court's recognition of the Article 226 alternative, the law of indirect effect was developed as if Article 226 simply did not exist.

(c) Chipping away at National Procedural Autonomy

The principle of national procedural autonomy governs the procedures which national courts must follow when enforcing rights conferred under Community law. The principle was laid down by the ECJ in a series of important constitutional cases in the 1970s. The principle provides that 'it is for the domestic legal system of each Member State to designate the courts having jurisdiction and to determine the procedural conditions governing actions at law intended to ensure the protection of the rights which citizens have from the direct effect of Community law'.[31] This principle was always subject to two conditions, known as the condition of equivalence and the condition of effectiveness. The first of these states that procedural circumstances required by national law may not be less favourable in the context of the enforcement of Community norms than they are with regard to norms deriving from domestic law. The second states that procedural circumstances required by national law will not be applicable if their effect is to make it impossible in practice to exercise the rights derived from Community law which national courts are obliged to enforce.

The principle of national procedural autonomy was never something about which the Court appeared to be entirely content. While a constitutional

---

for the national court to interpret and apply the legislation adopted for the implementation of the directive in conformity with the requirements of Community law, in so far as it is given discretion to do so under national law'.

[29] Case C–106/89, *Marleasing SA* v. *La Comercial Internacionale de Alimentacion SA* [1990] ECR I–4135.

[30] *Ibid.*, para. 8. Note that, unlike the direct effect of directives, this ruling is not limited to cases involving the state: in *Marleasing* both parties were private.

[31] See Case 39/73, *Rewe-Zentralfinanz* v. *Director der Landwirtschaftskammer Westfalen-Lippe* [1973] ECR 1039, para. 5. See also Case 45/76, *Comet BV* v. *Produktschap voor Siergewassen* [1976] ECR 2043.

lawyer would immediately recognize it as a cornerstone of federalism, clearly demarcating the boundaries of responsibilities as between the central European Courts and the various national legal systems, the ECJ repeatedly urged the Community legislature to adopt legislation harmonizing aspects of procedural law, such as causation, remoteness, interim relief, limitation periods, quantum in damages, and so forth.[32] This invitation, however, was not taken up.

In the early 1990s the ECJ decided two extraordinary cases which have caused the principle of national procedural autonomy to be significantly rewritten. Each of these cases represents a considerable advance for the cause of the individual enforcement of Community law. The first of these cases is *Factortame*.[33] This famous case concerned a challenge to the validity of certain provisions of the Merchant Shipping Act 1988. Factortame argued that the provisions of the Act were contrary to Community law, in that they effectively prevented several Spanish-owned fishing vessels from fishing against the United Kingdom's quota under the terms of the common fisheries policy, contrary to Article 43 (ex 52) EC. The national court referred this matter to the ECJ. In the meantime, Factortame sought an interim order from the national court, the effect of which would have been to order the Crown (in the form of the relevant government minister) to suspend the operation of the relevant provisions of the Act. In proceedings before the English courts, the House of Lords found that the applicants would suffer irreparable damage if the interim relief which they sought was not granted. However, the House of Lords ruled that, notwithstanding this finding, English courts had no jurisdiction to grant such relief, as the Crown Proceedings Act 1947, section 21(2) provided that 'the court shall not in any civil proceedings grant any injunction or make any order against an officer of the Crown . . .' . The House of Lords then referred to the ECJ the question whether this rule of national law should as a matter of Community law be set aside in circumstances where its application would deprive a party of the enjoyment of rights which were derived from Community law. The ECJ appeared to have little difficulty in answering in the affirmative. It ruled that:[34]

Community law must be interpreted as meaning that a national court which, in a case before it concerning Community law, considered that the sole obstacle which precludes it from granting interim relief is a rule of national law, must set aside that rule.

In reaching this conclusion the Court did not even mention its previous case law on national procedural autonomy, despite the fact that it had been cited to the Court by the United Kingdom in support of its submissions. In its judgment, the

---

[32] See A. Arnull, *The European Union and its Court of Justice* (Oxford University Press, Oxford, 1999), 151.   [33] Case C–213/89, *Factortame*, n. 14 above.
[34] *Ibid.*, para. 23.

Court relied solely on the principle of supremacy as laid down in *Simmenthal*,[35] and on the obligation of fidelity enshrined in Article 5 (now 10) EC.[36]

What is most extraordinary about this case, however, is not that the principle of national procedural autonomy was simply ignored: rather, it is that the entire decision was unnecessary. Before the case was decided by the Court, the Commission had brought an action under Article 169 (now 226) for a declaration that, by imposing the nationality requirements laid down in the Merchant Shipping Act, the United Kingdom had failed to fulfil its obligations under, *inter alia*, Article 52 (now 43) EC. While this Article 226 case had not at the time *Factortame* was decided itself been heard by the Court, at the same time as the Commission had lodged its Article 226 action with the Court's registry, it had also applied to the Court for an interim order requiring the United Kingdom to suspend the application of the nationality requirements of the 1988 Act. By an order of 10 October 1989 the President of the Court granted the application for an interim order,[37] following which the United Kingdom made an Order in Council amending the relevant provision of the Merchant Shipping Act with effect from 2 November 1989. All of this occurred well before *Factortame* was decided by the ECJ (judgment was handed down on 19 June 1990), or even before the case was argued before the Court (the oral hearing took place on 5 April 1990).

Thus, Community law had already been enforced by the ECJ in *Commission v. United Kingdom*. Why, then, did the Court decide that it needed to be enforced all over again, this time by the national courts? Why especially in a case of unusual political sensitivity raising the most acute constitutional questions in the country concerned? It seems odd that the ECJ had become so narrowly focused on the value of individual enforcement that it appeared wholly to have lost sight of the value of institutional enforcement. We shall return to this point further, below.

The second case to have dramatically affected the principle of national procedural autonomy is *Francovich*.[38] This case concerned Italy's failure to implement the terms of Directive 80/987, a measure which was intended to guarantee to employees a minimum level of protection under Community law in the event of the insolvency of their employer. The Directive provided in particular for specific guarantees of payment of unpaid wage claims. The ECJ found that the terms of this Directive were not in their entirety sufficiently precise and

---

[35] In Case 106/77, *Amministrazione delle Finanze dello Stato v. Simmenthal SpA* [1978] ECR 629, para. 17, the Court had ruled that 'in accordance with the principle of the precedence of Community law, the relationship between provisions of the Treaty and directly applicable measures of the institutions on the one hand and the national law of the Member States on the other is such that those provisions and measures . . . by their entry into force render automatically inapplicable any conflicting provision of . . . national law'. [36] See n. 27 above.

[37] See Case 246/89 R, *Commission v. United Kingdom* [1989] ECR 3125.

[38] Cases C–6/90 and–9/90, *Francovich*, n. 15 above.

unconditional for the Directive to be directly effective. However, in a ground-breaking ruling, the Court proceeded to rule that:[39]

[T]he full effectiveness of community rules would be impaired and the protection of the rights which they grant would be weakened if individuals were unable to obtain redress when their rights are infringed by a breach of Community law for which a Member State can be held responsible. The possibility of obtaining redress from the Member State is particularly indispensable where, as in this case, the full effectiveness of Community rules is subject to prior action on the part of the State and where, consequently, in the absence of such action, individuals cannot enforce before the national courts the rights conferred upon them by Community law. It follows that the principle whereby a State must be liable for loss and damage caused to individuals as a result of breaches of Community law for which the State can be held responsible is inherent in the system of the Treaty.

Accordingly, the Court ruled in *Francovich* that it is a principle of Community law that a Member State is obliged to make good loss and damage caused to individuals by breaches of Community law for which the state can be held responsible. The Court then laid down three conditions which must be satisfied before such liability may be imposed: first, the result prescribed by the directive should entail the grant of rights to individuals; secondly, it should be possible to identify the content of those rights on the basis of the provisions of the directive; and finally, there must be a causal link between the breach of the state's obligation and the loss and damage suffered.[40]

Whereas in *Factortame* the Court ignored its earlier jurisprudence on national procedural autonomy, in *Francovich* it was referred to, the Court stating that the new principle of state liability would be enforced by national courts 'on the basis of the rules of national law on liability' and that in the 'absence of Community legislation, it is for the internal legal order of each Member State to designate the competent courts and lay down the detailed procedural rules for legal proceedings intended to safeguard the rights which individuals derive from Community law'.[41] The absentee from the Court's judgment in *Francovich* was not the principle of national procedural autonomy, but Article 226. This omission makes the *Francovich* decision just as remarkable as was the Court's decision in *Factortame*. As in *Factortame*, so too in *Francovich* there had been an earlier action, brought by the Commission under what was then Article 169. It will be recalled that when *Factortame* was decided by the ECJ, the Article 226 case had not at that stage been heard, although interim relief had been granted. With regard to *Francovich*, however, the full Article 226 case had been not only heard, but decided, by the Court. Its judgment in

---

[39] Cases C–6/90 and 9/90, *Francovich*, n. 15 above, paras. 33–35. This conclusion was further buttressed, in the view of the Court, by the terms of Art. 5 (now 10).

[40] *Ibid.*, para. 40. The reach of the principles laid down here has subsequently been extended: see especially Cases C–46/93 and C–48/93, *Brasserie du Pêcheur SA v. Germany, R v. Secretary of State for Transport, ex parte Factortame Ltd.* [1996] ECR I–1029.

[41] *Ibid.*, para. 42. This partial safeguarding of the remnants of national procedural autonomy remains subject to the two familiar conditions: namely, those of equivalence and effectiveness: see para. 43.

Commission v. *Italy*[42] was handed down in February 1989: that in *Francovich* nearly three years later, in November 1991. In *Commission* v. *Italy* the Commission ran three arguments: that Italy had violated Community law in failing to implement Articles 3 and 5 of Directive 80/987 (concerning the setting up of guarantee institutions); Article 7 (concerning the guarantee of the payment of the benefits due to employees under statutory social security schemes); and Article 8 (concerning the guarantee of payment of old-age benefits). The ECJ agreed fully with the Commission with regard to all three claims and granted a declaration accordingly.

As we have seen, the Court justified its extension of principles of individual enforcement in *Francovich* on the basis that without the principle of state liability the 'full effectiveness' of Community law would be impaired. As with its decision in *Factortame*, so too here has the Court, it seems, completely lost sight of the fact that to be effective the enforcement of Community law does not have to come about at the instigation of individuals but could, and moreover in both of these cases actually did, come about at the instigation of the Commission, just as the Treaty had always imagined it would.

3. REACTION AND ASSESSMENT

The overwhelming reaction to the series of cases outlined in the preceding section of this essay has been to welcome them. Community lawyers love direct effect.[43] They seem equally delighted with the Court's creation of the principle of state liability. Consider the following representative assessments, first from Szyszczak:[44]

Without the ability of individuals to enforce Community rights in the national courts, the original enforcement mechanisms contained in Article 169 . . . are limited. Individuals have no part to play in the process; they cannot compel the EC Commission to commence proceedings . . . The Article 169 process is delicate, secret and often protracted. Even if the outcome is successful, there is no genuine sanction against a Member State which refuses to abide by the Court's ruling . . .

Secondly, consider this, from Steiner:[45] 'provision made under the Treaty for the enforcement of [Members States'] obligations was weak' because, despite Articles 169–170, 'no sanctions were provided to compel States to fulfil their

---

[42] Case 22/87, *Commission* v. *Italy* [1989] ECR 143.

[43] An illustrative example is the work of R. Craufurd Smith who has suggested that before the Court invented the doctrine of direct effect the mechanisms for the enforcement of Community law were 'without real bite': 'Remedies for Breaches of EU Law in National Courts: Legal Variation and Selection', in P. Craig and G. de Búrca (eds.), *The Evolution of EU Law* (Oxford University Press, Oxford, 1999), 289.

[44] E. Szyszczak, 'EC Law: New Remedies, New Directions?' (1992) 55 *MLR* 690, 690–1.

[45] J. Steiner, 'From Direct Effects to *Francovich*: Shifting means of Enforcement of Community Law' (1993) 18 *ELR* 3.

obligations . . . This omission posed a real threat to the uniform application of Community law, indeed to the Community's very existence.' If this last claim seems exaggerated, it is supported in part by our final extract, from Tridimas:[46]

As the internal market began to take shape in the aftermath of the Commission's White Paper of 1985, it became increasingly clear to political and judicial actors alike that reliance on traditional means of enforcement, mainly the doctrine of direct effect and the tardy procedure of Article 226 (ex 169) were inefficient. The right to reparation [laid down in *Francovich*] came to close the gap between rights and remedies and reduce the under-enforcement of Community rights which the Court perceived to be constitutional in nature.

The emphasis on mechanisms of individual, rather than institutional, enforcement is echoed in the textbooks. Weatherill and Beaumont devote twenty pages to Article 226, in comparison with the eighty-four pages they devote to Article 234 and direct effect.[47] Hartley devotes eighteen pages to Article 226, but 106 to preliminary references and direct effect.[48] Craig and de Búrca devote thirty-five pages to Article 226, but 147 pages to Article 234, remedies in national courts, and direct effect.[49]

However, while it is true that overall lawyers have tended strongly to welcome and to endorse the development of the mechanisms of the individual enforcement of Community law, one lawyer who has famously resisted this temptation, and who has crafted especially strong arguments against the Court's decision in *Francovich*, is Carol Harlow. In her formidable article, '*Francovich* and the Problem of the Disobedient State'[50] Professor Harlow attacked the Court's decision in *Francovich* principally for two sets of related reasons. These reasons might be classed 'constitutional' and 'administrative'.[51] The constitutional argument consists of a critique of the view, perennially fashionable among communities of lawyers, that no weapon is more potent than the rule of law as a technique of holding the politically powerful to account. In Harlow's words, 'the Rule of Law is a noble ideal but one which, unrestrained, is capable of degenerating into an ideology of law courts'.[52] Lawyers tend to imagine first that no constitutional problem is 'genuinely' solved unless and until it is judicially solved; and secondly that there is no constitutional problem which cannot be successfully solved by courts. Both tendencies are exaggerations, of

---

[46] T. Tridimas, 'Liability for Breach of Community Law: Growing Up and Mellowing Down?' (2001) 38 *CMLRev* 301, 302.

[47] S. Weatherill and P. Beaumont, *EU Law* (Penguin, London, 3rd edn., 1999).

[48] T. Hartley, *The Foundations of European Community Law* (Oxford University Press, Oxford, 4th edn., 1998).

[49] P. Craig and G. de Búrca, *EU Law: Text, Cases, and Materials* (Oxford University Press, Oxford, 3rd edn., 2002).

[50] (1996) 2 *ELJ* 199. This article was also published by the Robert Schuman Centre at the European University Institute as EUI Working Paper RSC 96/62.

[51] These labels are mine, not Professor Harlow's.

[52] C. Harlow, '*Francovich* and the Problem of the Disobedient State' (1996) 2 *ELJ* 199, 222.

course, and both are dangerous. They are dangerous because they inflate the role of the law at the expense of politics. Harlow again:[53]

The Rule of Law is a great ideal; it must be remembered, however, that its maturation in modern constitutional theory took place during a period before the flowering of fully representative government. Unrestrained, it is capable of blocking democratic evolution.

Harlow's second criticism of *Francovich*, the administrative argument, is that the imposition of a rights-based principle of state liability will prove extraordinarily difficult to accommodate within the varied domestic administrative law regimes of the Member States (whose courts will of course have to work out how to implement the new principle in practice), and that, ultimately, the imposition of the new principle will undermine what Harlow refers to as the 'fault lines' of liability as between Community and national law.

The suggestion here is that the rule of law rhetoric behind the ever expanding scope of individual enforcement has itself adversely contributed to the stymied polity of the European Community. Harlow talks of 'blocking democratic evolution', and this is indeed one famous aspect of the weakness of the Community's polity, that it has not evolved democratically. But another is its apparent failure to grasp the importance, or to appreciate the potency, of political, or institutional, enforcement. The blinkered focus on a narrow rule-of-law approach to the development of principles and processes of administrative enforcement has resulted in an undermining of the values of political, or institutional, enforcement, producing an impoverished and one-dimensional system of administrative law and regulation. The principal value of political or institutional enforcement, a value which is missing from the law of individual enforcement, is one which focuses on seeking to find ways first of identifying and then of facilitating and encouraging practices of good administration. (This is the vision of administrative law which Harlow and Rawlings have labelled greenlight theory.) It imagines that the purpose of administrative law is to try to make public administration better. This is an aim which is wholly absent from the Court's case law on individual enforcement. This case law, as we saw above, focuses on compensating aggrieved individuals (and corporations) for administrative wrongs suffered in the past, and says nothing about how administrators should conduct themselves in the future. No doubt a mature and sophisticated system of administrative law would aim to achieve both goals, but as things presently stand in the EC the unrestrained focus on what Harlow refers to as the rule of law has highlighted the one and eclipsed the other.

In the final sections of this essay, I will sketch out a way of taking Harlow's constitutional critique further, not by applying to *Francovich* abstract principles of constitutionalism, but more mundanely by returning to the basic, or constitutional,

---

[53] *Ibid.*, 223. For my own attempt to read principles of political responsibility into the still largely undemocratic fabric of European governance see A. Tomkins, 'Responsibility and Resignation in the European Commission' (1999) 62 *MLR* 744.

text of Community law, the EC Treaty, and by seeking to suggest a way in which Community lawyers might begin to re-imagine the balance between the rule of law and political enforcement. At present, as Harlow suggests, the rule of law trumps political enforcement. It ought properly to supplement it, and not to have supplanted it. Yet there is a relatively straightforward way of putting this right. The starting point will be to take Article 226, and Commission (i.e. institutional or political) enforcement of Community law more seriously.

4. Taking Article 226 more seriously

Lawyers tend to make three assumptions in respect of Commission enforcement of Community law under Article 226: first, that it is all about political discretion and therefore not really an issue for legal analysis; secondly, that it is a largely ineffective procedure, relying principally on administrative rather than judicial sanction, and therefore not really worthy of legal analysis; and thirdly that in any event the Commission lacks the resources it needs to be able to make Article 226 work as well as it might.[54] While each of these criticisms no doubt carries some weight, we would do well immediately to remember that, as Dashwood and White have argued, 'the procedure under Article 169 represents a considerable advance on the rules that normally apply in public international law where a State fails to fulfil its obligations under a treaty'.[55] Not only does prosecution fall to the Commission, and not merely to other Member States, but, moreover, Member States must accept the compulsory jurisdiction of the Court of Justice: there is no discretion not to accept it, as is the usual position in international law. Dashwood and White further argue that:[56]

Six out of every hundred recorded infringements reaches the stage of a judgment by the Court of Justice. This is a considerable achievement for a procedure concerned with the behaviour of States and is a clear indication that the proceedings exert effective pressure on Member States to remedy infringements.

It may be as well to remind ourselves at this stage of precisely the terms of Article 226. It provides:

If the Commission considers that a Member State has failed to fulfil an obligation under this Treaty, it shall deliver a reasoned opinion on the matter after giving the State concerned the opportunity to submit its observations. If the State concerned does not comply with the opinion within the period laid down by the Commission, the latter may bring proceedings before the Court of Justice.

In 2000 the Commission delivered 460 reasoned opinions, and referred 172 cases to the ECJ under Article 226.[57]

---

[54] On the resources point see Gil Ibanez, n. 9 above, chap. 8.
[55] See A. Dashwood and R. White, 'Enforcement Actions under Articles 169 and 170 EEC' (1989) 14 *ELR* 388.   [56] *Ibid.*, 411.
[57] These figures are broadly similar to those from previous years: in 1999 there were 460 reasoned opinions and 178 referrals to the Court; in 1998 the figures were 675 and 123 respectively.

Discussion of Article 226 procedure in textbooks on Community law tends to focus on three features: discretion, informality, and sanction. From such discussion, we learn first in terms of discretion that the Commission is not generally amenable to judicial review in the ECJ over its motivations for commencing, or for deciding not to commence, an investigation or a subsequent court action under Article 226.[58] Further, the Commission is granted by the ECJ generous latitude in terms of time limits, although excessive delay might constitute grounds for judicial review under Article 230 EC (formerly Article 173 of the EC Treaty).[59] We also learn that the Commission cannot be forced to open an investigation, nor to commence an action, not even by the complainant who has brought the suspected infringement to the attention of the Commission in the first place. The leading case on this point is the *Star Fruit* case in which the Court ruled that 'it is clear from the scheme of Article 169 of the Treaty that the Commission is not bound to commence the proceedings provided for in that provision but in this regard has a discretion which excludes the right for individuals to require that institution to adopt a specific position'.[60] This last instance of Commission discretion may seem odd, given the careful choice of verbs that those who drafted Article 226 adopted. It will be noted from that text that whereas the Commission 'may' bring an action in the ECJ, where the Commission considers that a Member State has infringed Community law, it 'shall' deliver a reasoned opinion. The Court's dilution of that word 'shall' to a mere 'may' in the *Star Fruit* case is unfortunate, to say the least. We shall return to this point, below.[61]

As regards the second theme, informality, we learn that the reasoned opinion has been held by the Court to be of no binding effect, and cannot accordingly be the subject of an annulment action brought under Article 230 EC.[62] The Court has underlined the informality of the reasoned opinion stage by holding that while the opinion must contain a 'coherent statement of reasons' it does not have to respond to every point made either by the complainant or in response by the Member State.[63] Nor does the Commission have to indicate in its reasoned opinion what steps should be taken by the state to remedy the breach.[64] However, slightly incongruously with authorities on such points, the Court has also ruled that once the Commission has delivered its reasoned opinion it may not substantially change its reasons if the case proceeds to the Court.

---

[58] Case 416/85, *Commission* v. *United Kingdom* [1988] ECR 3127, para. 9: 'it is not for the Court to consider what objectives are pursued in an action brought under Article 169'. See also Case C–431/92, *Commission* v. *Germany* [1995] ECR I–2189.

[59] Case C–96/89, *Commission* v. *Netherlands* [1991] ECR 2461.

[60] Case 247/87, *Star Fruit* v. *Commission* [1989] ECR 291, para. 11.

[61] For a full treatment of the problem of discretion under Art. 226, see Gil Ibanez, n. 9 above, chap. 7. [62] Case 48/65, *Lütticke* v. *Commission* [1966] ECR 19.

[63] Case 7/61, *Commission* v. *Italy* [1961] ECR 317.

[64] Case C–247/89, *Commission* v. *Portugal* [1991] ECR I–3659.

In order to comply with the Member States' procedural safeguards, if the Commission wishes to rely on new argument, it must start the entire Article 226 process again.[65] Perhaps it is little wonder, with the ECJ laying down rules such as these, that lawyers tend to view Article 226 as ineffective and inefficient!

It is with regard to the third theme, sanction, that there has been most significant reform, with the addition at Maastricht of Article 228. Illustrative of the problem which Article 228 was designed to solve is the notorious *Sheepmeat* affair. Hartley tells the story thus:[66]

[The *Sheepmeat* affair] began when France (with some justification on legal and social grounds) refused to admit imports of lamb and mutton from other Member States, principally Britain. The Commission brought proceedings and in due course the Court gave judgment against France. The French government, however, made clear that it would not comply with the judgment until the Council agreed to a Community support system which would protect French farmers, a measure blocked by Britain. The Commission then brought new proceedings and applied for an interim order requiring France to admit British lamb without restrictions. Surprisingly, this was refused by the Court on the ground that it would substantially duplicate the previous judgment and would not, therefore, be 'necessary', as required by Article 186 (now 243) EC. In fact, one suspects that the Court, knowing that any order it gave would be ignored, decided that it would be better to save what was left of its tattered authority by refusing the order. In the end, the case never went to a final judgment: Britain agreed to a Community regime for lamb and mutton in exchange for concessions on its budgetary claims; France then lifted the ban on imports.

Article 228 now provides that where the ECJ has in a case brought by the Commission under Article 226 (or by a Member State under Article 227) found that a Member State has infringed Community law, if the Commission considers that the Member State has not taken sufficient measures to rectify the infringement, it shall issue a further reasoned opinion to that effect and may bring further proceedings in the ECJ. If the Court finds that the Member State is continuing to infringe Community law and has not complied with its earlier judgment, the Court may impose a penalty payment.

Each year the Commission publishes a *Report on Monitoring the Application of Community Law*. At the time of writing, the most recently published report is that for 2000, published in July 2001.[67] It discloses that by the end of 2000 the Court had imposed a penalty payment under Article 228 in only one case, brought against Greece.[68] The case arose out of a complaint made to the Commission in 1987 concerning river pollution by the uncontrolled disposal of waste in the river Kouroupitos in Crete. In an application brought under

---

[65] See, e.g., Case 232/78, *Commission v. France* [1979] ECR 2279, and the other cases cited by Craig and de Búrca, n. 49 above, 415.

[66] Hartley, n. 48 above, 321, footnotes omitted. The relevant references are: Case 232/78, *Commission v. France* [1979] ECR 2729; Cases 24, 97/80 R, *Commission v. France* [1980] ECR 1319.

[67] COM(2001)309 final, 16 July 2001.

[68] Case C–387/97, *Commission v. Greece* [2000] ECR I–5047.

Article 226 the Court ruled in 1992 that the pollution constituted a violation by Greece of two directives.[69] Nothing was done to remedy the pollution, and consequently the Commission brought further proceedings under Article 228, resulting in the Court imposing a penalty payment of €20,000 per day. The Commission noted in its *Annual Report on Monitoring* that as of the end of 2000, while Greece was regularly paying the fine into the Commission's EC Own Resources account, it still had done nothing to comply with the Court's 1992 judgment.

In addition to the Greek case, the Commission is currently in the process of referring three further cases to the Court under Article 228, two of which, like the Greek case, are concerned with environmental matters (one of these is against Germany, the other against the United Kingdom), and one of which, against Italy, concerns sea transport. As of the end of 2000 these four cases constituted the only active cases in which the Commission had decided to make a second referral to the Court under Article 228. Since 1993, however, a total of twenty-one cases have been referred. Seventeen of those were terminated or suspended without the Court having to give further judgment, the Commission closing the proceedings because it had become satisfied that the Member State concerned had acted so as to remedy its earlier infringement of Community law.

While, as we have seen, lawyers have made much of Article 228, suggesting that it at last makes the Article 226 procedure effective as it is now accompanied by a 'genuine' sanction with 'real bite', it is too early to say anything meaningful about the effectiveness of the new procedure, as there are too few cases from which we could draw our conclusions. The fact, however, that the procedure appears to have been used in so few cases (only twenty-one in total) might be taken to suggest that perhaps the Commission does not consider non-compliance with Court judgments under Article 226 to be a significant problem. Perhaps the concern with sanction was principally only a cosmetic one? Before we leave the question of sanction, we should note that despite the imposition of a judicial penalty payment, the Greek case has not been resolved, raising at least a doubt that if we really want genuine sanctions with real bite perhaps we should not, after all, be going to court to look for them. We might also note that, despite the many difficulties of the case, the *Sheepmeat* affair was eventually satisfactorily resolved (and this in the days before Article 228, of course), but by political negotiation rather than by filing suit. Perhaps what Szyszczak referred to (above) as the 'delicate, secret' nature of the Article 226 process might be one of its strengths, rather than one of its limitations.

It is hard to assess the effectiveness of Article 226. Surveying the Commission's *Annual Reports on Monitoring*, one rapidly sees that the use of Article 226 is not uniform across the various sectors of Community law, and that in some areas it appears to be far more widely used than in others. Two

---

[69] Case C–45/91, *Commission v. Greece* [1992] ECR I–2509.

areas in which Article 226 is, it seems, extensively used, are environmental law and internal market law. Consideration of these two sectors constitutes a greater proportion of the Commission's report for 2000 than is taken up by its consideration of all of the following combined: business law, competition law, employment law and social affairs, agriculture, energy and transport, fisheries, regional policy, taxation, education, health and consumer protection, and justice and home affairs. Even within the two major areas of activity there is substantial variation. Within environmental law, for example, the Commission is much more active in the field of monitoring compliance with directives concerned with water pollution than it is with regard to the Environmental Impact Assessment Directive. As regards the former, the Commission stated in its 2000 report that 'monitoring implementation of Community legislation on water quality remains an important part of the Commission's work. This is due to the quantitative and qualitative importance of the responsibilities imposed on the Member States by Community law and by growing public concern about water quality.'[70] As regards the latter, however, the Commission stated in the same report that the 'most effective check' on infringements concerning environmental impact assessment was 'very likely to be at a decentralised level, particularly through the national courts'.[71] No doubt the reasons for such wide sectoral variation are complex: both analysing the reasons for the variation and evaluating the impact of Article 226 procedures on various sectors would make an excellent research topic; research data on such issues do not seem to be currently available.

There is also some variation (although less considerable in extent) as between Member States. The Commission regularly publishes league tables comparing the record of the fifteen Member States as regards transposition of directives, and such like. In 2000 top of the league was Denmark with a transposition rate of 98.5 per cent. Bottom was Greece, with a rate of 93.9 per cent, the Community average being 96.6 per cent. The Commission also publishes tables listing the numbers of Article 226 cases which are active as against each Member State. The latest data indicate that there are more cases against France (by a considerable margin) than there are against any other Member State. Italy and Greece also fare badly; indeed, 40 per cent of all Article 226 cases which were active as at the end of December 2000 concerned these three states. The states against which the Commission takes action the least are Denmark, Finland, and Sweden. As with the variation evident across sectors, so too here is it very difficult without extensive further research data to know what to read into these rather basic statistics.

While considered assessment of the Commission's various uses of Article 226 is something on which there is currently very little academic research, this is an issue which has been scrutinized by the European Ombudsman. In 1997 the Ombudsman exercised his power to undertake 'own-initiative inquiries' to

---

[70] *Eighteenth Annual Report on Monitoring the Application of Community Law (2000)*, COM(2001)309 final, 16 July 2001, para. 2.8.4.   [71] *Ibid.*, para. 2.8.2.

examine the Commission's administrative procedures for dealing with individuals' complaints concerning infringements of Community law by Member States.[72] The impetus behind the Ombudsman's inquiry was that he himself had received a high number of complaints about the way in which the Commission treated complainants. Three issues, in particular, were identified: the excessive time taken by the Commission to process complaints; lack of information and communication from the Commission on the progress of complaints; and absence of reasons offered by the Commission in support of its conclusions. As a result of the Ombudsman's inquiry, the Commission altered its procedures in two important respects: first, when closing a file it now informs the complainant of the reasons why it has found that there has been no infringement of Community law; and, secondly, complainants are now offered the opportunity to express views to the Commission about the reasons the Commission has offered, before the Commission commits itself to a final conclusion that there has been no infringement. The Ombudsman's efforts have been subjected to critical scrutiny by Rawlings, who described the inquiry as a 'wasted opportunity' and the procedural changes which were its outcome as 'tepid'.[73] Yet even if the Ombudsman's report was not as far-reaching as it might have been, it nonetheless remains a considerably more progressive and helpful contribution than has been made by the ECJ to the improvement of Article 226 procedures.

5. CONCLUSIONS

It was suggested above that in the standard legal analysis three principal problems with Article 226 are commonly identified, constituting three limitations on the effectiveness of the procedures of institutional enforcement: first, Commission discretion; secondly, informality and reliance on administrative rather than judicial sanctions; and thirdly, lack of resources. It will be seen from the preceding survey of contemporary practice under Article 226 that many of these problems are not of the Commission's making, but are to a considerable extent the responsibility of the Court. It is the Court which has held that the Commission's discretion under Article 226 is largely unreviewable. It is the Court which has held that the reasoned opinion is merely an informal, non-binding aspect of the procedure. In both instances the Court's reasoning is thin. There is nothing in the Treaty to require these conclusions, and the Court's cursory treatment of these issues stands in stark contrast to the teleological approach it famously adopted in cases on individual enforcement, *Van Gend en Loos* and *Francovich* especially.

---

[72] The Ombudsman's findings were reported in his *Annual Report for 1997*, 270–4.

[73] See R. Rawlings, 'Engaged Elites: Citizen Action and Institutional Attitudes in Commission Enforcement' (2000) 6 *ELJ* 4, 18.

Moreover, it is the Court which has manifestly failed to safeguard the rights and interests of complainants, not only in the *Star Fruit* case, discussed above, but again more recently in *WWF (UK)* v. *Commission*, an important decision of the CFI.[74] This case grew out of the decision by the Irish government to build a visitors' centre at Mullaghmore in the Burren National Park in the west of Ireland. The Irish government proposed to use structural funds to finance the project. The Worldwide Fund for Nature (WWF) lodged a complaint that this project would breach EC environmental law, and the Commission opened an investigation under Article 226. The Commission subsequently announced that it would not initiate infringement proceedings against Ireland, since in its view EC environmental law was not violated. WWF then sought access to all Commission documents relating to the examination of the Mullaghmore project. The Commission denied WWF's request, and WWF brought an action in the CFI alleging breach of the Code of Conduct on Access to Documents. The Commission argued that to disclose the documents sought by WWF would threaten what it called the 'proper progress' of infringement proceedings, and the Court agreed, ruling that 'the confidentiality which the Member States are entitled to expect of the Commission in such circumstances warrants, under the heading of protection of the public interest, a refusal of access to documents'.[75] In comparison with the judicial record, the Ombudsman's report was a rare breath of fresh air.

The judicial record in terms of seeking ways of improving Article 226 procedures within the Commission is abysmal. Viewed in comparison with the Court's extensive case law on expanding the frontiers of the individual enforcement of Community law, this all seems very odd. Whereas, as we have seen, the Court has since the Community's very inception gone significantly out of its way to develop a range of remedies available to citizens in national courts, it has done virtually nothing to help to make Article 226 more effective as a mechanism of the institutional enforcement of Community law, and indeed, in some jurisprudence, both the ECJ and the CFI have actually made matters worse. It is very difficult to understand why the Court has behaved in this way, particularly given that one of its stated aims is to secure the uniform application of Community law. By devolving the responsibility for the enforcement of Community law to national courts (subject to the occasional supervision, of course, of the ECJ through the preliminary reference jurisdiction under Article 234 EC) and by relying on the randomness, or at least the arbitrariness, of individual or corporate, private, litigation, it might have been thought that the Court had lessened rather than strengthened the possibility of securing the uniform application of Community law.

---

[74] Case T–105/95, *WWF (UK)* v. *Commission* [1997] ECR II–313.
[75] *Ibid.*, para. 63. This case is discussed by Rawlings, n. 73 above, 12–13, and by Tomkins, n. 4 above, 226–7.

One final point is worth reiterating. For all the criticism of Article 226 procedures, and for all the undoubted problems that continue to persist in its application, it should not be forgotten that Article 226 processes of institutional enforcement have scored notable, and hugely important, victories. As we saw above, in *Factortame* and *Francovich*, both immensely difficult and challenging cases from the point of view of individual enforcement, by the time these cases were decided by the Court of Justice, the Commission had already brought successful applications (in one case interim, in the other, final) before the Court under Article 226, and remedies had already been granted. Evidently, this was not enough to satisfy the Court of Justice, however.

EC administrative law has worked hard to give the individual European citizen a powerful voice in the enforcement of Community law, as long as the citizen (or corporation) is conceived of as a litigant before a national court, and not as a complainant before the Commission. No doubt there is a certain constitutional value to this development, but now that the law of individual enforcement has become so entrenched in the fabric of Community law it is time for attention to turn to the constitutional values which can come instead from the Commission and its processes and techniques of institutional enforcement. What the European Community so desperately needs is to fasten a genuine, inclusive, and vibrant polity onto its legal system. Taking Article 226 seriously cannot achieve this aim on its own, of course, but if administrative law is to play its part in the continuing constitutional development of the Community, Article 226 will have to come centre-stage.

Appendix
Carol Harlow QC, FBA:
Selected Writings

1. BOOKS

Compensation and Government Torts (Sweet & Maxwell, London, 1982)

Law and Administration (with Richard Rawlings) (Weidenfeld & Nicolson, London, 1984)

Pressure Through Law (with Richard Rawlings) (Routledge, London, 1992)

Understanding Tort Law (Fontana, 2nd edition, London, 1995)

Law and Administration (with Richard Rawlings) (Butterworths, London, 2nd edition, 1997)

Accountability in the European Union (Oxford University Press, Oxford, 2002)

2. EDITED BOOKS

Politics and Public Law (Sweet & Maxwell, London, 1986)

Lawmaking in the European Union (with Paul Craig) (Kluwer, Deventer, 1998)

Implementing Amsterdam (with Elspeth Guild) (Hart Publishing, Oxford, 2001)

3. CONTRIBUTIONS TO BOOKS

'English Administrative Law: A Personal Prospectus', in M. Chiti (ed.), *Il. Controlo giurisdizionale dell'attivita administrative in Inghilterra* (Giuffre, Milan, 1982)

'Power from the People: Representation and Constitutional Theory', in P. McAuslan (ed.), *Law, Legitimacy and the Constitution* (Sweet and Maxwell, London, 1985)

'Refurbishing the Judicial Service', in C. Harlow (ed.), *Politics and Public Law* (Sweet and Maxwell, London, 1986)

'Public Interest Litigation in England: The State of the Art', in J. Cooper and R. Dhavan (eds.), *Public Interest Law* (Basil Blackwell, Oxford, 1986)

'Les Tribunaux Anglais et les Procedures d'Immigration' in M. Flory and R. Higgins (eds.), *Liberté de Circulation des Personnes en Droit International* (Economica, Paris, 1988)

'Una rassicurazione simbolica: il ruola del controlo giurisdizionale in una democratzia liberale', in M. Chiti (ed.), *Cittadino e Potere in Inghilterra* (Giuffre, Milan, 1990)

'The Legal System', in P. Catterall (ed.), *Contemporary Britain: An Annual Review* (Institute of Contemporary History, Oxford, annually 1990–2)

'Public Law', in P. Birks (ed.), *Examining the Law Syllabus: The Core* (Oxford University Press, Oxford, 1992)

'Why Public Law is Private Law: An Invitation to Lord Woolf', in R. Cranston and A.W. Zuckerman (eds.), *The Woolf Report Reviewed* (Clarendon Press, Oxford, 1995)

'Ombudsmen: Access and Review—the Issues' in R. Gregory *et al.* (eds.), *Practice and Prospects of the Ombudsmen in the United Kingdom* (Edwin Mellen Press, Lewiston, 1995)

'A Special Relationship? The American Influence on English Public Law', in I. Loveland (ed.), *Lessons from America* (Clarendon Press, Oxford, 1995)

'Legal Services and the Alternatives: the LSE Tradition', (with Cyril Glasser) in R. Rawlings (ed.) *Law, Society and Economy* (Clarendon Press, Oxford, 1996)

'Public Service, Market Ideology and Citizenship', in M. Freedland and S. Sciarra (eds.), *Public Services and Citizenship in European Law* (Clarendon Press, Oxford, 1998)

'A People's Europe?', in R. Blackburn (ed.), *Law Reform Now* (Dartmouth, Aldershot, 1999)

'European Administrative Law and the Global Challenge', in P. Craig and G. de Búrca (eds.), *The European Union in Perspective* (Oxford University Press, Oxford, 1999)

'Citizen Access to Political Power in the European Union', published by the European University Institute as RSC WP No. 99/2

'Access to Justice as a Human Right: The European Convention and the EU', in P. Alston (ed.), *The European Union and Human Rights* (Oxford University Press, Oxford, 1999)

'A Common European Law of Remedies', in C. Kilpatrick, T. Novitz, and P. Skidmore (eds.), *The Future of Remedies in Europe* (Hart Publishing, Oxford, 2000)

'Discarding Dicey: Legitimating Legal Politics', in R. Barker (ed.), *Political Ideas and Political Action* (Blackwell, Oxford, 2000)

'Voices of Difference in a Plural Community', published by the European University Institute as RSC WP No. 3/2000

4. Contributions to journals

'Fault Liability in French and English Public Law' (1976) 39 *Modern Law Review* 516–541

'Administrative Reaction to Judicial Review' [1976] *Public Law* 116–133

'Remedies in French Administrative Law' [1977] *Public Law* 227–248

'Ombudsmen in Search of a Role' (1978) 41 *Modern Law Review* 446–456

' "Public" and "Private" Law: Definition without Distinction' (1980) 43 *Modern Law Review* 241–265

'Gillick: A Comedy of Errors?' (1987) 50 *Modern Law Review* 768–776

'La Distinction public/privé en droit anglais' (1988) *Revue Politique et Management Public* 199–215

'The Justice/All Souls Review: Don Quixote to the Rescue?' (1990) 10 *Oxford Journal of Legal Studies* 86–93

'A Cutting Edge? The Parliamentary Commissioner and the MPs' (with Gavin Drewry) (1991) 54 *Modern Law Review* 745–769

'A Community of Interests? Making Use of European Law' (1992) 55 *Modern Law Review* 331–350

'Towards a Theory of Access for the European Court of Justice' (1992) 12 *Yearbook of European Law* 213–248

'Changing the Mindset: The Place of Theory in English Administrative Law' (1994) 14 *Oxford Journal of Legal Studies* 419–434

'Accidental Loss of an Asylum Seeker' (1994) 57 *Modern Law Review* 620–626

'The National Legal Order and the Course of Justice: Some Reflections on the Case of the United Kingdom' (1995) 5 *Rivista Italiana di Diritto Pubblico Communitario* 929–945

'*Francovich* and the Problem of the Disobedient State' (1996) 2 *European Law Journal* 199–225

'Codification of EC Administrative Procedures? Fitting the Foot to the Shoe or the Shoe to the Foot' (1996) 2 *European Law Journal* 3–47

'State Liability: Problem Without a Solution' (1996) 6 *National Journal of Constitutional Law* 67–83

'Back to Basics: Reinventing Administrative Law' [1997] *Public Law* 245–261

'Accountability, New Public Management, and the Problems of the Child Support Agency' (1999) 26 *Journal of Law and Society* 150–174

'Export, Import: The Ebb and Flow of English Public Law' [2000] *Public Law* 240–253

'La Huronne au Palais-Royal or a Naïve Perspective on Administrative Law' (2000) 27 *Journal of Law and Society* 322–326

'Introduction' to Symposium on public administration and globalization: international and supranational organizations (2001) 76 *International Review of Administrative Sciences* 379–389 (guest editor)

'Public Law and Popular Justice' (2002) 65 *Modern Law Review* 1–18

Index